KV-637-675

FOREWORD

Budgeting is an adaptive process that is sensitive to the political and economic context in which revenue and spending plans are made and carried out. Although the basic routines of budget preparation and implementation typically continue from one year to the next with little change, governments periodically adjust established practices – both the formal rules and procedures of budgeting and the informal roles and relationships – to changing circumstances and requirements. Adaptation and reform are propelled by economic and political conditions, as well as by ideas in currency and the perspectives of budget makers. Change is usually partial and evolutionary, though reform is sometimes sweeping and comprehensive.

This report concentrates on budgetary practices in OECD countries. It is animated by the expectation that the international exchange of information and experiences, such as has been fostered by annual meetings of senior budget officials under the auspices of the OECD Public Management (PUMA) Committee, will stimulate and enrich the ongoing process of budgetary adjustment. The report emphasises diversity in contemporary budget practice, notes themes common to a number of countries, and discusses issues warranting further attention. It offers a glimpse of budgeting from the vantage point of senior officials in the central budget offices of OECD Member countries.

In view of the report's objective to promote the exchange of ideas, Part I focuses principally on recent innovations in budgeting. It provides a comparative perspective of developments in expenditure control and management across Member countries and updates material reported in the 1987 OECD publication, *The Control and Management of Government Expenditure*. The developments reported in Part I are drawn from three sources; *i)* certain material in the 1987 report that is relevant to current budgetary innovations; *ii)* papers and other documents prepared for the annual PUMA Meeting of Senior Budget Officials; and *iii)* the detailed country descriptions set forth in Part II of this publication.

Part II provides a detailed review of the budgetary practices of 22 OECD Member countries based on the contributions of Senior Budget Officials from Member countries. Each country chapter is developed around a common structure which examines: the Institutional Structure of Budgetary Decision-making; the Scope and Nature of Government Finances; Budget Formulation Strategy and Process; Expenditure Review arrangements; In-year Implementation of the Budget, and Recent Reforms.

The activity was undertaken as part of the OECD Public Management Committee's ongoing work in the area of public sector budgeting and financial management. It was directed by Terry Wall who is responsible within PUMA for comparative work on financial management reform in OECD Member countries.

The Secretariat is indebted to Dr. Allen Schick, Professor of Public Policy at George Mason University, Washington DC, United States for his major contribution to the preparation of Part I of this report. We also extend our thanks to the many officials from the OECD Member countries represented in this report for their help in compiling the chapters on their countries' budgetary systems.

This report is published on the responsibility of the Secretary-General of the OECD.

HJ7461 BUD

QMW Library

23 1088956 3

WITHDRAWN
FROM STOCK
QMUL LIBRARY

BUDGETING
FOR
RESULTS

DATE DUE FOR RETURN

Perspectives

on

Public Expenditure Management

ORGANISATION FOR ECONOMIC CO-OPERATION AND DEVELOPMENT

ORGANISATION FOR ECONOMIC CO-OPERATION AND DEVELOPMENT

Pursuant to Article 1 of the Convention signed in Paris on 14th December 1960, and which came into force on 30th September 1961, the Organisation for Economic Co-operation and Development (OECD) shall promote policies designed:

— to achieve the highest sustainable economic growth and employment and a rising standard of living in Member countries, while maintaining financial stability, and thus to contribute to the development of the world economy;

— to contribute to sound economic expansion in Member as well as non-member countries in the process of economic development; and

— to contribute to the expansion of world trade on a multilateral, non-discriminatory basis in accordance with international obligations.

The original Member countries of the OECD are Austria, Belgium, Canada, Denmark, France, Germany, Greece, Iceland, Ireland, Italy, Luxembourg, the Netherlands, Norway, Portugal, Spain, Sweden, Switzerland, Turkey, the United Kingdom and the United States. The following countries became Members subsequently through accession at the dates indicated hereafter: Japan (28th April 1964), Finland (28th January 1969), Australia (7th June 1971), New Zealand (29th May 1973) and Mexico (18th May 1994). The Commission of the European Communities takes part in the work of the OECD (Article 13 of the OECD Convention).

Publié en français sous le titre :

LA BUDGÉTISATION AU SERVICE DES RÉSULTATS
PERSPECTIVES DE LA GESTION DES DÉPENSES PUBLIQUES

© OECD 1995
Applications for permission to reproduce or translate all or part
of this publication should be made to:
Head of Publications Service, OECD
2, rue André-Pascal, 75775 PARIS CEDEX 16, France

QMW LIBRARY
(MILE END)

TABLE OF CONTENTS

Part I

COMPARING COUNTRY EXPERIENCES

Part II

INDIVIDUAL COUNTRY DESCRIPTIONS

Part I

COMPARING COUNTRY EXPERIENCES

Chapter 1

TRENDS IN PUBLIC EXPENDITURE

As instruments of government policy, budgets are designed to influence the performance of the economy. Fiscal policy has gone through several adjustments during the past 30 years. As the post-war boom faded, industrial democracies were beset by two oil crises, and lower growth rates became the norm in most OECD Member countries. One major adjustment has been sharpened awareness that the budget is affected by changes in economic conditions. The economy impacts the budget both in terms of the built-in changes in revenues and expenditures that accompany the cyclical rise and decline in economic activity, as well as by structural shifts in budget policy that are triggered by longer-term economic trends.

Table 1 divides the performance of the economy, as measured by real growth in GDP, into four periods: the early OECD years ending with the first oil shock in 1973; the turbulent decade from 1974-82 during which most Member countries suffered severe stagflation; the period 1982-90 characterised by renewed, though generally moderate, economic growth; and the most recent period 1991-93 when most OECD economies experienced severe recession. The four periods are not equal in length, nor do they fully correspond to economic cycles. They have been selected to shed light on the marked shifts in budget policies that have occurred during the past 30 years. These shifts are evident in Table 2 which reports on trends in government, receipts, outlays, and net lending during the years 1960-93.

Table 1. **Average annual changes in real GDP, 1960-93**

	1960-73	1974-82	1983-90	1991-93
Australia	5.2	2.4	3.7	1.7
Austria	4.9	2.3	2.6	1.3
Belgium	4.9	2.1	2.3	0.6
Canada	5.5	3.0	3.6	0.5
Denmark	4.4	1.5	2.3	1.1
Finland	5.0	2.7	3.3	−4.5
France	5.4	2.5	2.5	0.4
Germany	4.3	1.6	2.9	1.8
Greece	7.6	2.8	1.8	1.4
Iceland	5.5	5.2	2.7	−0.5
Ireland	4.4	3.9	3.9	3.3
Italy	5.2	3.0	2.7	0.4
Japan	9.6	3.6	4.3	1.8
Luxembourg	4.1	1.0	4.4	1.7
Netherlands	4.8	1.6	2.8	1.2
New Zealand	4.0	1.3	1.6	0.4
Norway	4.3	3.9	3.0	2.4
Portugal	6.9	2.9	3.0	0.9
Spain	7.2	1.8	3.6	0.7
Sweden	4.1	1.5	2.4	−1.7
Switzerland	4.4	0.4	2.6	−0.1
Turkey	5.9	4.1	5.6	4.4
United Kingdom	3.2	0.9	3.3	−0.3
United States	4.0	1.6	3.4	1.6
OECD Average	5.2	2.2	3.4	1.2

Source: OECD Economic Outlook No. 52 (December 1992) and No. 55 (June 1994).

Table 2. **Trends in government finance**

	Current receipts				Total outlays				Net lending			
	1960-73	1974-79	1980-90	1991-93	1960-73	1974-79	1980-90	1991-93	1960-73	1974-79	1980-90	1991-93
Australia	25.3	29.4	33.3	33.8	24.5	33.6	34.3	37.6	1.4	-2.1	-1.1	-3.8
Austria	38.6	43.9	47.2	48.2	38.7	46.7	50.0	50.6	0.7	-2.6	-2.9	-2.4
Belgium	32.2	46.2	51.2	50.5	34.1	52.1	60.4	57.6	n.a.	-6.9	-9.1	-7.1
Canada	30.0	36.1	39.0	43.0	31.6	39.2	43.5	49.5	-0.2	-2.5	-4.5	-6.6
Denmark	35.3	48.2	56.4	57.7	33.7	49.1	59.1	60.7	2.1	-1.3	-2.6	-3.0
Finland	32.6	38.2	45.7	53.2	30.3	36.3	42.5	57.9	3.1	2.1	3.2	-4.8
France	37.7	40.8	48.1	48.5	38.0	43.3	50.2	52.5	0.5	-1.1	-2.1	-4.0
Germany	37.5	44.0	45.0	46.1	37.4	47.5	47.1	49.2	0.6	-3.2	-2.1	-3.0
Greece	24.9	29.1	33.2	38.6	20.8	28.0[1]	41.7	51.4	n.a.	-2.5	-11.5	-12.7
Iceland	31.3	32.8	33.9	n.a.	29.6	34.4	35.1	n.a.	1.8	-0.6	n.a.	n.a.
Ireland	30.0	35.9	40.1	41.2	34.3	45.1	49.2	43.3	-3.5	-9.3	-8.2	-2.2
Italy	30.2	33.5	38.1	44.7	33.6	42.9	49.1	54.4	-3.1	-10.1	-11.0	-9.7
Japan	20.0	24.6	31.0	34.2	19.5	28.4	32.1	32.5	1.0	-4.2	-1.1	1.7
Luxembourg	35.2	50.1	n.a.	n.a.	34.1	48.2	n.a.	n.a.	2.2	2.9	n.a.	n.a.
Netherlands	39.4	49.8	51.8	52.2	40.7	52.8	56.7	55.1	-0.6	-2.9	-4.9	-2.9
New Zealand	n.a.	n.a.	n.a.	n.a.	n.a.	n.a.	n.a.	n.a.	n.a.	n.a.	n.a.	n.a.
Norway	40.0	49.8	53.9	54.9	36.6	48.5	49.0	56.6	4.1	2.4	4.9	-1.7
Portugal	21.0	27.6	36.3	45.4	20.4	33.0	42.2	51.6	0.5	-4.2	-5.9	-6.2
Spain	20.2	25.7	34.2	39.5	n.a.	26.8	38.5	45.0	n.a.	-1.7	-4.3	-5.5
Sweden	41.6	54.4	60.0	59.4	38.8	54.4	61.1	66.6	3.8	1.6	-1.1	-7.1
Switzerland	24.9	32.7	34.1	n.a.	20.3	29.2	30.3	n.a.	n.a.	n.a.	n.a.	n.a.
Turkey	21.6	n.a.	n.a.	n.a.	21.0	n.a.	n.a.	n.a.	1.0	n.a.	n.a.	n.a.
United Kingdom	34.8	39.0	40.2	37.0	36.7	44.4	42.2	42.5	-0.8	-3.9	-2.0	-5.6
United States	27.6	29.8	30.5	30.7	29.5	32.6	33.0	34.5	-0.6	-1.3	-2.5	-3.8

1. Only current disbursements.
Source: OECD Economic Outlook No. 52 (December 1992) and No. 55 (June 1994).

10

The first period predated the establishment of OECD and continued until 1974. It was characterised by strong economic growth and the steady expansion in the relative size of the public sector. The two trends went hand in hand, as economic well-being fuelled programme expansions. Real economic growth averaging about 5 per cent a year in the OECD community accommodated both rising disposable incomes and an enlarged public sector. Government expansion was not only in absolute terms, but relative to GDP as well. The share of government receipts and outlays in GDP was about 6 percentage points higher in 1974 than it had been in 1960, the year OECD was established. Despite the growth of government, net lending was very low, as a robust economy and tax increases enabled countries to finance their ambitions with current receipts.

The second period, stretching from the first oil crises (1973-74) through the second oil crises (1979-80) and the ensuing recession was characterised by economic stagnation, high inflation and high unemployment, and a steep rise in government spending as a share of GDP. Between 1974 and 1982, total government outlays in the OECD community climbed from 34.7 per cent of GDP to 41.7 per cent, a rise of almost one percentage point a year. During the same period, net lending rose from negligible amounts to 4.5 per cent of GDP in 1982. Evidently, many OECD Member countries had difficulty adjusting their budgets to the slowdown in economic growth. Some tried to spur economic improvement through demand-side stimulus; others found it difficult to slow the built-in momentum of rising expenditures despite the inadequacy of their revenue bases. Almost all countries faced a structural imbalance in revenues and expenditures.

The third period saw moderate economic recovery and stabilisation of the expenditure/GDP ratio in most countries. In fact, total government outlays in Member countries were a lower per cent of GDP in 1989 than they had been 7 years earlier. Moreover, there was a steady decline in the ratio of net lending to GDP during the period. But this period ended in 1990, a year during which economic conditions deteriorated in many Member countries.

Near the end of the 1982-90 growth cycle, and extending through the fourth period (1991-93), there were some signs, to be discussed shortly, of an easing of less effecting spending control in some countries. During this period, spending as a share of GDP increased by 4 percentage points which, with a cyclical weakening in revenue, led to a widening in deficits in OECD Member countries back to the levels experienced in the early 1980s.

The data in Table 3 suggest that the budgetary consolidation set in motion during the early 1980s ran out of steam by the end of the decade. In the early 1980s, many governments were highly sensitive to the recently experienced oil shocks as well as to failed efforts to stimulate economic activity and large fiscal imbalances. They came away from these policy failures determined to change course and to rein in public spending and the deficit. But as the recovery stretched on through the 1980s – most OECD Member countries went through 5 or more years without a downturn – and deficits abated, the resolve to constrain public spending may have weakened somewhat. Many faced demands for additional spending or tax reform, and the drive to curtail the deficit receded in importance.

Table 3 provides some confirmation of this pattern for the 1989-92 period during which most OECD Member countries experienced significant deterioration in financial balances along with rising expenditure/GDP ratios. Fourteen of the 19 countries displayed in the table had a less favourable balance than they had 3 years earlier. Significantly, budget conditions deteriorated in many of these countries despite an increase in revenues as a share of GDP. For the 19 countries, the revenue/GDP ratio averaged 0.7 per cent higher in 1992 than it had been in 1989. During these years, however, the expenditure/GDP ratio advanced 3.7 percentage points.

The June 1994 OECD *Economic Outlook* found that while part of the slippage in budgetary performance may have been due to the recession that began in 1990, most countries also had a significant increase in their structural deficit. At the end of 1993 structural deficits for the OECD as a whole were back to levels experienced in the early 1980s. But structural revenues and expenditures were around $3\frac{1}{2}$ to 4 percentage points of trend GDP higher than in 1979 and gross public debt had increased by around 25 percentage points of GDP, to more than 65 per cent in 1993; while net debt had increased by almost 20 percentage points to around 40 per cent of GDP. And if past patterns are repeated, cyclical pressures may once again contribute to structural imbalances. There is, accordingly, considerable pressure on OECD Member countries to again tighten spending controls in response to adverse budget conditions.

The late 1980s and early 1990s were characterised by another tendency that hints at some relaxation of the drive to curtail expenditures. Fewer budget innovations were introduced during this period than appears to have been the case earlier in the decade. The 1987 report on The Control and Management of Public Expenditure revealed more substantial innovation than occurred in the later period. To be sure, some of the reforms launched earlier in the decade, such as those in the Commonwealth countries, were still taking root. Moreover, the late 1980s were associated with some significant developments, such as the modernisation of the public sector in Finland and New Zealand's application of market principles to the conduct of government. But it seems

Table 3. **Changes in general government financial balance, 1979-92**[1]

	1979 Balance	1979-89 change		1989 Balance	1989-92 change		1992 Balance
		Revenue	Expenditure		Revenue	Expenditure	
Australia	−2.4	3.9	0.2	1.6	−1.4	5.0	−4.9
Austria	−2.4	0.1	0.5	−2.8	1.4	0.4	−1.9
Belgium	−7.4	−0.3	−1.3	−6.4	1.5	1.2	−6.1
Canada	−2.0	4.0	5.0	−3.0	3.7	6.4	−5.8
Denmark	−1.7	6.7	5.5	−0.5	−2.7	−0.7	−2.6
Finland	0.4	3.6	1.1	2.9	1.8	12.9	−8.2
France	−0.8	3.5	3.8	−1.1	−0.1	1.6	−2.8
Germany	−2.6	0.4	−2.4	0.2	4.6	8.3	−3.2
Greece	−2.5	1.0	16.2	−17.7	5.8	1.2	−13.2
Ireland	−10.6	5.5	−4.0	−1.1	−0.8	0.6	−2.5
Italy	−10.2	10.1	9.8	−9.8	2.1	3.4	−11.1
Japan	−4.7	5.7	−1.6	2.5	−1.0	0.2	1.3
Netherlands	−3.7	−0.7	0.7	−5.1	1.7	0.4	−3.8
Norway	1.3	0.8	0.7	1.4	1.3	6.1	−3.4
Portugal	−6.3	8.7	5.5	−3.1	1.2	3.5	−5.4
Spain	−2.1	10.1	10.8	−2.8	0.7	2.7	−4.7
Sweden	−2.9	6.5	−2.0	5.6	−4.9	8.6	−7.9
United Kingdom	−3.2	1.4	−2.8	0.9	−1.4	6.4	−6.6
United States	0.4	0.6	2.4	−1.5	−0.2	3.1	−4.7
Average[2]	−3.3	3.8	2.5	−2.1	0.7	3.7	−5.1

1. Amounts may not add due to rounding. A positive figure indicates a higher expenditure or revenue to GDP ratio; a negative indicates a lower expenditure or revenue to GDP ratio. In the balance category a positive indicates a surplus and a minus indicates a deficit.
2. Unweighted average.
Source: OECD Economic Outlook No. 52, December 1992, Tables 8, 9 and 10.

probable that economic improvement lowered the sense of urgency in some countries that the machinery of budgeting was in need of repair. If this is so, the adverse conditions of the early 1990s may spark fresh efforts at budgetary reform.

The effective control and management of public expenditure is likely to become increasingly salient in the years ahead as the proportion of elderly persons rises. In the OECD area, the old-age dependency ratio – the ratio of population aged 65 and over to the working age population – is projected to rise 2.1 percentage points in the 1990s, a much higher increase than occurred during the 1980s, but significantly lower than that which has been forecast for the early decades of the next century. This trend will be propelled by sizeable increases in the ranks of the very old – those aged 80 and over. This trend portends substantial increases in health and pension expenditures which will have to be accommodated in budgets that are already strained by fiscal imbalance.

The rising dependency ratio is associated with another trend that has long-term implications for the budgetary condition of OECD Member countries. Old-age assistance is typically in the form of social payments for pensions, care, and other income stabilisation schemes. Payments are also made for other social purposes such as unemployment assistance, family and children allowance, disability, and support to low-income households. The progressive rise in these payments has transformed government budgets over the past 30 years and has greatly complicated the task of expenditure control.

A few statistics tell the story. Since 1960, government spending in the OECD area has escalated about 50 per cent relative to GDP – from 28 per cent in 1960 to more than 40 per cent in 1990. During this period, however, there has been only a slight rise in the share of GDP accounted for by consumption expenditure the direct purchase of goods and services by government from 14.6 per cent three decades ago to 16.8 per cent at the start of the 1990s. But social security and related transfers have soared from 7 per cent of GDP to 15 per cent. Table 4 sums up this trend in terms of the shares of government spending allocated to consumption and transfer payments. In 1960, more than half of total outlays were devoted to consumption, twice as much as the share earmarked to transfers. By 1990, the shares were almost equal, and there is a high probability that early in the next century, transfer payments will take a larger portion of government budgets than will consumption expenditure.

It should be noted that this trend covers the consolidated public sector-the central government as well as provinces and local authorities. The shift from consumption expenditure to transfer payments is much more remarkable in central governments which, in all countries, have primary responsibility for social security and related income maintenance programmes. In some OECD Member countries, social transfers now account for upwards of 60 per cent of central government expenditure.

Table 4. **Final consumption as a per cent of total outlays**

	1960	1968	1974	1980	1986	1990
All OECD Member countries	51	49	46	43	41	38

	Social security transfer as a per cent of total outlays					
	1960	1968	1974	1980	1986	1990
All OECD Member countries	25	27	31	33	33	35

Source: "*National Accounts*", Volume II, detailed tables, OECD.

The long-term shift in the composition of government expenditure is also evident in investment outlays and debt interest payments. The former have declined both as a share of GDP and of governments budgets; the latter have progressively increased as a share of GDP and public expenditure.

A closer look at these trends for the 1979-90 period reveals that fiscal consolidation occurred largely through the curtailment of subsidies and reduced government purchase of goods and services, not from a restructuring of transfer payments. In all but one of the countries displayed in Table 5, social security and other social transfers increased their share of GDP between 1979 and 1990. In the total OECD community, these payments and interest charges account for just about all of the rise in relative spending during these years. The same trend emerges in changes in the changing composition of government outlays shown in Table 6. In 17 of the countries displayed in this table, social security and transfers accounted for a higher portion of total outlays in 1990 than in 1979.

Table 5. **Change in government outlays by economic category, 1979 to 1990**

Per cent of GDP

	Consumption	Social security and transfers[2]	Debt interest payments	Other		Government investment	Total change
				Subsidies	Transfers[3]		
Australia	−0.1	1.4	2.3	−0.6	0.3	−0.4	2.9
Austria	−0.5	0.2	1.7	−0.3	−0.2	−1.2	−0.3
Belgium	−3.4	−1.1	5.5	−1.6	−0.5	−2.3	−3.4
Canada	0.6	2.9	4.4	−0.3	0.0	−0.2	7.5
Denmark	−0.3	3.3	3.7	−0.3	−0.3	−1.8	4.4
Finland	3.1	1.4	0.4	−0.7	−0.3	0.1	4.0
France	0.7	3.1	1.7	−0.3	−0.2	0.2	5.2
Germany	−1.1	0.4	1.0	−0.3	−0.7	−1.0	−1.8
Greece	5.5	7.2	9.0	−0.5	0.0	−0.3	21.0
Iceland	2.2	1.4	2.7	−0.8	0.6	0.5	6.5
Ireland	−3.5	2.4	2.2	0.6	−1.0	−2.9	−2.3
Italy[1]	2.7	4.1	4.4	−0.6	0.5	0.4	11.5
Japan	−0.7	1.0	1.1	−0.6	−0.3	−1.3	−0.9
Netherlands	−3.2	1.5	2.5	0.3	0.3	−0.8	0.4
Norway	1.6	4.4	0.7	−1.0	0.0	−1.1	4.7
Portugal	5.9	0.5	5.8	−3.0	−2.3	−0.4	6.5
Spain[1]	1.6	2.1	2.9	−0.5	−0.1	2.9	9.0
Sweden[1]	−1.8	1.9	1.6	0.4	−0.9	−1.4	−0.2
Switzerland	−0.6	0.2	−0.6	−0.1	0.0	−1.1	−2.1
Turkey	1.5	1.1	0.0	0.0	0.0	−6.4	−3.9
United Kingdom	0.3	0.9	−1.0	−1.3	−3.6	−0.5	0.3
United States	1.2	1.3	2.4	−0.2	0.6	−0.1	5.2
OECD Average	0.4	1.5	2.0	−0.4	−0.1	−0.4	3.3

1. 1980 numbers instead of 1979 numbers.
2. Includes other current transfers.
3. Includes net capital transfers, capital transfers received from government less capital transfers to government, purchases of land, and of intangible assets.
Source: "Controlling Government Spending and Deficits: Trends in the 1980s and Prospects for the 1990s"; *OECD Economic Studies*, No. 17. Autumn 1991, Table 2, pp. 158-160.

Table 6. **Composition of government outlays 1979 and 1990**[1]

Per cent of total outlays

	Government consumption		Social security and other transfers[3]		Debt interest payments		Subsidies		Other transfers[4]		Government investment	
	1979	1990	1979	1990	1979	1990	1979	1990	1979	1990	1979	1990
Australia	52	48	28	30	6	12	4	2	0	1	9	7
Austria	37	36	40	41	5	8	6	5	3	3	9	6
Belgium	30	26	45	45	9	20	8	5	2	1	6	2
Canada	49	42	25	28	13	20	5	4	1	1	7	5
Denmark	47	43	32	36	7	13	6	5	1	1	7	3
Finland	49	51	29	30	2	3	10	7	1	0	9	8
France	39	36	45	47	3	6	4	3	1	1	7	7
Germany	41	40	40	42	4	6	5	4	4	3	7	5
Greece	50	41	27	30	7	21	7	3	0	0	10	5
Iceland	52	49	14	15	3	10	12	8	9	8	10	10
Ireland	39	33	30	37	12	18	8	10	2	0	9	3
Italy[1]	35	33	35	36	13	18	7	4	2	3	8	7
Japan	31	29	33	36	8	12	4	2	4	3	20	16
Netherlands	32	26	49	52	8	12	2	3	3	3	6	4
Norway	39	38	32	38	6	7	14	11	0	0	9	6
Portugal	38	46	28	25	8	20	12	4	3	-2	10	8
Spain[2]	38	34	43	39	2	9	6	4	4	3	6	11
Sweden[2]	47	44	31	34	7	9	7	8	1	-1	7	5
Switzerland	38	39	40	44	6	4	4	4	0	0	12	9
Turkey	40	50	18	24	0	0	0	0	0	0	42	26
United States	54	49	32	31	9	14	1	1	-2	1	5	4

1. Totals may not add due to rounding. Because of technical problems, the United Kingdom was not included, although it was included in the source table.
2. 1980 numbers instead of 1979 numbers.
3. Includes other current transfers.
4. Includes net capital transfers, capital transfers received from government less capital transfers to government, purchases of land, and of intangible assets.
Source: "Controlling Government Spending and Deficits: Trends in the 1980s and Prospects for the 1990s", *OECD Economic Studies*, No. 17, Autumn 1991, Table 2, pp. 158-160.

The continuing rise in transfer payments is not surprising. These often are tied to economic and demographic trends and are therefore highly sensitive to price changes, the age structure of the population, and the level of economic activity. Many of these income maintenance programmes are open ended entitlements, at least in the short-term, though once eligibility criteria and payment rates have been set, the total budgetary cost is determined by the number of eligible claimants who come forward and the amount each receives. The number is not always easy to forecast, even for short periods ahead, especially when conditions are turbulent and unanticipated changes occur. Moreover, it is hard to curtail these payments through legislative action. Such cash payments tend to be highly visible to recipients than services or public goods from which they benefit collectively rather than individually. A change in these payments will have an impact roughly equivalent to a change in workers' take home pay; cutting the payments is likely to evoke as much protest as cutting wages.

These payments are not only embedded in government budgets; they also are an increasingly critical portion of household income – more than 15 per cent in the OECD community. Hence a modification in eligibility rules and payment formulas will have a direct impact on the financial well-being of a broad swath of the population.

The increasing share of government expenditure that is substantially determined by the weight of existing obligations – such as debt interest and entitlements – impart a measure of structural rigidity to expenditure policies. This rigidity can impair the capacity of governments to adjust spending levels or allocations in response to changing circumstances or emerging priorities. The changing composition of government budgets has greatly complicated the control and management of public expenditure. Techniques and approaches appropriate for consumption expenditure may not be as effective in dealing with transfer payments.

This remainder of this part focuses on budgetary developments in the late 1980s and early 1990s. It takes the position that fiscal consolidation is not simply a by-product of improved economic performance but depends crucially on governmental efforts to strengthen the control and management of public expenditure. The innovations and practices described are means by which governments have signalled their determination to halt or slow the upward creep in the ratio of revenues, spending, or the deficit to GDP.

Chapter 2

THE SCOPE OF CENTRAL GOVERNMENT BUDGETS

This report deals with budget practices from the perspective of the central government office responsible for the overall control and management of expenditure. What is included in central government spending varies from country to country, but the main issues of scope are much the same. These issues pertain to borderline institutions on the boundaries of the public and private sectors; non-conventional transactions such as loans and guarantees; incentives that do not entail the direct expenditure of funds but have financial and other effects similar to ordinary expenditures.

These "scope" issues bring into consideration the long-established, though often-violated principle that the budget should be comprehensive, that is, it should cover all the financial inflows and outflows of the government regardless of their source or end use. Applied to central governments, this principle would, for example, require the budget to include grants to local government but not the expenditure by these governments of self-generated funds. It would also require the inclusion of social security, even if it is financed by special or trust funds, and state enterprises, even if they have access to capital markets.

The principle of comprehensiveness is not an end in itself but a means of accomplishing vital functions of budgeting. A comprehensive budget facilitates: *a)* the measurement of the economic consequences of government actions; *b)* control of the financial resources of the government; *c)* accountability of decisionmakers and managers in the public sector; and *d)* the efficient use of public resources. Despite the vital need for complete information on finances, few, if any OECD Member countries have perfectly comprehensive budgets that encompass all the financial flows of the government. Conventional expenditures for the operating expenses of government agencies and programmes are almost universally included in the statue budget. Exceptions arise only when law or practice treats a particular agency or programme as off-budget. More difficult issues arise when the expenditure is unconventional, as is the case when the government makes or guarantees loans or when it provides incentives or preferences through the tax system. This section does not consider social security, which it was previously noted is a growing share of total public expenditures in the OECD area. Interested readers may refer to the discussion of this subject in the 1987 report as well as to the country descriptions in Part II of the present report.

State Enterprises (SE). The boundary between public and private enterprises is not always straightforward or well defined. The degree of public control, ownership of the enterprise, and its reliance on public finance are important criteria in defining the boundary. But the lines are blurred when the government owns the enterprise but exercises little control, or conversely when it does not technically own the SE but nevertheless exercises significant managerial control. Further complications arise with regard to employment, pricing, and procurement policies, as well as the SEs access to capital markets.

When SEs are included in the budget, the most common practice is to account for them only in terms of the net flows between them and the government, or on a net basis (income minus expenses) rather than on a gross basis. A gross basis would strengthen government control of the enterprise, but it might distort the budget and lead to undue interference and rigid management. Netting income and expenses, on the other hand, shows the SE's contribution to the government's financial condition and facilitates control of SE borrowing requirements. In the *United Kingdom,* for example, the operational definition of public expenditure for control purposes includes the net external finance of nationalised industries and most other public corporations. Exceptions to the general practice of net budgeting for PEs is found in Austria where some enterprises (principally the traditional public service monopolies) are presented on a gross basis and in France where budget operations are still performed by departments, not the SEs.

Some countries draw a distinction between enterprises directly owned by the government and those established by it but operated as if they were private firms. In the *United States,* corporations owned in whole or in part by the federal government are included in the budget, in contrast to those sponsored (but not owned) by it.

Financial information on the latter – known as government sponsored enterprises or GSEs – is annexed to the budget but not included in the revenue and expenditure totals.

Privatization initiatives in various OECD Member countries have reduced the number and financial prominence of SEs. When enterprises are privatized, the funds earned by the government usually are budgeted as receipts or as deductions against expenditure. Either way, the government's short-term budget condition is improved. Despite the emphasis on privatization, some OECD governments still own major enterprises, especially in public monopolies such as transportation and communications.

Along with privatization, some governments have moved away from detailed ex ante budget (and other managerial) control to managerial discretion and accountability for performance. For SEs operating in competitive markets, the common practice is to give them considerable freedom with respect to standard managerial decisions such as pricing and the choice of inputs. In these SEs, budgetary discussions generally focus on state's contribution to the enterprise, whether for operating grants or capital financing.

The role of the budget office in overseeing SEs varies among OECD Member countries. In Austria, SEs engaged in manufacturing deal with the budget office through an umbrella organisation which submits requests for expenditures and financing. In Canada and France, discussions with the Budget Office occur under the aegis of the responsible minister. In the United States, the Office of Management and Budget has little involvement in SE operations. In practice, few budget offices exercise ongoing control over SEs. An exception is in France where some older nationalised companies have a resident comptroller who is an employee of the Finance Ministry and has access to all documents. Over the years, however, this role appears to have evolved from surveillance to maintaining communication between the Finance Ministry and the SE.

Ex post controls on SEs are largely exercised outside the budget process, typically through periodic audits. In recent years, the trend has been to expand these reviews to performance, not only compliance, issues.

Austria. SEs account for 15-20 per cent of the federal budget, even without counting nationalised firms operating in competitive sectors. Two groups of SEs are distinguished for budgetary purposes: 1) public service monopolies such as railways, post and telecommunications, and forests that are wholly owned by the state and generally are subject to strict budgetary and non-budgetary controls; and 2) SEs operating in competitive sectors which are at least 51 per cent owned by the state and generally autonomous, though the government may exercise some influence through the appointment of directors. All SEs in the first category are budgeted on a gross basis; those in the second category are netted.

The public service monopolies are budgeted in a manner similar to regular departments. Parliament approves their budgets, with separate limits on appropriations for wages, number of employees, investments, and operating expenditures. Rates of pay are also set by Parliament, though not through the budget process. These SEs are not permitted to borrow on their own account, and investments are budgeted on a cash basis as current expenditures. The second type of SEs – nationalised industries – are not subject to these detailed ex ante controls. The key channel of government control is the membership of public officials on the boards of these companies. Loans, grants, or capital infusions are processed through regular budgetary procedures. The Audit Bureau prepares yearly reports on public service monopolies and reports on other SEs over a 4-5 year cycle.

Canada. As of 1993, the Federal Government held a 100 per cent interest in 47 corporations with assets of $54 billion and employing more than 117 000 persons. The relationship between the government and PEs was modified by the Financial Administration Act of 1984 which altered the balance between central control and managerial autonomy. Under the rules currently in effect, each parent SE – those wholly owned by the government – must annually submit a five-year corporate plan setting forth its investments and borrowing, its objectives and strategy for achieving them, and results for the previous years (compared to objectives) and expected performance for the next year. These plans are tabled in Parliament and form the basis for annual appropriations requests. SEs must obtain annual approval (through the yearly corporate plan) to borrow, even when its enabling legislation authorises it to borrow.

Funds advanced by the government to SEs consist of budgetary funding which are not expected to be repaid and are therefore recorded as outlays (which are netted against SE revenues) and nonbudgetary funds which are expected to be repaid and are recorded on financial statements as assets. The budgetary funds are generally to provide cash subsidies or cover operating deficits; the non-budgetary funds normally are for capital investment, working capital, and similar purposes.

Finland has reformed the Central Government budget-linked enterprises to extra-budgetary ones. The reform process started in 1989, and has proceeded to cover a majority of enterprises. The new organisational form allows for wide operational flexibility to enterprises, while preserving the volume of investments and their finance as well as access to major functional choices in Parliamentary control. The new operational degrees of freedom are autonomy of operational management, pricing decisions and access to capital markets. Enterprises exposed to competition may be transformed to limited-stock companies, and sold to private investors. So far, three enterprises have been transformed into companies, and one has been sold. More enterprises will follow: a Bill has been submitted to Parliament on the reorganisation of the Posts and Telecommunications to a limited-stock company. The extra-budgetary enterprise may in future be an organisational form for producing compulsory Government services.

France. State enterprises play a significant role in the French economy and public sector. Two waves of nationalisation brought French SEs to their current scope and diversity, the first just after World War II, the second in 1981. Since then, the scope of the public sector has been significantly reduced by 2 privatisation programmes, one carried out from 1986 to 1988, and the other currently underway. In addition to "entreprises nationales" in which the state owns more than 50 per cent of the capital and voting shares, there also are various "societes d'economie mixte" which are partly public, partly private. Only the former are covered in these notes. The relationship between firms and the Minister of Finance depend on their date of nationalisation and on whether they operate as public service monopolies or in competitive markets. The size of the public sector has been appreciably reduced by the privatisations which came into being between 1986 and 1988 and by those currently underway.

Five main rules govern financial flows from the state to SEs: 1) capital grants are treated as current expenditures; 2) loans are recorded as temporary operations carried out through special treasury accounts; 3) dividends from SEs appear as receipts in the general budget while loan repayments are entered as receipts in the relevant special treasury account; 4) guarantees are budgeted only to the extent they lead to outlays; and 5) subsidies to SEs for the provision of social benefits are budgeted as expenses to the relevant departments when they are remitted to SEs.

Budget control is exercised over payments to SEs, the amounts and conditions under which some may borrow from the private sector, and the wages, prices, etc of some SEs. Relations between the SE and the budget office are channelled through the ministry responsible for the SE. Contributions from the state to public service monopolies and various other SEs for current operations are decided in the annual budget process. Investment policies of these SEs are reviewed by a special inter-departmental committee to insure that their financial plans are consistent with macroeconomic policy. In the case of SEs operating in competitive markets, discussions with the Finance Ministry pertain to overall borrowing or to specific requests for an increase in state-provided capital. But other matters are left to the managers of these companies or to government representatives on their boards of directors.

SEs nationalised in the 1940s or earlier have a resident official from the Ministry of Finance who monitors their operations, has access to documents, conveys the policies and preferences of the Ministry, and alerts the Ministry to developments.

United States. Although the United States appears to have a relatively small SE sector, it has a variety of institutions operating under diverse rules and financial arrangements. These can be classified into four categories. 1) Corporations owned (in whole or in part) by the federal government and included in the budget usually on a net basis. Most of these corporations get their capital from the federal government which bears the financial risk, and controls their budgets and other operations. Some of these entities have a line of credit at the Treasury, and most are subject to the apportionment of their funds by the Office of Management and Budget. All are subject to audit by the General Accounting Office. 2) A few SEs are owned by the government but are off-budget. The largest of these is the Postal Service which was removed from the budget in 1981. These are similar to the first category in important regards except for their budgetary status. 3) Government sponsored enterprises (GSEs) are created under federal sponsorship, but are privately owned and managed and are normally intended to be self financing. Most GSEs serve as financial intermediaries in credit-dependent sectors such as housing and agriculture. Some GSEs draw a portion of their capital from the government which bears financial risk either in the form of explicit guarantees or "moral obligation", the expectation that the government will come to their aid in case of distress. GSEs are excluded from the budget, but financial information concerning them is annexed to the budget. 4) Some private corporations receive federal subsidies either in the form of capital, operating subsidies or guarantees. The government generally exercises little control over these entities, but cash flows to them from the Treasury are budgeted as expenditures.

Loans and loan guarantees. Loans made to others (including state enterprises) are normally accounted for in the budget and included in any overall expenditure target. This cash basis derives from the fact that loans contribute the government's deficit or borrowing requirement in the same manner as conventional outlays. Moreover, the general lack of balance sheets and other financial statements inhibits the government from recording loans as assets, as they would be on business statements.

Treating loans as cash outlays has a number of serious shortcomings. One is that loans are made to compete with non-repayable expenditure such as grants in the decision making process. This treatment makes it appear that loans and grants of equal value entail equal cost to the government when, in fact, the true costs are unequal. Second, when a loan is budgeted as an outlay at the outset, there is no means for the budget to record any cost if the loan is subsequently written off, defaulted, converted to a grant, or forgotten. Third, the cash basis does not recognise that the terms of loans – the interest rate charged and repayment schedule – and the credit-worthiness of borrowers differ and greatly affect the true cost to the government.

Loan guarantees raise some particularly difficult budgetary issues. Inasmuch as cash payment by government occurs only if the borrower defaults, the general practice is not to include loan guarantees in expenditure plans or budget totals. In tendering the guarantee, however, the government does obtain a contingent liability pursuant to which it will have to make payment in the future if, as often happens, default ensues. At the point of default, it is too late for the government to control the cost, though it will have to record any cash payments in the budget.

Understating the cost of loan guarantees make it difficult to compare them to alternative financial instruments such as grants and direct loans, and also makes it difficult to assess their cost in terms of the risk to the government. Many governments have sought to compensate for the deficient treatment of guarantees by expanding the information on them in the budget and in other documents. In many countries, either the budget or standing legislation, limits the total volume of guarantees that may be outstanding or issued during the year.

The budgetary status of loans and loan guarantees has undergone considerable change in recent years. The most far reaching reforms, introduced in the United States and explained in the appropriate country description, aims at budgeting for both loans and guarantees on the basis of their estimated cost to the government. Other countries have sought to strengthen financial control by providing realistic assessments of expected cash payments in the budget. Other reforms have included charging borrowers a fee to recoup, or cover a portion of, the cost of the loan or guarantee to the government.

Australia. The volume of direct loans has declined since the late 1980s in consequence of policies that terminated Commonwealth borrowing for states and required government business enterprises (GBEs) to be self-funding. Most guarantees are issued to GBEs as a means of lowering borrowing costs and improving access to capital markets. GBE reforms adopted in 1988 withdrew explicit guarantees on new borrowing, but these enterprises still have implicit guarantees arising from the perception that the government will rescue them from financial difficulties.

Austria. No budgetary comparison is made of the cost of grants, loans, and guarantees. The Ministry of Finance applies a 7 per cent discount rate to measure the value of loans. The resulting estimated values are not entered into the budget. Ex ante appraisals of the financial soundness of borrowers minimise credit risks. State enterprises are not financed by direct loans, and it is rare for loans to be converted into grants. To minimise risk, guarantees are made only if they are provided for in laws that impose conditions on their issuance. Apart from export credit insurance, payments under guarantees have been very minimal. Loan guarantees have been issued to state enterprises, but their volume has been diminished by 1986 reforms that removed informal state guarantees on enterprises co-operating under the aegis of OIAG, the government holding company, and a 1991 law, terminating new guarantees to these firms.

Canada. Direct loans are a significant feature of public policy. These may be concessional loans, which are treated as grants and charged to the budget, or non-concessional loans which are at market rates and entail no subsidy. The loans are revalued each year, and mark-downs are taken if the credit risk or interest subsidy is found to be significant. Loan guarantees, which have increased in volume since the late 1980s, can be issued only if authorised by legislation and under terms approved by the Minister of Finance. Reference to loan guarantees must be expressly included in the budget estimates in order to obtain Parliamentary authority for the guarantee; however, the expenditure levels covers only cash payments resulting from defaults. When there is an expectation that loans might not be repaid, a reserve (generally equal to 25 per cent of the amount lent) is set up and recorded as a standard expenditure item in the budget. When loans by the private capital markets to State Enterprises or the private sector are expected to be fully repaid, they are presented off-budget. The Government is reviewing existing policies and practices with a view to establishing a new policy to reflect costs of loan guarantees in the governments summary financial statements.

Denmark. Direct loans are not a significant instrument of government policy, and amounted to only 2 per cent of expenditure in 1991. Loan transactions that create financial assets (receivables) are counted in the total budget deficit; repayments are treated as income in the financial transactions account. The subsidy cost of loans is not identified in the budget. No systematic comparison is made of guarantees to other forms of expenditure, but they are generally perceived as having a smaller subsidy than direct loans. Losses on some types of guarantees have been mitigated in recent years by higher premium charges.

Finland. Direct loans play a minor role as a budgetary instrument, amounting to less than 1 per cent of total expenditure. They are budgeted as outlays, while repayments are budgeted as income. Loan defaults, rescheduling, and other irregularities do not appear in the budget. With few exceptions, state guarantees are formally approved by Parliament. Detailed reports on these transactions appear in the annual Closed Accounts and the government's report on the Management of State Finances.

Germany. Direct loans amounted to slightly more than 1 per cent of federal expenditure in 1992. Loans are provided only if repayment is likely. There is no separate budget for financial transactions. Loan disbursements are handled as outlays, payments are counted as revenue. The budget approved by Parliament includes provision for the expected cash requirements arising from defaults on guarantees. Guarantees are issued in many sectors and are monitored by the Ministry of Finance.

New Zealand. Both direct loans and guarantees have diminished in importance as the government has moved, through deregulation, corporatisation, increasing contestability and other innovations, to introduce market principles in the public sector. The budget distinguishes between transactions that create assets and those that do not. Under the new accrual accounting system, write-offs of loans are recognised in financial statements. Guarantees are fully reported in the government's financial statements.

Sweden. The government proposes limits for the use of each loan guarantee programme, and these limits are decided upon by Parliament. A special section of the budget lists changes in loan guarantee limits and cash payments. The budget also provides estimates of expected payments on guarantees during the year.

Switzerland. In 1991, direct loans amounted to less than 2 per cent of government expenditure. When loans are made, a credit scoring system is used to rate the risk. The balance sheet distinguishes between loans that carry normal yields (so that their book value corresponds to their effective value) and those with low yields. The latter are revalued every year. There is a growing use of guarantees, possibly because they have no immediate impact on the deficit and are better suited to many situations. The effective subsidy on loan guarantees is close to zero because they are made only if the financial condition of borrowers is high and payment is probable.

United States. The Credit Reform Act of 1990 (which became effective with the 1992 fiscal year) made fundamental changes in the budgetary treatment of direct and guaranteed loans. Prior to the reform, the budget accounted for loans and guarantees on a cash basis. Direct loans were recorded as outlays when funds were disbursed and were netted in the budget against repayments of principal and interest on old loans. Loan guarantees were budgeted as outlays only when payment was made pursuant to default. In addition to this cash-based system, a separate credit budget, paralleling the regular expenditure budget, was introduced during the 1980s. This separate process provided for the congressional budget resolution to set forth total direct loan obligations and total guaranteed loan commitments for each fiscal year. It also provided for limits on annual loan activity to be set in annual appropriations acts. Some elements of this parallel budget process were continued by the 1990 reform.

The reform shifted the accounting basis for federally provided or guaranteed loans to the estimated subsidy costs of these transactions. The reform was aimed at putting direct and guaranteed loans on a comparable basis (that is, their respective subsidy costs) and to facilitate the comparison of these transactions to grants. The reform entailed complex procedures for estimating subsidy costs for each loan programme and for handling the unsubsidized portion of loans. The new system requires that budget authority and outlays be budgeted and that appropriations be made for subsidy costs. These costs are calculated on a net present value basis using a discount rate equal to the interest rate paid by the government at the time the loan is committed or guaranteed. In making this calculation, all future cash outflows and inflows are estimated, but the administrative costs of processing the loans or guarantees are excluded. In the case of direct loans, the outflows will be the amounts lent, and inflows will be repayments of principal and interest and recovery of assets pursuant to default. In the case of loan guarantees, the outflows are the payments the government will make if the borrower defaults and the inflows will be any recoveries. By discounting these flows to present value, the procedure enables the government to separate the subsidised portion of these transactions from the unsubsidised portion.

Chapter 3

GLOBAL BUDGETARY TARGETS

The growth of the public sector, the changed composition of public expenditure, a less optimistic view in some countries of the government's role in the economy, and concern over the rising debt burden, has contributed to significant shifts in the posture of governments toward public spending. There emerged in the late 1970s and early 1980s, recognition of the need to balance policy objectives against the financial capacity of government, as well as sharpened awareness of the potentially adverse impacts of chronic fiscal imbalances on the overall economy and the future freedom of the government to act.

These concerns led governments to predicate budgetary planning on global targets, typically extending several years ahead, to which annual spending decisions would be accommodated. While the precise links, if any, of these targets to actual budget decisions or outcomes depended on the willingness of political leaders and, governments to be, bound by preset norms, the targets helped to constrain demand at the start of the annual budget process. The targets put politicians, interest groups, bureaucrats, and other claimants for public funds on notice that there were limits to the responsiveness of government to their demands. The targets were important elements of an education process by means of which expectations were changed from expansion to cut-backs or stabilisation. Thus the targets were "top down" constraints imposed on the "bottom up" demands of spenders, their clients and supporters.

A government's global budget norms have to be expressed in simple terms, though they are likely to ensue from complex considerations regarding fiscal and monetary options, the size and role of government, the built-in momentum of revenue and expenditure, and sectoral policies and pressures. Targets that cannot readily be grasped by politicians, civil servants and the general public stand little chance of influencing decisions. To be simple enough to serve their intended purposes the targets must be summed up in a few numbers representing either future trends or the direction the government wants to go. In virtually all Member countries, the 1987 study on the Control and Management of Government Expenditure found, budgetary goals were expressed as specific quantitative targets, not as general qualitative statements of intent. Such precision provided a strong message as to the government's financial objectives, and restricted its ability to allow expediency to dictate aggregate revenue and spending levels.

The budget targets used in Member countries can be grouped into three categories, as set forth below. Some countries rely on two or more of the practices to influence budgetary developments.

1. A *ratio,* usually expressed as a percentage related to GDP or some other indicator of aggregate economic activity. The ratio may relate to the level of public debt, budget balance or government borrowing, revenue or expenditure, or a combination of these factors.
2. A *rate of change for expenditure.* A popular guideline has been zero real growth over the stated period, although the target could also allow some rate of increase or call for a reduction in real expenditure. Alternatively, the target may be expressed in nominal terms, and may be published alongside target ratios for the budget balance or revenue burden.
3. An *absolute value for the target variable in nominal terms.* Targets in cash terms can be expressed as either the future level of expenditure or the deficit, or as the amount of desired change from some baseline level.

Budget targets are not self-executing nor is it always within the grasp of the government to meet them, no matter how strong its determination. In pursuing stated fiscal norms, the government must be sensitive to the short-term performance of the economy. When recessions occur, fiscal targets will likely yield to the realities of economic conditions. Other shocks – the unification of Germany and the enormous cost of rebuilding and integrating the eastern sector was one of the most prominent in recent times – can force the government to retreat from carefully crafted fiscal objectives. Much also depends on the short-term control exercised by the government over key variables such as interest rates, and the cost of demand-led schemes.

OECD Member countries differ substantially in their fiscal performance measured against the targets they set for themselves. Leaving aside the recession which enfolded in the early 1990s, some countries outperformed their targets and some did a lot worse. In both these types of situations – doing better and doing worse – the drumbeat message of hard times and the need for belt tightening lost effectiveness in repetition. By the early 1990s, global targets were institutionalised in the budget practices of many OECD Member countries, but they were somewhat less influential as guideposts to budget policy and actions than they had been in the mid 1980s. One should expect, however, that given the toll which the recent recession has taken on the fiscal balances of democratic regimes, the emerging recovery will bring renewed emphasis on stringent targets as a means of fiscal consolidation.

Global targets are likely to be given some impetus among European Member countries by the provision of the Maastricht treaty that makes budget deficits below 3 per cent of GDP a condition of joining the European monetary union to be introduced by the end of the 1990s. Those EC countries with budget deficits above the Maastricht target may turn to global targets as a means of bringing their budgets into compliance.

Australia. Beginning in 1985, the federal government adopted a medium-term "trilogy" strategy of not increasing outlays or revenue as a proportion of GDP and of reducing the deficit/GDP ratio. In response to emerging balance of payments difficulties, these targets were tightened, with the Government committing itself to a real decline in outlays for the 1988-89 and 1989-90 budgets and to a zero net Public Sector Borrowing Requirement. After moving to surplus from 1987-88 to 1990-91, the federal budget returned to deficit with the early 1990s recession. In 1992, the Government announced a package of measures to provide a short-term boost to the economy, along with a commitment to return the budget to surplus by 1995-96. This target was subsequently deferred a year to 1996-97 and revised in the 1993-94 Budget to a deficit of around 1 per cent of GDP by 1996-97.

Austria. In 1987, the Coalition government adopted a medium-term programme aimed at reducing the deficit from 5.5 per cent of GDP to 2.5 per cent by 1992. Until the recession, this consolidation proceeded at a much faster pace than had been planned. But the recent deterioration in the economy has compelled a relaxation of fiscal targets and the current target is to achieve the 2.5 per cent/GDP ratio in 1994. In addition to reducing the deficit, fiscal policy aims to reduce the tax burden, holding the growth of public expenditure below that of GDP, and stabilising the debt to GDP ratio.

Canada. During the 1970s and early 1980s, the government sought to hold the growth of outlays to no more than the trend growth of nominal GDP. This gave way to a strategy that focused more on deficit and debt control. Since 1984, the government has sought to reduce the ratio of expenditures to GDP by holding the nominal growth of programme expenditures (not including debt service) to well below the growth of nominal GDP. In most years, the targets for expenditure have been significantly below inflation, implying real declines in programme spending. The 1991 budget introduced the Spending Control Act which sets legally binding limits on the growth of programme spending (excluding the self financing unemployment insurance and agricultural insurance funds) of an average of 3 per cent per year over the five years beginning in 1991-92. The 1994 Budget indicated the Act would not be extended once it expires in 1995-96. In conjunction with measures to lower the expenditure to GDP ratio, tax reform has increased the ratio of revenues to GDP. The medium-term strategy to reduce the deficit and debt-to-GDP ratio is based on revenues growing in line with GDP and expenditures growing by significantly less.

Denmark. Expenditure targets have generally been expressed in terms of real growth in public expenditure. The main fiscal objectives adopted in 1983 and pursued through most of the decade, were elimination of the central government deficit and zero real growth (exclusive of cyclical changes in expenditure on unemployment benefits) in public expenditure. By the late 1980s, rapid economic recovery had led to balance in central government finances and a substantial surplus in the consolidated public sector. Subsequently, however, rising unemployment expenditure and a slow rate of increase in tax revenue resulted in increasing deficits. The government that took office in 1993 set reduction of this deficit as an explicit objective. The target for expenditure is a growth rate significantly lower than the long term growth in GDP.

Finland. Beginning in 1977, the government set targets for gross tax rates and limits on State borrowing as part of its medium-term economy policy. The policy announced in 1985 called for stabilisation of the tax burden and the debt to GDP ratio through the remainder of the decade. With the breakup of the Soviet Union and developments in Eastern Europe, the Finnish economy was shaken and the previous fiscal targets proved inadequate. In 1990, the government adopted a new scheme of budget ceilings in which the Cabinet decides on expenditure ceilings for each ministry as formal guidance for budget preparation. The targets have thus shifted from overall central government expenditure to the components.

France. Following a brief period of expansion in the early 1980s, the government moved to a more restrictive posture, guided by two fiscal constraints: steadily lower central government deficits and reduced tax burdens. During the 1986-89 period, the actual deficit was consistently less than had been budgeted; in 1990-93, the opposite occurred and the government faced sharply higher deficit/GDP ratios, despite efforts at expenditure restraint.

Germany. The federal budget has incurred high additional expenditure to promote economic reconstruction in the new Lander and to finance social policy measures in support of unification. With one quarter of the spending budgeted for 1993 related to unification, the federal government has indicated the course to be followed: a three per cent limit on expenditure growth in the medium-term, a tight rein on public spendings and reductions in annual net borrowing. This consolidation covers regional and local governments as well, with the aim of bringing total public budget deficits down from 5.5 per cent in 1991 to 3 per cent in 1995.

Greece. The operational target for the budget is the ratio of the net public sector borrowing requirement to GDP. The 1991 stabilisation programme aimed at decreasing the central government's borrowing requirement from 13 per cent of GDP to 4 per cent in 1994. Although annual budgets are supposed to meet the targets set by the stabilisation programme, the programme has no binding effect, and the budget has often deviated from the fiscal strategy.

Italy. Policies adopted in the mid 1980s provided for reducing the total borrowing requirement of the extended public sector to about 7-8 per cent of GDP by 1990. The targets implied no real growth in current expenditure and holding real capital spending below the growth in GDP. These targets were not met, and the government presented successive budgets in the late 1980s and early 1990s containing cut-back packages. However, chronic deficit slippage has been a prominent feature of budgeting since the 1980s.

Japan. Although the government has not adopted aggregate spending targets for the public sector (or central government), since the early 1980s, it has pursued fiscal reforms aimed at phasing out debt-financing bonds and reducing the ratio of public debt to GNP. The main instrument of fiscal restraint has been strict guidelines which every ministry has to follow in preparing budget requests. Although the guidelines apply principally to operating costs – mandatory expenditure, national defence, and certain other important items are excluded – they have reversed the trend in debt financing.

Netherlands. Budgetary norms are typically enunciated in the coalition agreement negotiated at the start of a government to cover the four years it is scheduled to remain in office. Budgetary targets, expressed as a percentage of net national income (NNI) relate both to the budget deficit and the collective budget (which includes tax and social insurance payments and certain other revenue). The coalition agreement for 1991-94 set the target for the budget deficit at 4¾ per cent of NNI for 1991 declining to 3¼ per cent in 1994. This was the third in a series of coalition agreements, the first covering 1983-86 and the second 1987-90, which substantially reduced the budget deficit. The target for the collective burden during the 1991-94 period provided for it to be stabilised at 1990 levels.

Spain. Since 1983, the medium-term objective has been to control the public sector deficit and curtail public expenditure. With the movement to a single European market, budgeting in the early 1990s emphasised continued fiscal consolidation, and a shift from consumption to investment expenditure.

Turkey. The Five-Year Development Plan specifies targets for economic performance and public finance such as total public sector current and capital expenditure, transfers to other sectors, revenues, and fiscal balances. The Plan also targets ratios of total public expenditure to GNP. The budget is prepared in the framework of this Plan, but the outturn on the deficit has often exceeded planned levels.

United Kingdom. Since 1980, the Medium-Term Financial Strategy (MTFS) has provided the framework for monetary and fiscal policy. The MTFS is published with the annual budget and is updated annually. Each MTFS sets forth fiscal projections, usually for four years ahead, covering the public sector borrowing requirement in money (cash) terms and as a percentage of GDP. Under arrangements introduced in 1992 growth in "new control total" is to be constrained to a rate which ensures that general government expenditure (excluding privatisation proceeds) rose more slowly than the economy as a whole over time. On present assumptions this means that real growth in general government expenditure (excluding privatisation proceeds) should over time be no more than 2 per cent annually.

United States. During the early 1980s, the federal budget deficit soared both in absolute terms and as a percentage of GDP, while the public debt/GDP ratio also escalated. To arrest these trends, the Balanced Budget and Deficit Reduction Act of 1985 (the Gramm-Rudmam-Hollings Act) set specific deficit targets for each fiscal year 1986 through 1991. The Act contemplated that the deficit would be progressively lowered in each of these years and would be eliminated in 1991. The Act also devised semiautomatic procedures (known as sequestration) to reduce expenditures if the estimated deficit at the start of a fiscal year was above target. Congress amended the

Act in 1987 to adjust the targets and extend the year by which the budget was to be balanced to 1993. Despite some relatively small sequestrations, the actual budget deficit was above the Gramm-Rudman-Hollings target for each of the years from 1986 through 1990. Congress responded to this predicament in 1990 by shifting from deficit targets to controls on legislation affecting receipts and expenditures. These controls, initially effective for the 1991-95 fiscal years, divided spending into ''discretionary'' and ''direct'' categories. Discretionary spending is controlled by annual appropriations, which the 1990 reforms limited to preset levels. Direct spending, mainly for mandatory entitlements, was not limited in amount but was subjected to pay-as-you go (PAYGO) rules which require that legislated increases be offset by spending reductions in other programmes or by revenue increases. Initial experience with the new controls indicated that they somewhat restrained additional public expenditure but did not reduce the portion of the deficit due to past legislative decisions on revenue and expenditure. The Congress has now extended the discretionary caps and pay-as-you-go limits through fiscal year 1998. No legislative action was taken to restrain direct spending under current law. However, as part of the agreement, the President transmitted an executive order establishing caps on direct spending. If the caps are exceeded, the President will propose legislation to offset the increases.

Chapter 4

EXPENDITURE PLANNING: MULTI-YEAR AND ANNUAL BUDGETING

Aggregate budget norms and targets are typically expressed for several years, not only for the year immediately ahead. This multi-year dimension is essential because bringing the budget into conformance with acceptable fiscal objectives usually must be done in stages, with each year's budget progressing toward the stated target. If the annual budget does not subscribe to the global norms, they will not be achieved and the government will risk losing control of its fiscal condition. Yet there often arise tensions between medium-term budget commitments and annual budget pressures, so that rather than moving in the promised direction the budget reflects the realpolitik of the moment.

Multi-year budgeting (MYB) is the bridge between aggregate medium-term targets and annual budgets. MYB has also become an instrument of financial management reform in a number of OECD Member countries that have sought greater efficiency and effectiveness in the public sector by restructuring their budget practices. This feature of MYB is considered in subsequent sections of this report.

MYB's origins are in the perceived need of governments to address the growing size of the public sector and its influence on the economy, as well as the long-term implications of current decisions, such as defence and investment expenditure which often occur years after the budget makes provision for them. The early MYB systems were introduced during the 1960s and 1970s, a period during which the public sector was expanding rapidly and confidence in the capacity of government to steer the economy on a steady growth path was pervasive. In those years, MYB was a planning device, a means of identifying programme initiatives and setting aside funds for them in future budgets. MYB was itself an engine of expansion, as departments and others saw the plans as entitlements to future increases in budgetary resources. But as the rate of public sector enlargement became unsustainable, MYB was seen as an inappropriate approach. It did not make much sense to plan for expansions that could not be funded or to give rise to expectations that would not be satisfied. There also was concern that economic turbulence and unpredictability had rendered MYBs unreliable guides to future fiscal and programme policy.

In response to these concerns, various OECD governments reoriented their MYBs from plans to projections and from instruments of programme expansion to constraints on future spending. In some, such as the United Kingdom, this reorientation was signalled by the switch from planning in volume terms to cash planning. In others, it was reflected in rules dictating that the projections be based on unchanged policy, that is, that they merely estimate the future cost of existing programmes and not make room for any initiatives. A number of countries (the Netherlands, Sweden, and the United States), this baseline became the starting point for work on the budget. In most cases, the baseline conveyed a powerful message: that the built-in momentum of existing programmes had already claimed all future resources and that there was no margin for new spending schemes.

Cast as a baseline projection, the MYB functions as a financial constraint to which the annual budget must be accommodated. The constraint is often articulated in terms of the global target embraced by the government. It would thus show the budgetary implications, such as revenue increases or programme cut-backs, of staying on course to achieve the stated targets. To serve as a constraint on current budget policy, the budget must be linked to the annual cycle of expenditure planning. When MYB was part of an expansive planning apparatus, the process was often entrusted to a separate agency that had no direct role in preparing the annual budget. Accordingly, the common practice is to have the organisation responsible for preparing the budget make the multi-year projections. Linkage of the projections and budget has also been facilitated by shortening the time horizon of MYB to a frame that more closely corresponds to the period for which global budget targets have been established.

Australia. To start work on the budget, the Department of Finance compiles forward estimates of outlays in each of the next three years. These baseline projections include only the estimated costs of approved programmes in the absence of policy changes. The costs of expiring programmes that are likely to be renewed are separately identified. The Department of Finance then assembles the various projections into an overview that is adjusted to a consistent (budget forecast) price basis. Using these projections, the Cabinet indicates broad aggregate targets for the budget and forward years. Decisions made by the Government in the budget process are additional to the baseline forward estimates which do not include any allowance for policy changes. Budget decisions focus, therefore, on incremental adjustments – up or down – to this baseline. Although the Cabinet sets broad policy targets, detailed work is left to the Expenditure Review Committee (ERC), a subcommittee of senior ministers. In 1993-94, the Cabinet decided that most policy initiatives were to be fully offset by savings. However, certain high-priority proposals or those too costly to be fully offset were considered outside that constraint. Cabinet also endorsed a two-stage process in which portfolios were responsible for bringing forward both new policy and savings proposals. The first round called for Ministers to submit synopses of their proposals by May 1993. These were then sifted by Ministers who nominated items to be further developed in a second round. Detailed ERC consideration commenced at this point, producing expenditure figures for the budget tabled in August. However, this timetable will be altered from 1994-95 as the Budget will from this date be introduced into both Houses of Parliament in May of each year, in order to allow its passage prior to the commencement of the financial year in July.

Austria. The Government annually prepares a medium-term budget estimate covering three years beyond the current budget year. This estimate shows the financial implications of measures that have already been decided; it does not reflect other planned initiatives. On the expenditure side, the MYB indicates the financing required to meet approved goals and commitments; on the revenue side, it projects future receipts under unchanged policies. The MYB serves the Government's budget preparation, but is not acted on by Parliament.

Budget reform in the early 1990s provided for a multi-year financial programme to integrate the priority-setting, policy development, and expenditure management processes. Under this new arrangement, expenditure plans are set for each policy sector and Ministry.

Work on the budget, based on directives issued by the Ministry of Finance, starts in May of the previous calendar year. Recently, these directives have laid down strict demands for restraint, with a combined limit covering both discretionary and statutory expenditure. After agencies submit budget requests, negotiations are conducted with the spending ministries at three successively higher levels: in the budget department, by the Minister of Finance; and, if necessary, in the Cabinet Co-ordinating Committee headed by the Chancellor. The outcome of this process is the budget presented to Parliament in October.

Belgium. Budget preparation is launched in February or March by a call-in circular from the Ministry of Finance that has been approved beforehand by the Cabinet. The circular specifies guidelines, norms, and assumptions to be applied to budget requests submitted in May. These requests consist of current policy estimates along with separately documented proposals for new measures. The requests for on-going activities are based on current policy, defined as the legislation and regulations in force at a specified date. Proposals for increased spending are to include offsetting savings. Special attention is given in the requests to about 100 big items which together account for more than 80 per cent of total expenditure. Departments are instructed to provide additional information on these items. The requests are reviewed during June and July in bilateral meetings with the Budget Department after which the Cabinet decides on allocations to each of the big items and authorises expenditure initiatives or cut-backs. Capital projects include three-year estimates and are reviewed by an interministerial commission which recommends an investment programme to Cabinet.

Canada. The top-down fiscal planning system for establishing fiscal targets is expressed in terms of aggregate budgetary expenditures and net financial requirements. This top-down system interacts with a detailed bottom-up multi-year operational planning system (MYOP). The bottom-up system is initially expressed in constant dollars and deals with each element of spending. The Treasury Board manages the bottom-up operations while the Department of Finance deals with the fiscal planning system in consultation with the Privy Council Office.

Each year the Government reviews and rolls forward its fiscal plan covering the current year, the upcoming budget year, and the two following planning years. Projections of revenues, economic conditions, and status quo expenditures are evaluated in the light of governmental priorities, in particular, the medium-term strategy to reduce the expenditure to GDP ratio. The result is a planned multi-year expenditure path for each year that encompasses resources for the ongoing operations of government; central held reserves to fund government priorities, public debt charges, and variances from the forecasts for statutory programmes; and spending control measures required to achieve the deficit target. These, in global terms, are set out for the Budget year as part of the fiscal plan published in Budget Documents.

Each spending department develops an MYOP that is subject to review by the Treasury Board, leading to decisions on the resources required to continue existing programmes over a three-year period. The Estimates presented to Parliament reflect financial and authorities requirements for the first year of approved MYOPS, but are based on recognition of the multi-year costs involved.

At the same time, the Department of Finance updates the forecasts of major statutory payments and public debt charges based on the revised economic outlook. These forecasts, when combined with the results of the MYOP review, constitute the point of departure for the preparation of the Expenditure Plan with the first year serving as the basis of the Main Estimates.

The Estimates are presented to the Federal Parliament approximately one month before the beginning of the next fiscal year. In the Estimates, the Government seeks appropriations and reflects financial and authorities requirements for the first year of the approved MYOPs. There is also a recognition of the multi-year costs involved. Of the total Estimates, approximately 70 per cent has been previously authorised by existing statutory authority and is presented for information purposes. The balance is the amount for which resources are to be appropriated by Parliament.

Denmark. When the budget is passed by Parliament in December, an appendix to the Appropriation Bill projects expenditures for each of the next three years at the same price and pay basis as the appropriations. Work on the next budget starts shortly thereafter. The budget department in the Finance Ministry adjusts the multiyear projections to the pay and price assumptions to be used in preparing the next budget. In February, the Minister of Finance proposes to Cabinet a set of net spending ceilings, one for each Minister, and the new aggregate target. These ceilings set the framework for the drafting of budget proposals in the various ministries. In effect, the ceilings delineate an expenditure block for each Ministry, allowing it significant flexibility in arranging its budget proposals. Beyond this point, negotiations on the budget focus on accommodating new expenditures and cut-back options for ministries that have difficulty keeping within the agreed limits.

Finland. The system of medium-term activity and financial plans adopted in the 1960s remained relatively unchanged until 1990 when a new system of ceilings was introduced, the timetable for medium-term planning was aligned with the timetable for budget preparation, and the time span was shortened to 1 + 3 years. The ceilings issued by the Cabinet – not the expenditure demands of ministries – now govern the budget process. Budget proposals stress the results to be achieved, not the expenditure items, which was the case in the past. The role of medium-term planning has been redirected to give continuity and background in Ministerial and Cabinet decisions. The combined medium-term and budget timetable now has three major milestones: 1) ceilings in February; 2) budget proposals to the Ministry of Finance in May, and 3) the Cabinet budget conference in August.

The new system of expenditure ceilings and the concurrent results-oriented approach to budgeting implies a far-reaching delegation of detailed expenditure decisions to the line ministries and the agencies themselves.

France. No multi-year budgeting process existed until recently but certain expenditures (for example, defence and overseas provinces) are governed by multi-year legislation that largely determines the amounts to be included in the annual budget. For the first time in France, a 5-year orientation law now specifies desired targets for the State budget. This has been an important innovation in efforts to control public finances through the establishment of a medium term path for deficit reduction.

Formulation of the budget may be divided into four phases. 1) Early each year, the Ministry of the Budget (MB) prepares a preliminary estimate of next year's expenditures, including both a projection for the current year and an estimate of likely new expenditure. On the basis of this estimate, the Prime Minister, together with the Finance Minister and the Budget Minister decide on budgetary policy for the upcoming year. 2) The Prime Minister then issues "lettres de cadrage" to spending ministries in the Spring explaining the general policy framework for budget preparation. The main activity during this "phase de reconduction" is the rolling forward of the budget for the current year by updating the figures for approved measures ("measures acquises") and for "inescapable new measures" such as the financial consequences of new economic assumptions. The spending ministries submit their "budget de reconduction" to MB, along with proposals for new measures, thereby initiating technical negotiations. 3) In June, the Prime Minister issues "lettres plafonds" to each ministry, setting ceilings on total current and capital expenditures. These lettres go into considerable detail on the measures accepted or required in the next budget. The spending ministries then submit budget proposals and a second round of negotiations takes place, usually focusing on proposed initiatives and required cut-backs. Ministers are normally given considerable freedom to rearrange their budgets by cutting elsewhere to fund new expenditures. 4) The final phase is the technical preparation of the budget to be presented to Parliament.

Germany. Preparation of the annual budget is guided by the medium-term financial plan that is presented to Parliament each year. Both the plan and the budget are developed in the light of the fiscal intentions of the Lander and local authorities, as expressed in the Financial Planning Council where all tiers of government are represented. Proposals made by the Council relating to annual nominal growth of total expenditure and net borrowing are the basis for the top-down planning of the budget and financial plan.

Estimates of future federal revenue in the medium-term plan are based on macroeconomic projections and assumptions. The plan also indicates the Government's policy for federal budgetary balance, as well as for future expenditure in each of 40 large blocks. These blocks are aggregated from figures prepared in a bottom-up approach and agreed between the spending ministries and the Finance Ministry (and approved by the Cabinet) in the same detail as those compiled for the budget. In projecting cash needs for the last three years of the planning period, some blocks include allowance for price increases (such as for indexed social expenditures and interest payments). An unallocated planning reserve is set aside in each of these three planning years for further price increases and new programmes, as well as a global provision for pay increases.

The most important purpose of the medium-term financial plan is to set priorities in line with the Government's policies and to deter excessive demands on the budget. The detailed budget instructions issued by the Finance Ministry each year generally call for departments to keep expenditure bids within the upper limits laid down in the current financial plan. The Finance Ministry also provides special regulations concerning increases in current or administrative costs of departments.

Greece. Although there is no multi-year budget, each annual budget must be consistent with fiscal policy guidelines incorporated in the Programme for the Convergence of the Economy which aims at achieving the targets of the Maastricht Agreement. Within this framework, preparation of the central government budget takes place in several stages. Early in the summer, the Ministry of Finance issues instructions to all ministries and prefectures for the next year's spending proposals. After approval by the relevant Minister and review by the ministry's Ordered Expense Office, the proposals are forwarded to the General Accounting Office (GAO) which prepares and monitors the budget in collaboration with the General Directorates in the Ministry of Finance. GAO scrutinises proposals during the August-September period, and adjustments can be made by the Finance Minister (in consultation with the Prime Minister) to keep expenditure growth within fiscal policy targets. After revenue forecasts are prepared, the Ministry of Finance briefs the government on the budget outlook, and decisions are taken on changes in fiscal policy. Parallel procedures pertain to formulation of the public investment budget, but with two important differences. One is that the investment budget is prepared under the aegis of the Ministry of National Economy; the other is that the Finance Ministry must incorporate, without change, the recommended investment budget in the central government budget.

Ireland. Although there is no formal system of medium-term expenditure allocations, spending departments must forecast resource requirements three to four years ahead. These projections are rolled forward each year and provide input to medium-term economic and budgetary management.

Broad budgetary targets proposed by the Minister for Finance and adopted by the Cabinet provide the framework for negotiations between the Department of Finance (DF) and spending ministries and subsequently between Ministers. After targets have been adopted, DF issues guidelines setting forth the parameters for drawing up the next year's expenditure estimates. The Minister for Finance briefs the Government and negotiates with colleagues, individually or in Government, the estimates for the next year. When agreed by the Government, the detailed estimates are published in advance of the budget, though some final decisions are traditionally made on budget day.

Japan. There is no regular cycle of medium-term expenditure planning, though projections are sometimes used to assist preparation of the annual budget. Guidelines for the budget are decided by Cabinet at the start of each cycle, in the June-July period. Ministries rely on these in submitting requests to the Ministry of Finance by the end of August, following which MOF holds hearings and negotiates with spending ministries in hierarchical order, beginning with lower officials and proceeding, if appropriate, to Ministerial level. Intensive "revival negotiations" often take place in late December shortly before the budget, together with the Fiscal Investment and Loan Plan (FILP), is presented to the Diet. These negotiations do not alter the expenditure totals set in the draft budget. If additional funds are agreed at this stage, they are drawn from unallotted financial resources.

Netherlands. The Government maintains updated multi-year projections (MYP) which serve as a financial control for the Ministry of Finance. The MYP reflect expenditure projections for the budget year and the next four years based on policies agreed by the Cabinet, and they include estimates sensitive to macroeconomic developments, such as interest payments and unemployment benefits. At the start of the budget cycle, they represent the outcome of the last budget, adjusted for subsequent policy changes as well as changes flowing from re-estimates of existing policies and new economic assumptions. The MYP are rolled forward in an ongoing process; each change in budgetary developments results in a corresponding adjustment in the multi-year estimates.

With the MYP as a background, the Minister of Finance submits a "Framework Letter" to the Council of Ministers in March, thereby initiating formal preparation of the budget. The letter sets forth proposed allocations, including expenditure reductions, to various sectors. The letter may also spell out specific measures to achieve the sought cut-backs. The framework letter is discussed by Cabinet which takes decisions in March-April. Detailed budgets are then prepared under rules that generally allow departments to substitute other proposals for those made by the Minister of Finance, provided that the budgetary targets are not affected. Intensive negotiations on draft budgets take place in May-June, initially between the Director General of the Budget and senior officials in the spending departments, followed, if issues remain unsettled, by bilateral talks at ministerial level. Expenditure decisions are finalised by the Council of Ministers in July, but further decisions may be made until the budget is submitted to Parliament in September.

New Zealand. The financial management reforms implemented pursuant to the Public Finance Act of 1989 have greatly altered all aspects of government budgeting. Budget decisions are organised around a "baseline" process in which departments are invited to submit draft budgets at two periods, usually October-November and February-March. These baselines are reviewed by Ministers who make decisions as purchasers of output, on an accrual rather than a cash basis. The Government believes that output budgets better inform Ministers as to what is being achieved and enable them to judge whether the outputs meet priorities. In recent years, the baselines have been governed by rules which deny departments compensation for increases in input costs, require them to fund policy initiatives from reallocations within existing budgets, and permit extra funding only when it is demand-determined.

Norway. Preparation of the annual budget is initiated in February/March when the Cabinet approves preliminary expenditure ceilings for each ministry, as well as separate frames for policy initiatives. The ministries have the opportunity to propose adjustments. Final limits are decided by the cabinet in May/June. The ministries then develop proposals within the agreed limits in the beginning of August. The Cabinet resolves unsettled matters in September, at which time final policies on taxes and economic issues are decided.

Portugal. Although the State budget is annual, it may include programmes or projects that entail expenditure over a number of years. The budget presents an indicative schedule of the programmes and projects included in the investment and expenditure plan (PIDDAC), with a time horizon of four years. The State budget also takes into a account a reference framework drawn up by the Government for the medium-term. This framework is given in a Finance Ministry document known as QUANTUM (National Adjustment Framework for Transition to Economic and Monetary Union) which sets out no-change and adjustment scenarios for the 1991-95 period. The adjustment scenario aims at nominal convergence of the Portuguese economy to the European Community average within this 5-year period by means of a fiscal consolidation that produces a sharp and swift reduction in the public sector deficit and sustained reduction in the public debt. The time path of the policy variables set forth in QUANTUM constitute a political guideline and frame of reference for drawing up the annual budget.

Spain. Multiyear planning, which had initially been designed to extend investment planning beyond the budget year, has given rise to multi-year budget instruments that include macroeconomic and budgetary scenarios. These scenarios treat the annual budget as the first step in a four-year process and provide a framework for analysing the objectives of public sector action and possible effects on the economy. Within this framework, the Ministry for Economic Affairs and Finance (MEF) lays down guidelines for preparation of the budget. The Directorate General of the Budget then draws up corresponding instructions concerning the timetable and procedural requirements of the process. Three ministerial committees play significant roles in budget policy. The Functional Committee for the Budget offers proposals concerning the functional allocation of revenue and expenditure. The Programme Analysis Committee determines the financial requirements of expenditure programmes and ranks objectives according to the priorities laid down by the Functional Committee. The Public Investment Committee co-ordinates investment plans with the multi-year economic framework. After budget proposals have been submitted, the Cabinet may be involved in settling disputes between MEF and other ministries and in approving the draft budget for submission to Parliament.

Sweden. Each Spring, the Government presents medium-term projections of revenue, expenditure, and the budget balance in the "Langtidsbudgeten". The aim of this medium-term budget is to show the financial consequences of existing decisions and commitments for the four-year period ahead. Its scope has been extended to include other levels of government and social security, and to show the financial implications of the public sector for the private sector. This document is neither a programme nor a forecast, but serves as a discussion document for Parliament whose comments influence the Finance Ministry's instructions at the start of the annual budget cycle.

These instructions are transmitted in a general circular to agencies in February, approximately seventeen months before the start of the fiscal year. In addition individualised circulars, addressing matters of particular concern to the relevant agency, are transmitted to agencies operating under three-year budget frames. The

Government experimented with a triennial budget system in the mid 1980s and after several years of pilot testing decided to implement the new system in all agencies. Each agency must undertake a probing assessment of its activities and performance at the start of its three-year cycle, reviewing what it accomplished, in the previous period and setting forth its planned accomplishments for the next three years. This in-depth analysis is guided by a special circular which raises questions and asks for specific information concerning the agency's work and performance. In the intermediate years of the triennial cycle, agencies submit less detailed budget requests provided that the abide by the spending and performance path laid out for them.

Turkey. Budgeting takes place within the framework of the Five Year Plan submitted by the Government to Parliament. The approved plan and annual programmes are binding on the public sector and indicative for the private sector. The Sixth Plan for 1990-94 specifies targets for economic, social, and cultural development. The Plan also specifies ratios of total public expenditure to GDP.

The annual budget cycle begins in June, six months before the start of the fiscal year with a Budget Message by the Prime Minister setting forth a broad statement of principles for the forthcoming budget. On the basis of technical instructions from the Ministry of Finance and Customs (MF) in June, ministries prepare detailed proposals for current expenditure. These are discussed with MF over the next 2-3 months, culminating in decisions by the High Planning Council and the Prime Minister. A parallel process involving negotiations with the State Planning Organisation leads to preparation of an investment budget.

United Kingdom. The annual Public Expenditure Survey, introduced in the 1960s, sets plans for public spending over the next three years. The Government's overall objective for public spending – to reduce it as a share of GDP over time – is set in terms of general government expenditure. But in order to insulate the public expenditure planning process from the effects of variation in the economic cycle, the Government also defines a "new control total". This covers around 85 per cent of general government expenditure but excludes cyclically-related social security benefits and debt interest. The Government sets firm ceilings for the new control total at the start of each Survey, designed to ensure that the Government's public expenditure objectives are met. The aim of the survey is to allocate spending across programmes within these ceilings.

The Survey begins by establishing the baselines agreed in the previous Survey, if necessary incorporating classification changes or transfers of function between departments. Ministers in charge of spending departments then send the Chief Secretary to the Treasury an assessment of the pressures on their baselines, and the scope for offsetting savings. In the light of these submissions, the Chancellor and Chief Secretary report to the Cabinet in June and the Cabinet agrees new ceilings for the control total.

A sub-committee of Cabinet ministers, called EDX, is then charged with allocating spending between departments within ceilings for the new control total. EDX is chaired by the Chancellor of the Exchequer. Its decisions are informed by a series of bilateral meetings between the Chief Secretary and spending ministers; and ministers may also be invited to present their views to EDX. When these discussions are complete, EDX makes recommendations to the full Cabinet. Following agreement at full Cabinet, the new plans are presented in the Budget in November. The Budget on 30 November 1993 was the first to combine the presentation of the new spending plans with proposals for changes in taxation. Soon after the Budget, details of the new spending plans are published in greater detail in a series of departmental reports and a Statistical Supplement to the Budget. The plans set for the year ahead are used as firm control totals for the forthcoming financing year.

United States. The President's budget submitted to Congress early each calendar year presents "baseline" projections of receipts, expenditures and the deficit, as well as projections reflecting the President's proposals. The Congressional Budget Office (CBO) issues its own baseline projections, which may differ from the Administration's and are used by Congress in formulating a "framework" budget resolution. Until 1990, this resolution spanned the next three years; since then, however, it has been expanded to five years. Because the multi-year baselines are critical in computing the budgetary impact of legislation, strong efforts have been made for both the President and Congress to rely on common assumptions. For the FY 1994 Budget, the first budget of the incoming Clinton administration, the President announced that his budget would be based on CBO's macroeconomic assumptions.

Federal departments begin work on the annual budget 18 or more months before the start of the fiscal year. Each department has internal procedures for assembling its requests, but these must be presented to the President's Office of Management and Budget (OMB) in a standard format. During the summer, the President promulgates general budget guidelines and planned ceilings to guide agencies in the preparation of their budgets. Agencies submit their requests in the Fall, following which OMB prepares "passbacks" which notify agencies of the amounts to be recommended in the President's budget. Agencies have a brief period during which they can appeal these passbacks either to OMB or other presidential officers. On occasion, an appeal is made to the President who has the final say or the budget submitted to Congress.

Chapter 5

PARLIAMENTARY CONTROL

Legislative control of public expenditure is a fundamental principle of democratic government. There is no exception in the OECD area to the rule that government may spend public funds only pursuant to legislative authorisation. But the manner in which spending is authorised and the actual role of the legislature in dictating or influencing budget policies varies among OECD Member countries.

Annual appropriations are the traditional means of authorising public expenditure. Increasingly, however, parliaments also authorise expenditure in permanent or standing legislation. The changing composition of public expenditure – relatively more on transfer programmes and relatively less on operating expenses – has reduced the importance of annual appropriations (as a proportion of total expenditure) and given added prominence to spending authorised in standing legislation. Despite the decline of annually appropriated funds as a proportion of total expenditure, the vast expansion in the overall size of governments has meant a steady rise in the volume of appropriated funds.

The growth of government and related developments have wrought other changes in parliamentary practices. Democratic legislatures generally take a more independent stance on budgetary matters than they once did, though the degree to which they actually deviate from the Government's estimates depends on legal practices, tradition, and the overall relationship between the executive and legislature. Nowadays, it is rarely a question of confidence if parliament exercises some independent judgement and appropriates more or less than the government requested. On the matter of parliamentary independence in the voting of appropriations, practices range from the United States where Congress makes numerous significant changes in the budget presented by the President to the United Kingdom where supply is voted in the amount requested by the Government. Parliamentary independence is frequently expressed in the establishment (or enlargement) of legislative budget staffs and in the strengthening of legislative audit functions.

At the same time that parliaments have become more active on budgetary matters, the growth of government has eroded some of their traditional expenditure controls. At one time, the pervasive practice was for the government to submit estimates in the form of "line items", long lists of the resource inputs such as personnel, office supplies, utilities, and so on, to be purchased with public funds. Appropriations were often voted in the same detail, giving spending agencies little flexibility in using the resources provided to them. This form of detailed budgeting is still found in some countries (Germany for example), but the general trend is to reduce the number of items on which expenditure is legislatively controlled and to vote appropriations in broad frames, blocks, or portfolios. In recent years, Australia and Finland have been among the OECD Member countries joining this trend. Many countries have also loosened control over *virement,* the transfer of funds between votes. The overall result is a shift from parliamentary to bureaucratic control.

The growth of government has also weakened the annuality of legislative control. At one time, parliament decided on the amount to be spent each year through annual appropriations. But annual appropriations are not an effective means of regulating demand-determined expenditure, nor is it effective in controlling expenditure on long-term commitments such as investment projects. Quite a few OECD Member countries permit spending agencies to carry forward all or a portion of their appropriations to the next year or beyond. But despite the fact that annual appropriations may determine less than half of government spending in a particular year, parliaments retain annual control as one of their principal instruments for holding government agencies to account. But several countries that have embraced results budgeting have sought to devise means of combining annual appropriations with multi-year control mechanisms.

Belgium. The Government budget is highly detailed, totalling about 4 000 pages and organised into four parts: 1) the *appropriation law* setting forth aggregate amounts and authorisation of virement between certain items in the budget; 2) the *appropriation table* which is voted by Parliament and specifies the appropriations enacted by it; 3) the *apportionment table* which allocates appropriations to the organisations accountable for them; and 4) *supporting notes* which explain, sometimes in considerable detail, each appropriation contributing to a programme.

All expenditures are appropriated each year on a gross basis either as "split appropriations" which specify separate amounts for commitments and payments or as "unsplit appropriations" which specify only a single amount. Split appropriations are used for multi-year construction projects and some defence procurement, with the commitments authorised at the start of the project and outlays voted as the commitments come due. When appropriations are voted on an unsplit basis, the unpaid commitments may be carried forward to the next year without further Parliamentary authorisation to cover payments on unliquidated obligations.

Canada. The Government's plans are presented to Parliament in the *Budget Speech* which specifies revenues, proposed tax changes, and aggregate expenditures, and the Main Estimates which detail the proposed expenditures. The Main estimates consist of three parts: an overview of spending plans by policy sectors, economic category, and department; the appropriations act and the estimates for each ministry, department, and agency; and detailed departmental spending plans presented in a standardised format that describes programmes and their outputs and provides information on resources. The Part III expenditure plans take up more than 5 000 pages.

Appropriations are made in two forms: *annual appropriations* based on the estimates tabled in Parliament cover about 35 per cent of total expenditure, principally for operating costs and capital investments; and *statutory appropriations* for non-lapsing obligations such as debt interest charges, transfer payments and certain other special items. The latter are provided in separate acts of Parliament, and do not have to be renewed each year. Estimates for annual appropriations must be for services requiring payment during the year. Only statutory appropriations authorise spending in future years. Nevertheless, agencies may enter into contracts involving future payments provided these are conditioned on the availability of future appropriations.

Finland. All expenditure, including entitlements, is voted annually in an appropriations bill divided into ministerial portfolios, subdivided by agency or function, and further subdivided by economic category. Expenditures are appropriated as gross amounts, except in the case of commercial enterprises which receive net appropriations. Parliament makes three types of appropriations: fixed annual amounts; authorisations such as for investment projects, which may be carried forward for up to three years; and appropriation estimates which may be exceeded with the consent of the Cabinet's Finance Committee. The last type is used for pay and most transfers and accounts for approximately three quarters of total expenditure. In making appropriations, Parliament may add to expenditure, provided the amount is offset through spending cuts, or tax or borrowing increases so as to maintain budgetary balance.

The structure of appropriations has been altered by the introduction of results-oriented budgeting. The formerly separate items for salaries, other consumption, and equipment have been consolidated into a single item. Accordingly, there has been a steep decline in the number of expenditure items voted by Parliament. The number of expenditure items was less than 600 in the 1994 budget proposal , compared with more than 1200 in 1989.

France. The draft appropriation bill presented to Parliament is accompanied by voluminous annexes (totalling about 10 000 pages) providing details about the particular measure concerned. The blue annexes classify expenditure by title, chapter, and article, and provide information appropriate for each category. The Titles are standard classifications used by all ministries and differentiate operating expenditure, public intervention, investments and investment subsidies. The chapters are unique to each ministry – there were approximately 1 400 in a recent year – and are the level at which Parliament binds spending. The Government is legally bound to apportion appropriations according to the annexed distribution by chapters, as modified by Parliament. Spending is further divided into Articles, mostly organisational units or activities, and the level at which the Ministry of Finance binds spending. There may also be breakdowns of spending by paragraphs and lines – detailed items of expenditure – but these are only for informational purposes.

All expenditures are voted annually on a gross basis, and unless expressly identified as estimated or provisional, are fixed amounts that cannot, in principle, be exceeded without prior authorisation by Parliament. Estimated appropriations, such as for debt service and social security, account for more than one quarter of total expenditure and may be exceeded without further parliamentary authorisation as needed to settle legal obligations. Provisional appropriations are used for a small amount of expenditures that are difficult to estimate. These may be supplemented by drawing on a contingency reserve maintained by the Ministry of Finance. Appropriations are voted separately for "approved services" and "new measures"; the former are voted in the aggregate, the latter are divided into ministries and titles. In appropriating funds for capital expenditures, Parliament authorises both "commitments" which remain available for an unlimited period, and "outlays" which are, in principle only for the budget, but in practice may be carried forward almost automatically.

Sweden. The budget proposal submitted to Parliament consists of the draft appropriation bill and supporting material for each ministerial portfolio. Each portfolio is divided into "estimates" – about 800 for the central government – comprising an agency or a distinct investment or transfer programme. *Explanatory notes* for each estimate summarise what each agency has requested and the minister's response.

Expenditures are voted annually, with most non-tax revenues netted against expenditure. Appropriations may be fixed for a single year, authorisations which may be carried forward 2-3 years (or indefinitely for construction projects), or appropriation estimates which may be exceeded by decision of the Cabinet. The last type of appropriation comprises about 85 per cent of total expenditure and is used for operating costs and most transfers.

United Kingdom. Details of individual departments' spending plans are given in eighteen departmental reports and a statistical supplement published in the early spring. Departments have put a lot of effort into the development of useful performance information, which is reflected in the many indicators and targets included in the reports. Shortly before the start of the financial year, "supply estimates" are presented for voted expenditure and for non-public transfer payments. For each departmental portfolio, the supply estimates indicate whether the vote is a cash limit and define the "ambit" of the vote, that is, the purpose to which expenditure will be put, the net amount and the department accountable. This information is reproduced in the appropriation act. The Treasury has (in 1993) put proposals to Parliament which are intended to improve the coherence of the Supply Estimates and their integration with the information in departmental reports.

Voted expenditures cover about half of total expenditure and are authorised annually. Parliament also authorises expenditure for "standing services", non-lapsing authorisations for debt service and certain other payments. Parliament also enacts two or more supplementary appropriations each year, with any additional spending drawn from the unallocated reserve or offset by reductions in other programmes.

Chapter 6

EXPENDITURE MONITORING AND CONTROL

As a plan of expenditure for the period ahead, the budget is rarely implemented in exactly the form that it was prepared or approved by the legislature. Changes intrude, whether because of shifting economic or political conditions or because of numerous small adjustments in the details of expenditure. Yet as the authorised plan of expenditure, the budget must be put into effect with due regard to the commitments or expectations established by it and to the rules and limits enacted by Parliament. Implementing the budget thus requires a balance between adaptation to changing circumstances on the one hand and adherence to statutory and other strictures on the other. How this balance is struck varies greatly among OECD Member countries.

In all countries, there is provision for supplementation of expenditure, whether through additional appropriations or the transfer of voted funds from one use to another. In all, also, funds may be spent only as authorised by law and (with some exceptions) only up to authorised amounts. In most, concern about budget deficits and a sense of fiscal constraint have strengthened emphasis on adjusting to unanticipated needs by drawing on available reserves or by reallocating resources rather than by going to Parliament for additional funds. The United Kingdom and some other Commonwealth countries have relied on cash limits as a means of compelling spending institutions to make do with planned resources. The Netherlands has emphasised stringent rules of budget discipline that spell out how spending overruns are to be compensated. The United States has devised sequestration procedures for the automatic cancellation of resources if certain budget targets are breached.

Monitoring procedures have also gained prominence in many countries, propelled by advances in computerisation and in information processing capabilities. Many countries now regularly match the spending outturn against the plan, so that appropriate and timely corrections may be made when variances emerge. There is in some countries (New Zealand and the United States, for example) closer linkage of budgeting and accounting systems, not only to ensure that the two are on a consistent and uniform basis, but also to sensitise managers to the financial implications of their actions.

Somewhat different monitoring arrangements are in place for operating expenditure and transfer payments. The former are likely to be cash limited or require that offsetting savings be realised to pay for overruns. In these cases, monitoring is an instrument of expenditure control. It gives spending agencies and central authorities early warning as to the steps needed to avert or compensate overruns. The latter, however, tend to be open-ended, and the main purpose of monitoring is informational, to obtain early indication as to whether expenditure plans are on track. If they are not, supplementation will usually be automatic – no parliamentary action is needed – or routine – parliamentary authorisation will come in due course.

This distinction between operating expenditure (variously known as administrative expenditure or running costs) and transfer payments (variously known as entitlements, mandatory, or demand-led expenditure) has recently become more marked in some countries than was previously the case. Denmark is a notable exception to this trend, for it now combines both types of expenditure in the ''blocks'' used to control spending in ministries. In the United States, by contrast, the Budget Enforcement Act of 1990 established very different rules for controlling discretionary and other expenditure.

In the OECD community, there is a sharp difference in the control of administrative costs between those governments that exercise centralised, *ex ante* control, and those that have delegated control to the spending departments. The first camp is headed by France and Germany, joined by other countries (Belgium, Turkey, Greece) that require pre-authorization of administrative expenditure, such as for personnel and procurement, by inspectors posted in spending ministries but answerable to the Ministry of Finance. This form of control was once the near-universal practice in democratic regimes, and it continues to be used in various countries to ensure that spending is legal and prudent. This form of control is associated with itemised budgets and appropriations as well as relatively large Ministries of Finance.

The second group is headed by the United Kingdom and other Commonwealth countries and several Nordic countries (Denmark, Finland, and Sweden). At one time, governments in these countries exercised centralised control over spending actions. Devolution of control has come in two waves, the first in the 1960s when the growth of government impelled some finance ministries to cede some authority to spending departments, the second in the 1980s (and continuing into the 1990s) when the drive for efficiency and accountability in public expenditure impelled countries to delegate responsibility for spending within agreed budgets to departmental managers. The logic of these devolutions is more fully discussed in a later section on improving managerial accountability and programme effectiveness.

Australia. In line with the medium-term planning strategy and to allow greater flexibility and control of resource for programme managers, significant devolution of administrative costs to spending agencies has occurred. The Running Costs Arrangements (RCA) gives agencies flexibility to move administrative funds from one activity to another and to delay their usage to the following financial period or bring them forward from future appropriations. The quid pro quo for enhanced flexibility is that the amounts are cash limited, an efficiency return is provided to the Government and that agencies are accountable directly to Parliament for delivering programme outcomes.

These arrangements are backed by reliable, up-to-date information on actual spending. The Department of Finance (DOF) provides a computerised accounting service for all departments. DOF officials can access it to a certain level of detail, while each department specifies system requirements for its own monitoring and management purposes. DOF compares actual spending against budget estimates and reports on significant variances to the Finance Minister.

Supplementation of appropriations for unforeseen expenditure can be provided through a special fund appropriated to the Finance Minister (if certain conditions are met) or by additional appropriations in the second half of the year. Normally, departments seeking supplementation are required to offer, to the maximum extent practicable savings in other areas.

Austria. The Ministry of Finance has full control of the use of appropriated funds. Pre-authorization by MF is required for significant discretionary expenditures, as well as for subsidies and capital expenditure, MF also controls commitments and personnel costs. These controls are maintained via monthly allotments and reports. Spending ministries submit their financing needs for MF approval at the start of each month, and they report to MF on a monthly basis on funds previously spent. Increases or shifts in expenditure require parliamentary approval, but MF has limited authority to increase or shift authorised expenditures, provided that additional revenues are available.

Belgium. Spending ministries generally have limited discretion in using appropriated funds. Appropriations are divided into about 3,000 allotments, the level at which MF controls expenditures. MF approval is required for virement between allotments, but virement is not permitted between allotments for different objects – for example, between pay and other expenditure objects – even in the same programme.

To enforce *ex ante* controls, MF has Inspectors of Finance accredited to each spending department. These Inspectors closely monitor departmental operations and have access to all files and data. Although they only advise the spending ministries, the Inspectors play an influential role in budget implementation. All purchases and subsidies above threshold amounts must be submitted to the Inspectors for review. Advice by Inspectors may be appealed to the MF. In addition to these controls, all commitments must have a ''visa'' issued by Commitment Controllers (who work in the various ministries but are accountable to MF) certifying that sufficient funds are available.

The Government generally has limited scope to reallocate funds. In addition to the constraints imposed by the appropriations and allotment structures, departments are further limited by centralised personnel and procurement procedures.

Canada. Spending departments cannot switch resources between parliamentary votes without seeking Parliament's approval, but may reallocate resources across activities within a vote. These delegated authorities are subject to certain restrictions, such as the use of funds earmarked for essential capital which cannot be decreased by discretionary departmental actions. Commencing with the 1993-94 fiscal year, the federal government has introduced an Operating Budget (running cost) regime for managing resources dedicated to programme delivery. With the introduction of this regime, central control and monitoring will be significantly reduced. For example, separate controls and reporting on labour consumption (person years controls) are being eliminated, along with Treasury Board controls on funds earmarked for salary expenditures.

The budgetary system prescribes annual reviews of departmental multi-year operational plans which puts under scrutiny input and activity levels. There are no provisions for spending departments to report on actual expenditures to the budget office unless a department submits a request for supplementary funding at which time resource limits and the use of resources are analysed to determine if the supplementary funding will be recommended. Departments have to report on actual expenditures only if they request supplementary funding, in which case resource limits and use are analysed to determine whether the additional funds should be recommended. In certain cases, frozen allotments (portion of a vote) are established by the Treasury Board, even though the funding has been voted. Such allotments are only released upon satisfaction of conditions established by the Treasury Board.

Denmark. When Parliament votes an appropriation, it delegates authority to spend to the Minister concerned. Reforms during the 1980s increased the managerial responsibility of spending departments and reduced the number of items for which specific Finance Ministry and Parliamentary approval is required. MF runs a computerised paying and accounting service from which monthly data on payments are drawn. However, there is no *ex ante* central control of the payment profile over the course of the year. The formal monitoring arrangement since 1984 has each Ministry to report to MF three times during the year on how actual spending has conformed to – or deviated from – the agreed spending "frame." If overruns are envisioned, the responsible Minister is required to propose means of offsetting the overruns, including possible legislative changes. In practice, contacts between MF and spending departments is continuous and the two sides discuss the scope of remedial action whenever it is necessary.

Finland. A cash management system in use since the late 1960s was upgraded in 1991 to an on-line computer system. The new system offers tools for agencies, the Treasury, and the Ministry of Finance to plan their cash transactions more easily and accurately than before.

The traditional *ex ante* financial controls have been reformed, so they are no longer so detailed and input oriented but cover important legislation, decrees, and decisions that affect expenditure in future years, as well as overdrafts of estimated appropriations. The time span of transferable "reservations appropriations" has been shortened to one plus two years, and their volume has decreased since introduction of a new authorisations system that allows agencies to make commitments whose outlays are disbursed according to a cash outlay plan.

France. The Ministry for the Budget maintains detailed control over spending. It has "Contrôleurs financiers" accredited to each ministry. All proposed commitments are submitted to the relevant Controller who checks them for compliance (authority to commit, accuracy of calculations, correctness of account, accordance with financial management rules) and availability of uncommitted balances. Each spending ministry is responsible in an accounting sense for the propriety of its financial transactions, but approval of its Controller is required before payment is made. The Controller can refuse to authorise a commitment only for reasons of legality, but he can postpone his decision if he finds the commitment inadvisable, thereby forcing a dialogue with the minister concerned. There is no formal system of appeal of the Controller's decisions.

The Government has considerable freedom to move funds between different chapters of a ministry's appropriations by means of two procedures – transfer and virement. MF may transfer funds among chapters, as long as the character of the expenditure is not changed. However, transfers are precluded between current and capital expenditures, between personnel and other operating expenditures, and between various types of personnel expenditures. Shifts may also be made between ministries if the character of the expenditure is not altered. Furthermore, the Prime Minister may, by decree, authorise that appropriations be vired between chapters in the same ministry, even if the character of expenditure is changed. The vired amount cannot exceed 10 per cent of the original appropriation. These transfer and virement authorities are exercised centrally. Spending ministries have limited scope to make reallocations without approval of the Financial Controller.

Germany. A department's appropriation is specified in great detail in the budget law and apart from specially designated expenditure, there is no departmental authority to transfer funds from one item to another. Payments connected to the federal budget are processed through regional finance offices operated by MF which has sole responsibility for maintaining records and preparing each agency's annual accounts. These offices provide monthly analyses of actual spending to the MF, which also obtains reports from departments of probable needs over the next three months. The execution of the budget is thus continuously monitored and controlled.

When expenditures are likely to exceed the authorised total, the Finance Minister may make commitments or expenditures subject to his approval by blocks of expenditure, after having consulted the competent ministers. If the need for additional expenditure is deemed to be unforeseen and unavoidable, and supplementary appropriations cannot be enacted in time, or Parliament has waived the requirement for supplementary appropriations, MF can authorise excess and/or extra-budgetary expenditure. Moreover, the Government has legal authority to authorise additional expenditure to counter a recession without going through supplementary budget procedures. Conversely, MF can block expenditures or commitments in order to avoid overheating of the economy. Parliament must be informed of important departures from the budget plan, including excess and extra-budgetary expenditure.

Greece. MF has quarterly and monthly means of regulating expenditure. It decides on the percentage of certain annual appropriations that are to be spent in each quarter of the year, and determines the amounts that may be spent each month for certain categories of spending. Unspent balances lapse at the end of the year and are not transferred to the next year's budget. However, under certain circumstances, they may be used to cover overruns in expenditure.

Ireland. Public Expenditure may only be undertaken with the authority of Parliament given either in the annual Appropriation Act or in specific enabling legislation. In addition, it requires the sanction of the Minister for Finance which may be specific (for once-off expenditures) or delegated. In practice, authority for expenditure on continuing current programmes, which constitute the vast bulk of expenditure, is delegated to spending ministries subject to conditions and regulations governing their operations. Spending under delegated authority may not exceed overall cash limits specified in the annual supply estimates. Expenditures not having the sanction of MF cannot be charged against money voted by Parliament. If commitments lack this authority, the Department of Finance may withhold sanction if it determines that they should not have been incurred.

Each department prepares a profile of monthly expenditure (capital and current) at the start of the year; once agreed, this profile is used as a set of monthly cash limits, so that funds underspent in one month cannot be automatically reclaimed in a later month. A department can spend more than planned in a month only with the express approval of MF. Approved overspending in one month must be offset by savings later in the year. Unspent funds cannot be carried forward to the next year, but departments operating under the Administrative Budget Initiative launched in 1991 may have some savings in one year reallocated to it in the next year.

Japan. Each department is required to obtain MOF approval of its plans for incurring liabilities (contracts and other actions that lead to government expenditure). In addition, detailed profiles of expected disbursements by each departmental disbursing officer must be approved by MOF before the start of each quarter. The approval of the Finance Minister is needed for a department to transfer funds from one line item to another in its budget. The Finance Minister can also call for *ad hoc* reports on actual and prospective spending, and it can recommend corrective action that it deems necessary.

Netherlands. MF delegates substantial authority to spending ministries, but it retains the right to specify the items for which liabilities may not be incurred without its advance permission. During the year, departments operate under rules of strict budget policy that aim to keep spending within the intended totals. The rules prescribe how overspending is to be compensated by savings. During the year, also, periodic meetings are held between MF and each spending ministry about possible deviations from planned expenditure. In most instances, problems are resolved without Parliamentary involvement by shifting balances between sub-items, or under strict conditions (and to a limited extent) by shifting from one vote to another.

Norway. The appropriation and budget systems were changed beginning in 1986 to give spending institutions more discretion and flexibility in the use of appropriated funds. These reforms replaced a detailed control system with performance-based incentives to improve cost effectiveness.

Before the start of the year, each ministry issues an allotment letter to its subordinate agencies informing them of the resources at their disposal. Agencies are authorised to spend within their allotments, but they must regularly report on expenditure trends to their respective ministries. The Government (and for minor amounts MF) has been authorised by Parliament to increase expenditures by up to a preset amount.

Portugal. The Directorate-General for Public Accounts (DGCP) is responsible for monitoring implementation of the budget, and for this purpose compiles monthly information on expenditures. DGCP calculates safety limits for various categories of expenditure. If these are breached, it informs the Secretary of State for the Budget to ensure that appropriate measures are taken.

Certain changes to the budget, such as transfers between chapters in the organic classification or between functional categories, are within the competence of Parliament. But the Budget Law allows MF to transfer funds from the provisional allocation set aside to cover essential expenditure that was not foreseen when the budget was drawn up. Transfers between fiscal years may be undertaken, if provided for in the Budget Law, for investment expenditures and autonomous funds and departments. These funds and departments may implement budget changes that do not involve increased debt financial or increased transfers from the administrative sector.

Sweden. Virtually all executive activities are entrusted to independent agencies which carry out the policies developed by the ministries. After the budget is approved by Parliament, the Government issues Allotment Letters to the agencies specifying the conditions under which appropriated funds are to be spent. Each agency's Letter spells out the amount and type of appropriation, the purposes or activities for which the funds can be used, a budget specification splitting relevant appropriations into allotments (''anslagsposter''), specific limits or conditions, such as those pertaining to pay, and instructions concerning financial management and accounting.

The Allotment Letter may reserve a portion of the appropriation for further Cabinet decision. Agencies have considerable freedom in spending allotted funds. There are no general requirements for pre-authorisation by MF or Cabinet, but agencies must keep within general guidelines on procurement, personnel, and other administrative matters.

Because each agency is normally funded out of a single appropriation, there is limited scope for reallocation among agencies. Within each agency, however, there is substantial scope for shifting among activities, but there are restrictions on shifting between programme and administrative expenditure. Agencies operating under three-year budget frames are permitted to carry-over unspent funds to the next year or draw in advance on a limited portion of the next year's appropriation.

Agency use of funds is monitored by external auditing bodies. The National Audit Bureau provides the government with regular assessments of how the budget is developing against plans. This information is used both to manage the government's cash flow and to check budget outcomes against appropriated funds.

Turkey. The Ministry of Finance (MF) is empowered to regulate spending throughout the fiscal year. Shortly after the approval of the budget by Parliament, MF issues a circular to all agencies stating the main principles governing commitments of funds and the maximum percentage of appropriations to be released during the first six months of the year. Another circular, covering the second half of the year, is issued in June. The principles and percentages of the apportionments depend on general economic conditions; recent trends in revenue and expenditure; the need to spread current expenditure throughout the year; and the type of activities concerned. In addition, there is a separate control on the rate of outlays. MF also controls commitments in current and future years.

Inasmuch as Parliament appropriates funds at the programme level, its approval is required to transfer between programmes. However, transfers among items within the same programme may be authorised by MF. The transfer of investment expenditure within the same programme requires the consent of both the State Planning Organisation and MF. Unused funds lapse at the end of the fiscal year.

United Kingdom. When Parliament votes appropriations, it delegates to the Treasury authority to sanction payments from the vote in question. The Treasury in turn delegates authority to the spending departments in respect of most routine expenditures. This delegation is accompanied by arrangements regarding the information on expenditure that is to be provided by departments.

At the start of the financial year, each department provides profiles of expected spending, and as the year progresses they report actual spending through the Paymaster General's Office, which in turn provides monthly reports to the Treasury. These reports assist the Treasury in managing funds and assessing trends in total public expenditure. Care is taken not to dilute the responsibilities of spending departments to stay within cash limits and to provide early warning of likely variances in demand-led spending from agreed profiles.

Within each department, the Principal Finance Officer (PFO) appointed by the Permanent Secretary with the approval of the Treasury, is responsible for overseeing the management of expenditure. The Financial Management Initiative gave departments greater discretion in managing running costs and made them accountable for outputs and results. Building on this initiative, the Next Steps Initiative launched in 1988 extends the devolution of authority from departments to their constituent agencies. Each Next Steps agency has a Chief Executive who also serves as its accounting officer and is responsible to the competent Minister for the performance of the agency.

United States. Appropriations voted by Congress are not directly concerned with outlays or cash spending. Rather, they provide authority to enter into obligations that will result in outlays either during the current or future fiscal years. Outlays during a year may therefore be payment either for obligations incurred in prior years or the same years. The budget contains estimates of the outlays expected to ensue during the fiscal year to which it pertains, but these estimates are not cash limited, and they may be exceeded by actual payments.

After appropriations have been enacted, the Office of Management and Budget (OMB) apportions budget authority – authority to enter into obligations – to each agency, often by quarters of the year but sometimes for the entire year, or by activities to minimise the need for supplemental appropriations. A single apportionment is made for each of the approximately 1 100 budget accounts and for each of the various funds in the budget. Once budget authority has been apportioned, the responsibility for spending within budget and for authorised purposes rests with the spending agency. The Chief Financial Officers Act of 1990 established a Chief Financial Officer in the 23 largest federal departments and agencies and assigned this official broad responsibility for integrating budgeting with other accounting and financial management responsibilities.

Congress has established impoundment procedures governing instances in which appropriated funds are withheld from obligation or expenditure. These procedures distinguish between deferrals which delay the use of funds and are only permitted for routine management purposes, and rescissions which cancel previous appropriations. For both rescissions and deferrals, the President must notify Congress of his action. Rescissions take effect only upon the enactment of legislation by Congress.

Congressional approval is required for the transfer of funds between appropriation accounts. Shifts within the same account – known as reprogramming – may be made under procedures spelled out by the relevant congressional committee. Once funds have been obligated, they may be carried over to future years. Unobligated funds may be carried over only if they have been appropriated on a "no-year" basis or for a period beyond the fiscal year.

Chapter 7

BUDGETARY RESERVES

All countries make provision, within their overall expenditure targets, for unexpected requirements during the year. Some require spending departments to return to Parliament or the Finance Ministry to obtain additional funds or reprogramme previously provided resources. Others give spending departments considerable latitude in responding to unanticipated needs. One of the more widely-used methods is to establish an unallocated reserve that may be drawn upon as needed. Governments, with more or less rigor, embrace the view that it is the responsibility of spending departments to stay within the borders of their allocated budget, and that access to central reserves should be a last resort.

Different country practices indicate that central reserves are much more commonplace than departmental reserves, if only because the former enable the budget office to drive harder bargains. The *United Kingdom* and *Canada* have moved away from departmental reserves in favour of a central pool of unallocated resources. The UK Treasury concluded that departmental reserves weaken the government's ability to assess competing claims across the whole range of programmes. For its part, Canada simplified and centralised its Policy and Expenditure Management System by shifting from envelope-specific to government-wide reserves. Central reserves have one notable drawback: they may tempt departments to spend funds with less care than they might if the reserves were not available. Governments have sought to mitigate their danger through financial management reforms designed to hold managers accoutable for actions and results. These reforms give departments more flexibility in the use of funds on condition that they stay within agreed limits.

Where unallocated reserves are centrally maintained, the budget office (or Finance Ministry) will likely play a role in their distribution. In *Australia,* an Advance to the Minister of Finance is appropriated which may be utilised at the Minister's discretion upon application by spending departments meeting the urgent and unforeseen or urgent and in error criteria. In addition, a provision for Running Costs Borrowings is available for expenditure on running costs as long as funds are subsequently repaid to the Budget by the relevant agency. In *Canada* the contingency vote is used to adjust the pay bill for unbudgeted increases. In *Italy,* the Legislature votes reserves totalling 8-10 per cent of total spending, to meets the cost of new programmes and or cost overruns on established programmes. In *Turkey,* the Ministry of Finance and Customs has custody of funds for use in emergencies.

There are alternatives to a formal reserve. Since 1980, *Japan* has operated according to the principle of "scrap and build" which requires that new programmes be financed out of savings in old ones. In the *United States,* the President may propose supplemental appropriations for needs not provided in the regular appropriations. But the current practice is to require agencies to absorb the cost of unbudgeted pay increases, and not to finance them through supplemental funds.

Austria. The annual budget does not provide a general contingency reserve, but token funds may be set aside for a portion of the cost of future pay increases. The budget also provides for carrying forward unspent balances, usually for capital projects. In addition, the budget laws give the government some scope for overspending and permit the Finance Minister to activate a contingency budget in case of certain economic problems. During implementation of the budget, the Finance Ministry closely monitors spending rates and freezes a portion of appropriations to serve as a reserve for guarding against over-expenditure. This reserve gives the Finance Ministry room to manoeuvre to deal with unexpected or unbudgeted costs such as pay increases. Inter-year reserves, most commonly for capital projects and "earmarked" reserves for expenditures financed by hypothecated revenues, are controlled by the Ministry of Finance which regulates withdrawals.

Canada. The Policy and Expenditure Management System (PEMS), established in 1979, involved the preparation of a multi-year fiscal plan which specified annual spending limits or "envelopes" for each of the government policy sectors. Each sector contained a number of programmes linked in terms of their policy objectives. There was a policy reserve within each envelope to fund new or enriched programmes and a centrally-managed operating reserve to respond to contingencies associated with the existing policy framework. The reserves initially totalled about 6 per cent of planned outlays, but by 1986-87 this had been reduced to less than 3 per cent.

By the mid 1980s, PEMS had become rule burdened and bureaucratic. This was largely due to the fact that PEMS with its original policy envelopes fostered incrementalism, while concern was growing over the debt and deficits. In 1984 the Government fundamentally changed the PEMS system by abolishing the Ministries of State – the secretariats to the sectoral policy committees. This had the effect of strengthening the influence of the Privy Council Office and the Department of Finance.

By the late 1980s, the amount allocated to envelopes for new policy initiatives approximated one per cent of planned expenditure. Growing pressures to reduce the reserves, coupled with various expenditure reduction measures, led to frustrations as Ministers competed for increasingly limited resources. At the same time, special purpose contingencies provided centrally by the Minister of Finance became more common as the Government restricted its attention to a few key government priority areas. With the approval of the Cabinet Committee on Priorities and Planning resources would be earmarked in the framework for key policy initiatives. Decision making became more centralised.

In 1989, the Government abandoned the policy envelopes and reorganised the Cabinet structure. This reorganisation, while increasing the number of Cabinet Committees, did away with the "policy envelopes" and mandated the policy committees to "concentrate on policy", as opposed to getting bound up in transaction issues. Authority to authorise new expenditures was restricted to the Cabinet Committee on Priorities and Planning (P&P) in the case of new policy initiatives. Treasury Board would have authority in the case of the Operating Reserve. The reserves that remained were a central policy reserve managed by P&P, an Operating Reserve and a Reserve for Statutory Overruns. The latter reserve serves as a contingency for incremental requirements arising from changes in the demographic or economic assumptions underlying forecasts in statutory payments.

The centralisation of the expenditure management decision process is consistent with the increasing focus on expenditures as the mechanism for addressing deficit concerns, in particular the mid-term strategy of reducing expenditures as a percentage of GDP.

Netherlands. The annual budget presented to Parliament includes a central allowance for pay and price increases based on inflation forecasts issued by the Central Planning Bureau. The Ministry of Finance allocates sums to departments in compiling the Spring Memorandum early in the new financial year. These distributions are partly automatic, partly discretionary, and spending departments may have to absorb some cost increases within their cash limits. These cash limits are enforced by "rules of stringent budget policy" which govern the manner in which compensating cuts or savings are produced to avoid or minimise net additional expenditure. The basic rule is that offsets are to be sought in the department responsible for the overexpenditure. To assure that this is feasible, some departments withhold a portion of their funds when sub-allocating them to subordinate organisational units. When compensatory cuts are not found, general compensation – either on the basis of *ad hoc* decisions or formula – may be necessary. Although the rules of stringent budget policy have not prevented spending outturns from exceeding the budget, they have comported with the emphasis on collective decisions in the Dutch style of coalition governments.

United Kingdom. The annual public expenditure plans include an unallocated reserve within the planning total for each of three forward years. The purpose of the reserve is to ensure that spending above departmental plans – whether for programme initiatives, policy changes, unforeseen events, or revised estimates – is contained within the planning totals. The level of reserves is normally higher for the later years of the planning cycle than for the year immediately ahead. In the 1989/90-1991/92 cycle, the reserves were 2 per cent in the first year, rising to 5-6 per cent in the final year.

For the first year, the planning total becomes a cash limit, and the reserve is the last line of defence in preventing over-expenditure. All additional spending is charged to the reserve, while net savings are credited to it. The reserve is charged for excess spending by departments, excesses in demand-led programmes such as social security, and discretionary increases allowed by the Treasury. There are standing procedures for bids on the reserves which may be made by departments only after considering whether the excess can be offset by reductions in other areas or, if appropriate, by additional receipts. Within Treasury, claims on the reserve normally are decided at ministerial level. The Treasury monitors the status of the Reserve throughout the year, along with the projected outturn for public expenditure. If a claim on reserves is accepted for spending financed by Parliamentary vote, Treasury will present a supplementary estimate, and it may also have to seek adjustments in cash limits.

Future year reserves function as a cushion in the planning process, not as an operational control. It is typical for a portion of these reserves to be allocated as the years to which they apply draw near.

Chapter 8

BUDGETING FOR PERSONNEL

Public sector employment has broad economic and budgetary implications. Through the 1960-82 period, government employment growth in the OECD area exceeded employment growth in the private sector. By the early 1980s, governments in most OECD Member countries employed between 15 and 22 per cent of all workers, and their wage bill ranged between 10 and 14 per cent of GDP. The size and cost of public employment inevitably sharpened the interest of budget organisations in personnel policies and personnel expenditures, especially during the 1980s when restrictive fiscal postures were common. Controlling personnel was seen as an opportunity to improve budgetary balance while realising efficiency gains in the public sector.

Most of the instruments for controlling personnel – classification, recruitment, etc. – are not in the hands of the budget office. Among those concerning which budget officials may have a say, wage rates and personnel levels are the most prominent. Many governments have adopted specific targets with respect to aggregate personnel levels, either as a means of downsizing the civil service or constraining its further growth, or as an indirect means of forcing efficiency gains. These global limits are most likely to be applied to central government departments, with state enterprises exempted and certain other categories (such as defence forces) separately controlled. In some countries (Denmark and Iceland) agencies carrying out business activities are budgeted on a net expenditure basis which frees them from personnel controls.

Although personnel controls vary among countries, several patterns emerge. Some limit only the total number of positions while others also base controls on salary level or rank. Personnel targets are usually expressed in full-time equivalents or person-years. In general, personnel controls are exercised in the framework of or parallel to the annual budget process. Some countries have multi-year targets that aim to steadily reduce staffing levels over a period of years. Germany, Japan, the United Kingdom, and the United States are among the countries that have experienced a progressive decline in central government employment over the past decade.

Personnel expenditure is generally monitored and controlled on the same basis as other expenditure, with parliamentary approval required if appropriations are exceeded. Some countries have special personnel monitoring and control systems in place, with periodic reports on staffing, personnel expenditures, and related matters. Some flexibility in the use of personnel resources is prevalent in many countries, either by way of shifting among positions during the year, or transferring unused personnel expenditure to purchases of goods and services. Shifts from operating expenditure to personnel tend to be restricted, however, though countries that have undertaken ambitious financial management initiatives (the United Kingdom and New Zealand, for example) may provide more scope for redeploying resources, as deemed appropriate by managers, within approved budget limits. Additional flexibility may be available by drawing on personnel reserves, positions set aside for allocation during the year.

Australia. There are no longer any general personnel controls imposed on departments and agencies. Instead, a cash limited system has been provided, the Running Costs Arrangements (RCA), whereby agency managers have discretion over numbers and levels of staff, subject to service wide classification standards. Parliament approves changes to running costs budgets, but does not act on the detailed staffing levels. The Government does retain some specific controls over the number and level of Senior Executive staffing.

Canada. Prior to the 1993-94 financial year, person year (PY) controls were applied to full and part-time employment and were imposed on virtually all departments, though military staff and Crown Corporations were not covered. PY levels are established for each "programme", which generally corresponds to an entire agency in small departments and to a major organisational unit in larger ones. Person-year controls were discontinued as of 1993-94, with the government-wide introduction of Operating Budgets. The Treasury Board controls the creation and staffing of positions through Target Executive Count (TEC) controls. This system provides each department a base number of approved positions at the senior management and executive levels. Departments are allowed a "flexibility factor" of 1 per cent above this base to accommodate special situations.

Denmark. Personnel is controlled by means of multi-year limits on total pay including pension costs. Commercial enterprises and agencies which perform secondary business activities on a net expenditure basis are not subject to these controls. The Budget Department (BD) is responsible for total government personnel and the staffing levels of ministries. Within BD, the same staff handle personnel controls and the expenditure budget of the respective ministries. During budget formulation, BD exercises control by means of multi-year limits on total pay. These limits are confirmed by Cabinet at the same time it sets ministerial spending limits.

Within the limits, Ministers are free to set staffing levels of the various agencies and institutions. But more detailed central control is exercised by BD over changes in management positions. An annex to the Finance Bill sets forth for each agency and institution total person years for the budget year and the next three years, at each management level.

Finland. According to law reforms enacted in 1992, the agencies required to budget for results were entrusted with the power to establish, change and abolish positions for their personnel. Remuneration for the personnel of these agencies is budgeted under their running costs appropriations. Positions and the necessary funding may be transferred from one agency to another subject to the approval of the line ministry concerned, and between administrative branches of ministries by a Cabinet decision. Details of the 1 300 most senior positions (of which 1 000 constitute Judges) are required to be listed in the budget.

The numbers of personnel are regulated by ceilings issued in the annual budget process. On the basis of these ceilings, grand totals for personnel numbers are decided in the annual budget for the administrative branches of all ministries. The ceilings have also been used as an instrument to reduce personnel numbers. The Cabinet decided on 30 April 1991 to cut the number of personnel remunerated from the budget by 5 per cent (6 700 positions) over the period to 1996.

Germany. A single personnel structure covers the entire public service in the Federal Republic, including central, regional, and local administration. It also covers research and educational institutions, hospitals, and various state enterprises. A parallel system covers the Armed Forces. The federal budget approved by Parliament lists authorised posts. It also sets forth personnel allocations to administrative units, but does not assign staff to specific programmes. Changes in the number and grade of staff require the approval of both the federal government and Parliament. New staff can not be added unless authorised posts are open, even if funds are available. Conversely, the Ministry of Finance may provide funds from a special reserve to enable agencies to fill authorised posts. These rules generally apply to permanent staff, not to temporary employees.

The personnel and expenditure budgets are closely co-ordinated. The same administrative entities are involved in each case and the same procedures are applied. An important feature of the government's policy of consolidation is not to allow personnel levels to increase. When an increase in staffing levels is clearly necessary, attempts are made to find offsetting reductions elsewhere. Other means of restraining staff size is to require proportionate cut-backs in the number of posts by administrative entities or to approve new positions on the condition that they lapse after a specified number of years. Departments are generally free to manage posts as they see fit. The personnel budget is subject to verification by the Federal Audit Office in the same manner as the expenditure budget.

Iceland. Personnel control is the responsibility of the same Bureau of the Budget (BoB) staff that handle the expenditure budgets of the respective ministries. The Personnel Committee (chaired by the Director of the Budget, with representatives from Parliament and the Ministry of Finance) formally authorise new positions and the transfer of positions between organisations. The budget submitted to Parliament contains information on staffing, but Parliament does not vote on personnel limits or targets. There is relatively little control on personnel usage during the year as long as an organisation's net expenditure stay within the limits set in the budget. Hence, with the exception of positions at the highest policy and management levels, organisations may make in-year adjustments without consulting BoB. But in filling permanent positions, the responsible department must certify that the necessary funds are available.

Japan. The Total Staff Number Law, which was approved by the Diet, stipulates the maximum number of full-time employees. This law does not cover defence forces, government enterprises, the Diet, or courts – all of which are controlled by other regulations. The staff size of each ministry and agency is determined by Cabinet Order and the budget, within prescribed limits. Staff control is carried out mainly by the Management and Co-ordination Agency which is separate from the budget organisation. However, the Ministry of Finance does get involved in staff control through preparation of the salary budget.

Inasmuch as staff ceilings are set by law, any change in the upper limit can be made only by legislation. Since 1968, the Government has adopted a series of personnel reduction plans. The 7th plan, covering the 1987-91 period, provided for a 5 per cent reduction in personnel. In adopting this plan, the government also decided to seek comparable reductions in public corporations. The monitoring of staff size is carried out through quarterly reports by each agency and by personnel audits that parallel the spending audits.

Netherlands. Total civil service staff is controlled by ceilings on the number of person years (or full-time equivalents) and on expenditure for personnel in the various ministries. These ceilings are imposed by the Cabinet and laid down in the annual budget and the multi-year plans. The limits apply only to the central civil service; other parts of the "collective sector" are controlled indirectly through expenditure budgets. Enforcement of the personnel limits has been entrusted to the Interior Ministry's Directorate General for Management and Personnel Policy (DGMP). Decisions regarding a ministry's financial resources for personnel are made through tripartite discussions between the Finance Ministry, DGMP, and the relevant ministry. If not resolved at this level, the matter may be decided by the council of ministers. As part of the annual budget, personnel limits are formally approved by Parliament.

During the post-war period, public employment rose while private employment declined. To reverse this trend, the 1983 and 1987 Lubbers Governments adopted explicit targets for reducing the size of the civil service over a four-year period. The 1983 policy exempted certain sectors and fell short of its target, but the 1987 drive covered the entire civil service (though not the rest of the collective sector).

No reserves are set aside for adjusting the personnel levels after the financial year has started. The Finance Ministry monitors the utilisation of agreed expenditure budgets, including personnel spending, on a monthly basis, while the Interior Ministry monitors the use of personnel every three months. These central organs may intervene if overutilisation or other misuse of personnel is suspected.

Norway. Personnel use in the central government is controlled through: 1) limits on net new positions and 2) limits on total pay expenditures. The budget specifies net new positions in each organisational unit.

Decisions with respect to net new positions are integrated with formulation of the budget. Personnel ceilings are issued by the Budget Department to each ministry which, in turn, propose the allotment of personnel resources to agencies. After the budget has been adopted, major changes in personnel have to be formally approved by Parliament, in the same manner as changes in expenditure. Minor changes are in the competence of the Ministry of Finance.

Turkey. Position controls apply to civil servants, contract personnel, and permanent workers, but not to temporary employees. Controlled positions are created by the legislature and may be filled with approval of the General Directorate of Budget and Financial Control (DBFC). Certain positions within public enterprises are not subject to controls. Personnel expenditures, by programme, are determined by negotiations between agencies and DBFC during preparation of the annual budget. Parliament's Plan-Budget Committee considers personnel expenditure as part of its work on the Budget Bill. During the fiscal year personnel expenditures and position utilisation is monitored by Finance Inspectors and Budget Controllers; after year-end, the Court of Accounts (which is responsible to Parliament) audits expenditures and utilisation of unreserved positions.

United Kingdom. Costs of employing civil servants are controlled by running cost limits which cover pay and other recurrent costs of administration. Where pay bargaining has been delegated to an individual department or Agency, a control on the civil service paybill component of running costs is also agreed – from April 1994 around half of the civil service will be managed in this way. Provision for civil service pay and other running costs is discussed in the Public Expenditure Survey, where the presumption is that pay and price increases will be offset in whole or large part by improvements in efficiency, with year on year changes in the overall paybill where this is required to reflect significant workload changes. Provision for pay in other parts of the public sector is planned on the same basis, though different control arrangements apply.

United States. Total civilian employment in the executive branch is controlled on a full-time equivalent (FTE) basis. Some agencies or programmes are governed by laws establishing minimum employment levels. Permanent law limits the number of positions in the Senior Executive Service (SES). The Office of Personnel Management controls the allocation of these senior posts.

FTE requests are reviewed by the President's Office of Management and Budget along with agency expenditure estimates. The President's budget submitted to congress includes his recommendations for employment levels, and Congress often specifies FTE levels in Committee reports on the various Appropriations Bills. Inasmuch as most FTE ceilings are administrative rather than statutory, the executive branch has flexibility in shifting personnel resources. Within an agency, FTE's can be adjusted among bureaux or programmes, provided that the agency's total FTE allowance is not exceeded. The President sometimes announces a government-wide limitation on positions, but these targets are not enacted into law. The most recent instance was the promulgation by President Clinton in September of 1993 to reduce federal employment levels by 252 000 over a four-year period. The reduction is based on recommendations for government reform included in the six month national Performance Review, which was led by the Vice President and finished its work in September 1993.

Chapter 9

MANAGERIAL ACCOUNTABILITY AND PROGRAMME EFFECTIVENESS

The practice of budgeting is evolving in many OECD Member countries from a means of ensuring legality and propriety in public expenditure into an instrument for promoting managerial improvement and programme effectiveness in the public sector. This evolution has progressed at different rates in Member countries, as the previous discussion of expenditure monitoring and control indicates. It has advanced furthest in those countries that emphasise output or results-oriented budgeting and that have delegated substantial responsibility for expenditure management to programme managers. But it has taken hold to some degree in all Member countries and is reflected in the consolidation of expenditure objects into broader categories, relaxation of central controls, increased interest in outputs and performance. In no OECD country is the grip of centralised control as tight and pervasive as it was 30 years ago.

Several characteristics of this development warrant introductory comment. First, legality in public expenditure remains a bedrock requirement of public finance. It is a ubiquitous rule of democratic government that funds may be spent only as supplied or authorised by parliament, and only for allowed purposes. How this sine qua non of democratic rule is satisfied varies among countries, but its implementation has been transformed – not uprooted – by the addition of managerial functions to budgeting. Typically, it is accompanied by a shift from *ex ante* controls to internal controls, from pre-audits to post-audits, from auditing individual transactions to auditing systems, and from highly itemised appropriations to block appropriations. several of these developments are recognisable in the chapters on parliamentary control and expenditure management.

Second, the evolution has not been steady and relentless; rather, it has occurred in spurts. One of the most prominent of these was the introduction of planning-programming-budgeting systems (PPBS) and similar systems in the 1960s and 1970s. The most recent has been propelled by financial management initiatives and other reforms launched in the 1980s and continued early in the next decade. This development has not yet run its course; hence a full assessment of its application or accomplishments would be premature.

Third, the devolution of significant budget responsibilities to programme managers inevitably alters the role of the central budget organisation and its relationship to spending agencies. At this stage of development, it is easy to identify what has been yielded up by the budget office, but much more difficult to discern how it fits into the new order of things. Divested of routine controls, the budget office is to be recast into the lead institution for management improvement. Its new niche is to prod and energise, but it may not have the right levels for the job. Moreover, there may be a fundamental contradiction between the notion that spending agencies should (within agreed budgets) take charge of their own financial actions and the expectation that the same budget office which allocates and rations public resources should be the chief instrument of managerial and programme improvement. There will have to be much sorting out of responsibilities before the final verdict is in on this matter.

Finally, the reforms are focused on a vital but (in most countries) relatively narrow slice of the budget – the portion allocated to administrative or running costs. There has been no parallel development with respect to transfer payments, the fastest growing and least controlled part of government expenditure. At first glance, it may appear surprising that the most controlled portion of the budget is the prime target of contemporary management reforms, but there is a certain logic to this emphasis. For one thing, precisely because administrative expenditure is controlled, it may be safe to loosen the reins a bit and give spending agencies greater latitude in using these funds. For another, although they have been controlled, administrative spending has generally crept upwards over the years, and there is evidence that productivity gains in OECD governments have lagged comparable trends in the private sector. The devolution of spending control is typically accompanied by strict restraints on administrative costs, with agencies allowed increases below the rate of inflation. One widely-applied formula has been to hold annual increases in these costs two per cent below the rate of inflation. The two per cent rate has been favoured either because it is sufficiently small to be acceptable or because it mirrors long-term productivity improvement in business firms. But compounded over a period of years, this expenditure squeeze may impel agencies to retrench services or improve performance. Delegated budgeting and related managerial reforms aim at avoiding the first outcome and achieving the second. These innovations depend on a usually implicit (though sometimes explicit) quid pro quo: in exchange for giving agencies less real resources, the government gives them more discretion of their money.

While administrative costs may be a declining portion of central government budgets, they loom quite large in the everyday operations of agencies. The rules and procedures governing these expenditures have a lot to do with the behaviour and performance of managers. If the rules bind and constrict, it is argued, managers will operate by the book, giving primacy to the legalities of control and not caring very much about results. They cannot be held accountable for performance because they lack a genuine voice in how funds are to be applied, and they are prevented or discouraged from shifting resources from less to more productive uses. Managers cannot manage if they must repeatedly get approval from others before spending appropriated funds, or if their entreaties to shift resources are blocked by external controllers.

There are strong counter-arguments, of course, as evidenced by the governments that have retained central-ised control. Some of these are rooted in the political and administrative traditions of particular countries and may be difficult to change without remaking basic institutions of government. These considerations notwithstanding, some countries beholden to centralised administration may inch toward a more managerial posture in the years ahead.

Transforming the budget into an instrument of managerial and programme improvement depends on many changes in administrative practice that go far beyond the scope of the present study. But three budget-related reforms are vital, and they are considered in the sections that follow. Managers may be held accountable for performance when they have opportunity and incentives to spend authorised expenditure to achieve agreed programmes; they are held accountable for costs, including costs that under conventional accounting practices may not be charged to their budgets; and they are held accountable for results and performance, especially the results produced by public expenditures. These conditions are interdependent, though far greater attention has been paid to the last than to the other two, and far less progress has been made in accountability for cost than in managerial discretion and performance-based management. The linkage of the three reforms is most boldly recognised in the recent reform of the New Zealand public sector.

Managerial discretion. Recent changes in the budgetary systems of some governments reflect a shift from detailed regulations and managing for compliance to increased incentives and opportunity for managers to use discretion and initiative in achieving expenditure and performance targets. The institutional incentives that have been provided include: allowing spending departments to retain all (or a portion of) savings beyond centrally-determined targets; more discretion with respect to the mix of inputs (supplies, equipment, etc.) and the timing-of expenditures; greater freedom to reallocate funds between programmes or activities; and wider scope for levying user charges and applying the proceeds to relevant activities. The shift away from strict compliance has been accompanied by renewed emphasis on performance indicators, the negotiation and enforcement of strict spending limits, and new reporting and review requirements.

These managerial incentives have been introduced as a tool for expenditure reduction or restraint on the one hand and enhanced productivity on the other. In the countries that have moved in this direction, there is a shared feeling that a stringent fiscal environment has helped the reforms along. Higher productivity in the public sector is the key stated objective of giving operational flexibility to programme managers. Lower expenditure, decided at the centre, has been the main instrument to force or induce productivity gains. Reductions in resources have driven efficiency, not the other way around.

Assessments of progress in various countries indicate that some success has been achieved in containing or reducing administrative expenditures without major changes in programmes. Managers have been assigned responsibility for achieving planned shrinkage in expenditures; the precise distribution of cut-backs has not been dictated from above. The role of the budget office has been to foster a more performance-oriented managerial climate through the development of new measures and other reforms. But two obstacles have emerged in some countries. One is that the operational constraints on managers is still substantial, with separate controls still common on personnel and salaries, low caps on the resources that can be carried forward to the next year, and barriers to transfers between current and capital expenditure. This problem may cure itself over time as concern that managerial flexibility will weaken the overall control of expenditure abates. The second problem may be more troublesome. It is the propensity of headquarters's staff in ministries and departments to replicate, the controls divested by budget offices. This tendency has been confirmed by enough experiences to be considered one of the chief obstacles to the realisation of management reforms. To counter it, several governments have moved on to a stage of reform that demarks the relationship between the Ministry or Department and its constituent Agencies.

Australia. The Financial Management Improvement Program (FMIP) introduced in 1983 has been the Commonwealth's main vehicle for modernising expenditure management and emphasising value for money. A related but later development was the imposition of an "efficiency dividend" – an annual government-wide requirement to achieve efficiency gains by reducing salary and administrative expenditure by 1.25 per cent per annum. Further reform came in 1988 through Program Management and Budgeting (PMB) which reoriented the budget and appropriation focus from the level of expenditure on resource inputs to a focus on the objectives of government activity and on the efficient and effective achievement of desired outcomes.

Managerial incentives were provided through a new running costs system which sets cash limits covering all administrative expenditure in each appropriation and allowing for transfers between salaries and other administrative expenditure, as well as the carry-over and borrowings of expenditure between financial years. The efficiency dividend arrangement is currently under review. This system replaced an arrangement which separated staffing controls from financial controls and divided appropriations into up to 20 separate items for administrative expenditure. It represents, therefore, a substantial expansion in managerial flexibility. It is likely that additional reforms will be undertaken in the years ahead, especially in regard to programme evaluation, performance measurement and accrual accounting. In November 1992, Australian Government decided that departments should move to financial reporting on an accrual basis, as a further step in the Government's public sector reform programme. Ten departments produced financial statements on an accrual basis for 1992-93 with the remainder to do so for 1993-94.

In 1992, the Government's Management Advisory Board (MAB) launched an evaluation by an independent Task Force of the management improvements initiated since 1983. The Task Force's report was released in July 1993, and is titled "The Australian Public Service Reformed – An Evaluation of a Decade of Management Reform". The general conclusions contained in the Report are that the management reforms have been well directed, that their benefits have substantially outweighed their costs, and agencies need to take more active steps to fully integrate the reforms in the Public Service culture and to make them work more effectively.

Canada. The principal instruments for enlarging managerial discretion have been IMAA (Increased Ministerial Authority and Accountability) and Running Cost Budgeting. These arrangements devolve greater authority to department management, within an accountability framework, so as to concentrate on results rather than on process. They are a response to the piling up over decades of detailed rules and prescriptions that regulated the implementation of government policy and the expenditure of public funds. IMAA relaxes many central regulations for departments that negotiate contracts specifying what they will spend and accomplish over a 3-year period. IMAA involves departments from the start in identifying the room for man9vre they need and in getting their judgement on what can be done and of the resources needed to produce agreed results. In exchange for negotiating these performance contracts, departments gain limited carry-forward of capital funds, retention of savings achieved through their managerial initiative, and (in some cases) the use of revenue produced by user fees.

In the 1990's, the IMAA initiative has been overtaken by government-wide deregulation and decentralisation of Treasury Board administrative and personnel management practices and the promotion of Special Operating Agencies (SOA's). The latter extend the IMAA concept by identifying organisational units within departments that may enjoy additional delegated authorities in exchange for establishing a business plan and committing to performance targets. The Government is also aggressively promoting the development of service standards and performance reporting across all programmes.

Commencing with the 1993-94 budget, the government introduced a running cost regime for managing operating resources dedicated to programme delivery. This entails a unitary budget encompassing salary, other operating expenses, and minor capital resources which allows managers to choose the most cost-effective mix of inputs to carry out programmes. With this initiative, separate person-year controls have been eliminated, along with Treasury Board controls on funds earmarked for salaries.

Denmark. Since the mid 1980s, departments have had increasing scope to move money between votes; and agencies have had freedom to shift resources between items, except that they cannot increase expenditure on pay. Authority to carry forward unused investment funds has been extended to current expenditure as well. Uncommitted balances may be carried forward up to four years, provided their future use is specified. Most provisions for separate parliamentary approval of minor investment projects, sales of buildings, etc. have been abolished. The formerly detailed control on staff has been replaced by a multi-year limit on total pay, but the number of senior posts is still separately controlled.

In conjunction with budget reform, expenditure control was shifted from a gross to a net basis. The operative expenditure ceiling for each minister is now defined as a net amount, which means that increased revenues count as savings.

Ireland. Recent developments include the introduction of three-year administrative budgets in 1991 which aims at delegating greater authority to line departments (and within departments to line managers) for administrative expenditure and related matters. Each participating department negotiates a three-year agreement with the Minister for Finance stating the total expenditure to be available (in constant terms) in each of the three years, specifies the circumstances (if any) under which these amounts will be changed, allows the transfer of resources between subheads (within, not between, votes), allows some carry-forward of resources from one financial year to another, and arranges for monitoring the agreement and resolving any difficulties that arise. To ensure that the devolution extends to operating labels, each department must prepare a plan for internal delegation of authority over administrative expenditure. During the 1991-93 period, three-year agreements covered departments employing 80 per cent of the civil service.

New Zealand. The shift from appropriation of inputs to appropriation for outputs has given departments significant flexibility in the use of resources. Chief Executives, who are responsible for the performance of their departments, have authority to negotiate wages and conditions and have flexibility to transfer resources between input categories. In managing resources, Chief Executives are required to produce specified outputs (at specified levels of quality, quantity and timeliness) within the amount agreed by Ministers.

Sweden. As previously discussed, Sweden has adopted three-year budget frames for government agencies. Although funds are still appropriated one year at a time, agencies can carry forward savings in one year to the next and, within strict limits, draw in advance on future appropriations. The three-year frames are applied to administrative expenditure which has been subject to extended downward pressure for more than a decade.

United Kingdom. A succession of reforms, beginning with the Financial Management Initiative (FMI) in 1981 and extending through the Next Step Initiative in 1988 and the Citizen Charter in 1991, have progressively enlarged the scope of managerial flexibility and accountability. FMI called on each department to develop management systems and practices which give managers: clear objectives and means of assessing progress towards them; well-defined responsibilities for achieving value for money; and the necessary information and expertise. Each participating department was charged to tailor FMI to its own situation, so there was a great deal of variation in approach and in the pace of reform. FMI was oriented to budgeting by the Multi-Departmental Review of Budgeting (MDR) undertaken in 1986. MDR stressed the need for top management to set priorities, manage resources, and review performance. This was accompanied by running costs limits, also in 1986, giving departments greater control over administrative expenditure, thereby encouraging line commands to take a more managerial role than had been customary in assuring efficient and effective use of the staff and other administrative resources available to them. Senior managers were encouraged to delegate further within their commands so that operational levels were empowered to act as budget holders.

The Next Steps Initiative advanced the principles of FMI and MDR through the further enlargement of managerial discretion within a performance and accountability framework. The initiative involves the devolution, to the maximum extent practicable, by departments of executive functions to their constituent agencies. Each agency's chief executive, appointed by the Minister, is responsible for resources and results. In 1991, departments and their Next Steps Agencies were given the opportunity, depending on progress made, to gain greater responsibility for pay bargaining and greater scope to reward performance. The 1991 Citizen's Charter directly links managerial performance to the quality and cost of services provided citizens.

Accounting for Costs. Budget systems generally record expenditures on a cash basis, when payments are made, not when costs are incurred. Cash-based budgeting has two important advantages: it is easy to apply and simple to explain. There is no need for special record keeping or a separate accounting system; needed expenditure data can be derived from payroll records and other readily available sources. Moreover, expenditures represent actual rather than assumed or notional transactions, and there is no need to rely on assumptions. But cash-based budgeting misstates the true cost of carrying out government programmes and activities. It often assigns costs to the wrong activity or the wrong time period, such as when managers consume centrally-provided maintenance, printing or automotive services at no cost to their budgets. These "free goods" distort the allocation of public resources and drain managers of incentives to be efficient.

Costs also are misstated when they are recorded as bills are paid rather than when goods and services are consumed. This problem occurs in current budgets that do not charge for withdrawals from inventory and in capital budgets that do not charge for depreciation of assets or use of capital. Cash-based budgeting also misstates the cost of loans made by the government, as has been noted in the section dealing with this subject. It overstates the cost of loans when they are issued and understates the cost if they are defaulted or forgiven.

Accurate information on costs is crucial from a number of vantage points:

– in promoting freedom of managerial action in a decentralised budgetary environment, and holding managers accountable for results;
– in optimising resource allocation decisions, and assessing the cost-effectiveness of programmes;

- in facilitating comparison between public and private sector activities, so as to assess contracting out arrangement, user charges, and other market-type mechanisms;
- in evaluating the effects of government activity on the public sector's net worth.

Cash and cost accounting serve fundamentally different objectives. The former is concerned with allocating inputs to organisational units in such a manner that the legal control of expenditure is assured; the latter is concerned with efficiency in the allocation of public resources. The proper attribution of costs can be used in a number of budget-related tasks:

- in *programme evaluation* to assess the optimal mix of government programmes and activities;
- in *levying user charges* according to the principle that beneficiaries should bear the full cost of the services they receive;
- in *making budget decisions* to determine how much to spend for a wanted volume of goods and services;
- in *managerial reform* to encourage managers to take responsibility for their actions.

The last of these is especially pertinent for governments bent on modernising the public sector. The emphasis on productivity, performance, and effectiveness depends on means of allocating cost fully and accurately to specific programmes and activities. Performance has little meaning independent of the cost of producing it. Traditionally, however, input-oriented budgeting has not paid much attention to cost allocation. Intragovernmental services have often been provided centrally and at no cost to customers. Programme Managers have been free to use these at no cost to their programmes; and they could not substitute their "share" of the consumption of these goods or services for consumption of alternatives. The accountability requirements on which recent reforms have been conditioned call managers to account for the resources they consume in the process of producing outputs. The sought after enhancement in accountability will be lost or diluted if managers do not have full responsibility for costs.

Full attribution of costs requires far-reaching modifications in accounting systems, including the breakdown of the budget into cost/responsibility centres – discrete activities that can be held accountable for the work they perform and the resources they spend, as well as distinctions between fixed and variable costs and the development of other cost measures that allow units of input to be directly linked to units of output. It may also require new relationships between intra-governmental suppliers and their customers, and new methods for budgeting capital expenditures.

Canada. The government does not have a full cost allocation system, but it does attribute three types of costs to the programme or agency responsible for them: certain personnel-related expenses; rentals and accommodations, and centrally-provided financial accounting services. Some personnel costs, such as the government's contribution to supplementary health services for its employees, are appropriated in one sum for the entire government. This single appropriation is then "spread out" among departments and agencies in proportion to their share of total person-years in the government sector. This cost allocation is shown "below the line" in departmental budgets and is not included in their appropriations. Moreover, the amount charged to each department is estimated at the start of the year and is not adjusted for actual spending on supplementary health services. It should be mentioned, however, that certain personnel-related costs, such as the government's payment to pension and unemployment benefit schemes for its employees, are included in departmental budgets.

Rental and accommodation charges are allocated by the Public Works Department, the main operator of government office space, on the basis of equivalent market rates in the area where the building is located. In allocating costs, Public Works makes no distinction between government-owned or leased buildings nor does it base charges on its actual costs. Finally, the Department of Supply and Services apportions the cost of financial services among users on the basis of the number of cheques issued by each department.

In sum, the government allocates cost on the basis of mechanical "rules of thumb" that do not reflect actual costs and do not allow spending agencies discretion in the use of the resources charged to them.

New Zealand. Reform of the public sector has been reliant on a shift from cash-based to accrual accounting. The accrual basis provides for the full attribution of costs to the programmes or accounts incurring them and for costs to be charged to the outputs they purchase through a new accounting structure. The new system specifies four types of appropriations: 1) for capital contributions, that is, for public funds invested in a department; 2) for payments, such as grants, where no output is purchased; 3) for expenses of outputs purchased; and 4) for "Payments on Behalf of the Crown", that is transfers to other entities. Appropriations for "Payments on Behalf of the Crown" must in turn be identified as being for capital investments in other organisations, payments for outputs or unrequited payments.

The precise method used for attributing costs to output classes is left to individual departments. The department must demonstrate that it has a financial management system that is capable of providing timely and materially accurate financial information on an accrual basis, and that identifies the full cost of resources consumed, including, where appropriate, the cost of funds employed, and the allocation of overhead costs.

Managers have considerable flexibility in determining the mix of inputs in producing outputs, as well as freedom to manage balance sheets by buying and selling assets, provided that no unauthorised infusion of capital is required. As purchaser, the government has the opportunity to assess the quality, timeliness and full cost of the outputs produced and to compare with the outputs available from alternative suppliers. Cost attribution thus puts pressure on managers to produce outputs as efficiently as those available from other sources.

Sweden. A cost attribution system was introduced in 1973 to facilitate the comparison of government ownership and leasing of buildings. The system focused principally on appraising investment decisions, not on controlling the amounts charged to agencies for rentals and accommodations. The system was applied to cost control in the late 1970s and 1980s as part of the government's imposition of a 2 per cent reduction in administrative costs. The identification and apportionment of rental and other accommodation costs was an important aspect to computing the productivity gains each agency was required to achieve. The three-year budget frames tested in the 1980s and implemented government-wide in the 1990s have further enlarged the scope for cost allocation by giving managers greater discretion with respect to the resources, including rental costs, at their disposal.

United States. Although federal law enacted in the 1950s provides for cost-based budgets, the prevailing practice is to budget for cash and commitments. Two developments, however, point to more serious attention to costs in the future: one is credit reform which requires that direct and guaranteed loans be budgeted on the basis of estimated subsidy cost; the other is the establishment of the Federal Accounting Standards Advisory Board and the assignment to it of responsibility for recommending new accounting rules and practices. In the case of loans, the subsidy cost includes all estimated costs, except the administrative expenses of processing the loans. The concept of subsidy cost may be used as a model for other transactions where the cash basis provides an inadequate measure of the government's financial risk.

Although cash budgets constrained by spending limits are expected to continue to be the primary budget structure, OMB will be developing a recommendation for a capital budget presentation working with the Federal Accounting Standards Advisory Board. The presentation will be incorporated in the FY 1996 Budget.

Chapter 10

BUDGETING FOR RESULTS

The link between public sector performance and the overall performance of the economy is now widely recognised by the governments of OECD Member countries. The view that economic efficiency depends on the effectiveness of public programmes and policies has led to reappraisals of how public tasks are carried out and how performance and results are measured. This reappraisal has pointed in three closely-related directions: the measurement of performance, the freeing up of managerial discretion and initiative, and the use of the budget as a means of improving results. The second of these has already been discussed; hence, this section deals primarily with the two other developments.

Performance measurement in the public sector is not new. Many OECD Member countries have had experience with some form of planning, programming and budgeting system (PPBS) or with similar systems that tried to link budgets and performance. One of the principal lessons is that information obtained from performance measurement is only one of many elements in a policy decision. Another lesson is that it does not suffice to focus solely on the upper policy-making echelons. Care must also be taken to instil managerial responsibility and attention to results at all levels of management. In *Australia,* Program Management and Budgeting (PMB) has linked the aggregate control framework to the achievement of value for money by individual departments and managers. PMB has focused attention on planning objectives, budgeting, implementing strategies, and assessing programme outcomes. Evaluation has been the linchpin of the management cycle, providing a tool for managers to continuously improve the quality of decision making about achieving value for money.

While considerable work is underway on devising and sharpening quantifiable measures, the main emphasis is on overcoming obstacles to their use in managing organisations and allocating resources. As has been noted, considerable progress has been made in some countries in reorienting financial management from compliance to performance by freeing budget holders from most *ex ante* controls while demanding more accountability for what they accomplish and spend. The ultimate objective is, in some countries, to fashion the budget into a "contract for performance" in exchange for obtaining control of agreed resources, managers would commit themselves to specific outputs (or other performance targets) and (in some cases) to the results or outcomes ensuing from these outputs. In most countries, however, the drive for performance is less closely linked to budgeting but has a broader scope: to strengthen the capacity of managers to take initiative and responsibility for providing public services in a productive and effective manner.

In measuring performance, a distinction is often drawn between measures and indicators. Performance measures are quantified statements of outputs and results related to the objectives sought. Performance indicators, by contrast, are proxies for output and results that cannot be measured or are difficult to directly measure. Some countries also draw a fundamental distinction between outputs which are the direct results of government actions and outcomes which are the changes in social conditions that result from a combination of outputs. In an education programme, for example, the outputs may be measured by test scores and the percentage of students advancing to a certain level of proficiency in mathematics. The outcomes may be measured in terms of the percentage of students completing schooling or advancing to higher education. In drawing this distinction, governments typically assign responsibility for outputs to programme managers and responsibility for outcomes to senior officials or ministers.

OECD governments have identified a core of ideal characteristics for performance measures and indicators. These should be consistent over time and between units, and comparisons should be made only with similar programmes. They should be simple, well-defined and easily understood, and should emphasise those aspects that are important to decision making. Ideally, emphasis should be given to a limited number of key measures or indicators which reflect the programme's purpose or objective, or which signal whether the programme is worth continuing. It is fundamentally important that managers' performance should only be measured for those areas for which they have control. It also is a good idea to inform managers of the use to which the data will be put, and to avoid situations where considerable effort is expended in measuring performance but the collected data are then stored away without being used.

Increased effort is now being made to measure the quality of services, especially from the standpoint of taxpayers or consumers. This emphasis reflects rising concern about the quality and cost of public services. Quality of services has several measurable dimensions: timeliness, responsiveness to consumer needs, the manner in which it is delivered, etc. Quality may be measured by means of consumer (or citizen) surveys, as by more objective techniques. For example, the quality of garbage collection is gauged in some American cities through a photographic rating system in which the cleanliness of randomly selected streets is periodically evaluated. In the United Kingdom, the Department of Social Security has developed a Quality Assessment Package to measure the performance of its local offices. Some of the key features of the package are a postal survey of client attitudes and assessment of service by type of contact, such as office, telephone, correspondence, and home visits.

It is rare that performance measurement is an end in itself. Five gradations of managing for results can be identified, ranging from the publication of performance measures to budgeting for results.

Performance reporting is the systematic publication of data on results to citizens or clients. Being systematic means that key measures are selected in advance and reports on them are issued on a regular basis. Performance reporting goes beyond the descriptive information often found in the annual reports of governments or agencies. It examines results from the perspective of those who pay for or are impacted by public services and assesses how well their interests are being served. Performance reports sometimes concentrate on a specific policy area, such as school performance as measured by standard test scores, or hospital performance as measured by adjusted mortality rates (that is, rates adjusted for the age, sex, health, and other relevant conditions of patients). When concentrated in a single policy area, performance reports open the possibility for comparisons among institutions, such as schools or hospitals, providing similar services. Where consumers have choice in selecting the institution to provide the service, performance reports aim at turn them into informed ''shoppers''. Performance reports are also used to assess a broad range of government services at one period in time. In these instances, the reports become means of rating the overall quality of governmental performance.

Performance objectives take the process a big step further by specifying in advance the results expected or promised. The objectives can either be short-term targets tied the to current actions or long-term visions of where the government or agency should be heading. Performance objectives are intended to mould behaviour, that is, to mobilise the resources and attention of the government in the preferred direction. To affect behaviour, it is necessary that the objectives be carefully selected, that they pertain to matters of high concern to the agency or citizens, that they be as few as is reasonably possible, and that they be quantified. Publication adds weight to the objectives and conveys the sense that the government is committed to their attainment.

One type of approach applied in private sector firms to enhance performance against key objectives which is gaining increasing recognition but does not appear to have made much headway to date in the public sector, is benchmarking. *Benchmarking* involves an organisation in mapping its key operational processes; identifying crucial processes and key performance indicators; and then searching for best practice in terms of those indicators wherever it may occur. Benchmarks are performance objectives that represent the best practices (or results) found in organisations facing similar situations. Benchmarkings may be useful when many institutions provide the same service, for example, in motivating under-performing laggard hospitals to bring their practices up to the level of better-performing institutions. However, it is not necessary for an organisation to limit itself to benchmarking against similar organisations, for instance a hospital might enhance its performance through benchmarking its admission processes against those of a hotel. In the public sector, benchmarking may be a means of spurring agencies to identify ''role models'' whose performance they would then seek to match or surpass.

Performance auditing subjects statements by governments or agencies concerning their performance to review by auditors. This form of auditing is still in its infancy, and the precise role and scope of auditors in reviewing results is not well defined, but one may anticipate that financial auditing will be the model used in performance auditing. The specification of performance objectives and reporting on results will be a management responsibility. The task of auditors will be to review these statements to determine their reliability and accuracy. In order for auditors to carry out this role, it will be necessary to develop performance principles and standards similar to those applied in financial management.

Performance contracts specify the output or results that an agency or a manager is committed to produce with agreed resources. The signed contract is hammered out in negotiations between a spending agency and a central organ (such as the budget office) or between an agency and its managers. In some countries, the contract spells out the relationship between the ministry and its constituent agencies. The contract usually runs for three years or longer, during which performance is monitored to ensure that the terms are being met. A full review at the end of the contract period sets the stage for a new round of negotiations.

Performance contracts may be preconditions for easing *ex ante* controls on agencies, or they may be used as employment contracts for senior managers or executives. While performance contracts are a relatively new development, their use is likely to spread in the years ahead as governments devise means of linking operating conditions and results.

Performance budgeting is an implied contract that links resources provided to outputs promised. The linkage can range from a "lockstep" relationship in which a marginal unit of resources produces a marginal unit of output, to one in which the budget merely lists the expected results associated with the budgeted volume of resources.

No OECD country currently practices a form of budgeting in which quantified performance is the sole basis for resource allocation. New Zealand probably comes closest to this model in its system of output-based appropriations. The experiences of Canada, Australia, and the United States are more typical. In these countries, the prevailing view is that performance measurement is more useful in determining how to make best use of available resources than in determining what the allocation should be. A number of practical considerations have induced governments to shy away from a strict link between resources and performance. One is that there often is substantial uncertainty as to whether spending agencies can deliver promised improvements in performance even if they get the requested funds. The more explicit the link, the more visible will be the failure, and the consequent demoralisation or discrediting of performance budgeting, if departments fall short of meeting their targets. More importantly, the performance-orientation is aimed at changing management style and behaviour, not just at improving the budget process.

In most OECD Member countries, programme managers – not budget officials – are the prime users of performance measures. There is concern that excessive reliance on performance measures to allocate resources might generate controversy over the reliability of the data and deter managers from co-operating. If this were to occur, the supply of data might dry up or the quality might be impaired.

Budget staff have an important role in performance management, though one that generally stops short of a tight link of results and resources. The budget office typically has a strong role in designing performance systems and in prodding departments to adapt to the new managerial culture. It also has a voice in deciding which measures are appropriate and an opportunity to use performance data as one of the factors in making budget allocations.

Australia. The development of performance indicators has proceeded under the aegis of two related reforms: the financial management improvement programme (FMIP) and programme management and budgeting (PMB). As has been discussed, these reforms focus government budgeting and parliamentary scrutiny on objectives and outcomes, and encourage departments to assess and improve performance. PMB is the instrument for identifying objectives and placing them into an agreed framework that makes it possible to set performance targets for managers at all levels. The programme structure (programmes, subprogrammes, components, and subcomponents) arrays objectives in hierarchical order, with those at lower levels more capable of being quantified than those at higher levels.

The Department of Finance has issued a series of guidelines for the formulation of performance measures. Some address conceptual questions, such as the definition of various types of measures; others provide guidance on the use of measures in budgeting and other managerial activities. Use of performance measures is mandatory in the portfolio documentation presented to Parliament justifying departmental estimates. The portfolio documentation, known in 1993-94 as the Program Performance Statements, was refocused as part of Australia's decision to bring down its budget in May 1994, prior to the commencement of the financial year on 1 July 1994 (previous budgets were generally brought down in August). New policy proposals accepted by the Government, are highlighted in a new document, known as Portfolio Budget Measures (PBMS). Reporting of the contribution of those measures to the achievement of programme objectives will also occur within agency annual reports after the conclusion of each financial year. The government requires new policy proposals to be accompanied by statements of objectives, performance measures, and plans for future evaluations. Department of Finance guidelines suggest that the measures be as specific as possible so that they can contribute to decisions on programmes and priorities. The guidelines also suggest that the previous year's performance be reviewed in terms of the achievement of plans, targets or initiatives set for it. The PPS documents are linked intimately with Program Management and Budgeting and have become the primary vehicle for the presentation of programme performance information to the Parliament, and are thus an important element of Ministerial accountability to the Parliament. The early budget will mean a substantial change in Budget documentation, including the PPSs, but there will be a continuing emphasis in the new documentation on outcomes-focused performance reporting.

Canada. Departments have been required to measure and report on performance since the early 1970s, but this requirement has been given greater impetus by the IMAA (Increased Ministerial Authority and Accountability) reforms discussed earlier. Other relevant developments include publication of performance information in the

Estimates submitted to Parliament and efforts to improve financial management. Each department participating in IMAA prepares an annual management report that triggers an assessment of performance based on targets set forth in the memorandum of understanding negotiated by it and the Treasury Board. Every third year, an accountability review is conducted, pursuant to which specific directives may be issued to spur the efficient and effective use of resources.

Since 1982, Part III of the Estimates set forth planned and actual results as well as other performance data relevant to resource requirements. Treasury Board instructions advise departments to furnish information that assists Members of Parliament in understanding and assessing performance. The Comptroller General (in the Treasury Board) monitors preparation of the Part IIIs to see that significant evaluation findings are reported accurately. The Part IIIs contain a great deal of information of work activity and costs, but they vary considerably in content and quality. The Auditor General (who reports to Parliament) has conducted periodic assessments of the Part IIIs and has prodded departments to improve their performance measures. The 1977 legislation establishing this office empowers the Auditor General to report on whether funds have been spent with due regard to economy and efficiency, and whether satisfactory procedures are in place for monitoring effectiveness.

Denmark. Productivity improvement has been a key component of the fiscal constraint maintained since 1983. Greater efficiency has been sought by adjusting budget allocations for expected productivity gains; reorganising work to improve performance; and providing agencies with positive incentives to be more productive. Budget allocations for personnel expenditures are made in reference to productivity targets. Each agency's target is derived by examining its mix of personnel and computing the productivity gain that each type is expected to achieve, based on trends for comparable work in the private sector. Agencies may retain savings achieved by increasing their productivity above the budgeted target.

Since 1987, the trend data included in the supplementary material that accompanies the Finance Bill have been presented in a standard format. Quantitative data are reported, for all major accounts, for service, production and activity; resources and capacity; and productivity.

An improved format is introduced in the 1994 Budget. It establishes a consistent link between accounting data and performance data, and a separate identification of general management and auxiliary functions of each agency. However the coverage of performance indicators is still far from complete.

Finland. The new ''budgeting for results'' approach applied starting 1990 requires that the results to be achieved are described in the budget proposal with work, efficiency and effectiveness measures if possible. The line ministries agree with the agencies on detailed, and possibly adjusted, results targets and supervise their achievement. Results-oriented budgeting, which in the 1994 budget covers more than 80 per cent of the running costs of agencies, gives agencies much more flexibility to select the means of achieving their objectives than the former line-item budget did. This flexibility has allowed numerous agencies to apply management by results and other business management methods to improve their efficiency and effectiveness.

Starting from 1993, an amendment to the Constitution and the Budget Law allow the application of net budgeting to activities financed by user charges.

Sweden. Some efforts to measure performance are directly linked to budget decisions; others are independent of budgeting but have the potential to influence the allocation of resources. The main formal link is through the three-year budget frames described in previous sections. The triennial budget system calls for agencies to furnish trend data on performance during the previous five years, along with projections for the next three years. As has been noted, agencies entering the three-year cycle go through a more elaborate process in formulating their budgets, At the outset, each agency receives specific directives from its competent ministry, in addition to the general directives issued by the Ministry of Finance. The general directives require agencies to report on past performance, assess current objectives and arrangements, and to develop measurable targets for the work to be done and results to be obtained over the next three years. The special directives are tailored to each agency's circumstances and pertain to the evaluations to be undertaken, priorities and alternatives, and policy options. Although the three-year frames cover only administrative expenses, the review process extends to programme objectives and expenditures as well. Agencies are called upon to assess their total performance across their full range of activities. In effect, increased flexibility in administrative matters is offered as an inducement for agencies to make a broad, probing assessment of overall performance. The Agency for Administrative Development (SAFAD) and the National Audit Bureau have been assigned responsibility for devising procedures to be used by agencies in reviewing their performance.

United Kingdom. The development and application of performance measures are a central feature of the financial management initiative (FMI) and subsequent reforms. The reforms encourage quantification wherever feasible so as to facilitate assessment of the extent to which programmes have achieved their objectives and provided value for money. As the reforms have enfolded, spending departments have been given substantial responsibility for selecting the appropriate measures, collecting data on results, and publishing them in departmental reports. Inasmuch as FMI and the other initiatives discussed earlier are intended to spur managers to take responsibility for their actions and performance, they do not prescribe a uniform approach for all departments. Within FMI's broad objectives and guidelines, each department is free to develop the management style and system best suited to its circumstances. But as executive operations "graduate" to agency status under the Next Steps Initiative, they are expected to operate within an accountability framework that specifies resources and performance targets. The most recent initiative is the Citizen's Charter published in 1991. It emphasises qualitative aspects of performance and the responsiveness of public services to the preferences of their users. The Charter insists on published standards of service, such as guaranteed maximum waiting times for certain National Health Service procedures.

FMI and the initiatives following it conceive of the budget as a contract for performance in which departments commit themselves to concrete targets in exchange for agreed resources. The linkage of budgets and outputs is promoted by giving prominence to performance measures and targets in annual departmental reports. Though progress is somewhat uneven across departments, three trends can be discerned: 1) a shift from simple workload or output measures to more advanced performance measures; 2) emphasis on measures of service quality; and 3) greater emphasis on operational measures at Agency level.

United States. Performance measurement has a long history and is highly developed, but its application in budgeting and other decision processes has been quite limited. However, a spate of recent developments is likely to give significantly greater weight to matters of performance in the years ahead.

A 1992 survey of more than 100 federal agencies conducted by the General Accounting Office found widespread use of performance measures. All of the surveyed agencies claim to measure final outputs or products, 93 per cent say they have work or activity measures, 91 per cent claim to measure the timeliness of services, 83 per cent profess to have internal measures of quality, 71 per cent collect data on outcomes, and 63 per cent aver that they assess customer satisfaction. Few of these measures find their way into the federal budget, though some may play a role in influencing budget allocations. Performance measures are also collected in many American cities and state governments. It is now common for municipalities to publish standard test scores on school performance. An emerging emphasis is in issuing a comprehensive report on the quality of government. In 1992, for example, the City of Portland, Oregon issued its first annual performance report on six vital public services. The report also presented the results of a citizen survey and compared Portland's results to those of other cities. The State of Oregon has established a Progress Board that has set measurable objectives for the state at fixed periods: 1990 (the baseline year), 1995, 2000, and 2010.

Interest in performance-based government has been stimulated by some recent developments, including the following:

- Legislation enacted by Congress during 1993, the Government Performance and Results Act (GPRA), requires federal agencies to prepare annual performance reports comparing actual versus planned results, explaining why particular goals (if any) have not been met, and reporting on programme evaluations. The legislation also provides for pilot tests of performance budgeting and of new forms of managerial flexibility and accountability.
- The Chief Financial Officers Act of 1990 provides for the systematic measurement of performance, and annual reports on progress in improving financial management. Pursuant to this legislation, the Office of Management and Budget has issued guidelines for the development of performance measures to be appended to financial statements.
- The Governmental Accounting Standards Board, which has cognizance of state and local – but not federal – accounting practices has recommended the development of reporting and audit procedures for "service efforts and accomplishments" indicators of various governmental functions.
- The report of the National Performance Review strongly supports the GPRA, and includes numerous recommendations for implementing the Act as quickly as possible.

These and other recent developments lend support to the spreading belief that performance type budget systems will come to be more widely used in the years ahead.

Effective systems for the allocation, management and control of public sector resources are fundamental elements of good governance. The juxtaposition of the need for continuing fiscal restraint with demands for more and better public services is changing budgetary practices in OECD Member countries. The Budget is increasingly being used as an instrument for promoting managerial improvement and programme effectiveness in addition to its control and allocation functions. This report analyses budget practices and innovations in twenty two OECD Member countries. It describes how the practice of budgeting is contributing to a greater performance orientation in the public sector. It also provides standard summaries of the institutional framework and procedures governing budgeting in each of these countries.

Part II

INDIVIDUAL COUNTRY DESCRIPTIONS

AUSTRALIA

**Any changes which may have taken place in Australia
since March 1994 are not reflected in this chapter**

A. INSTITUTIONAL STRUCTURE OF BUDGETARY DECISION-MAKING

1. Political and organisational structure of government

Australia has a federal system of government comprising the Federal or Commonwealth government, the six State governments (and the Northern Territory and the Australian Capital Territory, to which Commonwealth laws give State like powers in most regards), and local government authorities which derive their powers and responsibilities from State governments.

The Commonwealth Constitution assigns certain functions and revenue raising powers to the Commonwealth government leaving the residual powers to the States. Commonwealth government functions are organised mainly around 17 portfolio departments. The current structure resulted from the machinery of government changes in 1987 which reduced the number of portfolios from 28. The agencies and statutory authorities which also contribute to government activity are all associated with one of these departments.

Departments can have either one or two Ministers depending on the size and nature of the portfolio. The Secretary of each department is a non-political appointment in the sense that the appointment is not limited by the lifetime of Cabinet; the same applies to the rest of the departmental personnel.

Parliament has two Chambers, the House of Representatives and the Senate. In the House 3 political parties and two independents are represented. The current Government is supported by one party having a majority position in the House of Representatives.

Elections for the House of Representatives and half the Senate are required to be held at intervals of no greater than 3 years. The last general elections were held in March 1993. The ministers are nominated to the Governor General by the Prime Minister from among the members of Parliament. A subset of ministers (currently numbering 17) form the Cabinet which is the main executive arm of government.

2. Main budgetary organs

Within Cabinet the Treasurer and the Minister for Finance assume the principal responsibility for the budget with the former being responsible for overall budget strategy, the majority of budget receipts and for borrowing while the latter is responsible for budget outlays and personnel resources. The Budget Speech is normally delivered by the Treasurer on behalf of the Government. Under the Treasurer are, inter alia, the Department of the Treasury and the Australian Taxation Office, advising on economic, monetary and taxation policies.

The Department of Finance is organised into six Divisions, and two ongoing Task Forces dealing with major asset sales. Four Divisions organised to reflect departmental groupings are responsible for liaison and budgetary negotiations with other Ministries. One division deals with accounting and financial management matters. The General Expenditure Division advises on budgetary strategy; co-ordinates the Government's budgetary processes; and has a lead role in promoting enhanced public sector resources management.

The General Expenditure Division is composed of some 80 staff divided into four branches of which the Expenditure Policy Branch performs the central budget expenditure policy and budget co-ordination functions with respect to aggregate outlays, and is responsible for management of departmental running costs.

3. Role of Prime Minister and Cabinet

The Cabinet is involved both at the opening stage of the budget preparation, communicating the government's policies to the spending ministries through the issue of guidelines, and at the closing stage when final examination of policy proposals and formulation of the budget take place.

The Expenditure Review Committee (ERC) reduces the workload of Cabinet in budget decision-making. The ERC comprises the Prime Minister, the Treasurer, the Minister for Finance and five other Cabinet Ministers who have spending responsibilities. The Committee develops the budget processes appropriate for each fiscal year, and any budgetary targets to be addressed. It also assesses proposals for new policy and for savings, and recommends to the Cabinet the proposals to be accepted. The assessment of proposals is undertaken in conjunction with the Minister whose portfolio is affected by the program.

Late in the budget cycle final decisions are taken by full Cabinet; these sittings of the Cabinet are called the "Budget Cabinet".

4. Role of Legislature

Only expenditure from the annual appropriations is subject to regular authorisation by the Parliament. The remainder of expenditure (about two thirds) is channelled via standing (or special) appropriations authorised under separate legislation by Parliament. These can be used to provide an automatic payment of funds where an entitlement exists, or to pay a specific amount separately identified from an annual appropriation bill.

The budget is debated in both the House of Representatives and the Senate. The Constitution limits the powers of the Senate in respect of appropriations for "ordinary annual services" like wages and salaries. Under an agreement between the two Houses in 1965, reflecting that limitation, appropriations are apportioned between "ordinary annual services" (Appropriation Bill No. 1) which the Senate may reject or defer but not amend, and "other than ordinary annual services" (Appropriation Bill No. 2) which encompasses most capital expenditure, Payments to the States and all major new initiatives. Further the Senate may not initiate bills imposing taxation or increasing any charge or burden on the people.

Previous budgets were generally brought down in mid-August. However, the 1994-95 Budget will be introduced into both Houses of Parliament on 10 May 1994 to allow its passage prior to the commencement of the financial year on 1 July. Once a budget is finalised the Budget speech is read simultaneously in both Houses of Parliament. At this stage the annual Appropriation Bills are introduced into the House of Representatives (HoR) and documents showing particulars of proposed expenditure in respect of each Bill are tabled in the Senate. These documents facilitate consideration of the Bills by Senate Estimates Committees (SEC's) and debate continues in the HoR while the SEC's consider proposed expenditure for each department and agency. There are six Estimates Committees covering all portfolios. To facilitate consideration by these Committees departments provide explanatory documents (which in 1994-95 will be titled Portfolio Budget Measures Statements (PBMS) – see Section E.2). The responsible Minister or his representative in the Senate and officials of departments are present to provide further information as required.

While the SEC's continue their deliberations the HoR continues debate on the bills in a Committee of the Whole (House). This committee reports to the Speaker (chairman) of the House and the Bills are passed by the House. In 1994, due to the early Budget, it is anticipated that this will occur before 30 June.

The Bills are then formally introduced in the Senate where, after debate in committee, the Senate invariably passes the Bills (in 1975 the Senate's refusal to vote on the Bills precipitated a political/constitutional crisis eventually leading to a change of government).

The annual appropriations are organised along portfolio lines and within each portfolio by department and agency. Running costs apart, the appropriations specify authorised expenditure limits in some detail. There are approximately 800 separate annual appropriation items. Supply Acts, which were previously required to be passed to authorise ongoing expenditure pending passage of the annual Appropriation Bills, will no longer be required as it is anticipated that the Appropriation Bills will be presented prior to the new financial year.

B. THE SCOPE AND NATURE OF GOVERNMENT FINANCES

On the basis of standard measures of international comparison, such as outlays as a percentage of GDP, General Government is relatively small in Australia compared with other OECD Member countries. Central Government is however, relatively big, taking into account its Federal character. This might be explained by the social security programs as they are organised mainly through the central government's budget, while in many other countries these programs are paid for from separate funds.

Table 1. **Budget outlays by function for 1992-93**

As a percentage of total

Defence	9.0
Education	8.4
Health	13.4
Social security and welfare	34.5
Housing and community amenities nec	1.3
Culture and recreation	1.2
Economic services	8.2
General public services	6.8
Not allocated to function:	
Assistance to other governments nec	12.8
Public debt interest	5.8
Other	−1.4
Total	100.0

Source: Budget Statement No. 3 1992-93, p. 3.284.

Both general and central government were net lenders from 1987-88 to 1989-90 reflecting large central government surpluses. However from 1990-91 general government moved back to being a net borrower.

The Commonwealth government has exclusive powers for matters such as defence, immigration, telecommunications and postal services and the collection of customs and excise. Social security expenditure is almost entirely dependent on the Commonwealth government's budget: no separate social security funds exist.

The Commonwealth raises about 75 per cent of total general government revenue (excluding borrowing) of which the dominant component has been personal income taxes. Around 30 per cent of Commonwealth general government revenue is passed on to the State and local governments in the form of general or specific purpose grants. State-type taxes include payroll tax and financial institutions duties. Local governments also raise their own revenue largely by imposing rates on land, residential buildings etc. However, since 1987-88 the State governments have been able to borrow in their own right, rather than relying on the Commonwealth to borrow and on-lend funds. Some Commonwealth and State statutory authorities (*e.g.* Telecom and state electricity commissions) local government authorities and government owned companies can also borrow on their own account subject to guidelines determined by the Australian Loan Council which comprises the Prime Minister, the Commonwealth Treasurer, the six State Premiers and two Territory Chief Ministers.

C. BUDGET FORMULATION STRATEGY AND PROCESS

1. Strategic aims and global norms

The broad aims of Government economic policy in recent years have been to enhance Australia's competitive position and generate stronger economic growth. Inflation has been reduced, a range of microeconomic reforms have been introduced and fiscal policy has been set to support a sustainable economic recovery. With a solid economic recovery now emerging, the Government's focus is on achieving steady reductions in the Budget deficit over the next few years.

The current government policies are also aimed at consolidating Australia's position in the ranks of the low inflation countries. The Government's current policy is focused on promoting sustainable economic growth consistent with the need to prevent a re-emergence of inflationary pressures and making further progress on the balance of payments.

With these aims in mind the Government has ensured that the growth in total budget outlays, and the higher Commonwealth Budget deficit in 1992-93, which has been caused by the current recession, will be unwound in future years as the economic recovery takes hold. The net Public Sector Borrowing Requirement (PSBR) is estimated to rise to 5.1 per cent of GDP in 1993-94, up from 4.8 per cent of GDP recorded in 1992-93. This increase partly reflects an expected turnaround from net lending to the more normal position of net borrowing by State/local Public Trading Enterprises (PTEs). Since 1988-89, the new PSBR as a proportion of GDP has risen substantially, mainly reflecting the increase in net general government borrowing as a consequence of the recession and related stimulatory action.

A special arrangement has been created in order to guide and control borrowings of the Commonwealth and State governments. Borrowing activities of all levels of government are co-ordinated and controlled by the Loan Council to ensure consistency with other macroeconomic targets. The Loan Council in 1984 established arrangements which provide for annual agreed limits on new money borrowings (broadly defined to include all forms of financing capital expenditure) by the Commonwealth and each of the States for their statutory authorities and local government bodies and government-owned enterprises. The limits are agreed outside the Commonwealth and State Budget processes, but are determined having regard to macroeconomic objectives.

The following table shows some Commonwealth budget aggregates since 1980-81, together with estimates for 1992-93.

Table 2.   **Fiscal indicators, 1980-81 to 1992-93**

As a percentage of GDP

	Outlays	Revenue	Balance
1980-81	25.9	25.2	–0.7
1981-82	26.2	25.9	–0.3
1982-83	28.8	26.1	–2.7
1983-84	29.4	25.3	–4.1
1984-85	29.9	26.8	–3.1
1985-86	29.5	27.1	–2.4
1986-87	28.8	27.8	–1.0
1987-88	26.6	27.3	0.7
1988-89	24.4	26.1	1.7
1989-90	23.8	25.9	2.1
1990-91	25.4	25.9	0.5
1991-92	26.7	24.2	–2.5
1992-93 (est.)	27.0	23.7	–3.3

Source: Budget Statement No. 5 1992-93, Table 3.

2.   Technical aspects of multi-year estimates

The Government has put in place an expenditure control framework which is based around a rolling three year estimates system. The forward estimates record the minimum cost of ongoing government policy, as adjusted from time to time by the Department of Finance for the effects of parameter and other necessary variations. They do not include any allowance for the introduction of new programs or expansion of existing programs unless decided by the Government.

The forward estimates are an integral part of the Budget process and have become an important part of the Government's approach to fiscal management. The formal linkage of the forward estimates and the budget estimates has:

- provided a consistent and ongoing basis for budget deliberations;
- freed Ministers from the need to determine base program estimates and allowed them to concentrate on policy issues involving substantive changes to programs;
- contributed to the control of outlays growth by ensuring that the estimates reflect the minimum requirement necessary to maintain existing policy; and
- given greater consideration to the medium-term effects of budget measures.

All variations to the forward estimates since the publication in the previous budget papers are summarised in the reconciliation of the published forward and budget estimates published as part of the budget papers each year. This information reflects changes made to the estimates during the year and facilitates public accountability.

3. Calendar of main points of decision-making and activities

It should be noted that the 1994-95 Budget timetable is considerably altered from previous years, as the budget is to be delivered on 10 May 1994, rather than in August. Stages and timing may also vary from year to year in the future, but Budgets will now continue to be delivered prior to the commencement of each financial year. This table reflects the process for the preparation of the 1994-95 Budget.

Months before start of FY (t)	Main events and activities
(Year t – 1)	
January	Mid-year review of current budget estimates prepared, forward estimates updated for changed parameters, Government decisions and other revisions.
February	Cabinet considers additional estimates, update of forward estimates and budget processes submissions.
	Expenditure Review Committee of Cabinet (ERC) considers Budget strategy. Portfolio's 1993-94 Additional Estimates and Program Performance Statements tabled.
	Trilateral discussions between the Minister for Finance, the Treasurer and portfolio Ministers on reviews, savings and new policy proposals.
Mid-March	Completion of Trilateral discussions. Loan Council meeting. Lodgement of material for consideration by ERC (*i.e.* portfolio budget submissions, review reports and other papers called for by ERC or Trilaterals).
End March to late April	ERC/Cabinet deliberations process.
26 April	Budget Cabinet.
10 May	Budget Night.
12 May	Debate begins in the House of Representatives and Portfolio Budget Measures Statements tabled (1994-95).
16 May	Senate Estimates Committee deliberations commence.
25 May	Key revenue bills introduced into the Senate.
June	Appropriation Bills considered and passed by the Senate, for Royal Assent by 30 June 1994.
(Year t)	
1 July	Start of fiscal year (t).
Sept./end-Oct.	Reports by departments and agencies on part-year performance tabled.
Early Nov.	Portfolio Additional Estimates Statements (1994-95) tabled.
Mid-Nov.	Senate Estimates Committee deliberations commence.

4. The annual budget cycle

The budget process is based on the forward estimates which provide the best available estimates of Commonwealth outlays over the next three years, and reflect current government policy. The forward estimates are continuously adjusted to take account of new decisions and other factors which affect current and later years. To help Ministers decide among competing priorities for new policy proposals, these decisions are concentrated in the period leading up to the budget each year.

In recent years the new policy proposal process has been undertaken in two stages:

• Ministers provide synopses of new policy and savings proposals to the Expenditure Review Committee of Cabinet (ERC). Trilateral discussions are held between the Minister for Finance, the Treasurer and portfolio ministers on reviews, savings and new policy proposals. ERC selects those proposals requiring further consideration given the current economic circumstances and the current focus of government policy.

• Ministers then provide full scale submissions on these proposals for final consideration by ERC and decision by Cabinet. Approved proposals are included in the budget.

In most instances, the only opportunity for amending the budget's Appropriation Bills is the additional estimates bills which allow for adjustment to budget figures for parameter variation (*e.g.* higher or lower inflation than expected), estimates variations due to other unavoidable changes in programs, or changes due to post budget decisions. The 1993-94 Bills were introduced into Parliament in early February 1994, but henceforth will be brought forward to November, reflecting the decision to introduce the Budget prior to the commencement of the financial year. This process, however, is largely a matter of revising budget estimates and appropriating extra funds as required. The budget formulation period remains as the major decision-making period.

Material prepared by Departments, Finance and Treasury is co-ordinated by the latter two into a series of Budget Documents for tabling when the Budget is presented. Since 1989-90 the forward estimates have been included in the Budget papers and are not published separately.

D.   EXPENDITURE REVIEW

In the annual budget context, policy reviews are undertaken by the Expenditure Review Committee of Cabinet, and cover examination of new policy proposals and savings proposals against existing programs. "Savings options" may be proposed either by the relevant Minister or the Minister for Finance.

These policy reviews may be based on Submissions and argument, on specially commissioned reviews by departments, or on formal program evaluations undertaken in the normal course of program administration. As part of the budgeting and management reforms introduced in recent years, program budgeting is now well established and the managing for results approach is broadly accepted by managers at all levels.

The Government's evaluation strategy requires annual portfolio evaluation plans (PEPS) to be prepared on a portfolio basis, to include those evaluations which have "major resource and/or policy implications", that is, which are likely to result in proposals for new policy initiatives, for extension or redirection of existing programs or which may identify potential savings. Besides evaluations initiated by the portfolio's own minister and executive, the PEP should include all evaluations and reviews commissioned by Cabinet (usually in the budget process) and those to be undertaken by other bodies such as Parliamentary committees, the Industry Commission and other research bureaux. In their evaluation plans, portfolios are expected to achieve a comprehensive coverage of all programs over a three to five year time horizon.

As part of the strategy, portfolios are required to report on the findings of major evaluations to their Minister and to the Minister for Finance, and the results of these major evaluations are normally published. In addition, annual reports (which from 1994 will contain significant program performance reporting elements, which previously appeared in Program Performance Statements) will be submitted to the Parliament's Committees for use in their oversight of program performance.

The PEPs are required to be submitted to the Minister for Finance in early November each year, and findings can be utilised in proposals in the subsequent budget process, commencing in January of the following year, if appropriate. For major new policy proposals, portfolios are required to provide an outline for an evaluation of the proposal if adopted by Cabinet.

To support the evaluation strategy, the Department of Finance has a co-ordinating role, providing advice on evaluation planning and on technical issues, and assisting portfolios to enhance their evaluation skills base.

Increasingly, portfolios' new policy proposals are utilising findings from evaluations in their design and as supporting argument. Savings proposals are prepared for the budget by the portfolio concerned (again often guided by evaluation or review findings) or in conjunction with the Department of Finance.

The greater availability of formal evaluation results has significantly reduced the need for reliance on more *ad hoc* means of identifying potential savings.

Recent budgets (1991-92 and 1993-94) indicate that between 40 per cent and 50 per cent of new policy proposals can be expected to be based to some significant extent on a formal evaluation. It is expected that in future the Expenditure Review Committee of Cabinet will increasingly have available the results and experience derived from formal evaluations to guide their deliberations.

E. IMPLEMENTATION OF THE BUDGET

1. Major instruments of in-year control

The Minister for Finance issues a monthly Statement of Commonwealth Financial Transactions. This Statement summarises all budget transactions showing budget estimates for the year, the monthly transactions, year to date figures, and the corresponding year to date figures for the previous years. Accompanying the Statement is a discussion of the reasons for and extent of significant variations from budget estimates and the likely impact on the full year's results.

In the midyear review, Cabinet considers the implementation of the current budget on a comprehensive scale. In certain circumstances supplementary funding is made available to meet prospective outlay overruns through the passage of additional appropriation bills. Supplementary funding can also be made available through the Advance to the Minister for Finance, a specific but limited amount appropriated to make advances that will be recovered through the year, and to provide additional funds to cover urgent and unforeseen requirements.

The government issues strict guidelines concerning access to supplementary funding and requires offsetting savings in other appropriations to the maximum extent possible.

The Commonwealth budget is cash based and some appropriations are cash limited, for example grants to other bodies. Cash limiting was applied in 1984-85 to within year administrative operational expenses (which do not cover salaries) of departments and certain agencies. However, more informal cash limits have been applied to certain other programs.

2. Managerial discretion

The Secretary of a Department and each head of other agencies are accountable to the Minister (and through him/her to the Parliament) for the efficient and effective performance of programs administered by the Department. The Secretary is required to present a departmental report annually to the Minister for tabling in Parliament. Departments are now responsible for the preparation of their financial statements. They must be presented in accordance with Financial Statements Guidelines for Departmental Secretaries, issued by the Minister for Finance.

Soon after the budget is handed down each portfolio Minister supplies the Parliament with Program Performance Statements (1993-94) [Portfolio Budget Measures Statements (PBMSs) in future years] in support of requests for budgetary funding. Such explanations of proposed expenditure are of long standing within the Commonwealth system of Government. PBMSs provide details of new budget measures or initiatives for each portfolio, including implications for achievement of the objectives of relevant programs. They will also identify the new or existing performance information with which their impact will be assessed. PBMSs will also explain any significant year on year variations in regular expenditure. In providing such information, the documents provide a broad "agenda" for the operations of Senate Estimates Committees and so are an important element of Ministerial accountability to the Parliament, representing the Minister's justification of how the requested budgetary funding will be utilised in terms of the effectiveness and efficiency of the programs for which he/she is responsible.

As part of the new budget arrangements, budget documentation will reflect two major stages of parliamentary scrutiny – the first being proposed appropriations in May; the second being past-year outcomes and performance from September, including hearings which will deal with additional estimates from November. PBMSs provide portfolio prospects for the first stage. It is anticipated that documentation produced by departments and agencies for the second stage of scrutiny will be much improved and consolidated within annual reports. There will be more emphasis on outcomes reporting, and less description of activities.

In recognition of the increasing need to make the most effective and efficient use of scarce resources, departmental managers have progressively been given both greater responsibility and increased flexibility in the management of resources appropriated by the Parliament. This has been achieved through a reduction in the number of appropriation items, the extension of cash limits, and a greater discretion in the use of staffing and administrative resources generally. The next steps in the process of devolution require the individual agencies to continue the process within their own organisations.

Funding authority can only be transferred between votes during the year with Parliamentary approval. Any expenditure obligation to be funded from annual appropriations that is incurred in respect of future years first requires the approval of the Minister for Finance or the Minister's delegate within the Department of Finance.

Annual appropriations, if not spent, lapse at the end of the year. The related funds are generally not allowed to be carried forward to the next budget year. The exception to this relates to running costs as described below.

3. The running costs arrangements

The running costs arrangements (RCA), introduced in 1987-88, comprises a package of measures which guide the expenditure of funds on salaries and administration required for the normal business of departments and agencies (as distinct from funding of programs). These measures provide an appropriate medium term framework and set of incentives to improve public sector operational efficiency and effectiveness, enhance accountability and streamline budget formulation.

The introduction of the RCA represents the culmination of a number of fundamental changes to controls over the administrative spending of government, and has resulted in a consolidated appropriation item which includes resources for expenditure on salaries, administrative expenses and property operating expenses.

All departments and non-commercial budget-dependent agencies are subject to compliance with the RCA.

On experience to date, the running costs arrangements have proven to be an effective vehicle for delivering the incentive, and providing the appropriate environment, for managers to maximise the efficient and effective application of administrative resources. It is, however, recognised that in some instances there has not been sufficient devolution to decentralised and lower level managers to fully realise the benefits attainable through the RCA.

4. Features of the running costs arrangements

The following provides a brief summary of major features of the running costs arrangements.

Cash limiting

Department and agency running costs budgets are cash-limited within the budget year, except for the effect of supplemented wage decisions, significant changes in workload and new policy initiatives. Running costs budgets also incorporate allowances for adjustments to non-salary expenses due to price variations.

Thresholds

Threshold arrangements require agency managers to cope internally with all changes below specified threshold levels. Requests for adjustments to running costs estimates will not normally be considered unless:

- the adjustment is non- recurring and exceeds 1 per cent of the total running cost provision;
- ongoing workload changes are greater than 0.5 per cent of the running costs provision.

No threshold tests apply to Cabinet endorsed new policy initiatives, wage or other parameter changes, Section 35 receipts (see section on retention of receipts below), transfers between notional items, and transfers into and out of running costs.

Provision for running costs borrowings

In the past borrowings from the following year have occasionally been restricted by the rigid time constraints imposed by the appropriation structure. In order to ensure that agencies benefit fully from the ability to borrow from future budget years, a provision was established in 1992-93, called the Provision For Running Costs Borrowings, which can be accessed when other funding sources are not available.

Carry-overs

The carry-over provision allows agencies to reallocate up to 6 per cent of their total running costs budget estimate (including funding from all sources) between years, subject to the Appropriation process, by saving or borrowing. Single year borrowings must be repaid before further borrowings are permitted. Carry-overs and borrowings across several years are also permissible, conditional upon appropriate resource agreements being signed, and the application of a notional rate of interest.

Efficiency dividend

Unless specifically exempted, all budget - dependent agencies are expected to provide an efficiency dividend of 1.25 per cent each year. This is applied to their running costs budget and intended to clearly demonstrate efficiency improvements gained through improved management and administrative practices, investment in technology, and the better utilisation of human resources.

The efficiency dividend is currently under review.

A portfolio Minister may seek approval to retain all or part of the efficiency dividend where it is offset by discretionary, measurable and ongoing program savings.

Minor capital payments

Items individually costing less than $250 000, and forming part of the nominal continuing activities of departments and agencies, have been transferred to the running costs appropriation. Individual components, costing less than $250 000, and forming part of a major new project costing $2 million or more in aggregate, will continue to be funded from outside the running costs appropriation.

Property operating expenses

Property operating expenses other than staff housing were incorporated in a separate notional item for the 1992-93 Budget, with full running cost flexibilities to be made available to Departments and agencies as property resource agreements are negotiated.

Retention of receipts

Funds raised by agencies through means other than their appropriation, may be utilised by annotating their appropriation (amounts are "deemed to be appropriated") in accordance with Section 35 of the Audit Act.

This feature of the running cost arrangements allows an agency to retain eligible proceeds from the sale of under-performing assets, the sale and rental of staff housing, user-charging, and other minor categories of receipts, providing that budget neutrality is not compromised. Amounts retained must be visible and, where appropriate, comply with the running costs arrangements.

The sharing of excess receipts and profit/losses is assessed on a case by case basis, having regard to the total cost accruable to the Commonwealth as a whole, as well as the ongoing funding required by agencies for particular activities. In general excess receipts will be made available for running cost purposes by DOF subject to individual agreements and provided that the extra efficiency dividend applicable is paid. In such cases there is a common presumption that such profits will be shared equally between the agency and the Commonwealth.

Supplementation for user charges is either budget neutral overall, or may involve a gain to the budget if less than full supplementation is provided. Charges introduced for new services are not supplemented. Where an agency makes a loss or underachieves, its budgeted level of receipts will also not be supplemented.

F. RECENT REFORMS

The framework providing the link between the budget system and enhanced value for money has been the Financial Management Improvement Program (FMIP). This program was launched in 1984. Since then, FMIP has been an umbrella program for many of the subsequent reforms in public administration.

1. Financial Management Improvement Program (FMIP)

The broad aims of the Government's budgetary and financial management reforms are:
- to focus attention more clearly on the purposes and objectives of particular programs;
- to develop and apply to the management of Commonwealth programs specific techniques aimed at improved performance and more effective and efficient resource use;
- to change the administrative procedures and practices to give managers more incentive to manage and greater awareness of resource costs; and
- to set up machinery to ensure that the effectiveness and efficiency of programs are reviewed regularly and that the results of such reviews are taken into account in the ongoing evaluation of budgetary priorities.

As part of the FMIP, commercial practices have been adopted where appropriate. User charging has been introduced widely and the provision of common goods and services to government organisations (where these goods and services are also usually available from the private sector) have been commercialised. In addition, the Government Business Enterprises' reforms have brought them closer to commercially run organisation.

The machinery of Government changes of 1987 which reduced the number of ministries from 28 to 18, while not a part of the FMIP, are nevertheless consistent with the FMIP because they encourage a broader perspective and greater coherence in policy and program development and provide greater scope for delegation of portfolios to decide on resource use through budgeting. Although subsequent Administrative Orders changes have occurred, the number of ministries remain at 18.

2. Program management and budgeting

Program Management and Budgeting is a central feature of FMIP. It focuses on the purposes of government activity and on the assessment of the effectiveness and efficiency of that activity rather than the level of expenditure on input resources. All Commonwealth departments and budget dependent agencies had adopted program management and budgeting by the 1988-89 Budget.

3. Evaluation of improvement in the Australian Public Service (APS)

In 1991, the Australian Government's Management Advisory Board (MAB) commissioned an evaluation of the last decade of public sector reform.

The Independent Task Force on Management Improvement completed the evaluation in December 1992. Their report, The Australian Public Service Reformed: An Evaluation of a Decade of Management Reform, was launched by the Prime Minister on 1 July 1993. The general conclusions of the report were that:

– the direction of management reforms since the early 1980s has been correct;
– these reforms have been well accepted and their benefits far outweigh their costs; and
– the reforms need to be more fully integrated into the culture of the entire Service.

Subsequent to the Task Force Report, the MAB published a report titled Building a Better Public Service, on the direction for further APS change. Building a Better Public Service emphasised the need for change in three key areas:

– making performance count: which includes locking in the reforms by encouraging further devolution of responsibility within agencies, and focusing on evaluation;
– enhancing leadership: which, in a devolved Service, includes clarifying the roles of central agencies; and
– strengthening the culture of continuous improvement: which includes improving staff development activities and making better use of contracts for Senior Executive Service (SES) staff.

As part of its continuous improvement initiatives, the Commonwealth Government announced in the 1993-94 Budget that benchmarking reviews would be conducted within the Department of Employment, Education and Training, Social Security, Veterans' Affairs and the Australian Customs Service. Benchmarking will involve each of the agencies in identifying areas within their organisations which offer scope for improvement in terms of cost and/or quality of service, identifying performance indicators and searching for best practice in terms of those measures wherever it may occur.

In pursuing the above mentioned policy objectives, the MAB noted that much will depend on the heads of public service agencies and their managers. The reform program of the last decade has given them more scope to manage, and they will be in the best position to judge what best suits their areas of responsibility. The MAB is working to stimulate APS discussion and debate of the issues raised in Building a Better Public Service and to increase awareness within the APS of the findings of the evaluation.

G. FURTHER INFORMATION

1. Documents related to the annual budget

The fiscal year runs from 1 July to 30 June.

The Budget Papers and Budget Related Papers published are released on budget night, which in 1993-94, will be 10 May 1994.

2. 1993-94 budget papers

Budget Speech

No. 1.   Budget Statements 1993-94
Contains detailed information on the budget figuring and measures, an historical perspective and explanatory material on the broader economic context.

No. 2.   The Commonwealth Public Account 1993-94
Contains information relating to the Consolidated Revenue Fund (including the Appropriation Bills No. 1 and 2 and Appropriation (Parliamentary Departments Bill), the Loan Fund and the Trust Fund.

No. 3.   Commonwealth Financial Relations with other levels of Government 1993-94
Provides information on Commonwealth financial relations with the States, Territories and local government.

1993-94 Budget Related Papers

No. 1.   Government Securities on Issue at 30 June 1993
Provides data on Commonwealth Government securities on issue on behalf of the Commonwealth, the States and the Territories.

No. 2.   National Income and Expenditure 1992-93
Gives estimates of gross domestic product, gross national expenditure and national income for the last five years.

No. 3.   Income Tax Statistics 1991-92 Income Year
Contains a summary of certain income tax data for individuals, companies and superannuation funds for the income year 1991-92.

No. 4.   Women's Budget Statement 1993-94
An assessment of the impact on women of the 1993-94 Budget, incorporating the implementation report on the new National Agenda for Women.

No. 5.   Social Justice Strategy 1993-94
An outline of the Commonwealth's overall social justice strategy including a summary of specific initiatives included as part of the 1993-94 Budget.

No. 6.   Australia's Trade Development Program 1993-94
Analyses Australia's performance within the international trade and economic setting and provides an outline for the further strengthening of Australia's trade future.

No. 7.   Program Performance Statements
20 volumes – Presents details of 1992-93 expenditure and estimates for 1993-94 on a program basis and relates these figures to program performance. (These documents are available from individual departments after the budget.)

Report of the Auditor-General

A report on the Financial Statements prepared by the Minister for Finance for the year ended 30 June 1993. (This document is to be released in November 1993.)

3. Other Documents

Annual Report (of each Department) describes goals, programs, information management etc. of the particular department and assesses performance over the past year.

Statement of Commonwealth Financial Transactions (monthly).

Running Costs Arrangements Handbook, Department of Finance, September 1992.

Australia's Budgetary and Financial Management Reforms, M. Keating and M. Holmes, Governance: Vol. 3, No. 2, April 1990, pp. 168-185).

Promoting Value for Money, the Role of the Department of Finance, Department of Finance, AGPS, April 1991.

Not Dollars Alone, Review of the Financial Management Improvement Program Report of the House of Representatives Standing Committee on Finance and Public Administration, AGPS, September 1990.

The Government Response to the Review of Financial Management Improvement Program, Report of the House of Representatives Standing Committee on Finance and Public Administration, Department of Finance.

Reports in the Management Advisory Board/Management Improvement Advisory Committee publication series.

NOTE

A Minister's portfolio includes the department and each agency for which he/she is responsible.

AUSTRIA

**Any changes which may have taken place in Austria
since September 1993 are not reflected in this chapter**

A. INSTITUTIONAL STRUCTURE OF BUDGETARY DECISION-MAKING

1. Political and organisational structure of government

Austria is a decentralised federal country with nine states (*Bundesländer*) and a hierarchy of local governments (*Gemeinden*) within each state.

Each state has its own constitution, parliament, government and administration. Each level of administration is autonomous and independent.

Federal government is headed by the Federal Chancellor, who is nominated by the Federal President. He chooses his cabinet. At present the federal government consists of 15 Ministers (including Federal Chancellor) and four Secretaries of State.

The government functions are organised around these ministries. Most of them include large operating services (*e.g.* education, science and research, defence, taxation, and public transport). Only a few ministries are small organisations with, mainly, regulatory activities.

With few exceptions ministries are organised in more than one department and a number of subordinated agencies and institutions.

Parliament has two chambers, the Federal Parliament (*Nationalrat*) and the Parliament of States (*Bundesrat*). The Federal Parliament is the actual legislative body. The Parliament of States is the federal institution through which the states participate in the legislation of the Federation. The Federal Parliament has 183 members, who are elected for four years; four parties are represented at present. The last election was in October 1990. At present the two major parties form a coalition and support the government on the basis of a coalition agreement.

2. Main budgetary organs

The central role in all budgetary matters is taken by the Ministry of Finance. The Minister of Finance is responsible for financial and tax policy and therefore responsible for the expenditure and revenue side of the budget in general. The responsibility for wage policy for civil servants and for personnel resources is shared with the Federal Chancellor.

Within the Ministry of Finance budgetary activities are co-ordinated by the Budget Department. It is responsible for general expenditure planning, general budgeting and expenditure control. The Budget Department with 50 professionals is split up in divisions. The Financial Management Division co-ordinates the preparation and implementation of the budget as well as accounting. The Budgetary Policy Division is responsible for policy oriented analysis, expenditure planning and forecasting. Seven divisions are engaged in preparing the budgets of the spending ministries and monitoring and controlling their implementation. Three divisions are responsible for manpower policy, staff budgeting and controlling personnel costs. Tax legislation and revenue estimates are formulated in another department.

3. Role of Federal Chancellor and Cabinet

All government decisions are taken collectively in the Cabinet. The outline of medium-term budgetary policy is formulated in the coalition agreement. All members of the Cabinet have to accept the global budget policy programme. Further involvement of the Cabinet in the budgetary decision process is more or less of a formal nature.

The annual budget guidelines are prepared by the Minister of Finance on the basis of the coalition agreement and submitted to the Cabinet for information and debate. The negotiations on expenditures (and consolidation measures) are held between the Minister of Finance, his Secretary of State and the responsible ministry. Issues which cannot be settled bilaterally are referred to the Cabinet-Co-ordination Committee, which is headed by the Federal Chancellor and consists of ministers and secretaries of the two coalition parties.

The Cabinet approves the government draft of the Budget, which is presented to Parliament by the Minister of Finance. The Federal Government has to elaborate mid-term budgetary projections and an investment programme every year, covering a period of four years. These surveys are submitted to Parliament for information only.

4. Role of Parliament

All central government expenditures and revenues have to be approved annually by Parliament. Parliament takes note of the multi-year estimates.

The draft budget is structured around approximately 1 900 appropriation accounts (1 200 for expenditures and 700 for revenues) on the basis of a modified economic classification. The structure of the main accounts is developed from the administrative structure, in most cases with separate accounts for each lower level agency and institution.

The draft budget is examined by the Parliamentary Budget Committee. This Committee has to discuss each appropriation item. It has the right to introduce its own proposals on matters dealt with in the draft budget. On the basis of a report from the Budget Committee a general debate is then held in Parliament. At its conclusion the budget is formally decided upon. These decisions constitute the basis for the execution of the budget. (Parliament has the authority to prepare its own budget, but this has never happened.)

B. THE SCOPE AND NATURE OF GOVERNMENT FINANCES

The responsibilities of each level of government are defined in the Federal Constitution. The central government is responsible for defence, law and order, for universities, research, high schools, regional policy, agriculture, postal services, telecommunications, railways and construction and up-keep of main roads. The central government also provides support for welfare, local transport and hospitals. The states have main responsibility for primary education, housing, health and welfare. The municipalities have the responsibility for kindergartens, administration of schools, local roads, water supply and canalisation. In addition, the large municipalities have responsibility for a wider range of services which normally include hospitals and social and cultural facilities.

Each government must bear the costs of its own activities. Thus, the sharing of responsibilities is matched by the principle of revenue sharing. All major taxes (*i.e.* wages and income tax, value added tax, business taxes on profits and capital assets, tax on bank interests, gasoline taxes and beer taxes) are joint taxes, *i.e.* they accrue jointly to the three levels of government. In 1989 the joint taxes yielded approximately two-thirds of total tax revenues. The exclusive central government taxes comprise the corporation tax, wealth tax, tobacco tax, stamp duties and custom levies and amounted in 1989 to about 28 per cent of total tax revenues. The state taxes consist mainly of land taxes, fire insurance tax, beverage tax and hotel accommodation taxes. The exclusive taxes of municipalities consist mainly of assigned taxes from the states plus business taxes on wages assigned by the federal government plus property tax. The taxes of local authorities amount to about 8 per cent of total revenues.

In addition to such tax revenues a system of intergovernmental transfers is used. Transfers are either for general purposes or for specific purposes, *e.g.* for housing or teachers' services. In addition where the states act as agents of the Federation, the Federation has to meet the resulting expenditures.

The social insurance funds are autonomous and fiscally independent. Their expenditures are financed by social security contributions and by transfers from the federal budget.

Federal public enterprises comprise railways, post and telecommunications, forests and theatres. These institutions are 100 per cent owned by the Federation and are included in the federal budget on a gross basis. This means that all enterprises' revenues are recorded in budget documents as state revenues. The subsidies granted to the federal railways are shown in the budget as their revenues, and as expenditures for the ministries concerned.

Total expenditures at all levels of government (including social security) have grown steadily during the post-war period, reaching over 56 per cent of GDP in 1987. Since then (see Table 1) expenditure growth has ceased and there has been a slow decline in total expenditure as a percentage of GDP. The functional disaggregation of current expenditure is shown in Table 2. It highlights the dominance of social security, health and education in the total current expenditure pattern.

Changes in the general government balance in Austria are dominated by the federal deficit (see Table 1). The states and municipalities incur only small budget deficits on an administrative basis, but show significant surpluses on a national accounts basis, which excludes net-lending from expenditures.

Table 1. **Fiscal indicators, 1985-90**

As percentage of GDP

	1985	1986	1987	1988	1989	1990
Taxes	43.0	42.8	42.3	41.7	40.6	40.7
Expenditures	55.0	56.4	56.7	54.8	53.3	53.3
Borrowing requirement	2.5	3.7	4.3	3.0	2.7	2.1
Outstanding debt	53.3	57.8	61.5	61.7	60.9	60.3
Federal deficit	4.5	5.2	4.7	4.3	3.8	3.5

Source: Ministry of Finance and Central Statistical Office.

Table 2. **Functional classification of general government current expenditures (1989)**

As percentage of total

General public services	6.8
Defence	2.4
Public order and safety	1.8
Education	9.5
Health	11.5
Social security and welfare	50.0
Housing	0.6
Recreation and culture	1.3
Transportation and communication	2.9
Other economic services	4.4
Debt service	8.8
Total	100.0

Source: Austrian Central Statistical Office.

C. BUDGET FORMULATION STRATEGY AND PROCESS

1. Strategic aims and global norms

An important objective of current fiscal policy is to gradually reduce the federal government deficit, to reduce the burden of taxation and to stabilise the federal debt-to-GDP ratio over the medium term. It aims to do this by keeping the growth of public expenditures below that of GDP. In implementing this strategy, high priority

75

has been given to reducing and cutting expenditures. Until now, the consolidation has progressed faster than planned and thus the cumulative deficit reduction was higher than originally planned. At the same time the most comprehensive tax reform after World War II was enacted. Thus the burden of taxation and the ratio of government expenditures have fallen (see Table 1). A further decline is planned for the future according to the coalition agreement of December 1990. The target is to reduce the federal government deficit below 2.5 per cent of GDP by 1994.

2. Technical aspects of multi-year estimates

The Government annually prepares a medium-term budget estimate covering three future years in addition to the current budget year. The purpose of the medium-term budget estimate is to show the consequences for government finance of measures which have already been decided on by Parliament and the Government.

On the expenditure side the medium-term budget indicates the size of the financial resources that will be required during the next few years in order to meet the commitments and goals that have already been approved. The revenue side indicates how the basis for taxation will develop if the existing fiscal regulations are applied without change during the period under review. The medium-term budget estimate is therefore less a plan or a programme for the coming years than a means of indicating the consequences of existing commitments. It thus serves as an instrument of budget policy by providing a basis for for decisions concerning, *e.g.* the need for further consolidation. The medium-term budget estimates are mainly for the Government's internal planning purposes, and Parliament is therefore not required to act upon them.

Multi-year expenditure estimates are prepared for each of the ministries on the basis of a detailed economic classification. The estimates mainly focus on statutory expenditures that are by far the largest category. It is compiled in the Ministry of Finance in co-operation with all other ministries.

Multi-year estimates are published once a year – in the spring – showing an institutional, functional and economic breakdown.

3. Calendar of main points of decision-making and activities

The fiscal year [FY(t)] is the calendar year (year t).

Months before start of FY (t)	Main events and activities
(Year t – 1)	
10-9 (March/April)	Ministries submit mid-term expenditure projection to MF.
9 (end April)	MF formulates budgeting guidelines.
7 (June)	Government agencies present request for next fiscal year to the competent ministry and MF.
7-4 (July-September)	Negotiations between the responsible ministries and MF.
4 (mid-September)	Cabinet finalises the drafted budget in the Cabinet-Co-ordination-Committee.
3 (end October)	Budget proposal is submitted to Parliament; "Budget Speech" by MF.
2-0 (mid-November-December)	Parliament debates and decides the budget.
(Year t)	
0 (1 January)	Start of fiscal year (t).
(Year t + 1)	
End February	Publication of preliminary outcome of the budget.
March-May	National Audit Bureau checks the accounts of the budget.
September	Publication of the outturn of the Budget.

4. The annual budget cycle

The budget procedure starts in the Government agencies during the spring (May) of the preceding calendar year. The work is done on the basis of directives issued by the Minister of Finance. In these directives the MF decides, against the background of the coalition agreement and available financial resources, on budgeting limits for the coming fiscal year. In recent years the annual directives have laid down relatively strict demands for restraint, rationalisation and review. In the past, several limits were set for several kinds of expenditures, but at present there will normally be only one limit for all expenditures, discretionary as well as statutory. Within each budgeting limit a limit on personnel resources is specified.

The agency requests have to be presented to the competent ministry. The ministries' budget requests are submitted to the Ministry of Finance not later than middle of June.

The next step in the budget procedures lasts until September and consists of negotiations between the ministries responsible for the activities in question and the Ministry of Finance. The budget requests are examined and discussed at three levels:

– by the division responsible in the budget department;
– by the Minister of Finance; and
– if necessary in the Cabinet Co-ordination Committee.

Budget negotiations at Minister level mainly focus on claims for increases to the budgeting limits. The Cabinet-Co-ordination Committee, headed by the Federal Chancellor, draws conclusions in matters of diverging opinions.

The outcome of this process is the draft budget, which is presented to Parliament at the end of October.

After the ''Budget speech'' the draft budget is referred to the parliamentary Budget Committee for discussion and approval. As noted above, Parliament has relatively little influence. It has the right to change the draft bill, but usually those changes are negligible. Parliament usually approves the budget in the middle of December. The budget act provides some regulations for flexible administration of the budget, in particular the competence of the MF to approve additional expenditures up to a limited extent, provided that these additional expenditures can be financed by cutting current expenditures or additional receipts, thus maintaining the deficit equally.

New expenditures due to new legislation or increases of limited expenditures put down in the budget have to be enacted by supplementary budgets and have to be authorised by Parliament.

D. EXPENDITURE REVIEW

There are no separate formal procedures for programme analysis and review, but the spending ministries are required to report once a year on spending developments. These reports, which replaced a more traditional system of expenditure monitoring, include an analysis of expenditure patterns, budgetary lags and the development of real variables and their financial implications. The purpose of their review is not merely to examine financial trends, but to assess the effectiveness of their own administrative policies. Much of the work of the Budget Department is concentrated on evaluating financial trends and on an assessment of the budgetary implications of existing and new policies. In addition to improving efficiency, in-depth studies of expenditure programmes of certain government operations have been undertaken.

E. IMPLEMENTATION OF THE BUDGET

1. Major instruments of in-year control

Immediately after approval of the budget by Parliament the Minister of Finance issues directives to all ministries and agencies concerning the implementation of the budget and ex-ante financial control.

A fundamental characteristic of the appropriation control system is that the Ministry of Finance has full control of the use of appropriated funds. Preauthorisation by the Ministry of Finance is required for each discretionary expenditure of any significance, for capital expenditure as well as for subsidies. Each construction project of any significance and all real estate transactions must be approved by the Ministry of Finance. The Ministry of Finance has further full control on commitments, personnel costs and manpower. The spending ministries are required to submit their financing needs month-by-month to the Ministry of Finance for approval at the beginning of each month and to report to the Ministry of Finance on a monthly basis on funds already spent.

The Minister of Finance is requested to report to the Parliament four times a year particularly on adherence to spending limits, on borrowings and other liabilities.

One or two supplementary budgets are passed every year, in which adjustments to expenditures and revenues are recorded.

2. Managerial discretion

Any increase or shift in expenditures requires the approval by Parliament of a supplementary budget law authorising such an increase. However, the Minister of Finance has limited discretionary authority (defined by the Federal Household Act and the Annual Budget Law) to increase or shift authorised expenditures provided that additional revenues are available. If revenues are less than expected, a special budget law has to be submitted to Parliament which authorises additional borrowing. However, the Minister of Finance can finance cyclical shortfalls in revenues of up to 5 per cent but has to report to Parliament on such operations.

F. RECENT REFORMS

A draft proposal for improving planning instruments will be brought before Parliament within this legislative period. This draft will provide that the Federal Government has to elaborate a multi-year financial programme at the beginning of each legislative period. The essential purpose of the financial programme is to achieve closer integration of the Government's priority setting, policy developments and expenditure management decision-making processes. Given overall Government priorities and fiscal policy considerations as well as the costs of existing and planned policies and programmes, expenditure plans have to be set for each policy sector. Planning figures have to be established for each year for each Ministry.

A cost information system is being introduced to enhance cost awareness in the public administration. As a part of it, cost studies have been undertaken in a number of sectors of the public administration on the basis of which general models for cost information systems can be designed. Associated with the cost-information system, it is also planned to provide each ministry with the necessary information technology infrastructure in order to derive cost calculations from budgetary data. Norms and standards for this purpose are also to be developed.

G. FURTHER INFORMATION

1. Documents related to annual budget

1. Federal Budget Law (*Bundesfinanzgesetz*), January year (t).
2. Financial Report of the Federal Minister of Finance (*Bundesvoranschlag*) containing the Budget speech and comprehensive statistical data, October, year (t – 1).
3. Multi-year budget estimates of the Federal Minister of Finance supplemented by the Federal Investment Programme, June, year (t – 1) (*Budgetprognose und Investitionsprogramm des Bundes*).
4. Annual Economic Report (*Wirtschaftsbericht*) of the Federal Government, June, year (t).
5. Quarterly Report on the excess expenditures (*Zusammenstellung der überplanmäsigen Ausgaben*).
6. Subsidy Report of the Federal Government (*Subventionsbericht*), annually, autumn.
7. Public Debt Report (*Finanzschuldenbericht*), published by the Austrian Postsparkasse, annually, July.
8. Federal Household Act (*Bundeshaushaltsgesetz*).

BELGIUM

**Any changes which may have taken place in Belgium
since September 1993 are not reflected in this chapter**

A. INSTITUTIONAL STRUCTURE OF BUDGETARY DECISION-MAKING

1. Political and organisational structure of government

Belgium is a federal state made up of of Communities and Regions. Three levels of public authorities can be distinguished: the central level, including the State, Communities and Regions, the lower level (provinces and municipalities) and social security bodies.

Communities and Regions only came into being in 1980. Many central government functions were then separated from the State Government.

The three Communities – French-speaking, Flemish-speaking and German-speaking – each have their own legislature and government. The same holds for the Flemish and Walloon regions, and for the Brussels-Capital region, which has some special features.

State government functions are divided among some 15 ministries. Ministries have in general one minister and in some cases one or more Secretaries of State. At a political level, the Minister's private office, which has no direct line management responsibilities, is also there to advise the Minister on major issues. The Secretary General of each ministry is a non-political appointment, as is the rest of the departmental staff. Ministers are usually members of Parliament.

Parliament has two Chambers, the Chamber of Representatives and the Senate. There are currently 13 political parties, four of which are split into Francophone and Flemish sections, the others being regional.

With rare exceptions, State governments have to be supported by a coalition of political parties. There is a coalition agreement, which inter alia currently includes detailed budgetary policy guidelines. Direct Parliamentary elections are held every four years. The next election will be in 1996 at the latest.

2. Main budgetary organs

Both the Minister of Finance and the Minister of the Budget are involved in budget policy matters. The Minister of Finance has primary responsibility for financial and tax policy formulation, whereas expenditure policies are in the domain of the Minister of the Budget. There is a Superior Council of Finances, which advises the Minister of Finance about financial and tax policies.

The Minister of the Budget is responsible for the Budget Department, which is part of the Ministry of Finance. The Budget Department with about 100 professional staff is headed by a Director General. It comprises five directorates. Apart from the Budget Study Directorate, there is a Budget Preparation Directorate and a Directorate which checks on expenditures. The Auditing Directorate prepares government decision-making and advises the Minister of the Budget on new departmental spending initiatives, drawing on information provided by the Inspectorate of Finance. It is represented on the Committee on the Orientation and Co-ordination of Government Procurement which prepares investment expenditure decision-making by government. Finally the Inspectorate of Finance Directorate is involved in preparing Ministry budgets and monitoring and controlling their implementation. Its staff is mainly located in the spending ministries, with a very small central unit in the Budget Department.

3. Role of Prime Minister and Cabinet

Preparing the budget is the sole responsibility of the the executive, in other words the Government, which submits a budget bill to the bureau of the Chambers. Within the Government, the Minister of Finance and the Minister of the Budget play an important role in drawing up the budget.

Every year, by February or March at the latest, these two Ministers send their colleagues a circular laying down guidelines for drawing up budget proposals for the fiscal year ahead.

Early in July, a ministerial Select Committee begins to meet under the leadership of the Prime Minister. The purpose of these meetings is an in-depth study of the budget proposals and the accompanying measures required to meet the objective set by the Council of Ministers with respect to net borrowing requirements. Once the ministerial Select Committee has completed its review of the budget proposals, they are submitted to the Council of Ministers for decision. The General Expenditure budget and the Ways and Means budget must be submitted to the bureau of the Chamber of Representatives or the Senate along with the Budget Memorandum. The latter contains a summary and analysis of the various budgets, together with information needed to brief the Chambers on the country's economic and financial situation.

4. Role of Parliament

Under the transitional provisions in the Constitution, Parliament approves the State budget.

The Ways and Means budget and the General Expenditure budget must be submitted to Parliament by 30 September; they must be considered together and adopted by the two Chambers at the latest by 30 November of the year preceding the fiscal year.

Included with the General Expenditure budget are administrative budgets prepared in greater detail by the Department.

Administrative budgets are subject to a separate review within the relevant specialised parliamentary Commissions, attended by the Minister of the departments concerned.

The Chamber and the Senate must both adopt motions demonstrating that the administrative budgets are in line with the content and objectives of the General Expenditure budget.

As with government or private bills, the Chambers also have the right under the Constitution to amend a budget. This, however, does not apply to administrative budgets.

If Parliament has not approved the General Expenditure budget within the set time, a system of provisional appropriations comes into force, with the exception of the prevailing rule that a specific item may be used up entirely, provided the overall percentage remains the same within the relevant budget section.

With respect to administrative budgets, Parliament is given a specified time (7 or 15 days) in which to make a declaration of non-conformity; if it fails to do so within that period, the administrative budgets concerned are understood to be in compliance with the General Expenditure budget.

With respect to revenue, the Ways and Means budget always contains a clause stipulating the renewal, for the coming fiscal year, of taxes existing on 31 December of the previous year. This renewal, or rather extension, is essential since, under the Constitution, any taxes accruing to the State, the Communities or the Regions may only be levied for one year and must be renewed annually.

According to the latest constitutional reform "aimed at completing the federal structure of the State" and intended to enter into force after the next general election, the reformed version of the Senate will no longer play any budgetary role; only the Chamber of Representatives will have the authority to adopt budgets.

B. THE SCOPE AND NATURE OF GOVERNMENT FINANCES

The Flemish Community, the French-speaking Community, the German-speaking Community, the Flemish Region, the Walloon Region and the Brussels-Capital Region are legal entities and as such are administratively autonomous, *i.e.* they are independent bodies managing their own budgets.

The Council or legislative body of each Community or Region adopts a budget every year and closes the accounts. The general account of each Community and Region is sent to their Councils with comments from the Audit Office. All revenue and expenditure is listed in the budget and the accounts. Once the budget has been adopted by the Councils, it no longer needs to be adopted elsewhere.

Responsibility for budgetary issues is exercised by the appropriate bodies in either the Community or the Region. This means that the authority of Parliament, the Government and the Ministry of Finance to audit is exercised respectively by the Councils, the Executive and Members of the Executive with authority over finance and budget matters.

Local authorities consist of provinces and communes. They have residual powers in all matters concerning their territory and the inhabitants thereof. Their tasks include providing services to the public (*e.g.* social assistance grants). In addition, they act as central government agents in performing certain tasks.

Local authorities are entitled to a share of the tax imposed on physical persons; they can levy certain local taxes and are authorised to borrow.

Social security is for the most part off-budget. The National Office of Social Security is in charge of collecting social security contributions. The payment of social benefits and the day-to-day management of different sectors (like health and disablement, pensions, family allowances and unemployment benefits) are taken care of by semi-public organisations, which are accountable to the government. Social Security contributions and rates of benefits are determined by Central Government.

The largest public enterprises are to be found in public transport, post and telephone, broadcasting and also include some public financial institutions. These enterprises are evolving towards greater autonomy and privatisations have considerably reduced the role of Parliament.

The following table shows the functional classification of government expenditure:

Table 1. **Classification of government expenditure (1992)**

As percentage of total

General administration	8.5
Defence	7.3
Public order and security	3.8
Communications	8.2
Commerce and industry	2.6
Agriculture	0.9
Education, culture and recreation	4.5
Social security and healthcare	24.9
Housing and physical planning	0.1
Not classified (excluding servicing of public debt)	39.3
Total	100.0

Source: Ministry of Finance, Belgium.

C. BUDGET FORMULATION STRATEGY AND PROCESS

1. Strategic aims and global norms

Budgetary targets are identified in the coalition agreement. They relate inter alia to the budget deficit, the total burden of taxes and social security contributions and public debt.

Budgetary targets are usually expressed as a percentage of gross national product (GNP). The net Treasury Borrowing Requirement (TBR) is broadly speaking the difference between revenue and disbursements by the Treasury for the State, Communities and Regions.

The following table indicates outturns for 1987-92:

Table 2. **Fiscal indicators, 1987-92**

As percentage of GDP

	1987	1988	1989	1990	1991	1992
Net borrowing requirement	9.2	8.5	8	6.3	5.7	5.3
Tax and social security contribution burden	44.8	43.7	42.2	42.7	42.6	43.0
Public debt	109.9	112.0	109.5	110.0	112.7	115.3

Source: Ministry of Finance, Belgium.

2. Technical aspects of multi-year estimates

The General Memorandum includes a multi-year estimate.

3. Calendar of main points of decision-making and activities

Months before start of FY (t)	Main events and activities
(Year t – 1)	
February-March	Minister of the Budget and Minister of Finance send their colleagues a circular setting out guidelines for drawing up budget proposals for the following fiscal year. The instructions have already been approved by the Council of Ministers.
March	On the basis of the guidelines in the budget circular, all the Ministers draw up, with the help of their officials, a budget estimate for their department, based on unchanged policies. The appropriations required for any new initiatives must figure separately in the budget estimate. The proposals are sent for his advice to the Inspector of Finance accredited to the Department.
April	The budget estimates are then reviewed in bilateral meetings (between each spending department and the Budget Department).
June	When all departmental budget estimates have been bilaterally reviewed, the Minister of the Budget presents a report on the outcome to the Council of Ministers at the end of June. The Minister of Finance does the same for the Ways and Means budget estimate.
June-July	Early July marks the beginning of a series of meetings held by the ministerial Select Committee headed by the Prime Minister.
Early August	Once the budget proposals have been reviewed by the Select Committee, they are submitted to the Council of Ministers for decision in late July-early August.
Late September	Submission to Parliament.
(Year t)	
1 January	Start of fiscal year (t).

4. The annual budget cycle

On the basis of norms and guidelines in a circular of the Minister of Finance and the Minister of the Budget, each Ministry prepares a budget request, based on unchanged policies (April-May).

Finance Inspectorates in each ministry co-ordinate preparation activities by drafting a "control report" which examines the unchanged policy expenditure levels. In bilateral meetings (June-July) with spending departments these estimates are examined by the Budget Department. Subsequently, Finance Inspectors draft a detailed "evaluation" report. On the basis of this report, inter alia, the Government decides the total extent and allocation of budget cut-backs.

Investment projects and their budgetary implications for the following three years have to be submitted to the Budget Department. The proposals are examined by the Commission on the Orientation and Co-ordination of Government Procurement, which drafts a report for final decision by the Government.

At the end of September, budget documents are submitted to Parliament, after which Parliamentary debates and decision-making take place.

D. EXPENDITURE REVIEW

For the past few years, the Government's aim has been to reduce public spending. This cannot be done without taking structural measures or abolishing the mechanisms which lead to automatic spending increases. All sectors of Government, including social security institutions, are concerned and affected by this exercise.

The Treasury Committee aims to co-ordinate and improve Treasury management. It analyses forecasts of cash requirements for the short and medium term, and examines the situation and financing of the Treasury.

E. IMPLEMENTATION OF THE BUDGET

1. Major instruments of in-year control

During the first quarter of every year, an audit is conducted to see whether any adjustment is needed in the Ways and Means budget or the general expenditure budget. Since the audit inevitably leads to changes in one programme or the other, the law stipulates that the Government, following the February-March audit, has until May at the latest to submit a bill adjusting the general expenditure budget.

Taking into account the economic context and scope for funding, as well as policy planning options, the Government sets out, again on an annual basis, a programme of commitments relating to public investment. Funds for each chapter are released in quarterly or six-monthly tranches only. Most public investment is now the responsibility of the Regions and the Communities.

Ministers must obtain the opinion of the Inspectorate of Finances on almost all expenditure proposals, with a few exceptions. These include contracts and transfers in which only a small amount of money is involved, certain kinds of personnel expenditure and expenditure resulting from organic regulations.

The major implementation report is incorporated in the Budget Memorandum for to the new budget. Every month in the *"Moniteur Belge"*, the Treasury Department publishes a "budget update", concerning both expenditure and revenue, and at similar intervals the Ministry of Finance publishes a press release giving details of trends over the past month in tax revenue and public debt.

2. Managerial discretion

The budget system is a dual one, in that appropriations must cover the commitment and the order to pay (*ordonnancement*) which precedes the actual payment.

Budget expenditure consists of differentiated and non-differentiated appropriations. Balances unspent at the end of the fiscal year are treated differently, depending on whether the appropriations are differentiated or not. Differentiated appropriations, as regards both commitments and orders to pay, are carried forward to the following year automatically and without any restriction. Conversely non-differentiated appropriations, which relate mainly to current expenditure, can only be carried forward if committed during the fiscal year referred to in the initial budget. Other unspent appropriations are surrendered.

Budget overruns can show up either in the check-up at the beginning of the fiscal year or during the preparation of a new budget or in examining cash patterns over the year. It may then be necessary to increase or transfer certain appropriations and to impose new budgetary adjustments which the Government has to submit to Parliament.

CANADA

**Any changes which have taken place in Canada
since October 1993 are not reflected in this chapter**

A. INSTITUTIONAL STRUCTURE OF BUDGETARY DECISION-MAKING

1. Political and organisational structure of government

Canada is a federal country with expenditure jurisdiction and revenue powers divided among the levels of government. The 10 provinces have responsibilities in the broad areas of health and education, welfare and social services, the administration of justice, and the disposition of Crown lands. Many major expenditure programmes administered by provincial authorities are jointly financed by federal and provincial governments. (See Section B for more information.)

Canada has a two-chamber parliamentary system of federal government in which the legislative function rests with the Parliament of Canada. The executive function is exercised by a Cabinet chosen by the Prime Minister. The two chambers are the Senate and the House of Commons. Cabinet Ministers, including the Prime Minister, are members of Parliament and are usually sitting members of the House of Commons, although Senators (non-elective) are occasionally appointed to Cabinet. There are three main political parties and the current government was elected in October 1993. Federal elections occur every five years; the next election is due in 1998.

Central government functions are divided amongst some 75 departments and agencies. A few of these report directly to Parliament (*e.g.* the Auditor General), however, most are responsible to one of about 23 Cabinet Ministers. The most senior public service positions (heads of departments or Deputy Ministers) are appointed by the Prime Minister. All other departmental personnel are appointed through a merit-based, competitive staffing process.

2. Main budgetary organs

Within the federal government, the Minister of Finance has primary responsibility for the formulation of macroeconomic policies. The Minister is also charged with recommending the appropriate fiscal framework, including the expenditure limits, for the broad policy areas consistent with the Government's priorities. The Minister also advises on the economic impact and effectiveness of new proposals. Responsibility for formulation of tax policies, providing recommendations on general revenue matters, as well as for debt management is held by the Minister of Finance.

The Treasury Board is a committee of several Ministers chaired by the President of Treasury Board. It is responsible for: the overall integrity of the financial and other resource control and management systems; the determination and approval of resource levels for all federal government programmes; the preparation of accounts and provision of reports on the status of reserves; the preparation and presentation to Parliament for formal approval of the resource estimates of programmes; and for policy advice on the effective and efficient management of public resources in general. The Treasury Board also has the role of ''employer'' for 240 000 employees of federal departments and administers the Public Service Superannuation Plan.

The Treasury Board is supported by two secretariats: the Treasury Board Secretariat (TBS) and the office of the Comptroller General (OCG).

The Treasury Board Secretariat provides analysis and advice to the Treasury Board Ministers on issues related to the management of the government's financial, human, and material resources. Within the TBS, the Programme Branch, with 143 professional and support staff, analyses and makes recommendations to the Treasury Board and Committees of Cabinet on departmental budgets and expenditure proposals as well as financial resources. This Branch is the centre for producing detailed expenditure plans including material presented to Parliament (see Section A4). Within Programme Branch, the Expenditure Management Sector has overall responsibility for the co-ordination, integration and analysis of the expenditure budget and government-wide management reforms encompassing programme delivery and departmental accountability.

The four other sections of the Branch are organised along portfolio lines, having lead responsibility for negotiations and relations with all spending departments and public enterprises. The Human Resources Policy Branch of the TBS, with a staff of 262, develops policies for standards and conditions of employment including training, and department organisation as well as conducts bargaining negotiations with the public service unions. Advice to Treasury Board on the development and monitoring of policies concerning the use of materials and services required by departments (e.g. standards for contracts, computer equipment, and travel expenses) is provided by the Administrative Policy Branch, which has a staff of 95. There are 61 people involved with the administration of the government's official languages policy and Employment Equity programme, which also fall under the purview of Treasury Board.

The Office of the Comptroller General is responsible for ensuring the establishment of management and financial practices in government departments. As part of its mandate, the OCG is responsible for preparing government financial and accounting policies and regulations, as well as the development of policies relating to comprehensive internal audits and programme evaluation. The OCG has 177 professional and support staff.

3. Role of Prime Minister and Cabinet

It would be quite unusual for a Canadian Minister of Finance to proceed with policy proposals which did not have the agreement and backing of the Prime Minister. The Cabinet Committee on Priorities and Planning (P&P), chaired by the Prime Minister, and including the Minister of Finance, President of the Treasury Board and Chairpersons of Cabinet Committees, is the main forum for setting the general directions and priorities of the Government and for approving the multi-year Fiscal Plan.

The Operations Committee, a committee of senior ministers which is chaired by the Deputy Prime Minister, was established in the 1989 reform of the Cabinet decision making process. This Committee is responsible for co-ordinating management of the Government's key agenda items on a week to week basis and for advising the P&P Committee on the handling of new policy initiatives.

4. Role of Parliament

Information about the federal government's planned revenues and expenditures is presented to Parliament in two forms:
1. the Budget of the Minister of Finance, and
2. the "expenditure budget" or Main and Supplementary Estimates tabled by the President of the Treasury Board.

The Budget, which contains in its supporting documentation summaries of planned expenditures and anticipated revenues, is usually delivered to Parliament approximately one or two months before the start of the fiscal year.

The Budget provides an opportunity for the Minister of Finance to make a statement of the government's economic policies and priorities, and to bring under review the entire financial position of government, present and prospective.

The Budget sets out the government's expenditure plan which provides the framework for the presentation of the detailed spending estimates to Parliament. In the absence of a formal Budget, the Minister of Finance may present an "economic statement" setting out the financial position of government, introducing fiscal measures, as necessary, and providing the expenditure framework for the presentation of the government's estimates.

Supporting documentation to the Budget may contain a statement of the government's assessment of the economic environment, including medium-term economic forecasts. This material provides Parliament with information concerning the state of the economy upon which the fiscal plan is based. In approving the Budget, Parliament assents to the fiscal policies of the government.

The Main Estimates, which provide the detailed expenditure plan for approved programmes, are tabled annually in Parliament approximately 1 to 1½ months prior to the start of the fiscal year. Although the Main Estimates are related integrally to the Budget, it is the details of expenditure contained in the Main Estimates for which Parliamentary approval is needed to authorise cash outlays. Parliament annually votes and approves less than 30 per cent of total expenditures, the balance being so-called "statutory" items, such as interest on public debt as well as most transfers to provinces and persons. Statutory items receive continuing authority under separate legislation. The 30 per cent of expenditures voted by Parliament is distributed over roughly 210 votes. Votes are organised by programme and type of payment (operating, capital, transfers) for each department and agency.

The Government must seek Parliamentary approval to increase the amount to be spent within any of these votes. Thus, in the course of the fiscal year, Supplementary Estimates may be tabled in Parliament to gain authority to provide for new initiatives or unanticipated expenditures. Recent years have seen as many as 3 or 4 Supplementaries each year, although two per year is the norm.

Parliament has the ability to propose deletions or reductions to the sums included in the Estimates tabled by the government. However, the Government, usually a majority government in Canada, would normally use that majority to reject such changes. Parliament is not able to amplify the ambit of a vote nor increase the amount proposed by the Government. The Main Estimates are considered by sectoral committees of Parliament during a four month period (March to June), including the first quarter of the new fiscal year (starting 1st April).

Parliament grants Interim Supply at the start of the fiscal year; generally authorising spending equal to one-quarter of the total proposed within the annual appropriations under consideration. Under the Standing orders of Parliament, the House and Senate, each sitting as Committee of the Whole must consider and vote on the Main Estimates by the end of June.

B. THE SCOPE AND NATURE OF GOVERNMENT FINANCES

Provincial and territorial governments are independent of the federal government with regard to their revenue and expenditure policies (*i.e.* there are no federal restrictions on provincial and territorial decisions in this domain). There are periodic meetings of the federal Minister of Finance and his provincial counterparts to exchange views on fiscal and economic policy. Local governments are incorporated by each province to perform certain functions falling within provincial jurisdiction. Generally, local government taxation revenues are limited to property taxes. Transfer payments from the federal government to other levels of government represent about 18 per cent of total spending. Almost 60 per cent of this is accounted for by federal contributions towards the financing of hospital insurance, medical care, post-secondary education, and social assistance payments which are the responsibility of provincial and municipal governments. In general, the federal government does not have authority over benefit or premium levels nor entitlement conditions for most of these programmes. Of course, the transfer payments themselves arise from federal legislation and are subject to federal control.

The major social security expenditures included in the federal budget are for universal pensions and unemployment benefits. These account for approximately 25 per cent of total federal expenditures. Federal legislation is the basis for these programmes, and benefit and contribution rates are (where applicable) subject to federal control.

Federal payments to Crown corporations (*i.e.* public enterprises) equal roughly 3 per cent of total spending. Most major commercial Crown corporations are authorised to borrow directly in the capital market, subject to the approval of the Minister of Finance.

C. BUDGET FORMULATION STRATEGY AND PROCESS

1. Strategic aims and global norms

A key focus of current fiscal strategy is reducing the federal government deficit and arresting the growth in outstanding debt. The medium-term objective is stabilisation and then reversal of the federal debt-to-GNP ratio by mid-decade and elimination of financial requirements by the latter part of the 1990's. The budget deficit differs from total financial requirements in that it excludes loans, financial investments and advances and certain specified purpose accounts (such as the Canada Pension Plan and pension accounts for federal employees).

In implementing this strategy, priority has been given to reducing expenditures. As well, tax policy changes are expected to generate increased revenues over the medium-term. Expenditure policies have been initiated to reduce total federal government spending from 26 per cent of GNP in 1984-85 to 21 per cent by 1990-91. To the end of the decade, the rate of growth in programme expenditures (*i.e.* excluding public debt charges) will remain below the rate of growth in inflation.

2. Evolution of the "expenditure planning" process

By the mid 1980s, the Policy and Expenditure Management System (PEMS) established in 1979 had become rule burdened and bureaucratic. This was largely due to the fact that while concern was growing over the debt and deficits, PEMS with its policy envelopes fostered incrementalism. Growing pressures to reduce the reserves, coupled with various expenditure reduction measures, led to frustrations as Ministers competed for increasingly limited dollars.

In the mid 1980s some changes began to appear. The first of these changes was the deferral and later abandonment of the Spring Operational Reviews in 1985 and 1986. In 1989 the Government abandoned the policy envelopes and reorganised the Cabinet structure. This reorganisation, while increasing the number of Cabinet Committees, did away with the "policy envelopes" and mandated the policy committees to "concentrate on policy", as opposed to expenditure transaction issues. Authority to authorise new expenditures was restricted to the Cabinet Committee on Priorities and Planning and the Treasury Board. Two of the new committees, the Operations Committee and the Expenditure Review Committee, were mandated to provide a central and co-ordinating role for the financial and policy dimensions of government expenditures. The Expenditure Review Committee was subsequently eliminated in 1992 and its role assumed by an *ad hoc* subcommittee of the Priorities and Planning Committee.

The roles of the key Cabinet Committees in expenditure management might best be described in terms more associated with the Programme Planning and Budgeting System. The Treasury Board is largely responsible for the A-base (status quo expenditure framework); the Cabinet Committee on Priorities and Planning for approving the B-budget initiatives (new policy); and the Expenditure Review and Operations Committees for X-budget initiatives (expenditure control and reduction). The Operations Committee is formally supported by a secretariat composed of key officials from the Privy Council Office, who work in close consultation with officials in the Department of Finance, and the Treasury Board Secretariat.

A major result of the annual fiscal planning exercise is the establishment of reserves, earmarking resources in those reserves for government priorities, and the setting in motion of expenditure reduction and control measures to enable the government to meet its spending targets.

3. Technical aspects of multi-year estimates

This section will provide an overview of the multi-year Fiscal Plan and Multi-Year Operational Plans (MYOP) along with their relationship to the preparation of the annual expenditure budget. The top-down (fiscal planning) and the bottom-up (expenditure management) time horizons are interactive, with each process providing information leading to adjustments in the other.

Multi-year horizons for fiscal and expenditure planning have been designed to facilitate the identification of policy issues for Ministerial consideration. They also provide for a thorough and continuous assessment of the requirements for, and consequences of, the funding of approved programmes. From the top-down perspective, the multi-year Fiscal Plan is the main instrument for establishing multi-year total expenditure levels. The fiscal planning process provides information about projected revenues and expenditures towards the development of overall government expenditure priorities. The planning process also encompasses the evaluation of sectoral policies and programmes in light of these priorities and assesses alternative means of achieving the appropriate fiscal stance. In principle, the Fiscal Plan, tabled in Parliament as part of the Budget, includes information on the upcoming and three future fiscal years. However, recent Fiscal Plans presented to Parliament have tended to vary the amount of information provided about future years. The Fiscal Plan includes reserves to provide for new policy initiatives, future wage and price increases and other operational contingencies and forecast errors.

Multi-Year Operational Plans (MYOPs) are the main bottom-up expenditure management vehicle. They are used to determine, on a government-wide basis, the resources required for delivery of approved and on-going programmes over a three-year forward planning period. Each department and agency provides a MYOP in October, which is reviewed by the Treasury Board Secretariat prior to decisions by the Treasury Board. These status quo planning documents include departmental requests for financial resources in constant price levels. Following negotiation and decisions by Treasury Board, they form the baseline estimates of future year programme costs. This provides an important input into the fiscal planning exercise.

The basic building blocks of the operational planning system are Planning Elements. These are discrete sub-divisions of a programme for which resource use can be identified, while conforming to a department's internal management and control structures for resource planning and utilisation. At present, there are roughly 375 Planning Elements. A Parliamentary vote can relate to one Planning Element, though it can also be divided into two (or more) Planning Elements. Planning Element resource allocations are expressed as Reference Levels, or the financial resources approved by the Treasury Board in order to carry out policies and programmes approved by Cabinet.

The annual review of Operational Plans considers the estimated cost of programmes for the upcoming fiscal year and for two planning years. The most recently approved Reference Level is used as the benchmark against which all changes are proposed. At this stage, the second planning year is added to the MYOP planning horizon based on departmental requests. The Reference Levels established for each Planning Element take into account workload changes, inter-element transfers, and policy approvals that have occurred since the previous MYOP review.

Each Planning Element is then adjusted, where appropriate, for allowances to offset increases in prices and other input costs for the upcoming year. At this time, provisions are not made for the adjustment of future reference levels for the impact of inflation. The first year of these adjusted Reference Levels forms the basis for the preparation of the Main Estimates. The Main Estimates are submitted for Parliamentary approval in the month of February, approximately 1½ months before the start of the fiscal year.

The resource levels for future years, as contained in the MYOP, are not published and thus are not considered nor approved by Parliament. The public information on planned expenditures is usually limited to a revised forecast for the current year and planned spending for the next five years.

4. Calendar of main points of decision-making and activities

The fiscal year is the period 1 April through to 31 March.

Months before start of FY (t)	Main events and activities
(Year t – 1)	
July-October	MF considers, in consultation with the President TB, changes to the fiscal plan and submits results to Cabinet Committee on Priorities and Planning.
	Departments finalise and submit their Multi-Year Operational Plans (MYOPs) and Main Estimates submissions for the three future fiscal years to Treasury Board by 1 October.
November-December	TB considers and approves revised multi-year reference levels and detailed departmental budgets for Main Estimates.
January-February	Budget submitted to Parliament by MF (Budget Day).
February	Main Estimates tabled in Parliament by President of TB.
March	Interim supply voted.
(Year t)	
1 April	Start of fiscal year (t).

5. The annual budget cycle

Departments finalise and submit their Multi-year Operational Plans (MYOPs) to Treasury Board by 1 October. These plans propose any desired changes to the most recently approved reference levels for the upcoming and the following fiscal years. In addition, levels are proposed for the future year to be added to the planning horizon. Following a review by Treasury Board Secretariat staff, reference levels are considered and approved by Treasury Board.

Resource planning cycle

	June/July	August	September	October	November
Priorities and planning Cabinet Cttee	Review of government priorities and status of fiscal plan.				Confirmation of budget strategy.
Treasury Board (President of TB)	Development of resourcing strategy for review of Multi-Year Operational Plans.				Approval of Departmental allocation of resources and resources and items to be included in M.E.
TB Secretariat	Review of spending pressures.	Technical instructions for Multi-Year Operational Plans (MYOPs).			Review of MYOPs.
Dept of Finance (Minister of Finance)	Budget consultation process begins.			Preparation of Economic and Revenue Forecast and Fiscal Strategies.	
Spending Depts	Review of Strategic and Operational Plans.		Preparation of MYOPs.	Submission of MYOPs to TB.	

	December/January	February	March	April	May
Priorities and planning Cabinet Cttee	Finalisation of Budget Details.				
Treasury Board (President of TB)		Approve items for final S.E. Tabling of M.E.	Tabling of S.E. Introduction of S.E. and interim supply bills.		
TB Secretariat	Preparation of estimates Parts I and II.		Preparation of S.E. and interim supply bills.		
Dept of Finance (Minister of Finance)	Budget preparation.	Presentation of Budget documents and Budget speech.			
Spending Depts	Preparation of estimates Part III.		Finalise new year operational plans based on M.F.		

Main Estimates (M.E.).
Supplementary Estimates (S.E.).
Source: Treasury Board, Canada.

During the period July through September the Minister of Finance considers, in consultation with the President of the Treasury Board, any necessary or desirable changes to the overall Fiscal Plan. These changes take into account, inter alia, an updated economic outlook and anticipated spending pressures. The Minister of Finance presents the results of this review to the Cabinet Committee on Priorities and Planning in the Fall to initiate the annual budget preparation process.

During the same period (July through September), departments prepare their MYOP and Main Estimates submissions, due at Treasury Board in October. These documents request changes to the most recently approved reference levels for the three future fiscal years. These changes are a result of operational pressures, new or enhanced programmes which have been recently approved, and adjustments to reflect wage and price changes during the upcoming year. In recent years, wage changes have been restricted by legislated salary controls and virtually no adjustment has been permitted for other price changes. In the Economic Statement of 1992, it was announced that salary levels for government employees will be frozen until the end of 1994. Treasury Board considers and approves revised multi-year reference levels and the detailed Main Estimates levels for the upcoming year in December.

In January or February, the Minister of Finance submits the Budget to Parliament, laying out the overall fiscal plan of the government and providing notice of any tax changes the government will be proposing in coming months.

In February, the President of the Treasury Board tables the Main Estimates in Parliament. These detailed expenditure plans form the basis of Parliamentary consideration and approval of appropriation bills that will be tabled by the government during the forthcoming fiscal year.

D. EXPENDITURE REVIEW

At any one time, there are likely to be numerous reviews underway regarding departmental or programme effectiveness. This may arise from internal departmental needs, from Treasury Board consideration of budget requests for on-going programmes, or from the need to respond to Ministerial requests for major policy reviews in selected areas. Departments are required to develop 5-year "evaluation plans" for the systematic review and assessment of their programmes, operations and results. Account is taken of major policy reviews and evaluation studies underway when considering possible changes to the multi-year expenditure plan.

E. IMPLEMENTATION OF THE BUDGET

1. Major instruments of in-year control

The multi-year spending plans include reserves to provide for contingencies and new initiatives. A Central Reserve for Statutory Overruns is intended to provide for unexpected cost increases in major statutory (entitlement) programmes. The Central Reserve is mostly used to cover unforeseen increases in transfer payments and it is not intended to fund cost increases due to policy changes. A policy reserve intended to cover the multi-year costs of new or enhanced programmes is managed by the Cabinet Committee on Priorities and Planning. A small Operating Reserve, with limited access and centrally controlled by Treasury Board, is intended to fund unavoidable increases in the cost of approved programmes. In the expenditure plan, for 1993-94, these reserves amounted to 1.6 per cent of total budgetary expenditures. In addition to these reserves, provision is made within the expenditure plan for those wage and price adjustments which may be approved in the future by Treasury Board. This provision has been greatly reduced in recent years with the government's policy restricting compensation for inflation and the legislation of multi-year wage control. As a general rule, departments are expected to live within the appropriations granted by Main Estimates each year. All exceptions must be approved by Treasury Board and ultimately Parliament (as noted earlier, statutory programmes are an exception to this requirement).

Regular monthly accounting statements are prepared by a central agency (Supply and Services Canada) on the basis of departmental reports. However, these monthly trends and detailed statements of spending are not closely monitored by the Treasury Board; nor is the system that controls monthly or quarterly apportionment applied to appropriations. Overall monthly cash requirements are monitored and forecast by the Department of Finance for purposes of the government's debt management programme.

There is no formal requirement for the Minister of Finance to provide an update report to Parliament on the most recently approved fiscal plan, although this may be done on occasion. As noted, Supplementary Estimates are tabled by the President of the Treasury Board throughout the fiscal year when Parliamentary approval is required for revisions to individual appropriations. In the Parliamentary supply process, the Supplementary Estimates are the manifestation of the reserves set aside in the Expenditure Plan for new policy initiatives and contingencies.

2. Managerial discretion

An appropriation provides the right to spend funds up to the approved vote level. Central, or Parliamentary approval, is not required if it is decided to spend less than the approved level. Departments can spend more on a given vote provided they have the approval of Treasury Board and Parliament. Thus, all transfers of funds between votes require Parliamentary approval. In addition, Treasury Board has the power to apply general restrictions below the level of detail specified in a vote. For example, separate allotments (subdivisions) may be created within votes. Other special allotments may be established by Treasury Board to control departmental access. Access to allotments "frozen" by the Treasury Board and all transfers of funds between allotments within a vote, require only Treasury Board, not Parliamentary, approval.

Appropriations lapse at the end of the fiscal year for which they were granted. That is, there is no appropriated provision for the carry-forward of spending authority. However, the Treasury Board has put in place policies that effectively permit the carry-forward of funds through the tabling of Supplementary Estimates. These measures include a carry-forward of Operating Budget funding of up to two per cent. On a case-by-case basis, up to 5 per cent of capital funding may be carried forward where funds not required for the project are set aside in a "frozen" lapsing allotment for the year-in-progress. Such a transaction does not bind Parliament as the future years level is still subject to Parliamentary approval. The government's expenditure plan for a given year explicitly recognises that a portion of the appropriation authority granted by Parliament will lapse.

F. RECENT REFORMS

1. Special operating agencies

In the last few years, the federal government has been encouraging the establishment of Special Operating Agencies (SOAs) within its departments. The SOAs are similar in nature to the Executive Agencies found in the United Kingdom. The aim of SOAs is to achieve improved efficiencies and better service to the public through the granting of special management flexibilities not common to the rest of the Public Service. A strengthened accountability framework, supported by a rigorous business plan, is also a critical requirement. As of January 1993, 12 agencies had been formally established.

2. Operating budgets

The adoption of Operating Budgets was announced in December 1990 as one of the initiatives contained within the White Paper entitled "The Renewal of the Public Service of Canada". An operating budget, or running cost model, allows managers to choose the optimal resource mix (salary, wages, other operating, minor capital) necessary to meet programme objectives. This change will enable managers to better take advantage of cost-saving opportunities, pursue more cost-effective programme delivery, and respond more efficiently to changing service priorities. Effective 1 April 1993 all government departments have been using Operating Budgets.

3. User fees

The idea of charging a user fee for government services is not new. However, this concept is being given renewed attention as a means to increase government revenues without harming the public good. User charges shift the responsibility for financing activities to those who benefit the most from that service. At the same time, it removes the obligation to involuntarily pay for a service that is not utilised by the taxpayer. When market forces become an important consideration, increased pressure is placed on the organisation to deliver a quality and costconscious service.

To assist departments with the implementation of user fees, several pieces of legislation have been introduced and approved by Parliament over the past few years. With this renewed interest in user fees, the amount of money received annually through user fees has doubled to over $3 billion in the last 8 years. In recognition of their importance, user fee revenue plans are now a key aspect of departmental Multi-Year Operational Planning.

4. Incentive-based management framework

A new management framework is beginning to emerge within the Canadian Public Service. This framework is increasingly based on incorporating incentives into policies to achieve efficiencies, rather than preparing cumbersome procedures and implementing costly control systems. In the coming years, all government policies will be reviewed to determine where appropriate incentives are better able to achieve the desired behaviour and results at a fraction of the present cost.

5. Council for administrative renewal

Established in November 1991 by a group of senior departmental officials in co-operation with central agencies, the Council focuses on streamlining administrative processes and systems that cross traditional functional boundaries of financial, personnel, materiel management, and other administrative areas. Three broad opportunity areas have been targeted: improve service delivery through the fundamental redesign of processes and/or information technology; promote common systems and best practices to support managers, reduce duplication, and achieve efficiencies; and improve the manner in which information is managed.

6. Carry forward policy

Prior to 1989, departmental managers would be inclined to spend the remaining portion of their budget at year end for fear that this money would be otherwise lost. In an attempt to reduce the incentive for spending at year-end in advance of need, the federal government established the carry forward policy. This policy enables departments to carry forward a portion (up to 2 per cent) of their operating funds to the following year.

7. Cash management

The cash management strategy is aimed at reducing the government's deficit through the improved management of cash flows. This has been achieved through the implementation of well designed business practices and the use of the newest technologies. Since 1985, smarter cash management policies and techniques have saved Canadian taxpayers nearly $1.5 billion.

G. FURTHER INFORMATION

All federal government documents are published in Canada's two official languages, English and French.

1. Documents related to the annual budget

Note: The fiscal year is the period from 1 April to 31 March (year t).
1. *Budget Papers.* A number of documents are published on Budget Day (in January or February, year t – 1) by the Minister of Finance. These Papers provide information on the economic outlook, details of the multi-year fiscal/expenditure plan, details of specific tax changes proposed, and a variety of other background analyses or options papers related to current policy issues or proposals.
2. *Estimates.* A large number of documents are published on the occasion of the tabling of Main Estimates. This occurs in February, year (t – 1), by the President of the Treasury Board. The documents are:
   - the Government Expenditure Plan, or Part I of the Estimates, which provides a summary of the multi-year spending plans and major elements within the Main Estimates;
   - the so-called "Blue Book", or Part II of the Estimates, provides detailed information on the upcoming year's spending, thus forming the basis for the appropriation bill considered by Parliament;

- the Departmental Expenditure Plans (approximately 85) form Part III of the Estimates. Each department prepares their Expenditure Plan, which provides details of departmental structure, programmes, spending, as well as performance indicators;
- the Supplementary Estimates provide the details of all proposed changes to existing appropriations (normally two Supplementary Estimates are published within a year).

2.   Other documents

3. *Public Accounts.* These are detailed, audited year-end financial statements for the government and individual departments. They are generally published in November of year (t).
4. *Report of the Auditor General.* This is an annual report to Parliament on the results of the Auditor General's on-going reviews of departmental operations and financial management practices and systems. It is published in November of year (t).

DENMARK

**Any changes which have taken place in Denmark
since September 1993 are not reflected in this chapter**

A. INSTITUTIONAL STRUCTURE OF BUDGETARY DECISION-MAKING

1. Political and organisational structure of government

Denmark is a unitary state, with Faroe Islands and Greenland having home rule within the Kingdom. Apart from central government, there are two levels of local governments: counties and municipalities.

Central government is organised in 24 ministries, each headed by a Minister. Each Minister is a member of Cabinet. In most cases a ministry is made up of one often quite small department and a number of executive agencies and institutions. Though their autonomy varies in practice, these agencies are all subordinate to the department and the Minister. A few ministries, among them the Ministry of Finance, are organised in more than one departmental portfolio.

The single chamber parliament has 179 members. The present government, is a minority coalition of the Social Democratic Party and two smaller non-socialist parties. The next election will be in 1998.

2. Main budgetary organs

The Ministry of Finance (MF) has one department which is composed of the Office of Finance and the Office of Negotiations. In addition to the Department, there are a number of subordinate agencies, among them a central accounting agency.

The Department is concerned with both sides of the budget and with economic policy including public expenditure planning, central government budgeting, expenditure control and manpower as far as total numbers and management positions are concerned.

The Office of Finance is made up of 10 Divisions. Each is responsible for both the budgets of a number of ministries and for one or several horizontal policy areas or functions (*e.g.* general expenditure policy and systems, public finance, public enterprises, government organisation and steering, performance measurement, administrative policy, administrative analysis of agencies and programmes etc.). Each group is staffed by an assistant secretary and on average 7 analysts (economists or political scientists) and supporting staff.

The responsibilities of the Office of Negotiations include personnel and pay policies, pensions and classifications, though most of the latter has been decentralised to spending departments. The Office of Negotiations is made up of 5 Divisions.

3. Role of Prime Minister and Cabinet

The major decision of Cabinet in budgetary matters is the allocation of ministerial expenditure limits in the initial stage of the budget preparation. Further involvement of Cabinet in budgetary decision-making is mostly of a more formal nature.

Most issues are settled either bilaterally by the Minister of Finance or in the Cabinet Economic Policy Committee.

4. Role of Parliament

The Finance Bill (*Finanslovforslag*) goes through three plenary readings in Parliament, as does any other bill. Between readings it is examined in the Finance Committee, which scrutinises the whole budget.

Parliament only takes one vote on the Finance Bill but this is preceded by votes on amendments to individual accounts, so that the proposal on which the final vote is taken may differ from the Finance Bill first presented by Government. Amendments usually number several hundred. Parliament controls expenditure at the level of about 1 000 individual accounts.

Following a long-standing practice, the Finance Committee may authorise supplementary "appropriations" during the implementation of the budget. Normally, such decisions are approved by full Parliament only after the end of the fiscal year. Any member of Parliament may, however, appeal an issue to Parliament and this is sometimes done.

All expenditure, including entitlements authorised under separate legislation, is annually appropriated; tax revenue estimates have to be approved as well. Multi-year estimates are not approved by Parliament.

If Parliament has not passed the Finance Bill before the start of the new fiscal year, a provisional Finance Bill is enacted, which enables government to continue activities on the basis of the previous Finance Act.

B. THE SCOPE AND NATURE OF GOVERNMENT FINANCES

Local governments take care of most services to citizens, in particular in the areas of utilities, social services, health and primary education. Therefore, only about 25 per cent of public manpower is employed by central government, of which one third is in the ministries of justice and defence and another third in the Post Office, the National Railroads and some minor public enterprises.

Apart from a few minor funds, social security spending is carried on the central government budget. Benefits are paid out by local government administration, except for unemployment benefits, as there is no independent social security administration.

Unemployment benefits are formally paid out by private unemployment insurance funds. However, except for administrative expenditure, their resources are fully controlled by central government. Contributions are determined by law.

Other major social security cash benefits, *e.g.* old age and disability pensions, child allowances, sickness benefits, are paid out by local governments, but mainly financed by central government. Pensions and child allowances in particular, are fully controlled and financed by central government and for this reason not considered as part of local government expenditure, though they appear as such in national accounts.

Most local government activities are regulated by legislation, but in most areas local government has considerable freedom in resource allocation and decisions on levels of service provisions. The vital revenue base of local governments is the proportional income tax. They are free to decide tax rates, but Government has in recent years strongly recommended that they do not raise them. Property taxes on land are only of marginal importance, as is borrowing which is restricted.

General grants to local governments were much reduced in the mid-1980s to offset growth in local government tax revenues, but have since been increased again by conversion of social reimbursements to general grants.

As part of the annual agreements with the Local Government Association on unchanged tax levels, Central Government has agreed to compensate cyclically induced expenditures by adjusting the general grants.

The expenditure of the Post Office, State Railroads and a few other enterprises is on the central government budget. Public ownership of companies is limited outside the communication and energy sectors. It has been further reduced by substantial sales of shares. On the other hand a number of new government-owned companies has been created by transforming on-budget enterprises (including the Postal Giro Bank) to companies and part of the shares sold.

Table 1. **Functional classification of general government expenditure (1990)**

As percentage of total

General public services and external affairs	7.5
Defence	3.5
Law and order and safety	1.8
Education	12.0
Health	8.9
Social security and welfare services	10.0
Housing	1.3
Recreational and cultural services	2.6
Energy	0.2
Agriculture and fishing	2.7
Manufacturing and construction	0.5
Transport and communication	3.1
Trade and business conditions in general	3.5
Other purposes	12.4
Total	100.0

Source: Ministry of Finance, Denmark.

Table 2. **Fiscal indicators, 1984-90**

	1984	1985	1986	1987	1988	1989	1990
General government expenditure							
Bill. Dkr	344.3	368.4	373.7	403.9	437.9	459.6	472.3
% of GDP	60.9	59.9	56.1	57.8	59.5	59.2	58.3
General government balance (– = deficit)							
Bill. Dkr	–23.2	–12.4	22.7	16.9	3.4	–4.2	–11.1
% of GDP	–4.1	–2.0	–3.4	–2.4	0.5	–0.5	–1.4

Source: Ministry of Finance, Denmark.

C. BUDGET FORMULATION STRATEGY AND PROCESS

1. Strategic aims and global norms

Expenditure targets have traditionally been expressed in terms of real growth in public expenditure. Throughout the 1980s, the medium-term expenditure target was zero real growth in public expenditure. The current target is a growth rate in public expenditure significantly lower than the long term growth in GDP.

Since 1985, annual targeting has been focused on the net expenditure of central and local governments respectively, and not on total public expenditure. The main reason for this change was the introduction of ministerial spending limits, which make individual ministers responsible for the total budget appropriated to them by Parliament. These annual targets are determined at given levels of unemployment and exclude debt interest.

2. Technical aspects of multi-year estimates

Multi-year estimates (MYE) are only published for expenditure and non-tax revenues. They are first published in August in an appendix to the Finance Bill, which shows comparable figures for the previous year (accounts t – 2), the current year (appropriations t – 1), the budget year (year t) and three forward years. Their function is both to provide information on multi-year consequences of the budget, and to control departmental spending plans. They are in the price and pay level of the budget year. MYE are not voted on in the final vote on the Finance Bill. A revised appendix is published shortly after the publication of the Finance Act. These final MYE reflect the future expenditure flowing from the measures approved by Parliament on the Finance Bill and not necessarily medium-term government policy.

3. Calendar of main points of decision-making and activities

Months before start of FY (t)	Main events and activities
(Year t − 1)	
12-11 (January-February)	MF prepares and negotiates proposal for ministerial spending limits and budgetary guidelines.
10 (early March)	Cabinet decides expenditure target for central government and ministerial spending limits.
10-9 (March-April)	Ministries prepare draft budgets which are submitted to MF early May.
8-7 (May-June)	Draft budgets are scrutinised by MF and decisions taken on how to eliminate excesses.
5 (August)	Finance Bill and related documents presented to Parliament.
4-1 (September-December)	Finance Bill goes through readings and amendments in Parliament before final vote middle of December.
(Year t)	
0 (1st January)	Start of financial year (t).

4. The annual budget cycle

The preparation of the annual budget begins shortly after Parliament passes the preceding Finance Bill. The revised multi-year estimates form the basis of the preparation of the new budget.

As a first step, the Ministry of Finance forms a view of the target for total central government net expenditure. The next major step is the breakdown of the target into ministerial blocks.

After bilateral probes, the Minister of Finance proposes a set of multi-year ministerial spending limits, each enveloping all net expenditure of one ministry. Except for repricing the first forward year of the multi-year estimates, spending limits are influenced by policy changes resulting in additional expenditure and by (tentatively) agreed cut-backs. The ministerial spending limits are usually decided in Cabinet at the end of February or early March. This is the major annual reallocation of resources between ministries.

By this procedure, the expenditure target is split up in about 25 blocks ten months before the start of the financial year. Once the limits are decided, each minister is expected to accommodate all cost changes (including increased expenditure on entitlements and decreased non-tax revenues) and to fund all policy changes within the allocated block. With few exceptions, ministers are free to arrange their budgets as long as they keep within the allocated blocks and estimate expenditures realistically.

Within the ministerial spending limits, two types of sub-limits are imposed on discretionary expenditure, *i.e.* roughly the quarter of total expenditure that is not entitlements. These limits are also decided in Cabinet, as part of the ministerial spending limits.

- Limits on discretionary expenditure
  These multi-year limits delimit ministerial blocks for discretionary expenditure. Only the total block, and not individual programmes, are repriced and rolled forward by general mechanisms at the start of each new budget round. Until now, the rolling-forward has included a "squeeze" in departmental multi-year limits, computed from productivity targets for various types of activities, as each new year is added. This "productivity squeeze" amounted to on average 2.5 per cent on pay. A new approach is currently being developed.
- Limits on pay
  Each ministry is also subject to a multi-year limit on total expenditure on pay, as a method of controlling personnel.

The ministries present their draft budgets to MF in early May. The main focus of MF scrutiny is on the realism of entitlement estimates, requests for reallocations between discretionary and other expenditure, the realism and feasibility of proposed cut-backs, and options for further cut-backs in those cases where the draft budget of a ministry exceeds the agreed expenditure limit.

During autumn, efforts are centred on securing support in Parliament for the Finance Bill and supporting legislation. This process used to lead to a large number of amendments, which are presented to Parliament by the Minister of Finance at the beginning of December, shortly before Parliament's final vote in mid-December. As a consequence of the change to majority government, most of the supporting legislation of the 1994 Finance Bill had already been passed by Parliament in June 1993.

On several occasions, elections have been called, when governments have been unable to secure support for the Finance Bill.

D.   EXPENDITURE REVIEW

Expenditure reviews (*"Budgetanalyser"*) are usually launched in February and September, after confirmation in the Cabinet Economic Policy Committee. The reviews are proposed and usually chaired by the Ministry of Finance, but with participation from spending ministries.

The reviews are integrated in the annual decision process on expenditure. They are timed so that the results may be used in January-February, when ministerial spending limits are first allocated, or in May-June, when the Finance Bill is being finished in government and decisions on legislation (mainly related to entitlements) have to be made.

Due to their integration in the budget cycle, most expenditure reviews have to be carried out in only two to four months. Therefore, they usually do not involve major research, but rather draw on available information on programme performance. The brief of the working parties, which carry out these reviews, will typically be to identify savings due to inefficient programme management, lack of co-ordination between related programmes in different spending ministries, etc. or to study the consequences of programme reductions or reorganisations.

E.   IMPLEMENTATION OF THE BUDGET

1.   Major instruments of in-year control

Since 1984, in-year control has been centred on the ministerial spending limits. The emphasis is on making the reallocations necessary to contain actual spending within the limit.

Twice a year – in May and September – the ministries prepare a comprehensive report on spending developments and likely future trends. If major overruns are envisaged, which almost invariably would be due to changing estimates of entitlements, the minister is expected to put forward a proposal for offsetting cut-backs, including suggestions for new legislation.

On the basis of the ministerial reports, budget updates (*"Budgetoversigter"*) are published. Budget updates are also published in August as part of the presentation of the next Finance Bill, and in December. The latter is based on the ministries' requests for supplementary appropriations.

The accommodation of expenditure developments from the decision on ministerial spending limits ten months before the start of the financial year and until it ends 22 months later is treated as a continuous process. Due to the limited size of discretionary expenditure, and the productivity squeeze imposed on this type of expenditure by the multi-year limits, the reallocations needed to offset new developments usually require legislation.

Apart from gross expenditure cut-backs in the ministerial spending limits, two other sources of offsets are allowed for: first, non-tax revenues can be increased, as the spending limits are defined as limits on net expenditure. Secondly, if new legislation or departmental orders induce direct savings to Local Governments, general grants are reduced correspondingly and the Ministerial spending limit in that case can be increased.

On the other hand, if ministries induce new or increased local government spending, the ministerial spending limit is reduced and the general grants increased.

2.   Managerial discretion

In general, agencies have one appropriation for their operational expenditures, which may include minor expenditures on grants, contribution and capital. Within this appropriation, MF imposes a limit on pay and on person-years at management levels. Apart from this, MF does not restrict managerial discretion and does not require pre-authorisation of spending decisions.

Major expenditures on subsidies, transfers, lending and capital are always carried on separate programme appropriations, except for public enterprises, which usually have only one appropriation for all expenditures and revenues.

In principle, appropriations are on a gross basis, but in practice most current non-tax revenues may be respent due to the following four arrangements:

a) all agencies may use minor additional revenues without prior authorisation;

b) non-commercial agencies with secondary commercial activities may expand these according to rules of price calculation that guard against distortion of competition. Such activities are not subject to pay limits;

c) some non-commercial agencies are fully net-controlled, but subject to pay limits;

d) public enterprises on the central government budget are controlled by a predetermined net financial result target and are not subject to pay limits.

Generally, ministries are allowed to transfer funds between appropriations on operative expenditure without previous approval by MF. Where authorisation is needed, the procedures are quite flexible.

Funds appropriated to specific investment projects may be carried forward to future years if projects are delayed. Unobligated balances on current expenditure may be carried forward provided their future use on a specific procurement or project is specified in the end-year supplementary appropriation bill. Finally, surpluses on net-controlled activities, *cf. b) – d)* above, may also be carried forward. The same holds for deficits, though only for a limited period.

F.   RECENT REFORMS

The budgetary system was thoroughly modernised during the second half of the 1980s. Ministerial spending limits, net control and carry-forward were introduced and personnel control was decentralised. Recently, the following initiatives have been implemented:

– *Further decentralisation of personnel control*
Until recently, savings on pay could only be carried forward for use on other operational expenditures, but may now also be used on personnel, though within narrow limits. Furthermore, MF now only imposes limits on person-years at the three highest management levels.

– *Multi-year budget agreements and "Contract agency experiments"*
A number of agreements have been made with major agencies on budgets and performances covering a four-year period. Further agreements are being prepared. A related initiative, sponsored by the Department of Management and Personnel, involves increased managerial discretion for instance in areas of pay and personnel, for a number of agencies, which in turn sign a multi-year contract on increased performance.

– *Improved cash management*
As part of both a more general effort to reduce central government borrowing requirements, and to introduce better cash management practices in agencies, a number of agencies now get their appropriations in monthly rates on interest-bearing accounts in the National Bank. The agencies keep half of the revenue earned by better cash management. This arrangement will gradually be expanded to include all agencies.

G.   FURTHER INFORMATION

1.   Documents related to the annual budget

The fiscal year (FY) is the calendar year (year t).

1. Finance Bill (*Finanslovforslag*), with two appendices on assumptions and details on agency budgets, activities and multi-year estimates, August, year (t − 1).
2. Finance Act (*Finanslov*), which include both appropriations and the appendices of the Finance Bill updated to incorporate amendments passed by Parliament, February, year (t).

3. Budget Updates (*"Budgetoversigt"*), published May, August, October and December, year (t).
4. Supplementary Finance Bill (*"Forslag til tillaegsbevillingslov"*), February, year (t + 1).
5. The Budget. English Summary of the Finance Bill, September, year (t − 1).

2. Other Documents

6. Finance White paper (*"Finansredegørelse"*), once a year.
7. Expenditure White Paper (*"Udgiftsanalyser"*), once a year.
8. Budget Manual (*"Budgetvejledning"*), latest issue February 1992.

FINLAND

**Any changes which have taken place in Finland
since October 1993 are not reflected in this chapter**

A. INSTITUTIONAL STRUCTURE OF BUDGETARY DECISION-MAKING

1. Political and organisational structure of government

Finland is a unitary state. There are three layers of government: state or central level, the municipalities and in between them strong municipal associations controlled by the lower level and relatively weak county administration steered from the central level.

Central government functions are organised mainly around the Prime Minister's Office and 12 ministries. Ministries have in general one Minister (4 ministries have 2 Ministers); the Secretary-General of each department is a non-political appointment, as is the rest of the departmental personnel. At present, the number of Ministers is seventeen. They form the Council of State, which acts as the Cabinet.

In accordance with the government's programme, intensified measures have been taken in Finland to reform the public services and administration. Significant public management reform was initiated by the past Cabinet (Holkeri's Cabinet) in 1987 and the new Cabinet (Ahos's Cabinet) appointed in April 1991 has continued the Reform.

Parliament has one chamber with 200 members. There are 9 political parties or other Parliamentary groups. The largest party (Central Party) has 55 seats. There are usually coalition governments: the present government is supported by four parties and has a majority in Parliament. The elections are regularly held in March every fourth year. The next elections will be held in March 1995.

2. Main budgetary organs

The central role in all budgetary matters is played by the Ministry of Finance (MF). MF deals with expenditure, taxation (or revenue) and borrowing policies, as well as with general financial and economic policy formulation and, additionally, organisational and State employer matters.

MF's position is changing following a reform of the system for financial management according to the principle of framework budgeting and results-oriented budgeting. MF's new task is to prepare politically binding budgetary ceilings for the government; the first time this took place was in October 1990.

Within MF, the Budget Department, among other things, co-ordinates budgetary activities and is especially involved in the expenditure side of the budget and non-tax revenues. The number of personnel in the department is 52, thirty of them having an academic degree. The Budget Department consists of four divisions, but after adoption of results-oriented budgeting a more flexible organisation schema will be adopted. The largest division is the Fiscal Policy Bureau, which is responsible for budget preparation and to a large extent also for budgetary control.

3. Role of President, Prime Minister and Cabinet

The Council of State (Cabinet) steers economic and financial policy-making with the help of two permanent Cabinet Committees, viz. the Committee on Economic Policy and the Finance Committee, both chaired by the Prime Minister. The Minister of Finance is a member of both committees. The Committee on Economic Policy discusses important economic policy matters and inter alia prepares the general economic statement on Economic Policy in which the Cabinet informs Parliament of the general economic and fiscal policy guidelines to be followed in its budget proposal in the following autumn. The Finance Committee of the Cabinet steers the implementation of the budget and other Ministerial decision-making in important economic and financial aspects. The Council of State as a whole discusses and decides the Budget proposal prepared by MF in its Budget conference chaired by the Prime Minister (late August) and in issuing budgetary ceilings in February and in May.

The President does not actively participate in the budget preparation, but formally submits the Budget proposal to the legislature. The Budget proposal is presented to Parliament by the Finance Minister in his budget speech on behalf of the Government.

4.   Role of Parliament

The Parliamentary treatment of the budget starts with a general debate, after which the proposal is sent to the Finance Committee of the Parliament. A detailed scrutiny takes place at the Subcommittees of Finance, after which the Finance Committee as a whole prepares its report on the Budget proposal. The role of the sectoral Special Committees is quite modest compared to the Finance Committee in the Parliamentary budget process. The Finance Committee is responsible for balancing the budget, if changes are made to the Government proposal. After the Finance Committee has given its report, the proposal is discussed and voted upon. Parliament may add to expenditure, but either an expenditure cut or a tax or borrowing increase has to accompany the expenditure increase in order to formally balance the budget. Parliament does not approve multiyear expenditure plans. Starting 1 March 1992, an amendment of the Constitution concerning State finances stipulates that the Parliament publishes the approved budget.

All expenditure, including entitlements, is appropriated annually. The budget is traditionally organised by ministries, subdivided by agency (or function) and finally, by type of economic activity (salaries, equipment, construction, transfers, lending etc.). In connection with the introduction of the results-oriented budgeting in agencies, the formerly separate items for salaries, other consumption and equipment are combined into one item for the costs of activity. The number of expenditure items voted upon is a little less than 600 in the 1994 budget proposal.

If Parliament has not passed the Budget at the beginning of the fiscal year, a continuation bill, based on the previous budget, is passed to enable the Government to continue routine activities until the Budget is passed and signed.

B.   THE SCOPE AND NATURE OF GOVERNMENT FINANCES

The increase of general government expenditure has been quite fast over the 10-year period since 1980 as compared to other OECD Member countries. The balance of central government finances is weakening.

The share of the local authorities within total final demand of the general government is about two thirds. More than a third of their revenue consists of transfers from the State, which are mainly expenditure-related, and linked to specific functions mandated to them by law (education, health and other welfare services). Their main source of revenue is a proportional income tax. Rates are determined by the local authorities themselves. The local authorities have free access to domestic capital markets. The municipal associations mainly perform those tasks of local authorities where co-operation is essential due to economies of scale or similar reasons (mainly regional hospitals, health centres, and certain vocational education). They are financed through transfers from member local authorities and the State.

The municipalities' financial position weakened very quickly over the period 1991-93. Taken as a whole, the local income tax proceeds declined during 1991-93; expenditure continued to grow up to 1992, but turned down in 1993. Transfers from the State grew in 1991-92 but declined in 1993 and 1994.

A new scheme of state appropriations based on objective criteria has been adopted starting in 1993.

The Social Insurance Funds are only partially run by the public sector. The National Pensions Institute manages the basic pensions and sickness insurance which are mainly financed through contributions made by the employers and the insured. The earnings-related and partly funded compulsory employee pensions scheme in the private sector is financed by employers, and mainly managed by several private insurance companies. The earnings-related pensions schemes for the State and local authorities' civil servants adopted a funded pensions system in 1990. Both the benefits and contribution rates of all these compulsory pensions systems are determined by respective laws.

Social security schemes, such as child allowances, war veterans' pensions and about two thirds of unemployment benefit, are mainly financed through the State budget.

Central government enterprise reform which started in 1989 with three minor enterprises has been continued in 1990-93 with reforms in several additional enterprises, including the State Railways and the Post and Telecommunications enterprises. New enterprise forms now covers a third of central government manpower. State lending and increases in shares in stock to state-owned companies are included in the Central government budget.

Funds outside the budget, among which are the State Pension Fund, amount to less than 10 per cent relative to the overall expenditure total of Central Government. The main part of their expenditure is financed from their own revenue (or borrowing).

Table 1. **Breakdown of functional spending categories (1994)**

As percentage of total

General administration	5.0
General order and security	3.0
Defence	4.4
Education, science and arts	13.7
Social security and health	27.3
Housing and environment	4.9
Labour	2.4
Agriculture and forestry	4.7
Transport	4.2
Industry and other business	9.0
Other (mainly debt servicing costs)	21.4
Total	100.0

Source: Budget Proposal 1994.

C. BUDGET FORMULATION STRATEGY AND PROCESS

1. Strategic aims and global norms

The main objective of economic policy is to maintain satisfactory economic growth and employment. That means, inter alia, that international competitiveness must be supported by budgetary policies aimed at reducing inflation and consolidation of State finances. The government has set targets in its economic policy statements for gross tax revenues (including social security contributions) and has limited the extent of State borrowing (both relative to GDP). Recently, more explicit concerns have been expressed as to the growth of public expenditure.

In its economic policy statement to Parliament in May 1991, the government said that the starting point for economic policy was unfavourable; the basic problem was the fact that both the internal and external balance of the Finnish economy had been shaken. The Government has emphasised that the growth of spending should permanently be decelerated, operating conditions of the open sector should be strengthened and incomes policy settlements should be moderate; the real growth rate of central government expenditure has to be zero per cent by 1995 and that of the whole public sector 1-2 per cent.

2. Technical aspects of multi-year estimates

The overall design of the budget formulation system of the Government has been thoroughly reformed starting from the preparation of the 1992 budget proposal. In Autumn 1990, the Government gave politically binding budgetary ceilings to Ministries for 1992 and the two following years. As part of this reform, the formerly separate process of multi-year budgetary planning was merged with the annual budget process. Although it is premature to evaluate the ongoing reform, one result of it is clearly a stronger political control of the budget process and more realistic budget submissions by the Ministries.

The new budget cycle is a multi-year loop, whose starting-point may be set at the annual budget conference of the Cabinet in August, where the Cabinet decides upon the budget proposal for the next year. The budgetary ceilings for two following years are decided in February. These ceilings are adjusted for economic changes, including price changes, in May. The agencies and the Ministries prepare their draft budgets and forward plans and estimates for the following three years for both expenditure and non-tax revenues of central government within the limits of these ceilings.

Expenditure estimates comprise, among other central government expenditure, interest payments and unemployment benefits. There is no unallocated reserve. Estimates are based on constant price and pay levels forecasted for the budget year. Estimates sensitive to macroeconomic developments, other than price and pay developments, are adjusted to be consistent with medium term forecasting results.

Estimates are built up from vote-level at the agencies and ministries. The process is both bottom-up and top-down. The top-down elements are introduced in the form of ceilings given by the Cabinet and detailed by the spending Ministry.

Previously, the MYE were published once a year, as an annex to the annual budget proposals showing a functional and economic breakdown. Every second year, MF publishes a report on medium-term prospects of the economy and government finances. In the reformed process, the Cabinet publishes their ceilings to Ministries.

3. Calendar of main points of decision-making and activities

The fiscal year [FY(t)] is the calendar year (year t).

Months before start of FY (t)	Main events and activities
(Year t − 2)	
September (t − 2)	Budget proposal is submitted to Parliament.
October (t − 2)-January (t − 1)	Government agencies and state institutions prepare their own proposals for medium-term plans and budgets. Negotiations.
(Year t − 1)	
February	The Government gives budgetary ceilings (frameworks) to Ministries.
March/April	Ministries draw up their final proposals for medium-term plans and budgets for their respective sectors.
May/June	MF prepares the budget.
July	Budget negotiations with the ministries.
August	The Government meets for the "thrashing-out" of its budget proposal.
September	The Government's budget proposal is submitted to Parliament.
October/November	Finance Committee processing.
December	The budget is passed by Parliament.
(Year t)	
January	Start of financial year (t).

4. The annual budget cycle

The combined budget and medium-term planning cycle starts with the budgetary ceilings for two years following the next budget year that are discussed and decided by the Cabinet in its conference in February. The Ministries are supposed to detail the approximately fifty ceilings given by the Cabinet as guidelines to the agencies reporting to them.

The ceilings are updated in February, taking into account the changes in economic outlook and economic policies, and adjusted to the expected price level of the following budget year. If necessary, they are adjusted in May when the draft budgets of Ministries have been submitted to the Ministry of Finance.

Ministries' proposals, submitted to MF at the end of April, are scrutinised by MF, which calls the spending Ministries into bilateral negotiations at end-July/August. At the end of August, the Cabinet has its Budget Conference, where the budget proposal is finalised and consequently submitted to the legislature in mid-September. The budget conference also discusses ceilings for the later years, which marks the beginning of the new budget cycle.

Parliament debates the annual budget proposals and approves the budget at the end of the year.

D. EXPENDITURE REVIEW

There are no separate formal procedures for programme analysis and review, but the combined budget and medium term expenditure planning process includes some features with the same purpose. Ministries may start reviews of their activities, and the Ministry of Finance regularly scans the activities and expenditure of Government for reallocation opportunities, and requests spending Ministries to initiate studies and measures for that purpose. These measures are linked rather informally to the budget process.

The Cabinet instructions for the preparation of new legislation include a requirement to provide for analyses of budgetary and economic consequences. This serves as background information which is submitted to Parliament as well.

E. IMPLEMENTATION OF THE BUDGET

1. Major instruments of in-year control

The implementation of the Budget is controlled using three interrelated instruments:
- The Cabinet issues General Instructions for the implementation of the budget, which establish the main rules concerning budget implementation and *ex ante* financial control;
- A detailed implementation budget (''the specification budget'') is prepared by spending Ministries and approved as a guideline for the implementation;
- Economically and financially very important expenditure decisions must be approved by the Finance Committee of the Cabinet (or, in less important matters, by the Ministry of Finance), even if necessary funds have been appropriated.

The formerly quite detailed budget implementation procedures have recently been simplified and adapted to the new results-oriented budgeting paradigm.

One or two supplementary budgets are passed annually, in which adjustments to revenue and expenditure (both decreases and increases) are recorded.

Parliament is informed about the implementation of the budget after the end of the fiscal year through the annual Accounts Report, the technical report incorporating the outcome of the budget, and the Report on the Management and State of Government Finances, which is more analytical in character.

2. Managerial discretion

The budget process has been kept rather traditional, with quite a limited access to discretionary transfers between the items decided in the budget. Balances can be carried forward up to two years after the end of the fiscal year, if Parliament has allowed for it in the Budget, which is customary for investments and similar appropriations with a multi-year character and, lately, for the activity appropriations of agencies budgeted in a results-oriented way. Transferable appropriations amount to 26 per cent of the budget total, and the balances actually transferred to 4 per cent.

F. RECENT REFORMS

Major reforms are taking place in the Finnish system of budgeting. The Parliament has passed an amendment to the Constitution concerning the State Finances. This amendment allows for, apart from transferring responsibility for the publication of the approved budget to Parliament, a considerable increase in the technical flexibility in budgeting (*e.g.* net budgeting). The subsequent amendments in the Budget Law have adopted new tools in practical budgeting starting in 1993. The Ministry of Finance is presently preparing the necessary amendments in the Budget Law in order to introduce the new tools in practical budgeting. Other recent developments in the Finnish budgetary reform and financial management system have been budgetary ceilings and results-oriented budgeting.

The new results-oriented budgetary approach to running costs was applied in 12 pilot agencies in the 1991 budget and covers three quarters of agencies in 1993. The Government has decided that the new approach will be extended to all agencies in the 1995 budget.

There is some work going on to improve accounting systems to support the results-related approach to budgeting and management. Moreover, there will be a continued reform of Government enterprises, refining cost attribution (personnel costs, office space and other premises, asset management including capital costing, internal pricing of services), legislative developments like the implementation of the amendment of Constitution concerning the State finances in the form of the changes in the budget law and the new law on user charges.

G. FURTHER INFORMATION

All documents are in Finnish and Swedish only, unless stated otherwise.

1. Documents related to annual budget The fiscal year is the calendar year

1. Budget Proposal (*Hallituksen esitys eduskunnalle valtion tulo- ja menoarvioksi*), budget policy and detailed proposals for annual appropriations and revenue items, September. The annexes: Economic Survey (English translation available), Report on Multi-year Projections of State Finances, and other occasional annexes.
2. Government Statement on Economic Policy to Parliament (*Valtioneuvoston talouspoliittinen selonteko eduskunnalle*), May.
3. Medium-Term Prospects. The Finnish Economy and State Finances to 1990, (biannual, English translation available), May.
4. Report of the Finance Committee of Parliament on the budget proposal (*Valtiovarainvaliokunnan mietintö hallituksen esityksen johdosta valtion tulo- ja menoarvioksi*), December.
5. The Budget accepted by Parliament (*Eduskunnan vastaus hallituksen esitykseen valtion tulo- ja menoarvioksi*), December.
6. The specification budget of the State (*Valtion erityismenoarvio*), February/March.
7. General Instructions for the Implementation of the State Budget (*Valtion tulo- ja menoarvion yleiset soveltamismääräykset*), concerning the rules of expenditure management, annual document, January.
8. The Annual Accounts of the State (*Valtion tilinpäätös*), April/May.
9. Report on the Management and State of Government Finances (*Kertomus valtiovarain hoidosta jai tilasta*), containing information about revenue, expenditure, activities, State as employer, financial support to other sectors, Government debt, annexes on cash receipts and outlays, personnel, salaries and pensions, lending, debt, guarantees etc., Autumn.
10. The State Auditors' Report (*Valtiontilintarkastajain kertomus*).

2. Other documents

Articles from the Monthly Bulletin of the Bank of Finland.

FRANCE

**Any changes which have taken place in France
since June 1994 are not reflected in this chapter**

A. INSTITUTIONAL STRUCTURE OF BUDGETARY DECISION-MAKING

1. Political and organisational structure of government

France is a unitary state. There are four levels of government: State or central level, the regions, departments and municipalities, the last three of these levels coming under the heading of local authorities. Regions each have their own executive and (one chamber) parliament. Central Government functions are organised around 20 to 25 ministries and a number of *"Secrétariats d'État"* (Secretariats of State – subdivisions of ministries). Ministries have in general one Minister and one or more Secretaries of State. On the policy-making level, Ministers have their own private staff (*Cabinet du Ministre*), who do not have line management functions, but who advise them on all matters of their concern. The directors of each ministry are non-political appointments, as are the rest of the departmental personnel.

Parliament has two Houses, the National Assembly (*Assemblée Nationale*) and the Senate (*Sénat*). Within the present coalition government there is broad agreement on the basic principles of financial policy, for example, privatisation, reducing government expenditure and taxation.

All Ministers are members of the Government; some Ministers do not have a budget of their own. Once appointed, Ministers have to give up their seat in the Assembly or Senate. Direct elections for the National Assembly are held regularly every five years, the next being in 1998. The next Presidential elections will take place in 1995. The President serves a seven-year term.

2. Main budgetary organs

The Ministry for Economic Affairs and the Ministry for the Budget play a central role in all economic and financial policy matters.

The Ministry for Economic Affairs is composed of several directorates. The Forecasting Directorate prepares macroeconomic projections. The Treasury Directorate is, among other things, responsible for public enterprises and servicing the public debt. The Ministry for the Budget consists essentially of the Budget Directorate which has about 250 staff and is divided into seven sub-directorates. Five of them monitor and control the budgets of the various government departments. There is a sub-directorate for civil service matters, while another is responsible for co-ordinating budgets, revenue and expenditure programmes as set out in the Finance Act. Tax matters are dealt with by the Directorate-General for Taxation and the tax legislation services. The Public Accounts Directorate is involved in the implementation of the budget as far as the disbursement of funds and the audited year-end financial statements are concerned.

3. Role of President, Prime Minister and Cabinet

The President decides certain *"grandes orientations"* and has a specific concern with defence and foreign affairs policies.

The Prime Minister determines the broad lines of budgetary policy on the basis of proposals put forward by the Minister for the Budget. These broad lines are incorporated in a "framework letter", which is signed by him and submitted to his colleagues. He also sends out the "ceilings letters" (see Section D3). He is called upon to arbitrate differences of opinion between Ministers.

Cabinet is involved in the last stage of budget preparation, *i.e.* approval of the Finance Bill before it is submitted to Parliament, as opposed to the earlier stages of budget preparation where the Cabinet is simply kept informed.

4. Role of Parliament

The Finance Bill submitted by the Government is examined by a Finance Committee, in both Houses, before being studied by sectoral committees.

Unlike other bills, the Finance Bill has to be first discussed and adopted by the National Assembly and subsequently by the Senate. If the two Houses do not agree, a joint committee of representatives from both Houses has to find a compromise which the Government can decide to resubmit to the two Houses. If there is still no agreement, the National Assembly has the final say.

The Parliamentary procedure to approve the budget is as follows. To begin with, Parliament has to approve Part I of the Finance Bill authorising the raising of revenue and defining the main categories of expenditure. Members of Parliament can change tax laws, so long as overall tax revenues are not reduced. Subsequently, Parliament has to agree on the so-called "equilibrium provision" of the Finance Bill, specifying the budget shortfall or borrowing requirement.

Discussion on Part II of the Finance Bill involves firstly approving the maintenance of expenditure under current legislation ("*services votés*"). Subsequently, new authorisations are voted by category of expenditure ("*titre*") and by Ministry. These new measures can also include cut-backs in the level of expenditure under current legislation. Parliament can only reduce expenditure; it cannot create or increase expenditure nor can it reallocate resources. In all, Parliament's control over expenditure extends to about 1 100 sections of the Bill ("*chapitres*").

Parliament has to approve expenditure annually, including expenditure authorised under separate legislation. However, appropriations for mandatory expenditure programmes are different in character: instead of a ceiling, they represent only an estimate which therefore can be exceeded without prior Parliamentary approval.

The Finance Bill is submitted to Parliament before the beginning of the new fiscal year. Under a special procedure it is automatically submitted to the Senate if the National Assembly overruns time limits and *vice versa*.

After approval by Parliament, Members of Parliament can submit the Finance Act to the Constitutional Council, which can annul some or all of the Act's provisions.

B. THE SCOPE AND NATURE OF GOVERNMENT FINANCES

Local authorities comprise the regions, departments and municipalities. Since the decentralisation programme of 1983 the regional level has been strengthened *vis-à-vis* the departments and municipalities.

Local taxes consist of property taxes, land taxes and a business tax. Municipalities are mainly concerned with primary education, cultural affairs and the registry service. Social welfare, school transport and secondary education (12-16 years) are the responsibility of the departments. The regions are responsible for education for 16-18 year-olds and for vocational training. Local authorities have access to capital markets, but only the bigger ones avail themselves of this facility. Their borrowing requirement is usually small.

The social security system comprises a number of different services. These fall into three main categories: retirement pension schemes, health insurance schemes and family allowances. These social partners are responsible for day-to-day management of these family allowance services. The State determines the scale of benefits and social security contributions. The State participates in the funding of the handicapped and disability schemes, while the departmental level of government is responsible mainly for the payment of social assistance benefits.

Government influence on certain private sector enterprises has long been more marked than in most OECD Member countries.

C. BUDGET FORMULATION STRATEGY AND PROCESS

1. Strategic aims and global norms

Following a substantial worsening of the deficit over the period 1991 to 1993, when the French economy was hit by recession, the government introduced a five-year guideline law (*"loi d'orientation"*) to curb public expenditure, with the aim of reducing the deficit by half a percentage point of GDP per year to 2.5 per cent by 1997. In order to do so, expenditure in terms of constant francs will be kept stable.

2. Technical aspects of multi-year estimates

The five-year guideline law enacted on 24 January 1994 sets out the parameters for government spending over five years. It is updated annually.

3. Calendar of main points of decision-making and activities

The fiscal year [FY(t)] is the calendar year (t).

Months before start of FY (t)	Main events and activities
(Year t – 1)	
January-March	Budget Directorate prepares budget outlook based on most recently revised economic assumptions.
April	The Minister for the Budget and the Prime Minister discuss and decide broad budgetary policy orientations; framework letter is sent to all Ministers setting out these orientations and giving instructions for Ministerial budget preparations.
May-June	Budget Directorate discussions with spending Ministries. Examination of scope for financing new measures. Prime Minister sends out letters specifying expenditure ceilings for each Ministry.
July-August	Budget Directorate meetings with spending Ministries to discuss the implementation of ceilings and the breakdown of expenditure.
August-September	Final budget preparations and fiscal policy decisions.
First Tuesday in October	Submission of Finance Bill to National Assembly.
(Year t)	
(1 January)	Start of fiscal year (t).

4. The annual budget cycle

There are four stages in the annual budget cycle. During the first stage (January-March) an outline of the next budget is prepared by the Budget Directorate. At the same time a budget projection is made on the basis of no changes in current legislation, and proposals are put forward for adjusting this projected budget so as to have an overall framework for submission to the Government. On the basis of this information, the Minister for the Budget and the Prime Minister discuss these budget proposals and, in April, decide the broad financial orientations for the following year (*e.g.* as in the preparation of the budget for 1995: a 1.5 per cent reduction in the number of civil servants and an 8 per cent reduction in operating costs). These orientations are communicated by the Prime Minister to all Ministers in his framework letter, which also sets out the norms and guidelines for the preparation of the next budget.

The following stage (May-June) covers the first round of meetings with the spending Ministries. The Budget Directorate and the Ministries try to agree on the costs of current programmes and discuss new policy measures and the costs and funding thereof. If they cannot agree, the Ministers (and their private staffs) and the Prime Minister step in to settle these differences.

As soon as the latest revenue estimates are available, the forecast budget outturns are studied in order to determine the scope for financing new measures. It is at this stage that cut-backs may be proposed.

The results of the negotiations undertaken at this stage are examined by each Minister and, if necessary, by the Prime Minister. Expenditure ceilings for major expenditure categories are communicated to Ministers in a "ceilings" letter, signed by the Prime Minister.

In July-August, a new round of meetings takes place between the Budget Directorate and the spending Ministries to make sure that all instructions and expenditure ceilings have been respected. Also, revenue forecasts are estimated anew.

During the last stage (August-September), the Finance Bill is drafted, a process which involves an update of economic assumptions, decision on fiscal measures and approval by the Council of Ministers. The Finance Bill and related documents are submitted to the National Assembly on the first Tuesday in October at the latest.

D. EXPENDITURE REVIEW

There is no central, systematic procedure for reviewing central government expenditure. However, the "*Cour des Comptes*" (Audit Office) has overall responsibility for seeing that public funds are properly administered.

E. IMPLEMENTATION OF THE BUDGET

1. Major instruments of in-year control

Once the budget has been approved, it can in principle be changed only by Parliament. However, there is an emergency procedure whereby funds can be released by decree ("*décrets d'avances*"), in principle, subject to other expenditure being trimmed by the same amount. These decrees have subsequently to be ratified by an amendment to the Finance Act.

On the other hand, the Government can decide not to spend, or set aside, certain appropriations in order to contain the growth in total expenditure. For this, no prior Parliamentary approval is needed.

Parliament is informed about the implementation of the budget by a so-called Amending Act which Parliament has to approve. In principle, spending Ministries are required to fund additional or new expenditure by reducing other expenditure.

A report on the implementation of the budget is presented to Parliament at least once a year, in November or December.

2. Managerial discretion

Transfers of funds between sections of the Finance Act are in principle not possible except with Parliamentary approval. There are, however, two exceptions:
- If not exceeding 10 per cent of the appropriation for the section concerned, funds can be transferred within the same expenditure category and within the same Ministry.
- Transfers between Ministries are allowed provided the nature of the expenditure is not changed.

Appropriations cannot be carried forward, except in certain cases. For example, capital expenditure appropriations that have not been used up by the end of the year can be carried forward. Appropriations included in certain sections of the Finance Act can be carried forward. For all other sections, only up to 10 per cent of the appropriation can be carried forward.

F. RECENT REFORMS

With the preparation of the 1994 Finance Bill, it has now become an accepted practice to adjust approved expenditure items and to scrutinise closely and individually all government "*intervention*" expenditure.

G. FURTHER INFORMATION

1. Documents related to the annual budget

The fiscal year (t) is the calendar year (t).

1. Finance Bill (*Projet de Loi de Finance*), setting out the broad lines of the budget (revenue and expenditure) and the funding of services, September/October, year (t − 1).
2. Economic and Financial Report (*Rapport économique et financier*), giving economic and budget forecasts, September/October, year (t − 1).
3. Supplement on "Ways and Means (*Fascicule 'Voies et moyens'*)", outlining central government revenue, September/October, year (t − 1).
4. Annexes (*Annexes*), detailing expenditures on existing services and new measures by Ministry, September/October, year (t − 1).
5. Approved Budget (*Budget Voté*) published after approval of Finance Bill, end January, year (t).
6. Social Security Accounts (*L'Effort social de la nation*), annual publication, financial results for the social security system as a whole, end October/November, year (t + 1).
7. Amendments to the Finance Act (*Lois des finances rectificatives*), at least one per year, November/December, year (t).

2. Other documents

8. Blue Papers (*Les notes bleues*), weekly publication of the Ministry for Economic Affairs, Finance and Privatisation:

NOTE

1. The term "*titre*" (meaning a category of expenditure, made up of a number of similar sections or "*chapitres*") has both a legal and economic significance.

There are seven categories. Current expenditure is divided into four categories:
1. public debt;
2. central Government appropriation;
3. operating expenditure;
4. government intervention.

Capital expenditure is divided into three categories:
5. central government investment;
6. investment subsidies;
7. war damage compensation.

GERMANY

**Any changes which have taken place in Germany
since September 1993 are not reflected in this chapter**

A. INSTITUTIONAL STRUCTURE OF BUDGETARY DECISION-MAKING

1. Political and organisational structure of government

The Federal Republic of Germany is a federal state and three levels of administration may be distinguished: the Federation, and after the reunification in 1991 sixteen *Länder,* and some 16 000 local authorities (Gemeinden/Kreise).

Each Land has its own constitution, Parliament, government and separate administration. The Federation and the *Länder* are legally autonomous and in principle independent in fulfilling their constitutional tasks.

Federal Government functions as defined by the Basic Law are distributed to ministries and several Federal agencies. Ministries are headed by a Minister, one or two parliamentary secretaries of state (being members of Parliament) and one or two (administrative) secretaries of state and are divided into several directorates.

Federal Government is headed by the Federal Chancellor who is elected by the *Bundestag* and who is formally the only member of government responsible to it. He chooses his cabinet by nominating Federal ministers for appointment (or dismissal) by the Federal President.

Parliament consists of two chambers – the *Bundestag* and the *Bundesrat.* The *Bundestag* (Federal Parliament) is the actual legislative body; the *Bundesrat* (Federal Council) is the federal institution through which the *Länder* participate in the legislation of the Federation.

The members of Parliament (about 660) are elected for 4 years. Since autumn 1982, three parties represented in parliament form a (majority) coalition supporting the coalition government on the basis of a coalition agreement.

2. Main budgetary organs

Within the Federal Government, responsibility for budget issues rests with the Federal Minister of Finance (MF). MF deals with the expenditure and revenue side of the budget in general. MF collaborates with the Federal Minister of Economics in overall economic projections which are the basis for tax revenue estimates, which are made by a working group of experts from the Economic and Finance Ministries, from the *Länder* and the local authorities as well as from scientific economic institutes and the *Bundesbank.* The chair is held by MF.

MF also chairs the Financial Planning Council which makes recommendations for the co-ordination of the budgets and financial plans of the Federal Government, the *Länder* and the Local authorities. This Council consists of Ministers of Finance of both Federation and *Länder,* the Federal Minister of Economics and representatives of municipalities (see Section D for more information). The *Bundesbank* also participates.

Another important Council, made up of representatives from Federal and *Länder* authorities and municipalities, is the Economic Policy Council ("Konjunkturrat") chaired by the Federal Minister of Economics, with a special Sub Committee on Public Borrowing, headed by MF. The Economic Policy Council, under the law to Promote Economic Stability and Growth, considers all measures required to achieve the aims of economic stability.

Within the MF budgetary activities are co-ordinated by the Budget Directorate (headed by the Director of the Budget) which has prime responsibility for the planning, (intragovernmental) co-ordination and implementation on the expenditure and revenue side of the budget. Taxation matters are with the Taxation and the Financial Policy Directorate. The Budget Directorate employs nearly 250. It comprises 4 sub-directorates with a total of 25 divisions, 17 of which being mirror divisions to spending ministries, the rest having general tasks. The "general division" has prime responsibility for the drafting of the annual budget and the financial plan and all necessary co-ordination.

3. Role of Federal Chancellor and Cabinet

The Federal Chancellor lays down the broad lines of government policy. He is the head of the Federal government and as such responsible to Parliament.

The Cabinet approves the government's draft budget and the financial plan as prepared by MF. The Federal Chancellor submits the government draft budget and the Financial plan to Parliament – the draft budget to be approved, the financial plan for information and debate only.

The Minister of Finance, member of all important Cabinet Committees, is in a rather powerful position regarding budgetary matters. On issues of financial significance, MF can lodge an objection against decisions taken by the Cabinet. This objection can be rejected only if the Federal Chancellor and the majority of all Federal ministers vote against it. This is an unprecedented event.

4. Role of Parliament

The budget bill is – like all other bills – approved by Parliament. To shorten the parliamentary approval time, appropriation bills and related budget documents are submitted to both Chambers of Parliament at the same time. This enables the Budget to be finalised, approved and published shortly before the start of the new financial year (*i.e.* the calendar year) to which it refers.

Once the budget has been presented to Parliament it is "out of the Government's hands" in the sense that the final decision with respect to the budget is made by the legislature, the final approval being from the *Bundestag*.

The *Bundesrat* may comment on the draft budget and is also able to propose amendments to it. Its proposals are then forwarded to the Federal Government which passes them on to the *Bundestag* together with its own (counter) Statement.

Once the *Bundestag* has decided to adopt the bill, it goes to the *Bundesrat* for the second time.

If the *Bundesrat* does not agree with the bill as adopted by the *Bundestag* (*i.e.* because it encroaches upon *Länder* interests) the *Bundesrat* may appeal to the Mediation Committee, which is made up of an equal number of members of the *Bundestag* and the *Bundesrat* and whose task it is to find a compromise between the resolutions of the two legislative bodies. If the Mediation Committee proposes an amendment to the bill, it must be put to a new vote in the *Bundestag*. After that, the *Bundesrat* is still entitled to enter an objection, but this objection can then be overruled by the *Bundestag*. Until now the *Bundesrat* has never appealed to the Mediation Committee in the case of the Budget bill.

Preparatory work for the decisions to be taken by the *Bundestag* is carried out by the Budget Committee of the *Bundestag*. The budget, registered on a cash-basis, comprises some 8 000 expenditure subheads, all of which are appropriated annually including borrowing authority and all regulations and explanations within the budget plan. Some 15 meetings of the Budget Committee are required to discuss them in detail on the basis of reports of committee rapporteurs for each of the single ministerial expenditure areas.

New programmes can be proposed and approved, although laws increasing expenditures or involving (or likely to cause) new expenditures (both compared to Government proposals) will require the consent of the Government. The Government may require the *Bundestag* to postpone its vote on such bills. In this case the Federal Government shall state its position to the *Bundestag* within six weeks. If the *Bundestag* after six weeks (at maximum) adopts such a bill the Federal Government within four weeks may require it to vote on that bill again. If the bill has become a statute the Federal Government may finally withhold its consent within six weeks time. This procedure practically is never used, since government would use the (coalition) majority to avoid votes of that kind against government opinion. In fact, most of the bills are discussed and prepared in committees of (coalition) parties, in which both government and members of Parliament participate.

B. THE SCOPE AND NATURE OF GOVERNMENT FINANCES

All levels of government are assigned tasks which are quite well defined in the constitution. The Federation, the *Länder* and local authorities meet separately the expenditure resulting from the discharge of their respective tasks by revenue from own taxes as well as by distributing the revenues of certain joint taxes to legally established formulas. In general, the principle of equalisation of revenues has been adopted, thus spreading the balances between financially strong and weak governments of various levels.

The local authorities receive funds required for performing their local tasks (including local social services and hospitals) from local taxes (mainly on real estate), from their share of income tax revenue and from Land grants and transfers.

The *Länder* are responsible for, among other things, cultural and educational affairs, the administration of justice, the police, and the health service. Another task of the *Länder* is the implementation of so called joint activities, a form of co-operation between *Länder* and Federation, regarding among other things regional economic structural policy. Most of the Federal laws (and tasks) are executed by the *Länder*.

These wide areas of *Länder*'s responsibility call for correspondingly large amounts of money. The *Länder* receive half the revenue from income tax (less the municipalities' share) and from corporation tax and a portion (37 per cent) of value added tax. In addition, the *Länder* are entitled to collect some taxes of minor importance; they have to pass on a certain amount of this revenue to the municipalities.

Federal Government's responsibilities include among other things defence and external affairs matters, social policy, development aid, the construction of federal roads and motorways etc. In order to finance its activities, the Federal Government receives part of the revenue from income tax, corporate tax and value added tax, and is entitled to the revenues of some other taxes.

The social insurance funds, as a rule, prepare their own budget. Their expenditure is financed by social security contributions of insured employees and employers, and in part by transfers from the Federal budget. On-budget social security covers war victims' pensions and related benefits and minimum relief for unemployed persons. Federal Government can influence entitlement terms and rates of social benefits via a bill presented to Parliament for approval.

Federal special funds operating as independent public-law enterprises are the Federal Railways and Federal Posts and Telecommunications. Federal Railways receive from the Federal budget current and capital grants. Federal Posts and Telecommunications pay an annual contribution to the Federal budget. Further important special funds are the "German Unity Fund" and the "Debt Processing Fund".

Table 1.   **Functional classification of federal government expenditure (1994)**

As percentage of total

Social sector	35.1
Defence	4.8
Transport	10.7
Education, science and technology	2.0
Personal services and benefits	11.5
Burden inherited from the former GDR	9.8
Interest on public debt	12.6
Other	13.8
Total	100.0

Source: Draft budget for 1994.

C. BUDGET FORMULATION STRATEGY AND PROCESS

1.   Strategic aims and global norms

The Federal Government's budgetary and fiscal policies are operated under the precondition to consolidate public finances, *i.e.* to put them on a sound basis. This consolidation strategy is at the basis of a multi-year Financial Plan (see below), which is decided and published annually.

Policy is aimed now at a reduction of the budget deficit by restricting nominal growth of federal budget expenditure.

For the current Financial Plan, the aims are:

- limiting total Federal nominal expenditure growth to a maximum of 2.3 per cent per annum during the five year planning period (*i.e.* roughly half of the nominal increase of Gross National Product);
- further reducing the Federal net borrowing requirement by 50 per cent.

The following table indicates current targets.

Table 2.   **Fiscal indicators, 1993-97**

	1993	1994	1995	1996	1997
Net Borrowing Requirement (in billion DM)	67.6	67.5	67.0	48.0	38.0
Total Federal nominal expenditure growth (%)	7.2	4.4	0.1	2.1	2.2

Source: Financial Plan 1993-97.

2.   Technical aspects of multi-year estimates

Multi-year estimates (MYE) for planning and control purposes are registered for expenditure, revenues and resulting budget deficits of Federal Government, in the Medium Term Financial Plan which is published annually with the budget. Though the multi-year estimates are consistent with medium term budgetary targets, the individual spending plans for future years usually add up to a smaller total than the aggregate total in the Financial Plan because of a general planning reserve for each of the future years to cover additional costs of new programmes and possible price increases.

The financial plan covers a five year period; the current year and the year to come, for which the budget bill is prepared and three future years. The macroeconomic assumptions of the estimates are based on the probable developments of macroeconomic parameters (including price and wage developments), which are developed by interdepartmental working groups, based on the Annual Economic Report of the Government.

MYE are prepared for each of the 8 000 expenditure items in the annual budget for each of the years of the planning period. The MYE are rolled forward each year. They are prepared and updated during the annual budget deliberations between MF and the spending ministries: simultaneously with the drafting of the annual budget, the expenditure estimates are fixed in cash terms for each of the single expenditure items and programmes for each of the future years. The total expenditure frame is set by the multi-year budgetary target based on a certain annual increase (top-down approach of planning). The difference between the sum of all expenditure estimates (bottom-up) and total expenditure by given the ratio of annual increase is the general planning reserve.

MYE are published in the Financial Plan, grouped by about 40 categories of functional spending. There is no publication of in-year updates of MYE.

3. Calendar of main points of decision-making and activities

The fiscal year [FY(t)] is the calendar year (year t).

Months before start of FY (t)	Main events and activities
(Year t – 2)	
13 (December)	MF gives detailed instructions to Federal ministries concerning budget preparations and adjustment of medium- term financial plan.
(Year t – 1)	
11-10 (February-March)	Federal ministries submit their bids for the budget and planning years to MF.
11-7 (February-June)	MF deliberations with each Ministry at all levels of officials up to Minister level.
7-6 (June-July)	Final Cabinet decision-making regarding draft budget and the Federal Financial Plan.
5 (August)	The Government's budget plus financial plan is submitted to Parliament.
4 (September)	MF delivers budget statement to Parliament at the beginning of the first parliamentary reading.
2-1 (November-December)	Final reading and vote on Government's Budget.
1 (December)	Signing by the Federal President and publication.
(Year t)	
0 (1st January)	Start of fiscal year (t).

4. The annual budget cycle

In December a circular issued by the Ministry of Finance gives detailed instructions to all Federal agencies concerning the preparation and the submission of agency budget estimates including estimates for the planning period. In general, the ministries are requested to keep their budget bids within the upper limits laid down in the current financial plan. The agency budget submissions are due at the end of February.

The budget requests are evaluated and discussed between the Ministry of Finance and the other Federal departments at three levels:

- by the head of division responsible in the budget directorate for a specific departmental budget;
- by the Director of the budget;
- finally if necessary at Minister level.

Going through various stages of review the original budget requests are examined and successively brought into line with a level consistent with economic and financial resources. Usually both the Financial Plan and the original budget bids are changed so as to make them consistent.

During budgetary negotiations within the government, MF may if required call for the Cabinet to take a decision of general principle laying down the basic data to be incorporated in the federal budget and the financial plan (rate of increase of aggregate expenditure, total budget volume, borrowing requirement). Cabinet is involved with the final decision of the Government's budget proposal and financial plan.

The final version of the draft budget is decided on by the Cabinet at the end of June/early July. The Government's budget bill must be submitted to the legislative bodies (*Bundestag* and *Bundesrat*) before the first reading in Parliament (September).

At the first reading, or general debate, MF delivers a budget speech outlining the government's considerations regarding the budget. Members of Parliament make their initial comments on the budget stating their fundamental points of view. After the first reading the bill is referred to the parliamentary Budget Committee as well as to the Programme Committees for discussion. At the second reading, (end of November/early December) the results of the Budget Committee's discussions are announced as the Committee's decision proposal to the plenary of the *Bundestag* by the Committee's rapporteurs and comments of the *Bundesrat* are available to the *Bundestag,* together with a counter statement by the Federal Government. This marks the beginning of a three-day discussion on the individual departmental budgets. The *Bundestag* comes to a decision, *i.e.* one vote on every departmental budget. At the third and final reading, (one day after the second reading) it is once again the budget as a whole which is the subject of debate, and, in conclusion, a vote is taken on its adoption.

After the *Bundestag* has voted on the bill it is submitted to the *Bundesrat* for the second time. The Budget that has to be approved consists of:

- the budget law (consisting of general regulations including total expenditure, total ceilings for guarantees, borrowing authority, etc.);
- the budget plan (as supplement to the budget law) containing item by item all authorised expenditure ceilings and estimated revenue plus explanatory notes.

D. EXPENDITURE REVIEW

There are re-examinations of various policy areas partly *ad hoc* and partly regular, *e.g.* by government reports to Parliament according to legal instructions. Budgetary consequences are normally taken into account in the following budget preparation phase. There is no general re-examination procedure regarding the budget as a whole (except within the Annual Economic Report which contains a broad description of the main policy areas with possible changes). A certain cross-sector analysis is made by the biannual report on subsidies. Its purpose is a description of the development of subsidies with the view to a continuous reduction of preserving measures as compared with those helping to cope with structural changes and inducing economic growth. Findings of the report reflect current budget policy and/or influence the next financial plan. Budget-wide cut-back proposals, if necessary, are prepared by MF alone, in the process of preparing the new budget draft and the medium term financial plan. (See Section F for more information.)

E. IMPLEMENTATION OF THE BUDGET

1. Major instruments of in-year control

At the beginning of the budget year, MF issues a Budget Implementation Circular (*Haushaltsführung-serlass*) with technical and administrative regulations for the spending agencies. Cash management and accounting rules allow for an intra-governmental control of the execution of the budget.

When expenditure is likely to exceed the authorised total the Federal Finance Minister may make commitments or expenditures subject to his approval by blocks on expenditure, after having consulted the competent Federal Ministers.

MF can under certain conditions (if the need for additional expenditure is unforeseen and unavoidable) authorise excess and extrabudgetary expenditure, although this only applies where owing to the urgency of the additional expenditure a supplementary budget cannot be enacted in time or where Parliament has already waived the requirement for a supplementary budget in the Budget Law (namely in cases where the additional expenditure does not exceed DM 10 million or where it arises from a legally binding commitment). In periods of retrenchment policy with relatively low expenditure ceilings, this happens quite often. Twenty to fifty cases (of more than DM 10 million) a year is quite normal.

Parliament is informed regularly (quarterly) about all important departures from the plan – excess and extrabudgetary expenditures.

Not for budgetary control reasons, but for considerations regarding overall economic development, the Government may apply the provisions of the Law to Promote Economic Stability and Growth (1967), if immediate action is necessary to prevent considerable economic damage and if such action cannot be taken through the enactment of supplementary budgets.

In the event of a substantial decline in general economic activity the Government may decide to authorise additional expenditure. Additional expenditure to counter an economic recession (*Konjunkturprogramme*) can be authorised by a simplified procedure without the need for a long drawn-out supplementary budget. The MF is authorised by law to raise credits up to DM 5 billion in excess of the provisions of the budget as adopted; taxation rates can also be decreased. Such economic programmes are prepared by the Government and require the consent of the Federal Parliament (last used 1975, as their effectiveness has come under question).

In order to avoid an overheating of the economy MF can block expenditure and the entering into commitments involving expenditure in future years (*Konjunktursperre*) as well as increase personal and corporate income tax rates or reduce depreciation allowances. Apart from this, the Federal Cabinet may limit borrowing by the Federation, the *Länder* and the local authorities. It was last used in 1971.

2. Managerial discretion

The detailed specifications, which are binding for the execution of the budget, are in many cases relaxed through budget regulations which permit additional expenditure on some items, provided that equivalent savings are found within certain specified items.

Investment expenditure and expenditure from specifically earmarked revenue may be carried forward. Other expenditure may be declared eligible for carry forward in the budget, if it is earmarked for a purpose covering several years and if this is in the interests of efficiency and economy. Funds in the originating budget year, as a consequence, may not be spent fully.

F. RECENT REFORMS

1. Improving the monitoring of efficiency in the Federal Administration

German budget legislation requires the principles of efficiency and economy to be observed both in preparing and in executing the budget.

In this connection, the Federal Audit Office has ascertained in the course of its examinations that the efficiency analyses needed to evaluate government measures are not being conducted to the required extent.

Following on from this conclusion, the Federal Ministry of Finance is taking steps to make the existing rules on efficiency analyses considerably more extensive and well-defined.

In future, efficiency analyses are to be carried out for *all* government measures by the persons responsible for these measures in each case, both at the planning stage and in the form of concluding and, where necessary, concurrent efficiency reviews. This will cover all government measures, ranging for example from procurements, investment projects, subsidies and social and tax policy measures to draft legislation.

Efficiency analyses do not necessarily have to be sophisticated cost-benefit calculations that are not readily comprehensible and are generally undertaken by experts from outside the administration. They should rather incorporate the natural application of efficiency checks to every type of activity and to all measures of the administration. The most simple and most economic method of analysis should be employed in line with the requirements of each case. The results of the efficiency check must be recorded in such a way as to be readily reproducible.

The persons responsible for preparing the budget in each ministry, the Ministry of Finance itself and Parliament can as needed call for information on efficiency checks. They may make the inclusion of a measure in the preparation and execution of the budget conditional upon the submission of efficiency analyses.

With this reorganisation, the observance of the principle of efficiency in the administration is to be:

- ensured across the entire range of administrative activity;
- facilitated by simple procedural rules;
- documented and thus rendered verifiable by third parties, for instance by the auditing authorities;
- made into a natural and virtually automatic constituent of the government's administrative activity.

2. Legislation mandated by the Federal Constitutional court to introduce rules to avert and to remedy acute budgetary crises

Under the constitutional rules governing public finance in Germany, the financially weak *Länder* receive revenue equalisation payments from the financially strong *Länder* and the federal government. During a constitutional controversy between the federal government and various *Länder,* the Federal Constitutional Court had, inter alia, to concern itself with the problem of how to deal with *Länder* that are in an acute budgetary crisis. The Court found that in deference to the federal principle, the federal government and the other *Länder* were under an obligation to help *Länder* in an acute budgetary crisis.

In this context, the Court found as a general rule that the federal government should lay down binding procedural rules and obligations that would:

- counter the development of acute budgetary crises, and
- where an acute budgetary crisis had occurred, serve to eliminate that crisis.

These rules shall be binding for both the federal government and for the *Länder.*

To this end, legislation should be enacted to create in particular the following arrangements for the federal government and the *Länder*.

1. Limits designated by financial ratios, for example relating to the volume of net borrowing and total indebtedness, are to be observed insetting up the budget.
2. Where these limits have been exceeded, binding rehabilitation programmes must be undertaken in order to bring budget management back within normal parameters.
3. These rules apply to the core budget including ancillary budgets.

The Federal government is currently examining ways in which the requirements of the Federal Constitutional Court can best be put into effect.

G. FURTHER INFORMATION

1. Documents related to annual budget

The fiscal year is the calendar year (year t).

1. Law on the Adoption of the Federal Budget (*Haushaltsgesetz*) supplemented by the Federal Budget Plan (*Bundeshaushaltsplan*), December, year (t − 1).
2. Financial Report of the Federal Minister of Finance (*Finanzbericht des Bundesministers der Finanzen*), containing the economic premises and the principal fiscal policy issues underlying the Federal budget (among others, the Financial Plan and comprehensive statistical data), August, year (t − 1).
3. Annual Economic Report (*Jahreswirtschaftsbericht*) of the Federal Government, responding to the annual report of the Council of Economic Experts (see reference 6 below), January, (year t), (English translation available).
4. Quarterly Report on the Excess and/or extrabudgetary expenditure (*Zusammenstellung der über und ausserplanmässigen ausgaben in ... Vierteljahr des Haushaltsjahres t*).

2. Other documents

5. Annual Report of the Council of Economic Experts for the Assessment of Overall Economic Trends (*Jahresgutachten des Sachverständigenrates zur Begutachtung der gesamtwirtschaftlichen Entwicklung*), November.
6. Report of the Federal Government on Federal Fiscal Aid and Tax Relief (*Subventionsbericht*), every two years usually in Summer.

Note: The above publications may be obtained from:
Bundesanzeiger Verlag
Postfach 1320
53003 Bonn

7. Federal German Budget Legislation (*Haushaltrecht des Bundes*), English translation available.
8. The German Budgetary System, (*der Bundeshaushalt - unser Geld*), 1984, English translation available.

Note: Documents referenced under 7 and 8 may be obtained from the point of contact.

NOTE

1. Art. 115 in the Constitution requires that Federal net borrowing shall not exceed total Federal investment expenditure estimates; however, "exceptions shall be permissible only to avert a disturbance of the overall economic equilibrium".

GREECE

**Any changes which have taken place in Greece
since September 1993 are not reflected in this chapter**

A. INSTITUTIONAL STRUCTURE OF BUDGETARY DECISION-MAKING

1. Political and organisational structure of government

Greece is a unitary state. The Greek general government is comprised of the central government, the local authorities and the Legal Entities in Public Law such as the Social Security Funds. It does not include any state-owned/controlled enterprises which are corporations.

The central government functions are carried out by 20 ministries and several peripheral bureaux. It also includes the 54 Prefectures (Nomarchia) which are central government agencies. Each Prefecture represents the central government in all its activities.

The one-Chamber Parliament consists of 300 members elected for a four-year period. Since the last election (April 1990) five parties are represented in the Parliament. Currently, the government is supported by one party with an absolute majority of seats. The Ministers appointed by the Prime Minister form the Cabinet headed by the latter. The Ministers are usually, but not necessarily, members of Parliament (MPs). Deputy Ministers and General Secretaries are appointed by their respective ministers and may not be MPs.

2. Main budgetary organs

The Minister of Finance (ranking seventh in the Cabinet) is primarily responsible for fiscal policy and is accountable to the Parliament for both revenues and expenditures of the ordinary budget. The Minister of National Economy (ranking fifth in the Cabinet) is responsible for overall economic and fiscal policies and drafts the investment budget, which is incorporated in the General Budget submitted to Parliament by the Minister of Finance.

The Ministry of Finance includes the State General Accounting Office (GAO), which prepares, implements and monitors the ordinary budget in collaboration with all the General Directorates of the Ministry of Finance.

The staff of GAO is organised in 18 directorates, of which the Budget Directorate is the most important one. It co-ordinates all budget activities and it is responsible for drafting the annual budget. It is comprised of subdivisions counterpart to spending ministries and other entities and monitors but cannot control ministerial decisions for the adjustment in public spending.

3. Role of President, Prime Minister and Cabinet

The President does not participate in budgetary decision-making.

The role of the Prime Minister is very important because he lays down the broad lines of government policy, according to which the Minister of Finance proceeds with the preparation of the annual Government Budget. Unsolved disagreements between the Minister of Finance and the spending ministers concerning, for example, expenditure cuts, have to be resolved by the Cabinet and the Prime Minister himself. The Cabinet also decides any change in tax legislation proposed by the Minister of Finance.

The final version of the Budget proposals needs approval by the Cabinet before submission to Parliament. The Cabinet does not set or approve guidelines at the beginning of the budget preparation, although it approves the fiscal target and the broad guidelines put forward by the Minister of Finance.

4. Role of Parliament

The Parliament does not participate in shaping the budget. A Parliamentary Committee prepares the debate, which usually centres around overall fiscal policy. The debate may last for a period of up to five days, after which voting takes place. The Parliament may not reject the principle of the budget, but votes on the individual annual appropriations per department, including expenditure authorised under separate legislation (*e.g.* social benefits). There is no in-year monitoring of the budget by the Parliament and any deviations are brought to Parliament for approval with the following year's budget.

According to the 1975 Greek Constitution, the Minister of Finance has to submit the budget to the Parliament at least one month before the beginning of the new fiscal year. If the Parliament has not approved the budget, for any reason, before the beginning of the new fiscal year, the government is authorised to submit a bill to Parliament which allows the government to continue collecting revenues and implementing current programmes. If the Parliament cannot vote this specific bill before the beginning of the fiscal year then by presidential decree the previous year's budget is extended for a four-month period.

B. THE SCOPE AND NATURE OF GOVERNMENT FINANCES

Public sector activities in Greece are carried out by an unusually large number of Government Departments, Agencies, Institutions, Funds, Public Enterprises etc.

The single most important component of the public sector is the central government budget. On a national accounts basis, outlays under the central government budget usually account for 50 to 60 per cent of general government outlays. Since 1952 the central government budget has been divided into two parts: the ''Ordinary Budget'' and the ''Investment Budget''. The first records all current receipts and outlays of the central government while the latter includes all capital spending (capital budget). The investment budget always runs a large deficit, while the ordinary budget was more or less in balance (''golden rule'') until the late ''70s''. Ever since, however, the ordinary budget has run sizeable deficits financed mostly by domestic borrowing.

Social security funds constitute the second largest component accounting for 30 to 35 per cent of general government outlays. Social security funds enjoy considerable fiscal autonomy. The major exception is the Farmers' Insurance Organisation (OGA) whose revenues are collected by the central government (earmarked taxes). Moreover OGA also receives subsidies from the ordinary budget. All other insurance organisations collect the major part of their receipts from employee and employer contributions or levies on the public at large. During the ''80s'', the financial situation of some major social insurance organisations (notably IKA, NAT) worsened considerably so the ordinary budget had to cover their annual deficits. In certain years bank borrowing was also used. As in most countries, social security outlays in Greece have exhibited, for the last thirty years or so, a strong upward trend.

Unlike the social insurance funds, local authorities (municipalities and communities) enjoy very limited fiscal autonomy in Greece. The state budget collects revenues on their behalf and transfers the proceeds to them. Another significant portion of local authorities revenues is collected through public utility bills (especially electricity) which do not appear in the central government budget. Moreover local authorities receive subsidies from the central government. Certain measures taken during the ''80s'' to give local authorities greater fiscal autonomy (fix their own tax rates etc.) have not proved so effective. In 1988 however, local authorities began borrowing in the capital markets, something which was not permitted before that year. The limited role of local authorities also follows from the fact that their spending accounts for less than 4 per cent of general government outlays.

Contrary to local authorities, public enterprises enjoy considerable autonomy, although their tariffs are controlled by central government. The government budget also provides (occasionally) grants to those enterprises which run deficits. Moreover, recently the central government took over part of the state guaranteed debt of certain public enterprises which were not able to serve it any longer.

Table 1 shows a breakdown of current expenditure by functional classification indicating the percentage share of total state budget expenditure.

Table 1. **Functional classification of public current expenditure (1989)**

As percentage of total

Administration	38.0
Defence	26.1
Justice	3.7
Health	11.1
Welfare	1.5
Education	15.5
Other	3.3
Total	100.0

Source: Provisional National Accounts of Greece.

C. BUDGET FORMULATION STRATEGY AND PROCESS

1. Strategic aims and global norms

Greece has already experienced a fiscal stabilisation programme (1986-87) and since 1991 a rolling 3-year stabilisation programme has been put into effect. The annual budgets are intended to meet the targets set by the stabilisation programme, although the latter has no binding effect. It should be mentioned however, that the targets of the 1991-93 programme were included in the March 1991 loan agreement between Greece and the EEC.

The operational target for the budget is the net PSBR/GDP ratio and in this sense represents a form of "top-down" budgeting. The net PSBR is the sum of the net borrowing requirements of the central government, the local authorities and the major social security funds and public enterprises supervised by the Ministry of National Economy.

The current stabilisation programme extends to 1994, setting a decrease of the net borrowing requirement of the central government from 13.1 per cent of GDP in 1991 to 4.1 per cent in 1994.

Table 2. **Net PSBR, 1985-90**

As percentage of GDP

	1985	1986	1987	1988	1989	1990
1. Central government	14.4	10.5	11.8	14.8	17.4	18.5
2. Social insurance and local authorities	0.8	1.4	0.3	0.6	−0.1	−1.0
General government (1 + 2)	15.2	11.9	12.1	15.4	17.3	17.5
3. Public enterprises	2.7	2.2	1.5	0.6	1.0	1.0
PSBR	17.9	14.1	13.6	16.0	18.3	18.5

Source: Bank of Greece, Governor's Annual Report.

2. Technical aspects of multi-year estimates

All budgets prepared by the Government are annual budgets. There is no multi-year budgeting practice although recently each year's annual budget must be coherent with the three-year stabilisation programme but no detailed estimates were provided, nor do they exist.

125

3. Calendar of main points of decision-making and activities

The fiscal year [FY(t)] is a calendar year (year t), as it is shown in the table below.

Months before start of FY (t)	Main events and activities
(Year t – 1)	
June	MF issues guidelines to spending Ministries and Prefectures, explaining the budget constraints and the limits within which they should form their spending proposals.
7-5 (July-August)	Ministries and Prefectures submit their expenditure proposals to GAO for examination. The GAO makes first round cut-backs and the MF consults with the Minister of National Economy as to the possible budget strategies.
5-3 (August-October)	GAO, under the instruction of MF, scrutinises proposals and holds discussions with each spending Ministry. Cabinet decides on the targeted budget deficit, based on both the expenditure and tax policies proposed by MF. (MF himself supervises the last round of expenditure cuts.)
2 (mid-November)	Finalisation and submission of the budget and related documents to the Parliament.
(Year t)	
0 (1 January)	Start of fiscal year (t).

4. The annual budget cycle

Preparation of the Central Government budget takes place in the following stages.

Early in the summer (usually June) the Ministry of Finance issues a circular with instructions to all Ministries and Prefectures, asking them to prepare their proposals for spending over the next year. The Financial Service in each ministry gathers the proposals of all services in the ministry which are usually accompanied by detailed (legal) justification on each spending item.

After the proposals have been approved by the Minister they are forwarded to the respective Ordered Expenses Office (OEO). The OEO submits them along with its own comments and suggestions, to the GAO by mid-August. The OEO personnel have the expertise to review these proposals in depth and make valuable suggestions. Prefectures, through Economic Administrative Sections, gather the forecasts from all their services and submit them to the Ministry of Interior. The Ministry of Interior assesses these estimates and forwards them to the GAO.

From August to October the Budget Directorate in the GAO scrutinises the proposals. The figures can be modified by the Minister of Finance, after he has consulted with the Prime Minister (or the Minister of National Economy). The purpose of these discussions is to contain the rate of growth of public expenditure within the limits of the fiscal policy targets. At the same time, the revenue section of the Budget Directorate with the Taxation Service estimate next year's tax revenue in the light of instructions given by Ministry of National Economy with respect to the estimates of expected GDP and inflation rates for the next year. The Ministry of Finance then briefs the Government and it is then decided if and how the proposed fiscal policy should be changed.

The above procedure holds also for the formulation of the public investment budget, which covers all types of investment expenditure including capital transfers and which is administered by the Ministry of National Economy. Once the Investment Budget proposals have been formulated, they are forwarded to the Ministry of Finance (GAO) to be incorporated – without the Ministry of Finance having the possibility to change anything – in the Central Government Budget.

The overall Government Budget once finalised (mid-November) is submitted to the Parliament. Discussion of the Budget and the Fiscal Policy of the Government in the Parliament takes place at the beginning of the second half of December.

D. EXPENDITURE REVIEW

Expenditure reviews are exclusively linked to the formulation and implementation Stage of the Budget (see Sections C and E).

E. IMPLEMENTATION OF THE BUDGET

1. Major instruments of in-year control

In the implementation of the Budget many officials and services are involved including the Ministry of National Economy who collaborates with the Ministry of Finance in deciding the measures to be taken. Implementation of the Budget, as far as the expenditure side is concerned, is a procedure where the Ministry of Finance is directly and continuously involved. The Ministry of Finance has the authority to regulate the flow of actual spending of appropriations by issuing decisions determining what percentage of certain annual appropriations may be spent in each quarter of the year (spending limits). If unspent balances result, overruns in some categories of expenditure may be covered by these balances. This, however, is not automatic.

The Ministry of Finance for the same reason issues a decision each month allowing the amounts which may be spent in each month for certain categories of spending, such as grants, government supplies, etc. (payments limit).

No overruns in annual appropriations or commitments are allowed for, without the consent of the Minister of Finance, declaring he will cover the overruns in cash from the reserve fund. The reserve fund is not appropriated, but it is entered in the budget as a total amount. Usually it does not exceed 2 per cent of the total current expenditure and it is used to cover unforeseen necessary expenditure where insufficient appropriations exist. Normally, it covers overruns in debt servicing or damages to agricultural production; generally it covers types of expenditure for which there can be no provision in the budget.

Though the Greek budget is cash-based, no commitment is allowed unless there is an appropriation for the specific expenditure. Overruns are justified only in cases where exact estimations are impossible.

Formally, the Parliament is informed about the budget implementation by the time the new budget is submitted for discussion. However, in practice the Parliament may be informed about the execution of the budget whenever they request.

2. Managerial discretion

Every Minister is accountable both to the Cabinet and to the Parliament for the policy followed in his Ministry and for the efficient use of resources allocated to his Ministry.

Unspent balances of appropriations are not transferred to the next year's budget. The fiscal year coincides with the calendar year but may be extended for a few months only to clear up commitments undertaken up to the end of the normal fiscal year. If a cash payment on a capital investment project is delayed beyond the extension period of the fiscal year, ending in March of the following year, the payment is made as a charge on the next year's appropriation. Commitments generating future capital expenditure can be undertaken if necessary for the continuation of the investment projects.

Appropriations cannot be transferred from one category of expenditure to another, unless approved by Ministry of Finance.

F. RECENT REFORMS

In the framework of the three-year stabilisation programme, recruitment in the public sector has been halted while a reallocation of personnel from overstaffed departments and agencies to understaffed ones is under way. The latter measure has met with stiff resistance from those being affected and the respective unions. In the 1992 Budget great attention was given to containing expenditure (excluding debt servicing payments which are expected to decline in real terms). More measures are being studied in order to cut expenditure even further.

IRELAND

**Any changes which have taken place in Ireland
since November 1993 are not reflected in this chapter**

A. INSTITUTIONAL STRUCTURE OF BUDGETARY DECISION-MAKING

1. Political and organisational structure of government

Ireland is a unitary state. There are two layers of government; central government, including the State-sponsored body sector and regional government which includes regional health boards and local authorities (municipalities) (see Section B for more information).

Central government functions are organised mainly around 16 Ministries and state agencies.

The Government consists of the Prime Minister (*Taoiseach*), the Deputy Prime Minister (*Tanaiste*) and thirteen Ministers. In addition, there are 15 other deputy Ministers (Ministers of State) who do not have Cabinet rank and who are appointed by the Government to discharge particular responsibilities delegated to them.

The legislature (*Oireachtas*) consists of the President, who is Head of State under the Constitution, the lower House (*Dail Eireann*) and the upper House (*Seanad Eireann*). Ministers must be members of a House of the *Oireachtas*. The Prime Minister, Deputy Prime Minister and Minister for Finance must all be members of the *Dail*. There are six registered political parties represented in *Dail Eireann* of whom two support the Government. The next regular elections are due in 1997.

2. Main budgetary organs

The Minister for Finance takes the lead role in budgetary matters. He has an overall authority and responsibility in relation to public expenditure and revenue and in relation to borrowing and debt management. The Minister has, however, delegated the exercise of the borrowing and debt management functions to a new statutory body called the National Treasury Management Agency (NTMA). The NTMA was established in December 1990. The Agency exercises its functions under the general control of the Minister for Finance and subject to directions and guidelines which the Minister may give to them. The Minister proposes strategy on public expenditure and budgetary matters generally to the Government and is responsible for the presentation of spending estimates and the annual budget to the Parliament.

The Department of Finance (DF) consists of five main divisions:

- Public Expenditure Division;
- Finance Division;
- Budget and Economic Division;
- Personnel and Remuneration Division;
- Organisation Management and Training Division.

The Public Expenditure Division is responsible for general public expenditure policy and the control and monitoring of expenditure by government Departments and State agencies. Policy formulation and monitoring and control functions are exercised in relation to some 70 per cent of Exchequer financed current expenditure and to all capital expenditure. The remaining 30 per cent of current expenditure arises mainly as debt servicing costs paid from the Central Fund (see Section A4) and is administered by the NTMA. The NTMA liaise with the Finance Division in relation to debt service expenditure and debt management policy. Finance Division is also responsible in the Budgetary context for forecasting and monitoring of certain non-tax revenues and capital receipts. Budget and Economic Division is responsible for the formulation of the annual budget, for macroeconomic forecasting and economic planning, for economic and budgetary aspects of Ireland's membership of the European Union and for taxation matters. The latter task is performed in co-ordination with the Revenue Commissioners who are given responsibility under law for the administration and collection of taxes.

Personnel and Remuneration Division is responsible for Civil Service Recruitment, public sector pay and non-pay policies, pay determination procedures and industrial relations generally. Finally, Organisation Management and Training Division is responsible for public service structures, reviews of staffing, organisation systems and procedures, promoting modern management and government accounting techniques and for operations research, computerisation and training. The central sections in each division, and the forecasting sections liaise formally and act in concert through a budget Co-ordinating Group which meets regularly to review the current year's budget and to plan for the following years' budgets.

3. Role of Prime Minister and Cabinet

The Prime Minister (*Taoiseach*) is responsible for the overall direction of Cabinet meetings. He exercises a pivotal role in all Government discussions. There are regular informal contacts between the Prime Minister, Deputy Prime Minister and Minister for Finance on budgetary and broad expenditure questions.

In recent years, the practice has been to specify general medium-term fiscal objectives, particularly in relation to the debt/General Government Deficit (GGD) ratio which do not require formal annual approval. The annual Estimates Circular seeks expenditure demands that comply with these medium-term objectives. Subsequently, the Cabinet decides on expenditure issues which remain unresolved between the Minister for Finance and his colleagues. Finalisation of the budget also requires Cabinet decisions on specific taxation changes and final adjustments to spending plans.

4. Role of Parliament

The budget statement is delivered in the *Dail*. Financial resolutions (proposals on taxation) which give effect to taxation changes requiring immediate approval are introduced in the *Dail* on Budget Day (see Section D).

The Government's annual expenditure estimates are presented concurrently to both Houses of Parliament in advance of Budget Day. Only the *Dail* has the power to amend legislation involving public monies; as noted below, however, it is not empowered to amend estimates – only to adopt or to reject them. Standing Orders (procedural rules) of the lower House preclude any addition or reduction in the annual estimates. The Upper House does not debate the budget per se; it does however consider the annual Finance Bill (taxation) and Appropriation Bill (expenditure) on which it may make recommendations which the *Dail* may either accept or reject. Government policy and administration may be examined and criticised in both Houses but, under the Constitution, the Government is responsible to the *Dail* alone. On all Bills, the overriding authority of the Lower House *vis-à-vis* the Upper House may be asserted.

All budget and estimates discussions take place in the *Dail* and are debated on the floor of the House. In 1993 five new *Dail* Committees were established whose remit includes the examination of Estimates for the areas of the Public Service for which they were designated responsibility. The new Committees are as follows:
- Finance and General Affairs.
- Legislation and Security.
- Enterprise and Economic Strategy.
- Social Affairs.
- Foreign Affairs.

Each of the Select Committees is empowered, subject to the consent of the Minister of Finance, to engage the services of specialists to assist it or any of its sub-committees. They may also invite submissions in writing from interested persons or bodies.

No Votes are taken in Committee on Estimates but the Reports of the Committees on the Estimates are presented to the *Dail* by the respective Chairmen.

Debt servicing expenditure and certain other expenditure such as contributions to the EC Budget and capital issues to State-sponsored bodies and local authorities do not have to be voted annually as they are met from the Central Fund under the standing authority of specific legislation passed by Parliament. All other Exchequer-financed expenditure must, however, be appropriated annually by Parliament. Taxation measures, announced in the Budget,* are given statutory effect in the Finance Act. Parliament does not approve multi-year estimates. Parliament controls the money to be spent by voting on the Annual estimates. The lower House passes about 44 votes covering all Exchequer-financed expenditure requiring annual appropriations. When passed, these are then included in the annual Appropriation Act. The Appropriation Act specifies: *a)* total (gross) expenditure; and *b)* Appropriations-in-Aid (receipts) for each Vote. Supporting information on the allocation of expenditure within each Vote is presented to both Houses of Parliament in the Estimates Volume.

To allow the continuation of services from one year to the next, Departments may, in any financial year, spend up to 4/5 of the previous year's appropriations pending parliamentary approval for the current year's estimates.

B. THE SCOPE AND NATURE OF GOVERNMENT FINANCES

The General Government sector is relatively large by OECD standards, with a big central government. General Government Borrowing as a proportion of GDP fell from 11.5 to 4.9 percentage points from 1983 to 1988.

Local authorities are responsible for such local services as provision of public housing, construction and maintenance of roads, water supplies and sanitary services, refuse collection, environmental protection and fire services. Approximately half of their spending is funded by Exchequer grants, most of which are specific grants and the rest of their funding is raised at local level. The principal source of local revenue is obtained from rates on commercial property which are levied by individual local authorities. Practically all of their capital expenditure is provided by Exchequer grants. Within broad policy parameters and cash limits on grants set by Government local authorities have freedom of operation. They have power to borrow funds subject to the approval of the Minister for the Environment. In practice regular borrowing is confined to the provision of temporary working capital requirements which is usually raised with banks acting as their treasurers.

Local authorities act as agents for Government in delivering social services only in the housing area and payment of education grants. Social services such as Education and Welfare Income Supports are provided directly by Government Departments while the major part of the health services are administered by the Regional Health Boards.

The nation's health services are administered on a regional basis. The Health Act of 1970 set up a regional administrative structure under eight health Boards which have responsibility for the day-to-day implementation of Government health policy. Of total gross public expenditure on health care about 70 per cent is spent by the Health Boards; the remaining 30 per cent is spent by other state-funded health agencies including voluntary hospitals and homes for the mentally handicapped. Almost all of the Health Board's expenditure is financed by the Exchequer.

Social security payments are either of a Social Insurance or a Social Assistance nature. Social Security spending provides comprehensive cover and extends to a wide range of services covering unemployment, sickness, retirement, old age and family support.

Social Assistance schemes, which are funded exclusively by the Exchequer, are means-tested payments. On the other hand, Social Insurance payments are paid from the Social Insurance Fund, an extra-budgetary fund, to people who satisfy certain contribution records. The Fund is financed by contributions from employers, employees and the self-employed at rates determined annually by the Government in the context of the Budget. Any gap between receipts and expenditure is bridged by the Exchequer via the Department of Social Welfare. Any changes in contribution rates, benefits or entitlement conditions requires Parliamentary approval.

State bodies are considered either commercial or non-commercial, the latter category defined as not being involved in the production and marketing of goods and services. Apart from relatively small amounts of own resources generated from the marketing of services to clients, the current and capital resources of the non-commercial State bodies consist of Exchequer grants channelled to them via their parent Departments. In principle the commercial State bodies are expected to operate without continuing Exchequer support. Trading activities of these bodies are not reflected in the budget accounts.

---

* The Budget, with capital ''B'', refers mainly to the Government's proposals for taxation.

The capital investment programmes of the commercial State-sponsored agencies are approved each year by the Government and provided for in the annual Public Capital Programme (see below) which specifies the mix of Exchequer capital, internally generated funds and external finance in total project financing. As stated above, commercial state bodies are expected to operate without continuing Exchequer support. However, as the State is normally the sole shareholder of these bodies the Exchequer has on occasions been obliged to provide (balance sheet) reconstruction finance by way of loans or share purchase under statutory authority for bodies which have encountered financial difficulties.

Most commercial State-sponsored bodies also benefit to some degree from a State guarantee of their borrowings. However, in line with Government policy of reducing the level of such guarantees, the proportion of commercial State-sponsored body debt under guarantee fell from 92 per cent at end-1986 to 75 per cent at end-1990. The dependence of non-commercial State bodies on the Exchequer for resources varies according to the nature of the body and the activities it is engaged in. Overall the non-commercial sector derives about 30 per cent of its funding from non-Exchequer sources. Since 1983 commercial State agencies have been required to submit five-year corporate plans to their parent department and to the Department of Finance. These plans must now also be rolled over annually.

The Government is prepared to consider private sector involvement in the commercial State-sponsored sector through, for example, share ownership or joint venture, if this is shown to be in the best interests of the company and the economy. In 1991, the Government reduced the State's shareholding in the former State-owned company Irish Sugar plc to 45 per cent while it reduced its shareholding in Irish Life plc to 34 per cent. In 1993, the State disposed of its remaining shareholding in the Irish Sugar Company (now Greencore) and sold off a further 18.1 per cent of its shareholding in Irish Life plc. Both companies now have Stock Exchange listings.

Both a current and a capital budget exist. The current budget comprises the Exchequer financed, current expenditure as well as all Central Fund financed expenditure. The capital budget comprises *i)* all loans, grants and investments, which lead to the creation of fixed capital under the Public Capital Programme; and *ii)* certain other capital payments relating mainly to the restructuring of commercial state bodies which are described as non-programme outlays.

The Public Capital Programme includes the planned investment of central Government, local authorities and State-sponsored bodies. This expenditure is financed both from Exchequer and non-Exchequer sources. The non-Exchequer comprises State-sponsored bodies' own resources (55 per cent) (trading receipts, depreciation funds), borrowing (34 per cent) and EC Structural Fund Receipts (11 per cent). (Percentages are based on 1991 budget figures.) Capital expenditure may be either voted or non-voted. In the former case, the annual Estimates/Appropriation Act provide the necessary authority for expenditure while, in the latter case, Parliament, having determined in legislation specific limits on capital expenditure/borrowing for particular State companies, does not also require the Government to seek authority for annual expenditure within these approved ceilings.

A breakdown of current and capital expenditure by functional classification indicating the percentage share of the total for each area in the 1991 Budget is set out below.

C. BUDGET FORMULATION STRATEGY AND PROCESS

1. Strategic aims and global norms

Medium-term targets are communicated in multi-year economic plans. For example, the economic plan, Programme for Economic and Social Progress, published in January 1991, covered the period 1991 to 1993. The Programme's objectives for the public finances were to maintain a significant rate of progress in reducing the Debt/GNP ratio towards 100 per cent, and as part of this, to achieve broad balance on the current budget.

2. Technical aspects of multi-year estimates

Although there is at present no formalised system of detailed medium-term expenditure allocations in operation, spending Departments, in submitting their annual demands for resources, must provide details of forecast resource requirements for three to four years ahead. These are rolled forward annually and form a valuable input into medium-term economic and budgetary management by the Department of Finance.

Table 1. **Functional classification of gross central government current expenditure (1991)**

As percentage of total

Debt service	22
Economic services	
Industry, tourism and labour	2
Agriculture, fisheries and forestry	4
Infrastructure	
Roads, transport and sanitary services	1
Social Services	
Health	13
Education	12
Social security	27
Housing and subsidies	2
Security	7
Other [1]	10
Total	100

1. Includes Central Fund Services other than debt service.
Source: OECD.

Table 2. **Functional classification of capital budget expenditure**

As percentage of total

Sectoral economic investment	
Industry and tourism	22
Agriculture, fisheries and forestry	10
Productive infrastructure	
Roads and sanitary services	16
Transport	15
Energy	10
Telecommunications, postal service and broadcasting	
Social infrastructure	
Hospitals	2
Education	3
Housing	8
Government construction	5
Total	100

Source: Budget Tables and the Public Capital Programme, published in the *Budget Booklet 1991* (see Section H).

Table 3. **Fiscal indicators, 1984-91**

	1984	1985	1986	1987	1988*	1989	1990	1991 (est.)
Current budget deficit [1]	7.0	8.2	8.3	6.5	1.7	1.3	0.7	1.0
Exchequer borrowing requirement [1]	12.4	12.9	12.8	9.9	3.3	2.3	2.0	1.9
Public sector borrowing requirement [1]	16.2	15.5	14.9	11.4	4.0	3.2	3.0	3.4
Aggregate current spending [2]+	6.7	7.4	7.9	8.0	8.0	8.0	8.4	9.0
Aggregate public capital expenditure [2]	1.7	1.7	1.6	1.6	1.3	1.4	1.7	1.8

* Includes Tax Amnesty.
+ Reflects net non-capital spending and central fund services.
1. As percentage of GDP.
2. £billion.
Source: Summary of Current and Capital Budgets, published in the *Budget Booklet* (see Section H); Public Sector Borrowing Requirement, Department of Finance.

3. Calendar of main points of decision-making and activities

The fiscal year [FY(t)] is the calendar year (year t).

Months before start of FY (t)	Main events and activities
(Year t – 1)	
9-7 (April-June)	Government approves targets for the CBD, EBR and PSBR.
7 (June)	DF issues guidelines to spending Departments, which inter alia explain the parameters with which the budget will operate and which seek appropriate adjustments to existing spending plans.
6-4 (July-September)	Departments submit draft expenditure estimates to DF for examination. Subsequently, DF briefs government, which makes decisions on detailed budget strategies.
4-3 (September-October)	DF discussions with departments.
2-1 (November-December)	Publication of detailed estimates after agreement by the Government, that provide the basis for seeking appropriations from Parliaments.
(Year t)	
0 (1 January)	Start of fiscal year (t).
(+) Budget Day, late January	The *Dail* deliberates and decides by way of financial resolution on those taxation proposals that require immediate decision and on any changes in expenditure allocations.
(+3) March	Revised Estimates are published.
(+4/+5) April-May	Enactment of Finance Bill.

4. The annual budget cycle

Work on the budget generally begins in the second quarter of the year. The Government is presented with an analysis of economic and budget prospects for the following year and on the basis of this information is requested to approve broad budgetary targets. Once the Government has adopted targets, guidelines are issued to other Departments by the Department of Finance (usually around June) setting out the parameters within which expenditure estimates for the following year must be drawn up (but see also Section D re Expenditure Reviews).

Draft estimates of expenditure are generally received by the Department of Finance in late August/early September and are reviewed in the context of the latest assessment of overall budget prospects. The Minister for Finance then briefs the Government and the broad outline of budget strategy is defined in greater detail. On this basis he settles with his colleagues, either individually or at Government level, the estimates for individual Departments. This process, part of which is carried out at official level, generally occupies the period September-October. The detailed estimates when agreed by the Government are published in advance of the Budget.

The final elements of the budget are refined right up to Budget Day. Certain additional expenditure allocations are traditionally made on budget day (*e.g.* provision for increases in rates of welfare payments) and the possibility of other expenditure revisions, downward as well as up, which might be required in the light of the most up-to-date assessment is not precluded. Decisions are made on specific changes in taxation and other financial adjustments within the broad parameters of tax policy settled earlier. These are announced on Budget Day. Detailed changes are incorporated in the annual Finance Bill which is introduced some two months after Budget Day. The Finance Bill must be enacted within four months of Budget Day. Changes to the published Estimates are incorporated in revised Estimates which are published usually in March.

D. EXPENDITURE REVIEW

Following the completion of the 1987 Budget, the Prime Minister initiated a system of expenditure reviews. The process required all Departments to carry out a policy-based review of their expenditure programmes.

Programmes were examined by an Expenditure Review Committee to see if they were justified on their merits and in relation to the Government's objectives for the economy. The Expenditure Review Committee comprised the Secretary and other senior officers of the Department of Finance, the Accounting Officer (usually the Secretary) of the Department concerned and an independent consultant economist. The Committee reported to the Government on the outcome of its meetings with the spending Departments and made recommendations for expenditure cuts to Cabinet for consideration and decision. The exercise was co-ordinated by the Department of Finance and was repeated each year up to 1990. In returning their estimates bids, Departments reflected all policy decisions made by the Government in the Review Process. Inevitably, the initial impact of this initiative quickly diminished, and the system of expenditure reviews was discontinued after 1990.

In 1988, the Government, again at the initiative of the Prime Minister, established the Efficiency Audit Group to examine the workings and practices of each Government Department with a view to recommending improved or alternative practices and methods which would reduce costs and improve efficiency. The Group includes senior representatives from the private and public sectors and reports to the Prime Minister whose Department provides the secretariat for the Group.

Among its activities to date, the Group has recommended a system of delegated administrative budgets for Departments which is now being implemented (see Section F) and has completed efficiency scrutinies of the Departments of Defence and Industry and Commerce. Further efficiency scrutinies of other Government departments are envisaged.

In addition to these higher level scrutinies, management surveys on selected programmes or blocks of work in spending Departments are carried out by the Management Services Unit of the Department of Finance, by locally-based qualified staff in Departments or by joint teams comprising representatives from both areas.

The Operations Research and Analysis Section of the Department of Finance also provides consultancy services to Departments in the areas of logistics and policy review.

At a parliamentary level, the Public Accounts Committee of the *Dail* examines and reports on the regularity and propriety of public expenditure which has been incurred by Departments; the Committee also deals with questions of economy and efficiency brought to notice by the Comptroller and Auditor General in his reports.

E. IMPLEMENTATION OF THE BUDGET

1. Major instruments of in-year control

Public expenditure may only be undertaken with the authority of Parliament given in either the annual Appropriation Act or in specific enabling legislation. In addition it requires the sanction of the Minister for Finance which may either be specific (for once-off expenditures) or delegated.

Expenditure not having the sanction of the Minister for Finance cannot be charged against money voted by Parliament. If spending Departments enter into commitments which do not have this authority, sanction may be withheld if the Department of Finance determines that the commitments ought not to have been incurred.

In Ireland, capital expenditure commitments for succeeding years are limited administratively to 65 per cent of the current budget year's allocation. This figure may, however, be varied with the specific approval of the Minister for Finance. All departments and State bodies under their responsibility report each month on the level of contractual commitments and other quasi-contractual commitments entered into for the following year.

To ensure tight control of expenditure and adequate notice of potential deviations from target departments are required to submit a profile of expenditure by month to the Department of Finance for approval at the beginning of the year, and monthly returns of actual and forecast expenditure including explanations of variations from profile.

If actual expenditure in any given month is less than the amount specified in the approved profile for that month, this will normally be regarded as a saving for the year, *i.e.* is not available for spending later in the year. Approval for expenditure in a particular month in excess of the approved profile is only given where there is a clear-cut understanding that it will be offset by specific compensating measures later in the year.

The transfer of savings from one Vote (area of expenditure) to meet overruns on another Vote is never permitted. The process of *"virement"*, the application, under the specific authority of the Minister for Finance, of savings on one or more subheads to meet excess expenditure on another subhead or subheads, is only permitted within an individual vote and under strict rules. Where additional resources are required for an individual vote over that originally provided in the budget, this is done by means of a supplementary estimate. Each supplementary estimate must be approved by the Minister for Finance and voted upon by Parliament. Government accounting is operated on a cash-based receipts and payments system.

The system is, therefore, a non-cumulative one and any unspent allocations remaining at the end of a year cannot be carried forward but must be surrendered to the Exchequer. An exception to this (but one which still requires surrender to the Exchequer at year-end) is the provision under the initiative on delegated administrative budgets (see Section F) whereby savings up to certain limits made by a Department on its administrative budget allocation in one year may be reallocated to it in the following year.

Data on Exchequer-financed income and expenditure is published twice monthly. At the end of each quarter in the fiscal year, the Government presents an analysis of the detailed budgetary data for that quarter, assesses the trends in the year to date and gives a view as to the likely outcome for the rest of the year. If corrective action to ensure adherence to budget targets is decided upon, information to this effect is provided to Parliament.

2. Managerial discretion

Under statute each Minister is responsible to Parliament for all policy matters. The civil service head of a Department (its Secretary) is normally appointed Accounting Officer by the Minister for Finance to be responsible to Parliament (through the Public Accounts Committee) for the proper expenditure of money from his Vote in execution of the policy of his Minister. The Accounting Officer is personally responsible for the safeguarding of public funds and property under his control, for the regularity and propriety of all the transactions in each Appropriation Account bearing his signature and also for the efficiency and economy of administration in his Department. This legal responsibility cannot be delegated to subordinate officers. However the Accounting Officer can and does delegate managerial responsibilities for the day-to-day administration of his Department and the areas for which it has responsibility.

F. RECENT REFORMS

There have been a number of initiatives in relation to Public Sector Management Reform in recent years. These include:

- a public service embargo on recruitment;
- a voluntary redundancy/early retirement scheme;
- the introduction of Three Year Administrative Budgets;
- the publication of expanded guidelines on financial management for Government Departments and Offices published in Public Financial Procedures – an Outline;
- the relocation of sections of Central Government Departments from Dublin to regional centres;
- the establishment by Government of an Efficiency Audit Group which is reviewing particular departments (see Section D foregoing);
- the introduction of a performance-related pay scheme for the Civil Service Assistant Secretary grade (*i.e.* the second level in the top management hierarchy); and
- the completion of strategic information technology plans for most Civil Service departments which has been accompanied by a significant increase in the level of investment in information technology by departments.

While each of these initiatives is expected to make a significant contribution to public sector management reform, the public service embargo and voluntary redundancy schemes and more recently the introduction of Three Year Administrative Budgets for most Civil Service Departments are seen as the most important budgetary initiatives impacting on the resource allocation process and in particular on human resource management.

An embargo on recruitment in the entire public service was introduced in 1987. Redeployment of surplus staff from declining work areas to more essential areas was used to minimise disruption to essential services. The success of this method was limited by the voluntary nature of such redeployment, under agreements with the trade unions.

In July 1987 a voluntary redundancy/early retirement scheme was introduced and made available in areas of the public service where it was clear that there were staff surplus to actual requirements. In November 1987 it was extended until end-1988 to personnel aged 50 and over in the Civil Service, non-commercial State bodies and health boards. In 1989 the scheme was again restricted to redundant staff and it was effectively brought to a close at end-1990. In the period 1987 to 1990 some 10 000 public service staff availed of the scheme at a cost of some £125 million.

In the light of a 15 per cent reduction in the non-industrial Civil Service since 1981 (from 32 100 to 27 300 at end 1990) and a reduction in the public service as a whole of about 9 per cent over the same period, the current emphasis of Government policy is on consolidating the reductions achieved. Accordingly, the embargo and early retirement programmes have effectively been replaced by the Administrative Budgets initiative.

The major policy objectives of the Administrative Budget initiative introduced in 1991 are to:

- reduce the cost of running each department by 2 per cent in 1992 and a further 2 per cent in 1993 in constant 1991 terms;
- improve efficiency and effectiveness in each department through:
  - delegating greater authority from the Minister for Finance to line departments in relation to administrative expenditure and related matters;
  - encouraging and facilitating the delegation of greater authority to individual line managers in departments in relation to administrative expenditure.

The Three Year Administrative Budget Agreement for each department:

- defines the expenditure areas covered by reference to the published book of Estimates;
- states the aggregate amount to be provided for these services in 1991, 1992 and 1993 in constant 1991 terms;
- specifies the circumstances in which these amounts will be increased/decreased;
- allows the transfer of resources from one subhead to another and the effective carryforward of savings from one financial year to another within well-defined limits and subject to clear conditions;
- provides for a monitoring group representative of the Department of Finance and the department concerned to oversee the operation of the agreement and resolve any difficulties arising.

Administrative Budget Agreements on these lines covering the years 1991-93 were in operation in twenty-three departments/offices employing some twenty-two thousand staff or 80 per cent of the civil service. The total expenditure covered by the Agreements was £560 million in 1991 terms. The only increases allowed in respect of this expenditure in any year are those associated with changes in pay rates which have been centrally negotiated. An extension of Administrative Budget Agreements to cover the years 1994 to 1996 was recently agreed upon with individual departments.

The introduction of this framework marks a significant change in the relationships between the Department of Finance and line departments and is in line with developments in other administrations. However it does not of itself ensure that the more fundamental delegation of authority to individual line managers will occur. In order to encourage and facilitate this further delegation the agreements between the Department of Finance and line departments require each line department to prepare a plan for internal delegation of authority in relation to administrative expenditure. Such plans are expected to have regard to the size, business needs and culture of the department in question. The implementation of change in this area is expected to be spread over several years. However, a start has been made in several departments in the identification of appropriate cost centres and corresponding budget holders. Work in this area is being supported from the centre by a training and research programme and by the development of a computerised financial management system, which it is expected, will be of particular benefit to the smaller and medium-sized departments.

Circular 1/1983 which outlines procedures to be followed in the appraisal and management of major capital projects is presently under review.

In addition the booklet on Government Contracts Procedures which codifies procedures which must be adhered to relating to the award of public contracts in Ireland, is being updated to take account of recent EC developments affecting public procurement, most notably progress towards the Single European Market.

G. FURTHER INFORMATION

1. Documents related to annual budget

The fiscal year is the calendar year (year t).

1. *Estimates for Public Services (Abridged Version),* otherwise known as The Abridged Estimates Volume, contains pre-budget estimates of Departmental Expenditure [November/December (t – 1)].
2. *Summary Public Capital Programme,* sets out in summary form the planned investment programme of government departments. Local Authorities and State-sponsored bodies and its financing [November/December (t – 1)].

3. *White Paper on Estimates of Receipts and Expenditure,* contains pre-budget estimates of total Exchequer receipts and expenditure, giving the opening budget position [January (t)].

4. *Revised Estimates for Public Services,* which is published on a post-budget basis is otherwise known as The Estimates Volume and contains fuller details of Departmental spending allocations, March (t).

5. *The Budget booklet,* contains the financial statement of the Minister for Finance, the principal features of the Budget and the financial resolutions to give effect to those taxation measures which are intended to have effect before the Finance Bill is enacted. It also contains *The Public Capital Programme* which sets out in detail the planned investment programmes of Government Departments, local authorities and state bodies. It also sets out the Exchequer and other financing commitments necessary for the implementation of investment plans for the year in question, March (t).

6. *The Finance Accounts,* give detailed information on receipts into and expenditure from the Exchequer in the previous financial year. They also include details of a number of Departmental funds/accounts and detailed statements of national debt and guaranteed borrowings, June (t).

7. *The Appropriation Accounts,* are the accounts prepared in each Department in respect of the monies voted by the *Dail* and administered by it in the previous year. The accounts when certified and reported on by the Comptroller and Auditor General are printed in a single volume and submitted to the *Dail,* by 31 October (t + 1).

8. *Report of the Committee of Public Accounts.* When the Committee of Public Accounts concludes its examination of the Appropriation Accounts for a particular year, it presents its final report on them to the *Dail,* no fixed publication date.

2. Other documents

Comprehensive Public Expenditure Programme (published periodically), sets out public expenditure in programme form together with policy statements and description of activities. Data on outputs and performance indicators are also included. The booklet, which first appeared in pilot form in 1983, now contains programme material for all public expenditure areas.

In years when no "Comprehensive" volume is published, a shorter volume "Summary of Public Expenditure programmes" is produced which presents financial data on public spending in a programme format. This volume does not contain detailed statements of programme policies or activities.

Programme for Economic and Social Progress, is an agreement between the Government and the Social Partners on a strategy to accelerate economic and social progress in the nineties. January 1991.

Public Financial Procedures – An Outline, gives a synopsis of Government accounting principles, procedures and terminology, covers the relevant constitutional and statutory provisions, and sets out the principles of financial management to be observed by Government Departments and Offices, August 1990.

NOTE: All the above publications are obtainable from Stationery Office, Dublin.

ITALY

**Any changes which have taken place in Italy
since May 1994 are not reflected in this chapter**

A. INSTITUTIONAL STRUCTURE OF BUDGETARY DECISION-MAKING

1. Political and organisational structure of government

Italy is a unitary State. There are four layers of government: State or central level, regional level, provincial level, and municipalities. The provincial level is by far the smallest of the four in financial terms.

Today, central government functions are organised mainly around 20 ministries and some agencies. Ministries have one Minister, and, in general, one (or more) Secretary of State. The head of a department is a political appointee, as opposed to the rest of the departmental personnel who are career civil servants.

Parliament has two Chambers: the "*Camera dei deputati*" (Lower House) and the "*Senato della Repubblica*" (Senate). In both Chambers three political groups (constituted by 13 parties and movements) are represented and one of them has an absolute majority in the Lower House. Today the 20 minister cabinet is based on a coalition of four parties and movements that are the expression of current majority. In general, Ministers are members of Parliament. Direct elections for both Chambers, to be held regularly every 5 years, were held in March 1994.

A coalition agreement is normally at the basis of every government. The current coalition agreement contains paragraphs on the budgetary policy to be conducted.

2. Main budgetary organs

The central role in all budgetary matters is played by the Ministry of Treasury, which is separate from the Ministry of Finance. The Treasury is responsible for both the expenditure and revenue side of the budget. The Treasury is also responsible for the debt-servicing programme.

The responsibility for economic and fiscal policy-making is shared between the Ministry of Finance and the Economic Planning Ministry: the first has the lead in fiscal revenue policies (taxes and other revenues), the second in macroeconomic forecasting. The Economic Planning Ministry also provides estimates in the budget of the costs of new public investment projects.

Most functions of the budget office are performed by a department within the Treasury, the State's General Accounts Department (*Ragioneria Generals dello Stato* – RGS). In addition to monitoring and controlling central government payments and receipts, RGS co-ordinates the medium-term planning process and the process for preparation of the budget. The central part of RGS is divided into nine Inspectorates, each of them dealing with a sectoral or regional spending area. Within the Budget Inspectorate, a central division co-ordinates the preparation of the budget.

RGS also operates decentralised accounting units in each ministry, region and province performing internal audit functions. Staff numbers are around 7 900, of which 690 are management staff.

3. Role of Prime Minister and Cabinet

The Prime Minister has no special prerogatives in budgeting, apart from his political role as leader of Cabinet.

Every year he presents to the Parliament the Goals Document, drafted by Treasury, Finance and Economic Planning Ministries. The Prime Minister heads the Economic Planning Committee (CIPE), composed of 12 ministers representing the main spending and financial departments. The main budgetary guidelines concerning, for example, stabilisation of fiscal pressure (*i.e.* government revenues), the reduction of current expenditure and the control of public debt, proposed by the Treasury and Economic Planning Ministers, are examined and approved by this Committee before submission to Cabinet.

The Cabinet agrees on the budget before it is submitted to Parliament following the same procedure as with any other draft bill.

4. Role of Parliament

Every year, the budget documents are submitted by the Government, either first to the *Camera dei Deputati* and subsequently to the *Senato della Repubblica,* or *vice versa.*

In both Chambers, a central role is played by the Budget Committee (in the Lower House) and the Treasury and Finance Committee (in the Senate). Both Committees prepare the discussion of laws in their respective Chambers. Their function is also to verify and to guarantee the financial coverage for all new expenditure laws.

The two Chambers have an equally important position regarding all sorts of laws, including budgetary laws. When Chambers disagree with each other the law is examined again (and modified) following the same procedure.

The Italian budget system contains four important elements: the Goals Document, the Finance Act, the annual budget (or Appropriation Act, the annual budget) and the multi-year budget.

The Goals Document presents medium term economic forecasts for revenue, expenditure and public debt, and identifies the measures necessary for them to become compatible. It identifies the main elements of the budgetary framework to be decided upon before more detailed actions are taken on the Finance Bill and the Appropriations Bill. The most important elements are the minimum increase in revenues, the maximum rate of growth for current and capital expenditure, respectively, and some specific rates of growth for detailed aspects such as staff, and current and capital grants.

The Finance Bill, introduced by the budget reform of 1978, and revised in 1988, is enacted by Parliament prior to the Appropriation Bill. The Finance Bill sets a framework for parliamentary debate and decision-making on the Appropriation Bill.

The Finance Act stipulates:

a) a ceiling on Treasury borrowing requirements in commitment-terms;

b) special reserves for new legislation likely to be passed during the financial year. All new legislation must be incorporated within the Finance Bill. These reserves amount to 4-5 per cent of global expenditure on average;

c) adjustments to multi-year expenditure. These adjustments are made in particular by deferring or advancing multi-year expenditure. Reference levels of multi-year expenditure are incorporated in an annex to the Finance Bill. When this Bill is approved, the (amended) reference levels are incorporated in the Appropriation Bill.

Until 1988, the Finance Act could change substantive legislation; this meant that it was possible to modify the existing laws or to create others ex-novo. Since the reform of 1988, the Finance Act cannot be used to change substantive legislation. To do so now requires special legislation, presented concurrently with the Finance Bill. When passed, the content of the Finance Act and Special Bills are incorporated into the Appropriation Bill by means of a "modifying note". This is a special amendment to the Appropriation Bill containing all the rules created and/or modified by the Finance Act and Special Acts.

Before appropriating funds, Parliament first decides the amount of total revenues and total expenditures. Annual budget funds are appropriated both in commitment and in cash terms. Parliament controls expenditure at the level of approximately 6 000 items.

All central government expenditure is appropriated annually. Both Chambers have the right to add to or modify proposed revenue and expenditure.

While enacting the Appropriation Bill, Parliament also approves the (amended) multi-year budget (for three years) in commitment terms: modifications and approvals do not relate to individual budget items but to economic and functional blocks of expenditure.

Budgetary laws, in comparison to any other law, can no longer be backed by a "secret vote". As a result it is now clear to other deputies to political groups and the public who votes in favour or against. "Secret vote" suppression reduces the capacity for deputies to vote contrary to their party's policy.

Parliament has to pass Appropriation Bills before the start of the fiscal year; under extraordinary circumstances it can provisionally authorise by law the budget proposed by the Government for a maximum period of 4 months.

B. THE SCOPE AND NATURE OF GOVERNMENT FINANCES

General Government expenditure is among the highest in the OECD area, as was its growth in the period 1974-94. Net borrowing remained high, for both general and central government.

The internal structure of the public sector can be characterised as follows. Local authorities (regions, provinces and municipalities) are dependent on central government's transfers and therefore their spending possibilities are limited. Local authority spending is also controlled by central government restrictions on capital market borrowing and on taxation capacities. Recently, central government has restituted limited taxation powers to regions in order to reduce, directly, the deficit in the health system. In general, the control on local authorities activities is restricted to aspects of legitimacy; local authorities are free to spend funds in whatever direction they like. Local authorities generally provide local services. Local governments act as an agent of central government in providing some services, mainly in the health sector, law and order and matters of primary education.

Apart from central departments, central government is made up of several subsidised autonomous agencies, enterprises, and funds. In general, central government establishes goals and targets to be achieved by authorities, provides them with the financial means, and leaves authorities free to devise the means to achieve their targets.

The social security and health system are mainly financed by contributions from employers and employees. Supplementary transfers are made by central government. The Cabinet proposes, and the Parliament determines by law, conditions of entitlement and contribution levels. The programmes are carried out by means of a special agency (National Social Security Institute – INPS).

Public enterprises, which sell their goods and services to the public, receive contributions and subsidies from central government to cover deficits. They can borrow funds to finance their investments, but in general, government authorisation is required.

C. BUDGET FORMULATION STRATEGY AND PROCESS

1. Strategic aims and global norms

The most important target is the Treasury Borrowing Requirement in nominal terms, which is to be stabilised from year to year. The Treasury Borrowing Requirement is defined to cover the so-called enlarged public sector, *i.e.* general government including autonomous and municipal institutions, governmental non-profit institutions, health service agencies and the national electricity corporation (ENEL). This concept of the deficit, expressed in cash terms, includes loans made by the government.

Current budget policies are aimed at progressing toward Maastricht targets:
  a) reducing the annual State borrowing requirement to 3 per cent of GDP by 1997;
  b) reducing public debt to 60 per cent of GDP by the same time. Both targets require reduction of borrowing and a serious budget policy aimed at primary surplus (excluding interest cost or accumulated debt).

The State Borrowing Requirement, established by the Finance Act, represents the difference between the total amount of revenue and expenditure in commitment terms. The following table indicates performance against this budgetary indicator:

Table 1. **Fiscal indicators, 1986-94**

As percentage of GDP
Annual Treasury Borrowing Requirement

1986	12.2
1987	10.2
1988	10.0
1989	9.8
1990	10.1
1991	9.9
1992	10.3
1993	9.7
1994 (estimate)	8.8

Source: Ministry of Treasury, Italy.

2. Technical aspects of multi-year estimates

Multi-year budgeting commenced with the introduction of the Finance Act, which was itself one of the results of the budget reforms (law) of 1978. Multi-year budgets are prepared in two versions each year. The first version, which is known as the "trend" version, is a projection of revenues and expenditures under current policy.

This multi-year "trend" budget is supplemented by a "planning scenario" version consistent with economic policy guidelines. Parliament approves the multi-year budgets, but approval does not mean authorisation to collect or disburse funds in this case. The multi-year budget "trend version" is a means to control new expenditure by the Treasury and by Parliament since it includes special reserves (global funds) for new legislation likely to be passed during the new fiscal year. The multi-year budget, when approved, defines the limits within which new expenditure for the second and the third year of the forecasting period may be proposed and approved.

Multi-year budgets are based on commitments. They reflect proposed government policy with respect to the new budget and its multi-year consequences. They cover a period of 3 years including the upcoming budget-year. The "trend version", based on current legislation, is initially prepared by spending departments and reviewed by the Treasury and updated once a year after the Finance Bill has been enacted.

Multi-year estimates are published once a year, showing the breakdown for expenditure according to institutional purposes and economic interventions. They are not updated during implementation of the budget.

3. Calendar of main points of decision-making and activities

The fiscal year [FY(t)] is the calendar year (t).

Months before start of FY (t)	Main events and activities
(Year t – 1)	
February-March	Treasury issues technical guidelines on the preparation of the budget.
April-May	Ministries submit their new budgets to the Treasury. Start of Treasury negotiations with each Ministry.
15 May	Prime Minister presents to Parliament the Goals Document drafted by Treasury, Finance and Economic Planning Ministries.
July	Treasury and Ministry of Economic Planning submit budgetary policy guidelines to the Economic Planning Committee (CIPE) and to the regions.
31 July	Cabinet agrees on budget and submits budget documents, based on the current legislation, to Parliament.
July-September	CIPE examines and approves budgetary guidelines, approves Overall Programming Report.
30 September	Cabinet agrees on Finance Bill, Special Bill and the multi-year budgets and submits them to Parliament to be enacted before start of fiscal year.
(Year t)	
0 (1st January)	Start of fiscal year (t).

4. The annual budget cycle

In February/March, the Treasury issues a circular which sets out the methods and basic criteria on which to base the annual commitment and cash budgets and the multi-year budgets.

The ministries send their budget bids to the Treasury in April/May and protracted consultations between the Treasury and departments follow. In general, budgets are based on current legislation and proposals for new policies which from a sectoral point of view are deemed necessary.

The first task of the Treasury is to evaluate the proposed budget as a whole and form a view of the guidelines necessary to make it consistent with the overall economic policy framework. In mid-May the Prime Minister presents to Parliament the Goals Document, drafted by Treasury, Financial, and Economic Planning Ministries. A first budget forecast is submitted to the Ministry for Economic Planning at the beginning of July and the proposal for main guidelines is then worked out jointly by this ministry and the Treasury.

The Treasury, in agreement with the Economic Planning Ministry, submits before the end of July the main guidelines for both annual and multi-year budgets to the Economic Planning Committee (CIPE). This committee examines and approves them before 15th September. It also approves the overall programming report, including the government's global budgetary strategy.

Before the end of July, the main guidelines are also presented to the regions and commented on by the Inter-regional Commission, a consultative body composed of the presidents of all the regions.

The budget based on current legislation is approved by Cabinet in July and presented to Parliament before 31st July.

In September, Cabinet agrees on the Finance Bill, Special Bill, and the multi-year budgets and submits them to Parliament to enact before the start of fiscal year.

D. EXPENDITURE REVIEW

An annual document attached to the General Report on Accounts constitutes a detailed instrument specifically designed to assess the effects of public policies. This document, called ''cost-benefit analysis'', presents data on economic trends and administrative activity in the current year, and in particular the costs incurred and the results obtained by each service, programme and project as compared with the aims and overall thrust of the government's programme. This document is required to serve not only as a means of reasserting the essential character of the financial results for the year but, above all, to fulfil the more decisive task of verifying the effectiveness of the totality of State intervention. This procedure can represent a critical means by which cut-back proposals for the new budget can be created.

E. IMPLEMENTATION OF THE BUDGET

1. Major instruments of in-year control

Once the Appropriation Act has been passed, any proposal to increase expenditure must, according to constitutional requirements, specify its source of finance, *i.e.* offsetting expenditure cuts or increased receipts. The same rule applies to reduction in revenues. The Treasury Borrowing Requirement is not allowed to increase during the implementation of the budget. The requirement to offset expenditure increases applies to every kind of expenditure; this constitutional requirement is applied to both the cash and commitments basis of expenditure.

Instruments for adjusting the budget approved by Parliament are the Implementation Act and the Budget Amendment Acts.

The Government is obliged to submit the Implementation Bill (before 30th June), which includes, at the least, changes arising from funds carried forward from the previous financial year. This coincides with the preparation of the General Report on the Accounts. Other amendments to the budget can be incorporated under this Act to take account of changing requirements.

The Budget Amendment Laws, which must be submitted before 31st October, are optional.

Parliament is informed about the development of the Treasury Borrowing Requirement and cash management trends every three months by means of a cash statement report. As an instrument of cash management, public entities are required to deposit their available resources with the Treasury, even though resources come from central government. In so doing, the Treasury's gross borrowing requirement, and related interest payments, can be minimised.

2. Managerial discretion

The different spending centres have responsibility for the effectiveness and efficiency of their expenditure programmes.

Transfers between votes are never possible at managerial level. Unspent funds may be transferred to the next fiscal year, only if liabilities have been incurred. If, by the nature of the expenditure item, a process of cash payments has been set in train, and not yet finished, funds can also be transferred to the next fiscal year.

F.   RECENT REFORMS

The Italian government has taken a number of measures to reorganise and improve the civil service in order to recover efficiency and functionality, to control expenditure and to reduce the deficit.

1.   Reform of public management

The reform of public management (law No. 421/92, legislative decree No. 29/93 and law No. 537/93) aims to reform traditional bureaucratic management patterns to reorient them more towards an enterprise model involving the careful appraisal of outcomes, of users requirements, and of speed and efficiency in delivering services and products.

This change is considered essential in order to modernise public management and the procedures of the civil service. Reforms will focus on:

1. establishing clearer responsibilities for management (defining goals, trends, programme and outcome measurement);
2. increasing managerial flexibility and autonomy with regard to day-to- day management and in the achievement of agreed objectives;
3. increasing managerial accountability with regard to the use of resources in terms of the achievement of outcomes.

An important element of the reform involves the devolution of autonomy in managing budgetary resources to individual line Ministries.

2.   Reform of control

Within the limits of the programme for reorganisation of the civil service the subject of control has been revisited (law No. 19 and 20 of 1994).

The Audit Office (*Corte dei Conti*) is the supreme body in Italy charged to verify administrative activity. The Reform aims to provide the Audit Office with efficacious instruments for the fight against administrative disorder and the waste of public money.

Recent reforms have two main elements:

a) the decentralisation of jurisdiction through the establishment of regional audit jurisdictions in order to follow more closely administrative activity and to facilitate an incisive check on the accountability of managers and public employees at the regional level.
b) the simplification of previous controls. Until now, obligatory *ex ante* controls were a cause for slowing the action of civil service without providing effective control. There has thus been an effort to ''shift'' the action of Audit Office from *ex ante* to *ex post* control of the legitimacy and merits of actions.

3.   Reform of public budget

There currently is a project underway to reform the State budget so as to separate it into two parts: a ''political budget'' (destined for parliamentary approbation) and an ''administrative budget'' (for management and control purposes).

The political budget, focusing on large groups of expenditure and State functions, will address demands for greater clarity in the budget. This presentation will enable the Parliament to focus more on strategic decisions concerning aggregate economic and fiscal activity. The aim is to re-orient parliamentary approval towards the broad functions and objectives of economic policy.

The "administrative budget" would be more detailed identifying the expenditure controls and limits, instruments and objectives which are responsibility of Ministries.

G. THE GOVERNMENT FINANCE OUTLOOK

1. Government finance objectives

In approving the 1994 annual budget, Parliament has provided the Government with the means to pursue its public finance objectives set out in the economic and financial Goals Document presented in July 1994 and approved by both Chambers along with specific resolutions.

These objectives are characterised by their continuity with previous budgetary policies: to reduce the State borrowing requirement (the difference between revenue and expenditure), to maintain a substantial primary surplus and to contain interest payments on the public debt. These are the conditions necessary to reverse the trend of the public debt/GDP ratio and to free the financial resources indispensable to economic growth.

The means of achieving these goals will be, firstly, to curb expenditure still further, while, on the revenue side, significantly lowering fiscal pressure, which will also take into account the downturn in the economic cycle; and, secondly, to speed up the process of privatising public enterprises.

The provisional results of 1993 confirm the trend towards a gradual improvement in government finance: the State borrowing requirement amounted to approximately L 153 trillion, which meant a significant drop in terms of percentage of GDP (from 10.5 to 9.8 per cent); the primary surplus was L 27 trillion, which was over three times higher than the previous year; and the inflation rate remained the same with a yearly average of 4.2 per cent, which was over one point lower than the 1992 average (5.3 per cent).

The Government's public finance targets for the three-year period of 1994-96 are shown in the following table:

Table 2. **The State sector programming account**

In absolute values and as a percentage of GDP

	1994	1995	1996
Revenue	540 203	567 600	598 100
	32.67	32.67	32.70
Expenditure [1]	508 403	521 500	532 600
	30.74	30.02	29.12
Primary surplus	31 800	46 100	65 500
	1.92	2.65	3.58
Interest payments	176 000	173 900	171 900
	10.64	10.01	9.40
Total borrowing requirement	144 200	127 800	106 400
	8.72	7.36	5.82
Debt/GDP ratio	121.4	123.3	123.2

1. Excluding interest and including net financial transactions.
Source: Ministry of Treasury, Italy.

The 1994 annual budget should further reduce the percentage of GDP represented by the State borrowing requirement, which should amount to L 144.2 trillion (8.7 per cent) and should consolidate the growth of the primary surplus.

The main effort will be directed towards reducing expenditure, which will also be accompanied by co-ordinated structural adjustment and institutional reorganisation in general government. This combined with the effects of the reforms already under way, should lower the ratio of expenditure to GDP.

On the revenue side, the tax burden (the ratio of taxes to GDP) imposed by the state sector should decrease by 1.2 percentage points (from 26.9 per cent in 1993 to 25.7 per cent in 1994); this trend should remain constant over the next two years. At the same time the tax system will be simplified and rationalised.

The overall budget should have the effect of maintaining low interest rates and consequently reducing the state sector debt burden (by approximately L 7.5 trillion for 1994 based on the present trend) which would in turn help to lower the borrowing requirement.

The current programme of selling off public assets and enterprises will contribute indirectly to achieving these objectives. The proceeds of the sales will in fact go towards reducing the public debt through a special debt amortisation fund which will allow for savings in future debt servicing expenditures.

2. The 1994 budget and the State balance

The public finance objectives are to be achieved with a smaller budget than in 1993. Excluding interest payments, the 1994 surplus is estimated at approximately L 31 trillion, which equals 1.9 per cent of GDP and from the standpoint of the state sector account can be broken down into an increase in net revenue of L 5 trillion (0.3 per cent of GDP) and a decrease in expenditure of L 26 trillion (1.6 per cent of GDP).

The corrective measures which are being taken through a variety of means primarily concern:

- in the direct taxation field, revision of the system of determining taxable earnings, offset in part by compensation for fiscal drag and lower taxes on primary residences;
- as regards indirect taxes, revision of the payment schedules and the increase in the intermediate VAT rate, as well as adjustment of the manufacturing tax on certain mineral oils;
- in the field of public employment, zero recruitment, staff restructuring, restriction of physicians' use of public health care facilities for part-time private practice and reorganisation of the educational system;
- as regards the organisation of the central government, a broad mandate to restructure ministries, stabilising expenditure on defence and security services, transfer of the funding of certain operations to the regions, restructuring of the postal service and renegotiating of public supply and procurement contracts;
- in social security, gradual raising of the compulsory retirement age, stiffer penalties for early retirement in public employment, and introduction of new forms of contributions for certain types of self-employed work; these steps are offset in part by measures aimed at raising the level of minimum pensions and combatting the job crisis;
- in health care, application of a ceiling to spending on pharmaceuticals, revision of the list of refundable pharmaceutical products and of the system of patients' co-payments, in addition to organisational measures to curb hospital spending;
- in capital expenditure, measures to cut back fixed capital formation, loans to private individuals and public enterprises and transfers to decentralised bodies.

3. The 1994 State budget in commitment terms

The public finance budget has an impact on both the revenue and the expenditure of the State budget. The forecasts in terms of commitments are as follows:

Table 3. **The State budget in commitment terms**

Trillion of lire

	1993 final	1994 provisional
Tax revenue	436 170	446 347
Other revenue	39 149	30 856
Total final revenue	475 319	477 203
Current expenditure (excluding interest payments)	354 666	370 849
Interest payments	183 159	173 000
Capital expenditure	76 204	75 304
Total final expenditure	614 029	619 153
Government savings	–63 268	–67 426
Net balance to be financed	–138 710	–141 950

Source: Ministry of Treasury, Italy.

The following table provides a function classification of expenditure:

Table 4. **The State budget in commitment terms**

Functional classification of expenditure[1]

Trillion of lire

	1993 final	1994 provisional
General government	18 843	18 447
National defence	20 482	19 765
Justice	6 283	6 693
National security	13 701	13 866
International relations	21 508	20 194
Education and culture	50 063	48 950
Universities and scientific research	11 389	11 083
Housing	3 055	2 971
Employment and social security	44 707	48 005
Public welfare	18 274	19 056
Hygiene and health	45 550	46 043
Transport and communications	32 927	34 643
Agriculture and food	5 232	5 722
Industry, trade and crafts	9 713	9 406
Measures in depressed areas	9 292	8 826
Various measures of an economic nature	7 250	6 794
Regional and local finance	65 706	66 854
Civil protection and disaster relief	3 316	2 680
Special and reserve funds	6 717	15 793
Unallocated costs	36 862	40 362
Total final expenditure excluding interest	430 870	446 153
Interest on debt	183 159	173 000
Total final expenditure	614 029	619 153

1. Excluding debts and health contributions transferred to the regions since 1993.
Source: Ministry of the Treasury, Italy.

4. Interest rates

The most substantial savings will be in expenditure on interest payments, which compared to 1993 should drop by approximately L 10 trillion in the State commitment budget and by approximately L 4 trillion in the state sector account.

For the first time there has been a drop in the absolute value of the public debt burden; this can be attributed to the sizeable decrease in interest rates which prevailed, with several interruptions, throughout 1993. Over twelve months the yield of Treasury bills went down by over 5 percentage points.

Expectations regarding a further major drop in interest rates are more guarded. The forecasts estimate that the yield of 12-month Treasury bills will go down by approximately one percentage point.

5. The public debt and the sale of public assets

The drop in the yield of government securities which occurred in 1993 and which is forecast to continue in 1994 is a strategic element for the improvement of government finances. It will help to contain the borrowing requirement, which in turn will reduce the progression of the debt and consequently curb expenditure on interest payments. In past years the combination of the debt service burden with the borrowing requirement had unleashed a destabilising spiral by adding a structural element to the process of degeneration of public accounts.

Continued lower inflation is essential to improving public finance: all things being equal, a slowdown in debtholders' loss of purchasing power will result in a corresponding adjustment of yields. Maintaining stable exchange rates is also of great importance, as it promotes the convergence of Italian exchange rates with those of the rest of Europe, which will reduce their level both in nominal and real terms. The major effort, however, is directed towards managing the public debt by lengthening the maturity of securities and reducing the stock of debt.

The publication of the annual programme of medium and long-term issues should make the market more efficient.

The so-called risk premium (the element which is added to the "normal" interest paid to savers) is determined not only by the size of the borrowing requirement to be funded, but by the stock of securities to be renewed. The disturbing need to renew a debt which is on average extremely short-term makes yields more variable in relation to temporary imbalances between demand and supply of securities and consequently increases the risk premium implicitly required of subscribers.

To reduce the stock of debt there is a need for early implementation of the policy of selling off not only financial assets but also real estate assets; as the proceeds will be used for early repayment of public debt, this will make it possible to reduce both debt service expenditure and the borrowing requirement.

6. Economic conditions and budgetary policy

The public finance budget for the 1994-96 period is based on the medium-term macroeconomic framework which has been presented here.

Whether these public finance objectives can be achieved will therefore depend on whether the forecasts actually prove to be correct.

For 1994 the expected cyclical upswing should make it possible to attain the planned targets provided that economic growth is in line with forecasts. Studies of the effect of variations in GDP on the public budget show that macroeconomic changes have a considerable impact on the borrowing requirement. Finally, these public finance objectives can only be achieved if savings expected from the reorganisation of the government administration are actually realised.

JAPAN

**Any changes which have taken place in Japan
since January 1995 are not reflected in this chapter**

A. INSTITUTIONAL STRUCTURE OF BUDGETARY DECISION-MAKING

1. Political and organisational structure of government

Japan is a unitary state. There are three layers of government: central government, regional governments, mainly "prefectures", and municipalities.

Central government functions are organised mainly among the Prime Minister's Office and 12 Ministries under which several Agencies and Commissions are set up. All ministries and some of the agencies have in general one minister, and one parliamentary vice-minister; the administrative vice-minister and the secretary-general of departments are non-political appointments as are the rest of the departmental personnel.

The Parliament (*Diet*) has two Houses: The House of Representatives and the House of Councillors. In both Houses several political parties are represented: The Liberal Democratic Party (LDP), which has a majority decision, the Social Democratic Party and the new party *Sakigake* are the parties in power. The elections for the House of Representatives are held every four years or in the case of dissolution. The last election was in July 1993. The elections for the House of Councillors are held every three years for half of its members. The last election was in July 1992.

2. Main budgetary organs

The Ministry of Finance (MOF) has main responsibilities concerning both sides of the budget and budgetary policy in general. Within the MOF, the Minister's Secretariat and seven Bureaux are established.

The Budget Bureau of the MOF is in charge of budget formulation. In the Budget Bureau, the Director General co-ordinates the budget-preparation, being assisted by three Deputy Director Generals. Twelve Budget examiners are in charge of budgets of the respective Ministries and agencies. The Budget Bureau holds almost 340 personnel (all grades and supporting staff).

Tax revenues are dealt with by the Tax Bureau of the MOF, which is in charge of the estimation of tax revenues, tax reform etc.

The Financial Bureau is in charge of the Fiscal Investment and Loan Programme (FILP, see Section B).

3. Role of the Prime Minister and the Cabinet

The Cabinet is empowered to prepare the budget and submit it to the *Diet*. The Minister of Finance has prime responsibility for the budget in the Cabinet.

At the beginning of a new budget cycle, the guideline for the budget requests and the general principles of budget formulation, which are the basis of principles of budget formulation and budget preparation, are decided by the Cabinet. The Prime Minister is also involved, if the revival (or second round) negotiations between the MOF and each Minister and Agency cannot be settled when a final decision is made by him.

4. Role of Parliament

The deliberation in the *Diet* of the Budget Proposal begins in the House of Representatives. The Budget Committee of the House of Representatives conducts deliberation on the Budget, and after approval at the plenary session of the House of Representatives it is sent to the House of Councillors around early March.

In the House of Councillors, the Budget Committee conducts deliberations first, and then it entrusts consideration to the respective committees under their jurisdictions. The Budget comes into force following its approval in the plenary session of the House of Councillors. The Budget Committees of both Houses are supported by the Budget Research Office, which provides information for the *Diet*'s deliberation on the budget. Both Houses of the *Diet* can amend the budget and make additions to the expenditures proposed.

When the House of Councillor's decision runs contrary to that of the House of Representatives, a joint conference of the two Houses is held. Subsequently, should the two Houses lack a consensus, the decision of the House of Representatives becomes the decision of the *Diet*, thus recognising the House of Representatives' greater authority regarding the budget.

When the expenditure budget is approved by the *Diet*, the budget is organised according to jurisdictions, organisations and items within a department. There are about 510 items in general account expenditure (FY 95 draft budget).

All central government expenditure is appropriated annually except expenditures previously approved as continued expenses, designed to plan for construction, production, and other projects which extend over several fiscal years before completion. Only in the case of continued expenses does the *Diet* approves multi-year figures.

If the *Diet* does not approve the budget before the start of the new fiscal year (1 April), there is a legal provision on the formulation of the provisional budget for a certain period of the new fiscal year.

B. THE SCOPE AND NATURE OF GOVERNMENT FINANCES

The national government's budget consists of the General Account Budget and 38 Special Account Budgets. The General Account Budget is the basic account to promote the major programmes of the government such as social security which includes transfers to local government's insurance funds and to the related Special Account Budget, and defence, public works, economic co-operation and energy measures. The single word "Budget" often refers to the General Account Budget. The Special Account Budgets are established by legislation. Some Special Accounts have their own distinct source of revenues (see below). The revenue of some Special Accounts may include funds obtained from borrowing.

With respect to the resource allocation to national government and local governments, the following revenues are transferred from the national government to the local public entities:

- Local Allocation Tax, which equals 32 per cent of the revenue from income tax, corporation tax and liquor tax; 24 per cent of consumption tax; and 25 per cent of tobacco tax, is distributed in grants through the Special Account for Allotment of Local Allocation Tax and Transfer Taxes. Local governments can use these grants at their own discretion;
- Local Transfer Taxes are directly received by the Special Account for Allotment of Local Allocation Tax and Transfer Taxes. This category consists of revenues of such taxes as local road tax, and 20 per cent of consumption tax;
- subsidies are provided by the national government to promote specific projects or to carry out programmes on a nation-wide basis.

When local authorities issue local government bonds, they must have the approval of the Minister of Home Affairs.

Budgets of the eleven government affiliated agencies must be submitted to the *Diet* for deliberation and vote. As for other major public corporations, 64 corporations in FY 95, their balance sheets are submitted to the *Diet* for reference during budget deliberation. Budgets, plans for projects and/or financial plans of the public corporations are to be approved by competent Ministers. Furthermore, in the case of most of the corporations, competent Ministers should consult with the Minister of Finance when such approval is given.

At the same time, public corporations subsidised by the government and financed by the Fiscal Investment and Loan Programme (FILP) are controlled indirectly through budget examination for subsidies or programmes.

FILP is formulated every year. It is not a budget, but the Programme is considered as important as the budget.

There are four sources of funds of FILP:

a) loan programme of the Trust Fund Bureau fund (which provide for about 80 per cent of the net total of resources);

b) loan programme of the postal Life Insurance Fund;

c) investment programme of the Industrial Investment Special Account; and

d) programme of government guaranteed bonds and borrowing of which the funds are used for public corporations and agencies, for example Japan Highway Public Corporation.

The FILP is submitted to the *Diet* for its approval since the four above fund sources are part of the budget.

About 5 per cent of the gross total of FILP funds is used to subscribe to Government Bonds. Institutions financed by FILP include certain special accounts of the Government, Local Governments and public institutions which are fully owned by the public sector. Over 70 per cent of the funds of FILP are allocated to the areas of housing, water supply and sewers, welfare facilities, education and to the promotion of small and medium-size enterprises, and agriculture, forestry and fishery. The remainder is made up by road, transport and communication projects. Loans are made available only to those projects which can repay the obligations. However, there are some programmes or projects which have a high priority, but no scope for adequate revenues to fully recover their costs. Such programmes or projects can be financed either by Budget expenditure, or by the FILP loans combined with interest subsidies, or combined with capital expenditure by the budget.

Almost all funds made available by the FILP, are provided as loans, rather than investments, with the exception of the Industrial Investment Special Account.

The functional structure of government expenditure is shown below.

Table 1. **Functional structure of the general account budget (1995)**

As a percentage of total

Social security	20
Education and science	9
National debt servicing costs	19
Pensions and others	2
Local finance (Local allocation tax grants)	19
National defence	7
Public works (General public works)	13
Economic co-operation	1
Small business	0
Energy measures	1
Foodstuff control	0
Miscellaneous	7
Reserves for salary increments	0
Reserves	0
Transfer to the industrial investment special account	2
Total	100

Source: The Budget (see Section G).

C. BUDGET FORMULATION STRATEGY AND PROCESS

1. Strategic aims and global norms

The "general" (mostly discretionary) part of the Budget is only allowed to grow little given that both debt servicing costs and the Local Allocation Tax Transfers are eating up a large share of total expenditure. Additional pressure on Government expenditure will arise as the rapidly growing share of the elderly in the total population towards the 21st century is also taken into account. Therefore, fiscal consolidation has been implemented by reconstructing both the expenditure and revenue side of the budget. In 1990, a new medium-term fiscal policy target was set. Its objective is to restrain the accumulation of outstanding national debt by reducing the dependence rate on government bond issues to less than 5 per cent and by accelerating the redemption of special deficit-financing bonds.

The following table indicates the performance of the budget aggregates:

Table 2. **Fiscal indicators, 1989-95** [1]

	1989	1990	1991	1992	1993	1994	1995
Deficit Financing Bonds (billion yen)	6 639	7 312	6 730	9 538	16 174	14 900	12 598
Dependence rate on Government Bond Issues (Deficit/Total Expenditure) (%)	10.1	10.6	9.5	13.5	21.5	20.6	17.7
Long-term Debt Outstanding/GDP (%)	47.1	46.3	45.8	48.2	52.6	58.4	57.3
Total General Account Expenditure (nominal growth rate %)	7.1	5.1	1.9	−0.1	6.1	−3.7	2.0

1. 1994: Revised Budget, 1995: Draft Budget.
Source: Explanation of the National Budget in detail (see Section H).

2. Technical aspects of multi-year estimates

There is no formalised system of detailed medium-term expenditure estimates in operation. The Ministry of Finance submits to the *Diet* every year the Medium-Term Fiscal Projection, a mechanical projection based on the system and policies of the newest budget and on technical assumptions as regards economic indices, etc. The figures in the projection are not binding at all on the formulation process of the following years' budgets.

3. Calendar of main points of decision-making and activities

The fiscal year (FY) begins on 1 April, ends on 31 March of the following year and is usually indicated as FY(t).

Months before start of FY (t)	Main events and activities
(Year t − 1)	
12-11 (April-May)	Ministries (and Agencies) start preparation of budget requests on next year's budget.
10-9 (June-July)	Cabinet discusses and agrees policy guidelines on budget requests, prepared by MOF.
8 (August)	Ministries submit budget requests to MOF. Ministries submit requests for FILP funds.
7-4 (September-December)	MOF holds budget hearings with Ministries and agencies about budget requests (including requests for FILP funds). MOF negotiations with Ministries take place hierarchically, from lower official levels to Ministerial level (if necessary).
4 (December)	Cabinet decides on budget draft (including FILP programme), taking also into account the macroeconomic outlook for the next fiscal year.
3 (late January)	Cabinet submits budget documents to the *Diet*. Finance Minister delivers his budget speech in both Houses.
1-0 (March-April)	*Diet* debates and approves the budget.
(Year t)	
0 (1 April)	Start of fiscal year (t).

4. The annual budget cycle

Each Ministry and Agency begins estimating around April or May of each year its revenue and expenditure for the following fiscal year's budget. They must prepare reports on expected revenue, required expenditures and other necessary matters under their jurisdiction and send them to the Minister of Finance not later than 31 August.

In June or July the guideline for the budget requests proposed by MOF is approved by the Cabinet. It contains instructions which each Ministry and Agency has to follow as it makes its calculations.

According to the Cabinet agreement on the guideline for the budget requests for FY 95, this guideline provided in principle a 10 per cent reduction for current expenditure and 5 per cent growth of investment expenditure, measured against the nominal expenditure level according to the previous budget. The guideline does not apply to national debt service costs and Local Allocation Tax Grants. The guideline also makes some exception to several programmes on account of the obligatory character of such programmes.

After the process of examinations which include hearings and reviews by the MOF from September to early December, the MOF prepares its proposal and submits it to Ministries and Agencies in late December. After the notification of the proposal to Ministries and Agencies, the "revival negotiations" between the MOF and each Ministry and Agency take place. For nearly a week financial decision-making takes place through negotiations at three official levels ending up at ministerial level.

The Budget proposal includes unallotted financial resources which are distributed to specific programmes in the course of the revival negotiations so that the total amount of the expenditure in the Budget Draft of the MOF does not change after the revival negotiations.

At the end of December, the Economic Planning Agency prepares the "Outlook and Basic Policy on the National Economy" for the following fiscal year through consultation with relevant Ministries including the MOF and it is decided by the Cabinet. At nearly the same time, "General Principles of Budget Compilation" are decided by the Cabinet as well. Finally, the Government approves the budget for submission to the *Diet*. Usually the deliberation process of both Houses ends in early April.

D. EXPENDITURE REVIEW

Efficiency or effectiveness reviews of expenditures are secured mainly by examination in the course of budget formulation. Departments are rather systematically urged to review their current activities, mainly through three mechanisms:

- guideline for the budget request: the guidelines, which set the limit of budget requests before the submission of these requests to the MOF, have been launched since 1961. The guideline has become strict and now implies a 10 per cent reduction on current expenditure and 5 per cent growth of investment expenditure (see Section C4);
- scrap and build: Under the principle of "scrap and build", a new organisation is "built" only when an existing organisation that has become out of line with the need of the times, is "scrapped". It is considered that this principle has contributed to the restraining of the expansion of public administrative organisations;
- sunset: For new subsidy programmes a termination period of not more than five years is set as a rule; and when the termination date arrives, the programme must be reviewed strictly.

E. IMPLEMENTATION OF THE BUDGET

1. Major instruments of in-year control

The head of each Ministry and Agency must formulate plans for incurring liabilities (contracts and other activities that lead to government expenditures) based on the allotted budget for public projects and other specified expenses, and must get approval of the Finance Minister. In addition, based on the allotted budget, the head of each Ministry and Agency must draw up (cash) payment plans which make clear the required expenditures for each disbursing officer in every quarter of the year, and must get approval of the Finance Minister. The Cabinet informs the *Diet* about the implementation of the budget and the situation of the treasury every quarter (see Section G, documents No. 11 and 12).

2. Managerial discretion

Spending managers cannot transfer funds from one line item to another within an item, unless with the approval of the Finance Minister. Balances cannot be transferred from one item to another by spending managers without parliamentary approval.

There are four situations in which unspent appropriations can be carried forward to the following fiscal year:

a) expenses previously approved can be carried over to the following fiscal year (carried over expenses);

b) where liabilities have already been incurred in the current fiscal year and where cash payments have not been (fully) realised due to unforeseen circumstances;

c) yearly expenditures are approved as continued expenses (see Section A4);

d) on the specific provisions of the law of special accounts (*e.g.* the Foreign Exchange Fund Special Account).

In cases *a)* and *b)*, approval of the Finance Minister is required. In case *d)*, no such approval is required and the competent minister can carry forward by notifying the Finance Minister and the Board of Audit.

F. RECENT REFORMS

At present, no major reforms in the Japanese budget system are being prepared.

G. FURTHER INFORMATION

1. Documents related to annual budget

The fiscal year (FY)(t) begins on 1 April (year t) and ends on 31 March of the following year.

1. The Budget in Brief (*Yosan-no-Hanashi*) English translation available, June/July, year (t).
2. The Budget (*Yosansho*) appropriation bill, presented to the diet, February of year (t – 1).
3. Explanation of the Budget (*Yosan-no-setsumei*) presented to the *Diet,* February, year (t – 1).
4. Explanation of the National budget in Detail (*Kuni-no-yosan*) commentary on the current year's budget, November/December year (t).
5. The Settlement (*Kessansho*) presented to the *Diet,* January/February, Year (t + 1).
6. References for the Budget Specified by Article 28 of the Finance Law (*Zaiseihou-dai-nijuuhachi-jou-ni-yoru-yosansankou-shorui*), Reference materials annexed to the Budget, February, year (t – 1).
7. Public Finance of Japan in Charts (*Zusetsunihon-no-Zaisei*), describes plans, explanation of the current budget, budget system, fiscal policies etc., June, year (t).
8. Budgetary Statistics (*Zaisei-Tokei*), containing historical data, September/October, year (t).
9. An Outline of Japanese Tax, English translation available, October/November year (t).
10. Monthly Finance Review, contains information on current economic, budgetary and financial situation, English translation available.

2. Other documents

11. The Situation of Appropriation (*Yosan shiyo no Jyokyo*) about the implementation of the budget, presented to the *Diet* quarterly. The contents of this document are published in the Official Gazette.
12. The Situation of Treasury (*Kokko no Jyokyo*), presented to the *Diet* quarterly. The contents of this documents are published in the Official Gazette.

NETHERLANDS

**Any changes which have taken place in the Netherlands
since September 1993 are not reflected in this chapter**

A. INSTITUTIONAL STRUCTURE OF BUDGETARY DECISION-MAKING

1. Political and organisational structure of government

The Netherlands is a unitary State. There are three layers of government: state or central level, provincial level and municipalities with the provincial level by far the smallest of the three in financial terms (see Section B for more information).

Central government functions are organised mainly around 13 ministries and several agencies. General government services are mainly provided centrally, rather than decentralised. Ministries have in general one Minister, and a State Secretary; the Secretary-General of each department is a non-political appointment, as are the rest of the departmental personnel.

Parliament has two Chambers, the Second Chamber and the First Chamber (or Senate). In the Second Chamber some ten political parties are represented, not one of them having a majority position. Therefore coalition cabinets are a common phenomenon. The current (majority) coalition is based on three political parties supporting a 14 minister Cabinet. Ministers cannot be a member of Parliament at the same time. Direct elections for the Second Chamber are held regularly every four years. The next election for the Second Chamber will be held in 1998. A so called coalition-agreement – covering all four years the government is supposed to remain in office – is normally the basis of a (new) government, currently with a strong focus on the budgetary policy to be conducted.

2. Main budgetary organs

The central role in all budgetary matters is played by the Ministry of Finance (MF). MF deals with the expenditure and revenue side of the budget (*i.e.* taxation) as well as with general financial economic policy, the latter responsibility shared with amongst others the Ministry of Economic Affairs. MF is, except for his own ministry's budget, responsible for the debt-servicing programme.

Within the MF, budgetary activities are co-ordinated by the Directorate General of the Budget, which has prime responsibility in controlling the expenditure side of the budget and non-tax revenues. The Directorate General of the budget, employing almost 250 (all grades and supporting staff), comprises three Directorates and the Central Auditing Service. One Directorate, the Inspectorate of State Finances is built up of 14 sections, most of which deal with one department. Another Directorate deals with finances of (lower) public bodies. Remaining budgetary activities (the general budgetary items) take place within the Directorate of Budgetary Affairs; *e.g.* the Budgetary Policy Division and the Financial Management Division co-ordinate the preparation and implementation of the budget.

3. Role of Prime Minister and Cabinet

The Cabinet plays a very important role in the budget process. The total extent and allocation of cut-backs in the budget, for example, is discussed and decided upon by the Cabinet, on the basis of proposals that are put forward by the Minister of Finance. A Cabinet sub-council chaired by the Prime Minister can precede full cabinet discussions and decision-making. Usually the MF and the Ministers of Economic Affairs, of Social Affairs and of the Interior participate. Because the Ministers have agreed upon the coalition agreement, they have accepted the main lines of medium term budgetary and economic policy (including possible budget cut-backs) to be conduced in the four year period the Cabinet will be in office. Of course, the character of coalition agreements is necessarily a global one, because not all details can be decided four years in advance.

4. Role of Parliament

The annual budget consists of seventeen chapters. Each chapter is made up of two laws. One for the revenue-side and one for the expenditure side. Usually the budget documents submitted by the government are examined by a committee of the Second Chamber which is in charge of the policy area of the budget chapter under discussion; generally speaking each budget chapter covers spending and revenues of one ministry. In actual fact, this committee prepares the discussion in the Second Chamber.

Annual appropriation of all central government expenditure by Parliament is required including entitlements authorised under separate legislation. Furthermore Parliament approves all commitments to be taken on in the budget year concerned, also if the commitment leads to expenditure in a later year. Parliament does not approve multi-year estimates. If Parliament has not passed the Appropriation Bill at the beginning of the new fiscal year, departments may spend up to 4/12th of the amount appropriated in the previous year pending parliamentary approval for the current year's estimates. Appropriation of expenditure takes place by budget chapter, comprising a great number of detailed sections (articles). In total, Parliament controls at the level of about 900 votes. The Second Chamber can change budget figures by means of amendments, usually at detailed sector level. The First Chamber lacks the right to amend the budget. Motions – intentions of will – do not necessarily have to be carried out by Cabinet. Motions usually deal with a broader policy area, as opposed to amendments that relate to a particular section or item of the budget. Whenever Parliament has enacted the budget, it can only be changed by supplementary budgets.

B. THE SCOPE AND NATURE OF GOVERNMENT FINANCES

Compared to other OECD Member countries, the Dutch public sector is large due to relatively high social security outlays (around 40 per cent of public expenditure). Central Government's budget deficit increased considerably in the years 1974-83, as has central government net borrowing. Since 1984, however, the deficit has fallen significantly.

The internal structure of the public sector can be described as follows. Local authorities (provinces and municipalities) spend less than one third of total public expenditure. They are limited in their spending by means of regulation and by central government supervision to a great extent. Restrictions on capital market borrowing and on taxation capacities, and block and specific purpose grants are all instruments that central government uses to control spending of local authorities. Except for providing local services, lower tiers act as an agent of central government, mainly in the housing sector, the (on-budget) social security provisions, in law and order affairs and in matters of education. Currently more responsibilities are transferred to local authorities, as part of a large decentralisation programme (see Section F).

Social security is only to a minor extent on-budget. Social insurance funds take care of the larger part, financing their expenditure (some 35 per cent of total public expenditure) by levying non-tax, or social premium, contributions. Central government controls total social security spending to a large extent, determining the social premium rates, the nominal size of the social benefits and the conditions of entitlement.

In recent years all state enterprises except the Royal Mint have been transformed into private companies, some of which have been (partly) sold off. In general, public ownership of enterprises is limited outside the transport (including the post, telephone and telegraph enterprise) and natural gas sectors and will be even more reduced by sales of shares.

Table 1. **Functional classification of central government outlays (1992)**

As percentage of total

General administration	3.1
Defence	6.9
Foreign relations (excluding development co-operation)	4.3
Development co-operation	2.9
Justice and police	3.2
Trade and industry	2.4
Agriculture and fisheries	0.9
Education and science	16.7
Cultural affairs and recreation	1.1
Social services	22.7
Health and environmental protection	1.9
Housing	5.4
Interest payments on central government debt	13.1
Block grants to local authorities	8.1
Not classified	1.2
Total	100.0

Source: Budget Memorandum, 1992.

C. BUDGET FORMULATION STRATEGY AND PROCESS

1. Strategic aims and global norms

Budgetary targets are identified in the coalition agreement. They relate to both the budget deficit and the public burden. There is no explicit expenditure target.

Budgetary targets are usually expressed as a percentage of net national income (NNI). The definition of the budget deficit differs from net borrowing in that it includes net credit accommodation and some off-budget items concerning loan guarantees in the housing sector and in the area of development co-operation (the loan guarantees currently included in the definition equal about 0.1 per cent of NNI). Separate guidelines have been set, controlling the budget balance of social security funds. The so called public burden is defined to cover tax and social premium payments and some non-tax revenues, mainly non-tax, non-export natural gas revenue, and environmental levies.

The coalition agreement for the period 1991-94 set the target for the budget deficit at 4³/₄ per cent of NNI for 1991, declining to 3¹/₄ per cent of NNI in 1994. In the budget of 1992 a significant package of budget cuts and related tax measures was presented.

As to the public burden, this target should be maximally at the projected 1990 level (53.6 per cent NNI) during the term of this Cabinet. Currently the public burden is estimated at 52.2 per cent (NNI) in 1994.

Also in the light of the discussions on the European Economic and Monetary Union (EMU) the Cabinet has recently decided to give more attention to capital expenditure by means of information on the economic classification of government expenditure.

The following table indicates realisation of target variables.

Table 2. **Fiscal indicators, 1990-96**

As percentage of NNI

	1990	1991	1992	1993	1994	1995	1996
Budget deficit	5¹/₄	4³/₄	4¹/₄	3³/₄	3¹/₄	3.1	3.0
Public burden	52.2	52.9	53.4	52.5	52.2	52.0	52.0

Source: Budget Memorandum 1992.

2. Technical aspects of multi-year estimates

Multi-year estimates (MYE) for control-purposes are registered for both expenditure and non-tax revenues of central government. There is no link to a medium-term fiscal plan; MYE serve as a means of control for MF, rather than as proclaimed resources for the spending ministries. They reflect (expenditure) projections according to policies that have been agreed on by Cabinet (which might include a future change in policy). MYE, linked to the current year (t − 1), cover the budget year (t) and four future years.

MYE include estimates sensitive to macroeconomic development, such as interest payments, unemployment benefits and grants. A provision is made for rising costs according to the forecasted price and pay level of the budget year. MYE therefore remain on a constant price and wage basis. These estimates are as far as possible based on macroeconomic forecasting results, also for future years.

MYE are built up from the level of articles, or sometimes an even more disaggregated level. In fact MYE are rolled forward in an almost continuous process: each change in (multi-year) budgetary developments has to be checked by the MF and after agreement by MF will result in a change of the budget/multi-year estimates. Usually, changes refer to estimate failures and are therefore not the result of new policy initiatives. However, new policy initiatives are incorporated in MYE. The new final year is constructed bottom-up by Ministries. MYE are published once a year, in an annex to the Budget Memorandum, the so called horizontal (year on year) explanation. The Spring Memorandum (see Section E) and the Budget Memorandum for the next budget year include an annex which presents all changes in the MYE, as compared to the previous year's Budget Memorandum, the so called vertical (Memorandum on Memorandum) explanation. In both the horizontal and vertical explanation, the presentation of MYE is a policy-oriented grouping of sections.

Besides MYE for expenditure and non-tax revenues, projections are made for tax revenues, so as to monitor the realisation of the budgetary targets in the medium term.

3. Calendar of main points of decision-making and activities

The fiscal year [FY(t)] is the calendar year (year t).

Months before start of FY (t)	Main events and activities
(Year t − 2)	
13-11 (December-February)	MF – Updating MYE; – If necessary, selecting cut-back proposals; – Preparations for "Framework letter" (accessing budget targets and possible problems).
(Year t − 1)	
10 (March)	MF sends "Framework letter" to Cabinet.
10-9 (March-April)	Cabinet decides on the basis of the "Framework letter" on total and allocation of resources and on possible budget cut-backs and whether or not room is available for new policy initiatives.
9 (up to 1 May)	Ministries prepare draft budgets to be submitted to MF before 1 May.
9-7 (May-June)	MF (mainly the Inspectorate of Finances) discussions with each Ministry on all levels of officials and if necessary on Ministerial level.
7-6 (first part of July)	Cabinet decides on expenditure side based on macroeconomic forecast and "unsolved issues" letter of MF (comprising if necessary an update of MY estimates and macroeconomic forecasts).
5 (last part of August)	Cabinet decides on remaining issues, *e.g.* tax measures social premium rates, effects on distribution of purchasing power, based on "August letter" of MF.
4 (third Tuesday of September)	Submission of budget and related documents, such as the Budget Memorandum.
3 (October)	Second Chamber discussion upon the general political and financial economic policy lines.
2-0 (November-February)	Both Chambers of Parliament discuss and decide upon each "budget chapter".
(Year t)	
0 (1 January)	Start of fiscal year (t).

4. The annual budget cycle

The preparation of the budget starts in February-March year $(t - 1)$. In March the Minister of Finance submits a letter (the so called "Framework letter") to the Council of Ministers, putting forward proposals concerning the allocation of resources to the various parts of the public sector. These proposals are usually based upon the expected medium-term development of the economy and upon the updated multi-year estimates for expenditure and non-tax revenues. Furthermore a multi-year projection is made for tax revenues. In the last decade this allocation has involved expenditure reductions, in order to realise the budgetary targets set by successive Cabinets. In case of budget cut-backs not only the allocation, but also specific measures to achieve these cut-backs, may be part of the letter.

This letter is discussed and decisions are taken by Cabinet in March-April.

In the following three months detailed budgets take shape; in general departments are free to curtail programmes or outlays other than those proposed by the Minister of Finance provided the budgetary targets (mainly the budget deficit) are not affected. The drafting of budgets is monitored by the Inspectorate of Finances. Intensive consultations take place between the departments and the Inspectorate. In May-June first drafts of the budgets are discussed by officials of senior rank of the spending departments and the director-general of the budget; if necessary, bilateral talks take place at ministerial level. The Council of Ministers makes a final decision in July about the expenditure side of the budget.

In July and in August decision-making takes place about a range of other measures and issues, like social premium rates, additional tax measures, etc., and taking into account the other (non-budgetary) goals of government policy (for example, income policy considerations).

The third Tuesday of September Cabinet submits to Parliament the draft-budgets of the spending departments and the Budget Memorandum, which sets out the financial-economic and budgetary policy for the budget year.

In October Parliament discusses the general political and financial policy lines set out by the Cabinet. During the next three or four months all budgets are discussed and decided upon, turning them into Annual Appropriation Acts, after possible amendments by Parliament (see A4).

D. EXPENDITURE REVIEW

1. Reconsideration Procedure

The main instrument of policy review is the so-called Reconsiderations Procedure which was introduced in 1981. This procedure aims at fundamentally reviewing existing policy areas within the public sector so as to develop policy alternatives that can facilitate the process of curtailing public expenditure. Only alternatives costing the same or less can be considered, with a mandatory 20 per cent funding level reduction included as one option.

Subjects for Reconsiderations are decided by the Council of Ministers. Preferably reconsideration reviews should start 1 November so the results can be brought together for a first assessment prior to the actual budget preparation. Nevertheless, reviews may be started at any time of the year. Both the responsible Minister(s) and the Minister of Finance can take the initiative and decisions need not be submitted to full Cabinet if no general cabinet policy is involved and provided the Ministers concerned have reached agreement.

All reports are made public by submission to Parliament. In addition, a summary report is published for each round of Reconsiderations, which also serves as a basis for the above-mentioned political assessment of results. Decisions made in the process of budget preparation on the basis of Reconsiderations reports are described in the budget-proposals of the different departments, and are summarised in the Budget memorandum.

The whole procedure is guided by a small, Ministerial Commission, consisting of the Prime Minister, the Vice Prime Minister(s) and MF. Advice and administrative support is provided by MF.

As mentioned, the Reconsideration Procedure is the main (ongoing) review process. In the last decade several other reviews have been carried out. They have had a reasonably great budgetary impact. The most recent review programmes are the revision of the entitlement programmes and of the subsidy-policy and the so called Efficiency Operation.

2. Entitlement programmes

In 1988 a start was made on evaluating entitlement programmes, *i.e.* regulations under which individuals and organisations, etc. are entitled to receive money from the authorities simply because they meet the stipulated requirements and which contribute to the exceeding of public spending limits. Following the carrying out of a survey, attention has turned to the analysis of risk factors, the realism of the estimates and the scope for tightening up the regulations.

3. Subsidy policy

The integrated subsidy policy is another result of the evaluation of policy. In this evaluation, which began in 1991, two approaches can be discerned. The first concerns the management of subsidies in general and efforts to prevent and combat abuse and misuse. The plan for the second approach outlines a framework for assessing the relevance, effectiveness and efficiency of subsidies. This assessment is carried out partly by means of the Reconsiderations Procedure.

4. Efficiency operation

As part of the so-called efficiency operation, the size and performance of the civil service are undergoing a fundamental review. The operation is aimed primarily at improving the efficiency and quality of the civil service. It involves the question whether current government responsibilities are still necessary on the one hand, and an inquiry to determine the best administrative and organisational structure on the other.

In preparation for the formulation of concrete efficiency proposals, analyses have been made of the tasks performed by government departments. Attention has also been devoted to the manner in which these tasks are performed and the organisational capacity this requires.

Attention has also been paid to the possible overlapping of the responsibilities of different ministries, relations with other tiers of government and ways of decentralising, privatising, hiving off tasks, increasing the degree of self-management, or reorganising them on an interministerial basis. The underlying idea is that the civil service should restrict itself as far as possible to core responsibilities, overall policy and to ensuring the proper allocation of resources.

5. Periodic evaluation

In addition to these three special forms of policy evaluation, more general forms of assessment are also carried out. To promote this, it has been decided that the explanatory notes on votes and accounts should include information on the facts represented by the amounts. The government wants to lay greater emphasis on the periodic evaluation of policy and the use of indicators in policy and budgetary decisions.

E. IMPLEMENTATION OF THE BUDGET

1. Major instruments of in-year control

The general treatment of changes in the budget is dealt with in the so-called Rules of Budget Discipline. These rules constitute procedures regarding what to do in case of set-backs and windfalls both of expenditures and non-tax revenues. The rules governing compensation for items are formulated in such a way that normally speaking any excess in expenditure is compensated for by corresponding reductions in expenditure. In general specific budget overruns (*i.e.* concerning a department's expenditure) are to be compensated specifically, that is to say that each department should compensate any excess in expenditure on its own budget chapter. Certain increases in expenditure are labelled as "general", which means that compensation for these is prescribed for all departments. Such general budget overruns are usually the result of macroeconomic developments, though Cabinet may also decide to label certain overruns of a specific nature as general.

During the implementation phase of the budget, Parliament is informed by Cabinet several times. After submission of the draft budget to Parliament in September, the Spring Memorandum is released in May. In the budget Memorandum, released in September, Cabinet informs Parliament not only on next year's budget, but also on the provisional outcome of the implementation of the current budget. In the Fall Memorandum, which is sent to Parliament in November, Cabinet presents the presumed results. The February Memorandum released in February of year $(t + 1)$, contains the provisional account of the previous budget year, while the Budget memorandum for budget year $(t + 2)$ presents the final account of budget year (t). All these Memoranda are accompanied by proposals for supplementary Appropriation Acts.

F.   RECENT REFORMS

1.   The financial accountability operation

Controlling public expenditure requires more than general standards and overall frameworks. Elements such as proper budget preparation, efficient implementation and proper accounts are indispensable. To this end, the "financial accountability operation" was launched in 1986. The basic aim is that every ministry should bear primary responsibility for the structure and organisation of its own accounting system, with the Minister of Finance playing a co-ordinating and supervisory role.

The chief objectives of the operation are:

- The establishment of an accounting system in the ministries which permits efficient and legitimate implementation of budgets, incorporating both commitments and cash disbursements.
- Ensuring that auditor's reports cover the whole of a ministerial accounting system and that the rendering of accounts is accompanied by a favourable auditor's report.
- Establishing a system for the supply of financial information between the various ministries and the Ministry of Finance and between the civil service and Parliament such that information on budgetary preparation, implementation and accounts can be provided rapidly and efficiently.
- Altering the structure and presentation of draft budgets, supplementary budgets, accounts and budgetary statements so that Parliament is better able to exercise its right to approve the budget and its right of authorisation. Both the 1976 Government Accounts Act and regulations deriving from it will be amended.

2.   Result-oriented management

As a result of this operation, management can be made increasingly subservient to policy, and greater attention can be devoted to the efficiency of the civil service. The government has adopted the recommendations of the working group for the review of management rules contained in the report entitled "Towards More Result Oriented Management". This report, which tries to steer a middle course between the need for management at macrolevel and permitting greater authority at microlevel, makes a number of proposals.

The proposals concern firstly the reassessment of rules governing financial and personnel management. For instance, it is recommended that civil service management be given wider responsibilities and ways are suggested of placing less emphasis on what is called the obsession with cash figures. Secondly, the working group has formulated recommendations for streamlining the budgetary process. The underlying idea is that by securing the close involvement of central and political bodies in policy and budget preparation and by ensuring that detailed accounts are rendered afterwards, the procedural burden during implementation can be lightened.

The third area covered by the working group's proposals is the introduction of agencies in order to widen the range of forms of self-management. Agencies are more independent parts of the civil service, and are considered to be ideally suited for ensuring that the emphasis is shifted from a resources-oriented authorisation to a performance-oriented account afterwards. Agencies typically have greater managerial powers and responsibilities than "normal" civil service departments. Examples are broader facilities for handling the budget, possibly in combination with accrual accounting and commercial bookkeeping.

3.   The decentralisation programme

The government has given fresh impetus to the decentralisation of responsibilities and resources to lower tiers of government. This decentralisation programme has led to an extensive package of proposals. The new style of decentralisation, i.e. decentralisation to urban regions, is also under discussion. The measures as a whole will lead to lower tiers of government being given greater responsibilities for policy and its implementation. The number of specific payments, the volume of regulations and various obligations which lower tiers of government still have at present (e.g. the submission of plans) will decrease. The measures are based on a careful examination of the tasks of the state, in which the central question was whether the tasks could be carried out more efficiently by lower tiers of government.

G. FURTHER INFORMATION

1. Documents related to the annual budget

The fiscal year (t) is the calendar year (t).

1. Appropriation Bills (*Begrotingswetten*), mainly concerning spending departments, third Tuesday in September, year (t – 1).
2. Budget Memorandum (*Miljoenennota*), summarises economic background to the Budget, describes the medium-term financial strategy, summarises the tax proposals and gives all the key figures for revenues, expenditure and the public sector borrowing requirement, third Tuesday in September, year (t – 1). English summary available.
3. Report on macroeconomic forecast (*Macro Economische Verkenningen*), third Tuesday of September, year (t – 1).
4. Spring Memorandum (*Voorjaarsnota*), reports on the implementation of the budget, Spring, year (t).
5. Autumn Memorandum (*Najaarsnota*), reports on the implementation of the budget, Autumn, year (t).
6. Report on the provisional results of the budget (February Memorandum) (*Voorlopige Rekening*) (*Februari Nota*), in February, year (t + 1).

2. Other documents

7. The Eighth Report of the Study Group on the Budget Margin (*8-ste Rapport Studiegroep Begrotingsruimte*), Towards sound Public Finance, 1989.
8. The Report entitled "Towards More Result Oriented Management" of the Working Group for the Review of Management Rules.

NEW ZEALAND

**Any changes which have taken place in New Zealand
since January 1994 are not reflected in this chapter**

A. INSTITUTIONAL STRUCTURE OF BUDGETARY DECISION-MAKING

1. Political and organisational structure of government

New Zealand has a centralised, unitary form of government; it has no system of state or provincial government. The central government sector consists of Ministers, departments, Offices of Parliament, Crown entities (CEs), and State-owned Enterprises (SOEs).

A main feature of central government in New Zealand is that there is only one legislative chamber, the House of Representatives, or Parliament. Members of Parliament are elected every three years. The last elections were held in November 1993. The party which has the highest number of representatives elected is invited by the Governor General to form the Government. Those not in Government form the Opposition.

In the November 1993 election New Zealanders voted to change their electoral system to a proportional representational system: this change becomes effective at the next election. Governments from the next election are consequently more likely to be formed as a result of a coalition, with the parties not in the coalition forming the opposition.

The leader of the Government is the Prime Minister, who selects Ministers of the Crown who, in turn, form the Cabinet. The current Cabinet consists of 20 members; in addition, there are five Ministers outside Cabinet. Cabinet Ministers are allocated a number of Votes (groupings of one or more appropriations)[1] to manage and this is known as their portfolio. Cabinet is responsible for initiating most of government policy and consequent legislation.

The State Sector Act 1988 and the Public Finance Act 1989 provide the legislative basis for the financial management system of the core central government (Ministers, departments and CEs). Departmental Chief Executives are hired on fixed term contracts and are accountable directly to a Minister (the Responsible Minister). They are accountable for delivering the outputs they agree with Ministers to produce and for the financial performance of their department. Departments and most CEs operate within the budget sector.

The State Owned Enterprises Act 1986 provides the legislative basis for the operations of SOEs. Under the Act, SOEs have a statutory responsibility to ''... operate as a successful business...''. SOEs also operate under the jurisdiction of the Companies Act 1955. They have a Board of Directors who are accountable to two shareholding Ministers for the day to day operations of the Company. The shareholding Ministers (the Minister of Finance and the Minister of State-owned Enterprises) are prohibited from involving themselves in the day to day decision-making of the SOE. SOEs and a few CEs operate outside the budget sector.

Separate from central government is New Zealand's system of local government, made up of territorial and special purpose local authorities.

Territorial authorities provide for community facilities such as roads, water supply, sewerage, recreational and other services by a mixture of levying rates on property, raising loans and charging for services. Local government elections are held every four years and are separate from parliamentary elections. This precludes central government from being directly involved in local government decision making.

Special purpose authorities provide specific services, usually on a user pays basis. Examples are transport operations, ports, airports and electricity supply. In recent years most special purpose local authorities have been corporatised (turned into companies owned by territorial authorities).

There is no explicit revenue sharing between central and local government although both contribute jointly to some activities, most notably roads.

2. Main budgetary organs

Within Cabinet, the Minister of Finance has the principal responsibility for the budget. The Budget speech is normally delivered by the Minister of Finance on behalf of the Government. The Minister of Finance is the Responsible Minister for the Treasury department.

The Treasury is the principal economic and financial adviser to the Government. It reports on most expenditure proposals before the Government and is often asked to participate in more general reviews of policy issues where there are resource use implications.

A significant part of the department's work involves advising on the content of the Government's annual Budget, as well as assisting with the preparation of Budget documents and associated legislation. As part of the Budget preparation process, the Treasury co-ordinates reviews of expenditure programmes, undertakes fiscal analysis, prepares revenue and expenditure forecasts and monitors revenue and expenditure flows.

The Debt Management Office of the Treasury manages the Government's debt portfolio and its borrowing requirements. This Office is also responsible for the disbursement of cash to departments. Departments are responsible for disbursing cash to other government entities and private sector contractors.

The Treasury is also responsible for the development and broad implementation of financial management policy in the public sector and for the preparation of the Financial Statements of the Government of New Zealand.

3. Role of Cabinet

The Cabinet is the highest council of government, it decides on administrative and legislative proposals and policies, and co-ordinates the work of Ministers. Ministers take collective responsibility for budgetary decisions.

The Cabinet Expenditure Control Committee (ECC) undertakes the detailed scrutiny of departmental budgets and expenditure proposals. ECC is a sub-committee of Cabinet and comprises most senior Ministers, including the Minister of Finance. It is chaired by an Associate Minister of Finance. ECC is supported by a committee of officials from the three central agencies; the Department of the Prime Minister and Cabinet, the State Services Commission, and the Treasury.

4. Role of Parliament

New Zealand operates under the conventions of the Westminister parliamentary system. Accordingly, it is Parliament's role to monitor the activities of the Executive (that is, the Ministers) by authorising its use of resources.

Parliament grants "supply" (authority or command over resources) to individual Ministers through the passing of Appropriation Bills, which "vote" money for specific purposes. No expenditure of public money can be made except through Parliamentary appropriation. There are two forms of appropriation: annual and permanent.

Annual appropriations, as the name implies, provide authority only for the financial year to which they relate. There are four types of annual appropriations:

- **Appropriation for outputs**: authority for the Executive to incur a specified amount of expense (measured on an accruals basis not a cash basis) for the production of a specified good or service (output).
- **Capital Contribution Appropriation**: authority for the Executive to invest a specified amount of capital (by way of an injection of cash) into a specified department.
- **Appropriations for other expenses**: authority for the executive to incur expenses other than as a cost of departmental outputs (such as revaluation expenses and loss on sale of fixed assets).
- **Appropriation for Payments on Behalf of the Crown**: these provide authority for the Executive to make payments to parties other than departments for either:
  • outputs to be produced by those parties; or
  • injecting capital into a CE or SOE; or
  • welfare transfer payments.

Permanent appropriations (or permanent legislative authorities) enable the expenditure of public money without the need to seek annual approval from Parliament. These are used in cases where:

- an assurance of the ability of the Government to commit resources is essential, such as debt servicing obligations;
- Parliament wishes to establish the independence of specific expenditure from the Executive, such as paying salaries for the judiciary; and where
- they are technically desirable, for example where a department earns trading revenue. A permanent appropriation authorises the department to spend such revenue on the costs of producing further outputs.

The introduction of the first Appropriation Bill in any financial year is also the occasion for the presentation of the Budget speech. In accordance with the Public Finance Act 1989, the Government is required to introduce the first Appropriation Bill (*i.e.* its budget) no later than 31 July each year. The financial year begins on 1 July.

Debate on the Budget is conventionally adjourned to the next sitting day but Budget-related legislation may be introduced for immediate passing.

Two documents are tabled – the Minister's speech and the fiscal tables related to it and the Main Estimates which show the Government's spending plans for the current year. The function of the Estimates is to elaborate the expenditure plans contained in the Appropriation Bill and to document the output and financial performance targets of departments for the year.

The Estimates presented by the Government are scrutinised in detail by one of the Parliamentary Select Committees on the House's behalf. A Vote cannot be passed until it has been examined by a select committee. The examination of each Vote involves the appearance of the chief executive and other senior managers of a department administering a Vote before the Committee. They are required to provide detailed information on the financial management of the resources under their control and answer any questions the Committee puts to them.

Recent amendments to Parliament's Standing Orders have effected some changes in the way Parliament scrutinises departmental Estimates and annual reports. The number of days – thirteen – currently provided for the Estimates debate is unchanged but has been reallocated as follows:

- three days for debate on the main Estimates;
- six days for a Financial Review debate in February/March of each year. The debate will be based on select committee reports of their examination of the annual reports and financial statements of departments and Offices of Parliament;
- four days for debate on select committee reports of their examination of the annual reports and financial statements of CEs and SOEs.

The changes enable projected performance for the current financial year to be scrutinised separately from actual performance for the financial year just ended.

B. THE SCOPE AND NATURE OF GOVERNMENT FINANCES

1. Current Status

An indication of the current scope and nature of New Zealand Government finances is provided by Table 1. This has been prepared on a cash basis.

Government expenditure patterns continue to be dominated by debt servicing costs and the provision of health, education and social services. Health, education and social welfare services and transfers are almost totally funded and/or provided by central government. This reflects the long-standing "welfare state" responsibilities of the New Zealand Government.

On the revenue side there has been a shift towards a balance between direct and indirect taxation since the mid 1980s. This contrasts with the heavy reliance on income tax that existed prior to that.

Public debt levels continue to be significant with the 30 June 1993 debt representing 47.9 per cent of estimated 1992/93 gross domestic product.

The recent financial management reforms have resulted in a much greater awareness of the contingent liabilities and guarantees of the Crown. These are now regularly reported as part of the Crown's Financial Statements.

Table 1. **Classification of government financial net expenditure
by economic transaction, 1992-93**

$ million

Administration	3 098
Foreign relations	1 534
Development of industry	1 094
Education	4 504
Social services	10 697
Health	3 874
Transport	718
Debt services	3 899
Total net expenditure [1]	29 418

1. Financial net expenditure excludes lending minus repayments which is an IMF government Finance Statistics'
   term referring to net repayment of loans and net sales of equity.
Source: New Zealand Treasury.

2. Implications for future finances

In the period since late 1990, there has been a refocussing of social service expenditure. This has included a rationalisation of welfare benefit levels and the introduction of partial user charges for health services. The latter is part of a comprehensive reform of the health sector whereby a series of Regional Health Authorities will contract with Government owned hospitals and other health providers for the delivery of agreed health outputs.

Reform is also underway in state funded housing with the introduction of an ''Accommodation Supplement'' and a move away from the provision of subsidised rental accommodation. These reforms have included the restructuring of the Housing Corporation along commercial lines and the sale of the prime rate mortgage portfolio run by the Corporation.

C. BUDGET FORMULATION STRATEGY AND PROCESS

1. Strategic aims and global norms

The budget process has undergone significant change as the Financial Management Reforms have been implemented following the Public Finance Act 1989. The process was substantially modified in 1989 and 1990 to reflect output budgeting and progressive implementation of accrual accounting and budgeting. Substantial modifications were also made in 1991 and 1992 to reflect the improved information available on departmental and Crown entity outputs, assets and liabilities.

These changes to the process reflect the strategic objective of ensuring that the budget process is congruent with the financial management system in which government agencies operate.

Fiscally, the Government's stated objectives are to:
- move towards surplus in the adjusted financial balance;
- control debt levels;
- reduce government expenditure as a percentage of GDP.

Fiscal projections made in the 5 October 1993 Economic and Fiscal Update show that significant progress will be made in these objectives over the next three years. The adjusted financial balance is expected to be close to surplus by 1995-96. Net debt is anticipated to decline from 47.9 per cent of GDP in 1992-93 to 44.6 per cent in 1995-96. Government financial net expenditure as a percentage of GDP is expected to fall from 37.9 per cent in 1992-93 to 34.6 per cent in 1995-96.

2. Technical aspects of multi-year estimates

Three-year projections are available to Ministers at the beginning of the budget round. This information on trends in the overall fiscal position provides the backdrop for Ministers as they develop their Budget strategy. Departmental three-year Budgets are drafted in line with that Budget strategy.

3. Calendar of main points of decision-making and activities

Budget (Main Estimates)	Supplementary Estimates	Final Supplementary Estimates	Budget
July	March/April	May/June	July
Strategic phase	Agreement and budgeting phase	Collective review phase	Production phase

4. The annual budget cycle

Budget decisions are organised around a "baseline" figure and two out-year forecasts. The baseline is determined by previous years' forecasts and Government decisions. In subsequent years the out-year forecast becomes the baseline and the forecast is extended. These forecasts are subject to strict guidelines that limit their growth over the previous years' baseline.

These baselines are reviewed by Treasury, individual Ministers and Cabinet committees before being included in the First Appropriation Bill/Main Estimates (July) or Second Appropriation Bill/Supplementary Estimates (April/May). A Third Appropriation Bill/Additional Supplementary Estimates is usually introduced in May/June to make minor adjustments to output costings for the year. It normally does not contain any new policy.

Ministers generally do not make decisions at the level of net fiscal impact. Rather, decisions are generally made on individual output purchases or ownership decisions. These items are generally expressed in accrual terms rather than cash. Once decisions are made departments calculate their cash impact and incorporate this figure in their draft budgets. In cases of disagreement about the costing of budget measures, departmental figures have been accepted as the base with Treasury left to challenge their validity.

In the 1991/92 budget process an Officials Committee on Expenditure Control was established to review departmental budgets and develop saving options for consideration by Ministers. The Committee was chaired by a Treasury Deputy Secretary and also included representatives from the Department of Prime Minister and Cabinet and the State Services Commission.

Presentation of departmental budgets on an outputs basis has helped inform the Officials' Committee and Ministers as to what the government is achieving with particular expenditures. It has also facilitated expenditure reductions in some areas because it enabled Ministers to make a judgement about whether the outputs being delivered met their priorities.

The second major innovation was the preparation of *guidelines* or ground rules for the re-submission of departmental budgets. These guidelines were endorsed by Cabinet and issued to departments as a basis for the preparation of their budgets. The guidelines have recently required that:

- departments were to receive no compensation for increases in their input costs;
- extra funding would only be provided in cases where expenditure was to be determined by statute and demand (for example welfare benefits);
- new policy initiatives would have to be funded from re-allocations within existing budgets;
- capital injections would be restricted.

This represented a fundamental departure from the previous practice of allowing Chief Executives to prepare unconstrained budgets as bids. It is difficult, in the absence of a clearly defined forecast baseline, to establish how much the guidelines saved in fiscal terms. However, in previous rounds expenditure creep, disagreed bids and excessive inflation adjustments had cost in excess of $400 million.

This approach was continued in the 1992/93 budget round. For the first time, the 1992/93 projection contained in the department's 1991/92 three year forecast was used as the "*baseline*" for 1992/93 departmental budgets. Previously a new bid was developed. Not only has this limited expenditure creep, it has ensured that greater effort will be applied to developing realistic three year forecasts.

From the 1993/94 budget onwards, the budget will be prepared on an accruals basis. However, it is expected that *ex ante* accrual based information for the consolidated Crown will begin to be produced within 2-3 years. Existing cash based fiscal measures will continue.

D. EXPENDITURE REVIEW

The predominant vehicle for expenditure review is the annual budget process outlined above.

From time to time *ad hoc* reviews of specific areas of expenditure are undertaken. The catalyst for these are either new policy objectives (as was the case with the 1988 Royal Commission on Social Policy) or expenditure pressures. These *ad hoc* reviews usually operate outside the budget process but are often initiated within it.

On a day to day basis departmental Chief Executives are accountable for the financial performance of their departments. As they are funded on an outputs basis they have only a limited ability to pass on increases in input costs. Consequently, most departments now have reasonably active management systems for reviewing and minimising input expenditures.

In addition to processes within the Executive, the Audit Office undertakes "value for money reviews" on areas of expenditure of its choosing. These are reported to Parliament.

E. IMPLEMENTATION OF THE BUDGET

1. Internal monitoring

Departments are required to provide monthly monitoring reports to their Ministers and Treasury. These consist of actual against projected comparisons for:
– appropriations by type;
– operating statement, cash flows and balance sheet;
– net fiscal impact.

On a quarterly basis they are required to report the actual outputs produced, and the quality, quantity and cost of each, against projected output production for that quarter.

On a regular basis Treasury prepares fiscal position and forecast updates for the Government to monitor its overall position.

2. External financial reporting

Departments and the Crown are required to prepare annual financial statements (and also half yearly financial statements for the Crown) for tabling in Parliament. From 1 July 1992, the Crown's financial statements have been prepared on an accruals basis and in accordance with Generally Accepted Accounting Practice. The financial statements, which are required to be audited (with the exception of the Crown's half yearly statements) consist of:
– Financial Position (Balance sheet).
– Operating (accrual income and expenditure).
– Cash Flows.
– Objectives (output and financial performance targets as specified in the Estimates; not required for the Crown).
– Service Performance (outputs produced; not required for the Crown).

- Borrowings (not required for departments).
- Commitments.
- Contingent Liabilities.
- Unappropriated Expenditure.
- Emergency Expenditure (expenditure under national emergency legislation).
- Accounting Policies.
- Trust Money (not required for departments).

Since 1992-93 the Crown's Financial Statements have consolidated financial results for the wider central government sector including SOEs and CEs.

3. Supplementary appropriations

There are normally two supplementary appropriations during the year. They are used to:

- alter the mix of outputs being delivered or the cost of those outputs;
- inject new capital into departments;
- reflect increases in the amount of appropriation required for non-discretionary payments such as welfare benefits;
- provide appropriations for new policy initiatives.

Supplementary appropriations are generally limited to switching resources within the overall budgetary level set at the time of the Main Estimates. This is necessary as a separate appropriation exists for each output class. If more of one output class and less of another class is desired this requires a change to the appropriation.

4. Managerial discretion

As outputs rather than inputs are appropriated, departments have significant flexibility in the use of inputs. Subject to a limited number of government policies relating to particular inputs, Chief Executives are able to establish the input mix they consider most appropriate to the business of their department.

Individual Chief Executives have the authority to hire and fire staff and negotiate individual wages and conditions. They also have the flexibility to transfer resources between other input categories, for example between office supplies and travel, or staff and consultants.

Appropriations are not required for capital expenditure by departments unless additional capital is required. The Public Finance Act 1989 provides authority for departments to fund the purchase of new assets with the proceeds of the sale of existing assets. They have near complete flexibility to manage their balance sheet as they see fit.

In managing their inputs they are constrained by:

- the outputs they are required to produce and the amount Ministers are prepared to pay for those outputs;
- the financial performance targets (*e.g.* rate of return) they are required to meet.

F. RECENT REFORMS

1. Existing reforms: the past five years

The New Zealand Public Sector has been significantly reformed in the period since 1986. Government's commercial activities have been established as State-owned Enterprises with commercial objectives and the core departmental sector has moved to an output, accrual based focus. The latter has been accompanied by a delegation of day to day control over input selection and use to departmental management.

This has meant a change in roles and responsibilities for all the key players: Parliament, Ministers (both individually and collectively), Central Agencies and Departments. There have been significant changes to the budgetary and appropriation system. These are explained in a separate article contained elsewhere in this publication.

2. Future reforms: the next five years

Further development of the existing reforms is expected. This includes refinement of the "Capital Charge Regime" currently being implemented amongst departments. This regime involves a charge, levied by Government, for the capital employed in departments. The capital charge recognises the cost of the capital the Crown invests in departments and allows the full cost of producing outputs to be assessed. It also encourages the efficient use of fixed assets because the cost of idle capacity has to be met.

Other areas of development include: improving the processes for output contracting between departments and Ministers; enhancing the strategic focus of budgetary processes; further developing the monitoring of the Government's ownership interest in agencies; and a greater focus on the management of the Crown's balance sheet as a whole.

The principles which have been applied to the reform of the inner budget sector are being applied to the outer budget sector: health, education, housing and Crown Owned Entities. The gradual implementation of improved financial management practices to those areas is also expected over the next five years.

NOTE

1. A "Vote" is a grouping of one or more appropriations for:
   - classes of outputs; or
   - capital contributions; or
   - benefits or grants; that are the responsibility or one Minister of the Crown and administered by one department.

NORWAY

**Any changes which have taken place in Norway
since December 1993 are not reflected in this chapter**

A. INSTITUTIONAL STRUCTURE OF BUDGETARY DECISION-MAKING

1. Political and organisational structure of government

In Norway there are three layers of government: the central government, counties and municipalities.

The central government currently consists of 15 ministries, a number of central agencies and local state authorities. Each ministry is headed by a minister, an exception being the Ministry of Foreign Affairs which is headed by three ministers and the Ministry of Health and Social Affairs having one minister for each field. The 18 ministers, along with the Prime Minister, constitute the Cabinet. In addition to the cabinet minister, there are usually one to three political appointees in each ministry, including one State Secretary, who are not members of Cabinet, nor responsible to Parliament.

In general, the ministries are rather small, with on average about 160 employees in each. Other state agencies are normally subordinated to a ministry, and subjected to its instructions in all matters.

The Parliament (*"Storting"*) has one chamber, split up in two parts for the purpose of considering new legislation. It operates as a one chamber body when budget matters are considered. Parliamentary elections are held every 4 years. The last general election was held in September 1993.

2. Main budgetary organs

The Government's most important financial and budgetary policy functions are executed by the Ministry of Finance (MF). In addition, the Finance Minister has prime responsibility for economic policy formulation, planning and taxes and tariffs.

MF is divided into several departments: in addition to the Economic Policy Department and the Budget Department, the Department of Policy Analysis and Planning is responsible for the Long Term Programme and medium and long term analyses of structural matters – including development of public expenditures. Tax legislation and tax revenue estimation – the income side of the budget – take place in the Tax Law and the Tax Economy Departments, while indirect taxes and tariffs from foreign trade is the responsibility of the Indirect Tax and Tariff Department. The Budget Department, with 60 professional staff, managed by a Director General, is split up into divisions. Three divisions are involved in analysing, monitoring and controlling expenditure of five or six ministries each. Accounting matters are the concern of Public Accounts Division.

3. Role of Prime Minister and Cabinet

In February, the Cabinet meets for several days to discuss the main guidelines for economic and fiscal policy in the following budget year. Ministers are invited to endorse major guidelines as well as budget total expenditure limits for each Ministry's area of responsibility. The ministries work out proposals within the agreed limits. In September, when budget proposals have been submitted to and reviewed by the Budget Department, unsettled matters are decided by the Cabinet. After the Budget proposal has been approved, the Cabinet transmits the budget and economic policy documents to Parliament and the Minister of Finance delivers the "finance speech".

The Prime Minister participates in the formulation of economic policy, and as head of Cabinet, draws conclusions in matters of diverging opinions.

4. Role of Parliament

After the "finance speech" is delivered by the Minister of Finance, the *Storting* proceeds to consider the (preliminary) budget proposal in 12 permanent committees which generally correspond to the division of central government in ministries. It should be emphasised here that the status of the budget proposal differs from that of a bill. Under the Norwegian constitution, bills and budget proposals from the cabinet are treated quite differently in Parliament.

The 12 committees appraise each appropriation item and may propose alterations. Committee proposals are discussed in plenary assembly and preliminary votes are conducted. Parliament controls expenditure at the level of about 1 600 budget items. Amendments to budget items are usually both additions and reductions, their size generally being small in relation to total expenditure. On basis of these amendments, the Ministry of Finance works out the proposal for a Final Budget. This proposal also includes updated short-term economic forecasts, if necessary, and includes proposals for the borrowing requirement for the coming year. This time, the Parliament votes on the total budget in the middle of December. Auditing of the budget is performed by a separate agency directly controlled by the Parliament.

B. THE SCOPE AND NATURE OF GOVERNMENT FINANCES

Local governments (counties and municipalities) rely on taxes and transfers from the Central Government budget. Among the important taxes are a proportional income tax and a wealth tax, both with upper limits fixed by law. Property taxes are levied by some local authorities. Transfers by the Central Government include funds for health care, social welfare programmes, basic and secondary schools, cultural purposes, etc.

Central Government has some effect on local authorities' capital expenditure by allocating loans through the Municipal Bank. Otherwise, capital outlays of local authorities are financed through other types of borrowing, taxes or operating revenues.

Social security is organised through the central government, the social security system (*Folketrygden*) and local governments. *Folketrygden* is completely controlled by the Central Government (and the Parliament), as they determine the benefits and social security contributions of the social security schemes. Municipalities act as an agent of central government in delivery of social help (safety net provisions).

The most important public enterprises are in the areas of electricity, railways and postal and telephone services. These are included in the budget on a net basis. The deficits of the State companies are covered by the budget.

C. BUDGET FORMULATION STRATEGY AND PROCESS

1. Strategic aims and global norms

Main fiscal indicators are important inputs for the evaluation of macroeconomic and overall fiscal policy.

Fiscal indicators for the budget year are presented in Report No. 1, the so-called National Budget, submitted to the *Storting* in the Autumn. These short term indicators include:
- Central government budget balance before loan transactions.
- Central government surplus before loan transactions adjusted for oil taxes and transfers from Norges Bank and Central Governments petroleum activities (the share of the oil sector in the national economy is estimated 16 per cent of GDP in 1990).
- Central government spending total:
  • contribution from the budget balance to monetary growth;
  • fiscal indicators adjusted for activity showing the real macroeconomic impact of the budget.

The following table shows performance from 1990.

Table 1. **Fiscal indicators, 1990-94**

As percentage of GDP

		1990	1991	1992	1993	1994
A.	Revenue [1, 2]	45.7	46.1	45.2	43.9	43.7
B.	Revenue excl. oil	48.2	47.9	47.1	45.5	45.8
	1. Taxes and excises	35.1	35.2	35.0	33.3	33.3
	2. Interest revenue	6.0	5.9	5.1	4.6	3.9
	3. Other revenue	7.2	6.8	7.0	7.6	8.6
C.	Expenditure [1, 2]	45.2	49.0	50.2	51.0	49.9
D.	Expenditure excl. central government petroleum activities	53.9	58.4	58.3	58.3	57.5
	1. Purchase of goods and services	13.7	14.3	14.4	14.2	14.0
	2. Transfers	40.2	44.1	43.9	44.1	43.5
	– Deficit in stateowned enterprises	0.3	0.3	0.0	–0.0	–0.0
	– Interest payments	3.3	2.9	3.0	3.3	3.3
	– Other transfers	36.6	40.9	40.8	40.8	40.2
A-C.	Surplus before loan transactions [1]	0.5	–2.9	–5.0	–7.1	–6.1
B-D.	Surplus before loan transactions, adjusted for oil taxes and transfers from Norges Bank and central government's petroleum activities	–5.7	–10.5	–11.2	–12.8	–11.7

1. Per cent of GDP, otherwise GDP excl. oil and ocean transport.
2. Excl. transfers (from) to *Statens petroleumsfond*.
Source: Ministry of Finance.

In addition, every fourth year, the Long Term Programme includes longer term analyses and indicators of government expenditures. In the Revised National Budget, presented to the Parliament each spring, medium term fiscal indicators are presented. Work is now under way to present more systematically structural indicators.

2. Calendar of main points of decision-making and activities

Months before start of FY (t)	Main events and activities
(Year t – 1)	
February-March	Cabinet endorses preliminary expenditure ceilings for each Ministry.
March-April	Ministries prepare draft budget proposal under each budget item, including proposals for new policy.
May-June	The Cabinet decides final spending limits for each Ministry.
August	Ministries develop revised proposals under each budget item, within the revised limits set by Cabinet. Draft budgets are scrutinised by MF. Bilateral negotiations between MF and ministries.
September	The Cabinet gives the final approval on budget expenditures and revenues including deciding on unsettled matters. Final decisions on central government revenues and expenditures are also made.
October	Cabinet's budget proposals are submitted to Parliament.
December	Final consideration and amendments in Parliament. Final voting in middle of December.
(Year t)	
January	Start of financial year (t).

3.   The annual budget cycle

As already mentioned the Cabinet meets in February/March for several days to discuss the main guidelines for fiscal policy and to endorse budget expenditure ceilings for each Ministry's area of responsibility. The Cabinet also endorses separate frames to finance new policy initiatives. The ministries can give comments on the preliminary ceilings. Final limits are decided by the Cabinet in May/June.

The ministries then work out proposals under each budget item within the agreed limits, and include proposals financed under the frames for new policy initiatives. Some major items, especially new items, are discussed between each ministry and MF. In September, after having submitted and reviewed the ministries proposals, the Budget Department transmits the budget proposal to Cabinet, for deciding unsettled matters and final decisions on central government expenditure. Final decisions on Central Government revenue and economic policy are also made.

In October the Cabinet's budget proposals are submitted to Parliament. During October and November the Parliamentary Committees consider and amend the proposals, and make preliminary decisions. On basis of these preliminary decisions and new information on economic development the Ministry of Finance works out the proposal for a Final Budget. After final consideration and amendments in Parliament final voting is held in middle of December.

D.   EXPENDITURE REVIEW

In 1986 the government established a program aimed at modernising the public (state) sector in Norway. Some measures were also taken to improve public sector efficiency. A central part of the program was to commence a process of establishing specified policy goals for the ministries and state agencies and to make sure that these goals were supported by "management by objectives" systems at an organisational level.

All public organisations have to produce "institutional plans" (virksomhetsplaner) on a one year basis. "Institutional plans" as a management tool have been developed from the more traditional methods of "management by objective". The directorate of public management has established detailed guidelines to ensure that institutional plans are actually carried out and in a more or less standardised manner. These guidelines describe ways/efforts to overcome problems of measuring performance in the public sector, and some indicators of performance have been developed.

In addition to the one year plans public organisations also have to produce strategic plans on a three to four year basis to support the achievement of the specified policy goals. Practically all the public institutions concerned have been through the process of making such plans.

The process of setting up policy goals and connecting them to more operational goals in the organisations is normally done in co-operation between the ministries and their respective departments and agencies. Performance targets are set by the organisations, but the ministries influence the choice of different goals as well as ambitions.

At the organisational level, management is responsible for developing relevant performance measures. In most institutions it is considered to be a fairly important process where staff and staff representatives contribute. The most common process is to arrange seminars where objectives, performance measures as well as targets are discussed.

Most ministries have set up a specified reporting system to consider whether objectives actually are taken into consideration by the organisations, but the quality of this practice varies to a large extent.

To improve the tools for budget decisions, the Ministry of Finance is involved in the process of making available performance measures for the Parliament. In addition, the Ministry of Administration in co-operation with the Ministry of Finance puts forward recommendations for organisational forms of control.

The system of planning presupposes that client/customers needs, and information related to this, should be a base for the setting of goals. The organisations themselves define who their clients are.

The performance measures are firstly meant to be used by the organisation itself to achieve a more efficient internal allocation of resources. Introducing performance measures make centralised control of public organisations easier and allows a more decentralised organisational structure.

When the appropriation and budget system successively were changed from 1986 it gave spending institutions more freedom and flexibility in the use of appropriated funds. By replacing a detailed control system with some incentives to improve cost-effectiveness, however, the Ministry of Finance and the Ministry of Administration (Civil Service department) had to attempt to establish measures to indicate actual performance.

When spending institutions are reporting preliminary results to ministries/directorates during the budget year, these figures are not official.

By and large the most important receiver of performance measures is the Parliament. Performance measures should and are meant to be presented in the Government's budget proposals and budget reports to Parliament as long as the quality of the measures are considered to be reasonably good. Norway is now experimenting with different ways of presenting performance measures in documents to the specialised committees in Parliament. All these documents (budgets and reports) are published and open to the general public.

E.   IMPLEMENTATION OF THE BUDGET

1.   Major instruments of in-year control

Immediately after the Parliament's approval of the Budget, the ministries issue directives to their subordinate agencies, informing them of the resources at their disposal the following year (''allotment letter''). On this occasion, the ministries may choose to withhold funds in certain areas (*e.g.* investments in infrastructure), for instance for financial purposes. After having received the allotment letter, the subordinate agencies have the authority to spend within the instructed limits.

Agencies report expenditure developments to ministries on regular basis and ministries attempt to analyse expenditure developments of their agencies. The Ministry of Finance is informed through bimonthly reports of each agency on funds already spent.

Parliament is informed twice a year about implementation of the budget, through rather technical reports.

Parliament has granted authority to the Government (and MF) to exceed appropriated expenditure amounts, if necessary. The Government is allowed,for each decision concerning a budget item, to spend up to a maximum of 3-4 million Kroner. The Ministry of Finance is authorised to allow additional spending up to a maximum of about 1 million Kroner.

2.   Managerial discretion

In principle, appropriated funds cannot be transferred from one budget item to another, the budget item being defined as the homogeneous economic category within a vote. However, transfers between current expenditure items are possible to some extent, in particular between wages and other current expenditure, and from wages and other expenditure to investment expenditure.

Carry-forward of funds, committed and uncommitted, is allowed for, if it is so declared in the budget, *e.g.* for investment expenditure. In addition, 5 per cent of wages and other current expenditure items in the budget can be carried forward.

Each Ministry can allow subordinated agencies to use additional revenues up to 2 per cent of current expenditure without prior authorisation.

F.   RECENT REFORMS

To hire a person in the central government there must be a vacant position for the purpose, established by the Parliament. The ministries have earlier been given authority to change positions between different types of executive officers. The authorisation has recently been extended to also include administrators.

PORTUGAL

**Any changes which have taken place in Portugal
since July 1994 are not reflected in this chapter**

A. INSTITUTIONAL STRUCTURE OF BUDGETARY DECISION-MAKING

1. Political and organisational structure of government

Portugal is a unitary state in which there are various forms of decentralisation which affects the budgetary structure.

In budgetary terms there are three components: the Central, Regional and Local Administrations and Social Security. In Regional Administration there is budgetary independence substantiated in the preparation, approval and implementation of the respective budgets which are not included in that of the State.

Nevertheless, the State Budget sets up provisions as regards indebtedness and draws up allocations for costs resulting from the insularity of Madeira and Azores and for the coverage of any deficit.

Although local Administration may not levy taxes it is granted budgetary independence since the establishment, approval and implementation of the budgets are carried out by their own entities.

These budgets are not included in the State Budget but State budget transfers are submitted to the Assembly of Republic (Parliament) for approval.

Social Security has administrative and financial autonomy. This budget is integrated in the State Budget from which it receives funds to cover the deficits of the non-contributory schemes and of social welfare.

Budgets of state companies, though under some supervision by both the Sectorial Ministry and the Ministry of Finance, are not included in the State Budget. However, the State Budget grants subsidies for the payment of costs imposed by public service and for investment.

Since the revision of the 1989 Constitution, Central Administration Budgets for agencies and autonomous funds form part of the State Budget and are thus submitted to the Assembly of the Republic for approval.

The Central Administration is composed of 16 Ministries and nearly 360 agencies of which 160 belong to the National health Service and 100 to the higher education sector. Each Ministry is headed by a Minister and a number of Secretaries of State.

2. Main budgetary organs

As regards Budgets the major intervening bodies are as follows: the Assembly of the Republic, the Government and the Court of Accounts.

The Assembly of the Republic is responsible for political functions whereas the Government is entrusted with executive functions and the Court of Accounts is in charge of jurisdictional and auditing functions.

As regards the Government, the Ministry of Finance performs a key role.

Taking into account the macroeconomic scenario and the pluriannual framework for budgetary policy – currently the European Union Programme of Convergence – the Ministry of Finance submits the guidelines for the budgetary policy to be followed namely, the nominal ceilings for the outlays of each Ministry and for the most important functions, as well as taxation measures and revenue forecasts.

The Ministry of Planning and Territorial Administration is responsible for drawing up the annual and pluriannual investment scheme to be included in the State Budget taking into consideration the restrictions resulting from the Programme of Convergence and from the ceilings as laid down by the Ministry of Finance.

In the Ministry of Finance the main responsibility for drawing up the Budget rest with the Secretary of State for the Budget in co-operation with the Secretary of State for Tax Affairs in matters related to tax revenues, and the Secretary of State for the Treasury in matters related to finance.

Within the departments dependent of the Secretary of State for the Budget, the Directorate General for Public Accounting co-ordinates and establishes the budget for expenditure.

3. Role of Assembly of the Republic, Government and Court of Accounts

The Plenary of the Assembly of the Republic approves the general outlines of the budget and the revenue and loans to be raised in detail. In the Assembly of the Republic the Committee for Economy, Finance and Planning approves expenses, in detail. However members of Parliament can call for a final decision by the Plenary of proposals having been decided by the Committee. The Budget must be approved until the 15th December. If this is not possible before the beginning of the new fiscal year, the corrected Budget of the former year remains in force. Should this be the case, planned revenue can be collected and expenditure may be carried out in accordance with the one twelfth principle (not more than a twelfth of the annual amount, per month).

The Ministry of Finance submits the major budgetary political outlines to the Prime Minister and the final decision is made by the Cabinet which sets the ceilings for each Ministry. The Cabinet approves the draft budget to be submitted to the Assembly of the Republic.

Table 1. **Administrative public sector accounts (1993)**
(National accounts)

Estimated percentage of GDP

	State general account	Autonomous funds and services	Local and regional administration	Social security	Total
1. Current revenue	21.62	6.82	3.63	12.20	36.76
1.1. Taxes on income and property	8.21	0.00	0.80	0.00	9.00
1.2. Social Security contributions	0.00	0.00	0.00	10.29	10.29
1.3. Taxes on goods and services	11.39	0.34	1.08	0.08	12.89
1.4. Nontax revenue	2.02	6.48	1.75	1.82	4.58
of which: From other general government sectors	0.03	5.11	0.91	1.45	
2. Current expenditure	25.39	6.48	3.47	11.81	39.65
2.1. Public consumption	9.45	4.54	2.87	0.48	17.35
of which: Personnel	8.29	3.34	1.80	0.30	13.73
Goods and services	1.16	1.20	1.07	0.18	3.61
2.2. Subsidies	0.77	0.19	0.05	0.00	1.01
2.3. Interest payments	6.32	0.06	0.29	0.00	6.66
2.4. Current transfers	8.85	1.69	0.26	11.32	14.63
of which: To other general government sectors	7.18	0.10	0.01	0.22	
3. Current balance	−3.78	0.34	0.15	0.39	−2.89
4. Capital revenue	0.61	2.77	1.48	0.92	3.27
of which: From other general government sectors	0.04	1.63	0.81	0.03	
5. Capital expenditure	3.44	3.24	1.95	1.33	7.46
5.1. Fixed Investment	0.77	1.49	1.73	0.07	4.07
5.2. Capital transfers	2.66	1.75	0.22	1.26	3.39
of which: From other general government sectors	2.13	0.03	0.00	0.35	
6. Overall balance	−6.61	−0.13	−0.32	−0.02	−7.08
7. Primary balance	−0.29	−0.08	−0.03	−0.02	−0.42
8. Net financial assets	−0.10	0.23	0.04	0.00	0.16
9. Overall balance with financial assets	−6.50	−0.36	−0.35	−0.02	−7.24

Source: OECD.

The Court of Accounts, an independent court, checks whether or not public expenditure and accounts are legal. In addition, it gives an appreciation of the State General Account and deals with financial infractions.

B. THE SCOPE AND NATURE OF GOVERNMENT FINANCES

Budgetary measures are part of a medium term strategy in which the reduction of the deficit, the weight of public debt and current expenditure are the main objectives. The State Budget Framework Law (Law 6/91, February 20th) lays down: The State Budget must allow the resources necessary to cover all expenses and must avoid any outlay being financed by the creation of money.

The primary balance, (*i.e.,* the difference between total revenue and total expenditure excluding public debt interest) must not be negative.

The maximum limit of increase in public debt intended to meet financial needs resulting from the implementation of the State Budget, including agencies and autonomous funds, is set annually by the Assembly of the Republic in the budget State Law.

The State Budget, in its narrowest sense, is broken down into public expenditure for the operating costs of the public administration and for the financing of the Investment programme "Planned Investments".

Operating expenses are disaggregated by economic, organic and functional classification. As regards planned investments there is also a classification by programmes and projects which makes up the annual tranche of programmes and projects. Revenue are disaggregated by economic classification. The revenues and expenditure of agencies and autonomous funds are disaggregated in the same way as those of the State Budget. Social Security revenue and expenditure are disaggregated by a specific classification according to the specificity of the subsector.

C. BUDGET FORMULATION STRATEGY AND PROCESS

1. Technical aspects of the multi-year estimates

Though the State Budget is annual, it contains, as an indicator, the pluriannual programmes and projects which are included in PIDDAC (Investment and Development Expenditure Plan for Central Administration).

The forecast generally covers the budget year and the three following years.

2. Calendar of main points of decision-making and activities

The fiscal year corresponds to the calendar year and there is an additional period to pay expenses until 31st January of the following year.

Months before start of FY (t)	Main events and activities
(Year t – 1)	
May/June	Macroeconomic guidelines.
June	The Ministry of Finance presents the first Budget estimate.
July	Ceilings are discussed and approved by the Cabinet.
July	Circular from the Directorate General for Public Accounting (DGCP) with norms to be observed for each government department in the drawing up of its budget.
July/August	Preparation by the Services of the draft budgets.
August	The Directorate General for Public Accounting analyses the draft budgets presented by the Services without autonomy and by agencies and autonomous funds and checks if they are in accordance with the ceilings attributed to them and the directives set out in the circular.
June/September	Drawing up the Budget report.
By 15 October	Drawing up the Draft Bill and its approval by Cabinet.
By 15 October	The Government submits the Budget to the Assembly of the Republic.
15 October/15 December	The Assembly of the Republic discusses and approves the Budget.
(Year t)	
January	Start of financial year (t).

179

D. EXPENDITURE REVIEW

Within a perspective of analysis of efficiency and effectiveness, the drawing up of the State Budget pays particular attention to budgeting by activities. It allows for the setting up of management indicators, namely means, products, results and environment.

These instruments enable information to be obtained as to the best combination of available resources *vis-à-vis* the intended objectives and subsequently their comparison with the results achieved.

E. IMPLEMENTATION OF THE BUDGET

1. Main instruments of in-year control

The monitoring of the budget out-turn in the Services without financial autonomy is based on elements relative to budget allocations, commitments, expenditure authorisations and degree of accumulated monthly out-turn.

This data is provided, at a global level, by each Ministry and Service and by economic and functional classification.

These tables allow a first analysis of deviations through comparison between the degree of effective out-turn and the security pattern. Monthly reports are also drawn up by each Ministry to explain the respective budget out-turn.

A reserve allocation to be used by order of the Ministry of Finance, is included in the budget of the Ministry of Finance in order to cope with contingent, urgent and unpostponable expenses. This provisional allocation comprises also the estimated amount to pay adjustments in the Civil Service which are approved after the drawing up of the budget.

The follow up of agencies and autonomous funds is carried out through quarterly balances prepared on a public accounting basis to facilitate the drawing up of consolidated overall accounts. this information allows for assessment of the budget out-turn and possible deviations. As personnel expenditure accounts for nearly 85 per cent of public consumption, surplus in these allocations may not be used by Services for other expenses without the prior agreement of the Ministry of Finance.

As regards planned investments, any financing by the Ministry of Finance is made according a plan of application by programmes and projects and by economic classification.

The level of additional net debt of organisations with a legal capacity for indebtedness is also monitored with a view to not exceeding the limits laid down annually by law.

2. Managerial discretion

The Assembly of the Republic, the Government and the managing bodies of the Central Administrative may carry out budgetary alterations.

The Assembly of the Republic is responsible for the alterations which determine any increase in the total expenditure of the State Budget, each Ministry, or of a functional nature. Parliament is also responsible for the budgetary alterations of agencies and autonomous funds which may determine an increase in the limit of the overall net debtedness.

F. RECENT REFORMS

The perspective of management by objectives which was recommended in the introduction of activities (in 1987) was reinforced in the Revision of the Portuguese Constitution (1989) and in Law No. 6/91 – State Budget Framework. In fact, this regulation makes provisions for the Budget to be structured by programmes. Moreover, the State Budget Framework also laid down that the Budgets of the agencies and autonomous funds should be approved by the Assembly of the Republic.

Basic regulations concerning the budgetary reform are as follows:

– Basic Law for Public Accounting (law No. 8/90 of 20 February);
– Decree Law No. 155/92 of 28 July which stated the guidelines relative to the New System of the State Financial Administration;
– Decree Law No. 275 – A/93 of 9 August which established the State Treasury unit.

The implementation of budgetary reform will bring about:

a) abolition of Services which have no financial and administrative autonomy;
b) reduction of a "*a priori*" control in favour of an "*a posteriori*" check with a view to evaluating results;
c) accurate characterisation of agencies and autonomous funds and their reduction;
d) the setting up of a treasury unit and the introduction of an electronic payment system which will considerably improve the drawing up of the budget and budgetary control.

The instruments designed for these purposes in the area of accounting statements, staff management and administration of assets have been put into effect throughout the Ministry of Finance. Budgetary reform has been introduced into the Ministry of Finance and will be subsequently extended to other Ministries.

The use of an accounting system in line with the National Accounting Scheme and applicable in private companies is also foreseen.

Finally mention should be made of the introduction in 1995 of the new scheme of functional classification of public expenditure following the budgetary reform which has already been implemented and which included economic classification of public revenue and expenditure (1988).

SPAIN

**Any changes which have taken place in Spain
since December 1993 are not reflected in this chapter**

A. INSTITUTIONAL STRUCTURE OF BUDGETARY DECISION-MAKING

1. Political and organisational structure of government

Spain is a unitary State where authority is vested in a parliamentary monarchy. There are three tiers of government:

– central government;
– the autonomous communities (regional tier);
– provincial and municipal authorities (local tier).

Each region (or autonomous community) has or may have a constitution (*Estatuto*), parliament and government of its own, with a separate public service. Each tier of government is in principle autonomous in performing the functions assigned to it under the Spanish Constitution.

The functions of central government are essentially constructed around the relevant ministerial departments and a number of autonomous organisations and agencies. Each ministry is headed by a Minister, with in some cases one or two State Secretaries. Ministers and State Secretaries are political appointees. The number of Ministers may vary, but remains fairly stable; there are 16 at present.

The Parliament (*Cortes Generales*) is made up of two chambers, the Chamber of Deputies (*Congreso*) and the Senate (*Senado*). Members of Parliament are elected for a four-year term. In the last parliamentary elections, the Socialist Party lost its absolute majority, but still holds a sufficient number of seats to secure a relative majority.

2. Main budgetary organs

Under the Constitution, the budget is prepared by the Government, and the Minister of Economic Affairs and Finance holds the main budgetary powers and responsibilities, including general ones for revenue, expenditure and macroeconomic forecasting.

The Ministry for Economic Affairs and Finance is divided into:

– a State Secretariat for Finance;
– a State Secretariat for Economic Affairs.

The State Secretariat for Finance holds main responsibility for the whole budget process.

It contains a Secretariat General for Planning and the Budget, within which budget activity is co-ordinated by the Directorate General for the Budget, which has prime responsibility for preparing, co-ordinating and implementing the budget with regard to expenditure and revenue.

A significant role is played in preparing the budget by a number of committees:

– the Functional Committee for the Budget, with an open membership, is chaired by the State Secretary for Finance and co-ordinated by the Secretary-General for Planning and the Budget and includes a number of management centres. Its purpose is to analyse the budgetary repercussions of policies concerning revenues and the functional allocation of expenditure in the budget;

- the Programme Analysis Committees, which determine the financial requirements of the expenditure programmes in relation to objectives and ranks objectives in accordance with the priorities laid down by the Functional Committee for the Budget;
- the Public Investment Committee, which co-ordinates the investment plans of government services within the multi-year economic framework.

3. Role of Cabinet

The Cabinet (*Consejo de Ministros*) plays a fundamental role in the budgeting process. It approves the general directives for the preparation of the budget and sets guidelines for the central government's economic, financial and monetary policy. It settles disagreements over appropriations between the Minister for Economic Affairs and Finance and other Ministers. At the conclusion of the preparatory stage, it takes decisions concerning amendments to tax provisions and approves the draft budget for presentation to Parliament.

4. Role of Parliament

The Central Government is responsible for drafting the General State Budget. Parliament is responsible for examining it, amending it as necessary, and approving it. The Government is required to submit the General State Budget to the *Congreso* not less than three months before the end of the current budget period.

When the budget papers have been submitted to Parliament, they are reviewed by a Budget Committee of the *Congreso*. When the *Congreso* has voted on the Bill, it goes to the Senate where the approval procedure is the same as in the *Congreso*.

The Senate can amend the Bill, make additions, or vote it down; in the latter case, the Bill goes back to Congress. The Senate veto can be overridden by absolute majority in a second round voting in Congress. Otherwise, in a third Congress round two months later, a simple majority will suffice to lift the Senate veto. In the absence of this, the Bill would be sent back to the Government. The Budget Act cannot create new taxes, but it may modify existing taxes in cases where a provision exists in a previous taxation law.

If Parliament has not approved the Finance Bill by the start of the new budget period, the current budget is automatically carried forward until Parliament votes appropriations for the new period.

B. THE SCOPE AND NATURE OF GOVERNMENT FINANCES

The macroeconomic and budgetary scenarios guide the medium term action of the central government, and the annual budget is its reflection for the first of the four years covered by these scenarios. The latter are not formally approved during the budgeting process, and hence have no statutory force.

Under the Finance Act, the public sector comprises two parts, general government and public undertakings. The General State Budget comprises estimates for central general government (State, autonomous organisations of administrative nature, social security and certain public entities) and state-owned public undertakings (autonomous organisations of a commercial, financial or similar nature, public undertakings and corporations).

The local and autonomous authorities, undertakings which they control, and private establishments controlled by the State are not included in the General State Budget.

Social security is chiefly funded by contributions from employers and employees (affiliation is mandatory), with part coming from the State budget.

There are substantial financial flows from central government to the other tiers of authority and public undertakings.

Table 1 shows the consolidated expenditure of the State, the autonomous organisations and social security under spending heads, providing a general view of the functional breakdown of expenditure.

Table 1. **General State budget. Expenditure by policy**

As a percentage of GDP

Policies	1992	1993
Justice	0.36	0.36
Defence and foreign affairs	1.37	1.30
Internal security	0.88	0.84
Pensions	9.03	9.63
Unemployment protection and other social benefits	4.82	5.05
Employment promotion	0.52	0.53
Health	4.26	4.80
Education	1.65	1.64
Housing	0.17	0.16
Transport subsidies	0.45	0.40
Infrastructure	1.33	1.24
Research	0.34	0.30
Agriculture	0.97	1.24
Energy and industry	0.37	0.34
Tax administration	0.22	0.21
Financing of regional and local authorities	4.50	4.75
European Communities	1.17	1.31
Public debt	5.93	6.60
Other	1.87	1.81
Total	40.23	42.57

Source: *Presupuestos Generales del Estado, 1993.* Informe Económico y Financiero.

C. BUDGET FORMULATION STRATEGY AND PROCESS

1. Strategic aims and global norms

The strategy and objectives for the budget are set out in the macroeconomic and budgetary scenarios, and reflected in the short term in the annual budget. Budgetary policy is conditioned by the need to adjust the Spanish economy to the requirements of the European Union. From this standpoint, the objectives for the 1993 Budget are:

1. To continue the process of convergence with the other European Union members.
2. To keep the effort in social protection.
3. To keep the effort in public investment.
4. To continue the process of fiscal harmonization with other European Union members.

Table 2. **State budget indicators, 1984-92**

As a percentage of GDP

	1984	1985	1986	1987	1988	1989	1990	1991	1992
Revenue	15.5	15.6	17.6	19.5	19.7	21.2	20.4	20.5	21.0
Expenditure	20.8	20.9	22.1	23.2	22.6	22.9	22.7	23.0	24.3
Deficit	−5.3	−5.3	−4.5	−3.7	−2.9	−1.7	−2.3	−2.5	−3.2

Source: Intervención General de la Administración del Estado: *Actuación económica y financiera de las Administraciones Públicas.*

2. Technical aspects of multi-year estimates

Multi-year planning in Spain, which had initially been designed to overcome the difficulty of investment planning beyond the annual budget period, has over recent years given rise to a series of multi-year budget instruments and papers which indicate the improvements that have been achieved:

- The macroeconomic and budgetary scenarios: they treat the annual budget as the first step in a four-year process and provide an appropriate framework for analysing the objectives and circumstances of public sector action and its possible effects on the economy. The scenarios cover general government, comprising the State, social security and the autonomous administrative organisations, hence differing from the budget framework which further includes the commercial organisations and certain public entities.
- Annex on public investment: this sets the annual volume of investment and contains estimates for the three subsequent years.
- Budgeting by expenditure programmes: a four-year span is also found here, although the budget paper contains only the objectives and appropriations for the coming year.

3. Calendar of main points of decision-making and activities

The budget period is the calendar year (year t).

Months prior to start of budget year (t)	Main events and activities
(Year t – 1)	
10-9 (March-April)	The Ministry for Economic Affairs and Finance (MEF) Directorate General for the Budget draws up technical directives for the preparation of the budget.
9-8 (April-May)	Evaluation of objectives for the budget year in relation to macroeconomic objectives. Expenditure and revenue proposals are submitted to the Ministry for Economic Affairs and Finance (MEF) by management centres, and are examined by MEF and the Government.
7 (June)	The proposals by the management centres are consolidated in MEF and aligned on the directives and priorities set by the Government. Meetings of the Functional Committee and the Programme Analysis Committees.
4 (September)	MEF draws up its Budget estimates in line with economic objectives and the Cabinet's directives, and presents the Finance Bill to the Cabinet. The Bill is approved by the Cabinet and submitted to Parliament before October 1.
3 (October)	Parliamentary sittings on the Finance Bill begin.
(Year t)	
0 (1 January)	Start of the budget year (t).

4. The annual budget cycle

During the early months of the year, after analysing the actual course of the economy and adjusting the macroeconomic programme, the Ministry for Economic Affairs and Finance (MEF) lays down guidelines for the preparation of the budget. The MEF then draws up the corresponding instructions as to the method to be followed, the schedule to be observed and the documents to be presented. The management centres and the various committees (Functional Expenditure Committee, Programme Analysis Committees and Public Investment committee) and the administrative units concerned with the preparation of the budget then draw up the papers concerning the monitoring of expenditure and revenue and projections for the preparation of the budget to be submitted to MEF.

When the recapitulations of objectives and the papers concerning revenue and expenditure for individual programmes and management centres have been provided, MEF launches an ongoing process of discussion and exchange of information (June and July) involving intensive data inputting and computer simulations in order to adjust the range of proposals to pre-established priorities and secure compatibility.

The culmination of this stage is reached in September with MEF preparing a preliminary draft budget. This goes to the Executive and, after acceptance or amendment, goes to Parliament before 1 October as the Finance Bill.

D.   EXPENDITURE REVIEW

Steady efforts have been made to improve the efficiency of the procedures for preparing and executing the budget since the system of budgeting by objectives was introduced in 1984.

Since 1989 the annual budget has been prepared in the framework of multi-year planning by programmes, covering a rolling four-year period. The whole process of budget preparation is designed to provide clear identification of the objectives to be achieved.

Objectives for expenditure programmes are set according to the Budget Policy priorities given by the Functional Committee for the Budget. Then, the Programme Analysis Committees determine the resources to be allocated to the different expenditure programmes, on the basis of the above-mentioned objectives as well as financial restrictions.

The computer systems introduced in recent years (SICOB – Accounting and Budgetary Information System), staff training and the use of discussion methods in the preparation of the budget have all helped make the budgeting process more rational.

E.   IMPLEMENTATION OF THE BUDGET

1.   Major instruments of in-year control

Improvements in budgeting methods and in the structure of the budget have called for, and facilitated, a greater degree of monitoring of the execution of the budget, based on:
- Spot checks using an integrated computer system which provides continuous accounting data on the execution of the budget and various other aspects, providing information on investment projects at any point in their implementation.
- Since 1989, a system has been set up to monitor objectives. It initially covered eight programmes (four on the creation of public infrastructure and four on the provision of public services). In 1993, the system was extended to an additional eight programmes (a total of sixteen). This process will be extended to all programmes where it is appropriate.

Far-reaching administrative reforms are currently being planned; the aim is a clear-cut modernisation of administrative structures and methods, and the management of revenue and expenditure will clearly be affected.

2.   Managerial discretion

The different spending centres have prime responsibility for the effectiveness and efficiency of their expenditure programmes.

A spending manager can transfer funds from one vote to another without Parliamentary approval, with restrictions specified in law. Balances can be carried forward to the next fiscal year, but approval of MEF is always needed.

F.   RECENT REFORMS

The 1983 budgetary reform will eventually transform the traditional budget of means, into a budget of ends or goals. Such an integrated system will enhance the consistency and quality of budgetary decision-making. A number of steps have been taken to change organisation, and procedures, among which are:
- Design of an integrated target budget system;
- Automation of budgetary data-bases and development of applications software;
- Unification of management and administration of personnel costs, by creation of a new Directorate General of Personnel Costs;
- Preparation of budget rules for the public sector.

G. FURTHER INFORMATION

Significant documents on the annual budget for the calendar year (year t) include:

1. The Finance Act (*Articulado de la Ley de Presupuestos Generales del Estado*).
2. Statement of revenue for the State, autonomous organisations, certain public entities and social security (*Presupuesto de ingresos*). This contains consolidated estimates of revenue for the year.
3. Expenditure. Budget by programme and statement of objectives (*Gastos. Presupuestos por Programa y Memoria de Objetivos*). Twenty volumes with schedules of government expenditure listed by programmes, not by their allocation to management centres. There are two annexes, describing objectives and indicators (*Anexo de Inversión Vinculantes*) and listing the projects in the Inter-Territorial Compensation Fund (*Anexo de Proyectos que componen el Fondo de Compensación Interterritorial*).
4. Financial statements and accounts of the commercial, industrial and financial autonomous organisations (*Estados Financieros y Cuentas*).
5. Operating and capital budgets and financial statements for certain public entities and state corporations (*Presupuestos de explotación y capital y estados financieros*).
6. Economic and financial report (*Informe económico financiero*) providing information on the Spanish economy, the prospects, expenditure policies and major budget items in the context of the national economy and flows with the European Community.
7. Consolidated budget (*Presupuesto consolidado*). This provides an overall view of revenue and expenditure, by chapter, for the Budget of the State, the autonomous organisations, social security and public establishments.
8. Annexes on the staffing of both government and autonomous organisations from an organic and a functional point of view (*Anexos de Personal, Estructura orgánica y funcional*).
9. Interim report on the budget outturn for the current year (*Avance de la liquidación del presupuesto*).

SWEDEN

**Any changes which have taken place in Sweden
since September 1993 are not reflected in this chapter**

A. INSTITUTIONAL STRUCTURE OF BUDGETARY DECISION-MAKING

1. Political and organisational structure of government

Sweden is a unitary state. There are three layers of government: the State or central government, county councils and municipalities.

Central government currently consists of 13 ministries (known collectively as the Government Office) and about 250 agencies. The ministries are very small – few have more than 200 employees – as their task is mainly to assist the minister in policymaking. The implementation of policy is the responsibility of independent agencies, formally reporting to the Cabinet and not to individual ministers. All deliberations between government and the agencies are public. The borderline between formulation and implementation of policies is drawn by government, through collective Cabinet decision-making, thus preventing an individual minister's intervention in specific cases or in the implementation of policies that have been delegated to agencies.

Ministries have in general one or two ministers, and there are at present 21 Ministers. The Under-Secretaries, the highest official rank in each ministry, are political appointments, as are a small number of other appointees, but the large majority of departmental personnel is non-political.

Parliament has one Chamber (*Riksdag*). The present government is a single party minority Social Democratic government. Elections are held regularly every four years, with the next elections due in 1998.

2. Main budgetary organs

The Ministry of Finance has prime responsibility for expenditure and taxation policies and for fiscal and economic policy, as well as personnel policy and wage determination for central government. The MF includes a Legal Department (responsible for tax legislation), the Economic Policy Department, an international department (responsible for Nordic co-operation, relations with international institutions etc.) and financial markets regulation, consumer policy and the Budget Department. The Ministry of Finance is also responsible for the administration of grants to Municipalities and county councils.

The Budget Department, headed by a budget director, has approximately 40 staff (all grades and supporting staff). Five divisions work in the budget department, each having both controlling functions with regard to sectoral spending areas and "general" tasks, like budget forecasting, general budgetary issues and monitoring of the three-year frames for agency appropriations as well as internal personnel policy.

The National Audit Bureau which is formally responsible to the Minister for Finance, although its independence is stressed, has main responsibility for taxation and other revenue estimates. The Bureau is also engaged in other activities concerning the budget process, such as development of financial management systems and regulations, training of agencies and ministerial personnel, and audit of agencies activities.

3. Role of Prime Minister and Cabinet

All government decisions are taken collectively in Cabinet.

The Prime Minister's Office is involved in the most important stages of the budget cycle. The government's stance on economic policy and expenditure policy, published twice a year with the Budget and the supplementary estimates, is decided by the Cabinet.

Policy guidelines issued by MF are also first decided on by Cabinet. Thus Cabinet is involved at all stages of the budget process, although the negotiations on expenditure as a rule are held between the MF and the responsible ministry.

4. Role of Parliament

Parliament approves the annual appropriations of all central government expenditure, including entitlements authorised under separate legislation. The parliament does not approve multi-year estimates, but can decide upon multi-year planning frames such as a five-year frame for defence, multi-year authorisation for investment purposes etc. Expenditure is controlled at the level of some 900 votes, *i.e.* as an average about 75 per departmental spending area. The budget documents, submitted by government to Parliament, are considered by the Finance Committee and by a number of sectoral committees. The Committees can vary budget estimates both up and down, and the Finance Committee has no superior role to other sectoral committees in formulating the budget. Each committee has a staff of three to five officers. Decisions are made by the Committee responsible for each sector.

By constitutional law, Parliament has to approve the Budget before the start of the fiscal year. If the Parliament is for some reason not in session and does not approve the budget, the Finance Committee has emergency power to release funds, but this has never occurred.

B. THE SCOPE AND NATURE OF GOVERNMENT FINANCES

The percentage of GDP represented by total outlays of government in Sweden has long been one of the highest in the OECD area, although general government financial balances, while in deficit from the late 1970s through to the mid-1980's, moved into surplus in the second half of the decade. However there was a deterioration in the state of public finances in the early 90s, in part cyclical and partly related to the implementation of taxation reforms, putting pressure on public spending.

One of the main characteristics of the Swedish public sector is the large extent to which county councils and municipal governments make up total public expenditure. This is also reflected in the high consumption expenditure level of local authorities relative to that of the public sector at large. The municipalities are in charge of schools, for which they act as an agent of central government. Other areas of importance are child day-care and support to the elderly. The county councils, operating at regional level, are responsible for hospitals and primary health care and operate quite independently from central government.

The main source of regional and local government revenue is the proportional income tax, at present averaging about 30 per cent. Legislation in 1991-93 froze levels of local taxation. Regional and local governments also levy fees for services and receive grants from other tiers of government. A new system of general grants for local authorities is to be introduced from 1993, replacing a number of differentiated specific purpose grants. The new system is intended to create more equal financial conditions between local authorities, recognising the differences in their structural circumstances. The new system will also reduce the level of central government regulation of local authority activity. The central government will set guidelines for local government which primarily relate to the overall financial framework and transfers from the centre. The aim is to give the authorities greater freedom of action to manage resources more efficiently. Local authorities are permitted to have access to capital markets and have often made use of this possibility.

Social security is organised through both budget and off-budget funds. From a policy point of view there is no difference between off-budget and on-budget financing. Parliament has to approve the compulsory payroll tax contributions, or wage-bill related fees, as well as other parameters, like eligibility terms. To the extent that there is a deficit in most social security funds, it is covered by central government. The social security system comprises basic and supplementary pensions, health insurance, occupational injury and unemployment insurance. Basic pensions and occupational injury insurance are provided through central government's budget. In addition, central government provides grants in aid (transfers) to social security funds. Supplementary pension funds for old age retirement schemes with general, mandatory coverage, are controlled by an independent board. In autumn 1992 the former liberal-conservative government met a principal agreement with the social democratic party then in opposition concerning significant changes to the social security system. One of the most important parts of the agreement was that the responsibility for health insurance and working injury insurance should successively be transferred from the state to become a matter for negotiations between the employers' federations and employee organisations. The aim is for these counterparts, over a period of time, to assume the full responsibility for both the future financial construction as well as levels of benefits. The state will however by legislation guarantee a minimum level of compensation in the system.

190

Public enterprises (for example telecom and the railway traffic enterprise) established by public law, and state owned companies are required to finance their current operations from receipts and to conduct their operations in a commercially viable way. Public enterprises have to fund investment from their surplus or from market borrowing. There are borrowing facilities in the national debt office for enterprises. Government guarantees on borrowings are explicit, and require a parliamentary decision and are also subject to a 1 per cent annual fee. The overall level of loan guarantees is published with the budget documentation. No borrowings from the foreign market are allowed. Where an enterprise or company is required to provide a particular service or level of service by the government in the nature of a community service obligation an appropriation will be made to cover the costs incurred. A programme of privatisation has been established, with the first enterprise to be sold being the state owned steel company.

Tax expenditures are significant in some areas, for example in relation to housing mortgage expenses and some business expenditure.

Table 1. **Functional classification of central government outlays in 1991-92**

As a percentage of total

Defence	8
Education	13
Social security	31
Housing	8
Recreation and culture	4
Communication	5
General public services	5
Public order and safety	5
Public debt interest	19
Other	3
Total	100

Source: Ministry of Finance, Sweden.

C. BUDGET FORMULATION STRATEGY AND PROCESS

1. Strategic aims and global norms

The Government is pursuing an economic strategy aimed at enabling Sweden to become an economically strong member of the European Community and to keep inflation permanently low. Key elements of the strategy are improved conditions for sustainable economic growth through measures to promote investment and employment, a more competitive and flexible economy, and restored balance to public finances. The long term strategy is to eliminate the deficit in public finances over the business cycle, to make certain strategic reductions in taxation, which impose very stringent requirements on economic policy, and to pursue economic policies which will permit fulfilment of the convergence criteria for participation in Economic and Monetary union within the EEC.

The following table provides overall figures on the fiscal position of general government:

Table 2. **Fiscal indicators 1987-93**

As percentage of GDP

	1987	1988	1989	1990	1991	1992	1993
General government							
Total outlays	57.8	58.1	58.3	59.1	61.3	67.2	71.3
Current receipts	62.1	61.6	63.7	63.3	60.2	59.8	58.3
Surplus (+)/deficit (−)	+4.2	+3.5	+5.4	+4.2	−1.1	−7.4	−12.9

Source: OECD Economic Outlook.

2. Technical aspects of multi-year estimates

The main basis for long term expenditure strategy is the multi-year estimates published in the Medium-term Calculation of Consequences. The calculations of expenditure and revenue estimates are made on a constant policy basis – that is, that government policy decisions and commitments remain the same for the period, the starting point being the next fiscal year with projections covering a further four years. The estimates are based on background material and constructed bottom-up by spending ministries and agencies for each of the 900 votes on a constant price basis and updated annually on a rolling basis. MF however makes the final calculations and has the responsibility for publication. No in-year updates take place. The multi-year estimates originally covered central government only, but projections now include the entire public sector.

Multi-year estimates (MYE) for both revenues and expenditure have mainly been developed to project budget-deficits and to highlight the fiscal implications of government programmes on a same policy basis. They are not used for control purposes, and are not a forecast of likely events or a statement of future government expenditure policy.

Macroeconomic forecasts (the Medium Term Survey) are also produced, which present scenarios for developments in the Swedish economy over the same period, and provide a second important base for the development of a long term expenditure strategy, as well as providing the assumptions which underpin the budget estimates.

MYE are published once a year as an appendix of the Revised Budget Bill, both at functional levels and in economic categories (constant price and pay level). The economic forecasts are also published as an appendix to the Revised Budget Bill, when no separate long run analysis report is published (*i.e.* two years out of every three).

3. Calendar of main points of decision-making and activities

Months before start of FY (t)	Main events and activities
(Year t – 1)	
January	Presentation of Budget Bill for the year commencing July 1 to Parliament.
February-April	Consideration of long-term expenditure policy strategy for the following year. Analysis of agency reports on previous year activities. Guidelines for budget preparation issued to Departments and Agencies.
April	Government presents Revised Budget Bill to Parliament with the economic and budget policy of the government together with MYE of preceding budget round and three year economic development assessments which are the basis for government budget policy formulation. Parliament discusses policy-guidelines suggested by government.
May-June	Budget Bill passed by Parliament. Government outlines the objectives to be achieved by the agencies over a three year period.
(Year t)	
July	Start of fiscal year (t).
September	Agencies present budget requests to ministries and MF. Ministerial frames for the budget to be presented in January decided by Cabinet.
October	Agencies report on performance during the year just ended.
October-December	The line ministries issue frames for individual appropriations based on principal agreement with MF about sectoral priorities the most important sectors within the budget frame of within individual ministry's. Negotiations between ministries and MF on the contents of the budget bill to be presented to Parliament in the following January.

4. The annual budget cycle

The fiscal year runs from 1 July to 30 June, with the main events as shown in the calendar above. The preparation of the budget starts shortly after the presentation, in January, of the draft budget prepared for the preceding cycle, which covers the year commencing 1 July.

The structural framework of the budget process is result-based management, which operates from the level of agency objectives drawn up by the government to internal agency management at all levels. Recent changes to the process, however, are placing greater emphasis on evaluation and analysis at the broad sectoral level. This involves the establishment of a long-term spending strategy for the public sector, a total public sector spending frame, and its distribution in separate budget frames among the various Ministries, together with strengthened demands for result-analysis at all levels.

Key features of the preparation of the Swedish budget are the three year budget frames provided to Agencies, which outline the objectives to be achieved over that period, and the annual review of the results obtained. The intention behind the three year frames is that, while appropriations are provided for one year only, each agency would only be subject to major analysis and evaluation of its performance once every three years. In this way, a full review would be conducted into one third of the agencies every year. However, the three year review cycle is not adhered to inflexibly, and major changes of government policy will mean modification of the three year frames irrespective of the stage in the cycle.

The annual reviews normally take place from October, after Agencies have submitted their budget requests (September) and provided a report on results achieved in the year just ended, and are critical to more recent developments in the budgetary process. These reports are more than statements of financial results: agencies are also asked to report on their performance against the targets set, using a range of indicators. The review of performance, based on these reports, will determine in part whether the agency's three year budget frame needs major review.

The next step in the budget procedure lasts until December, and essentially consists of preparation of the budget bill by ministries and MF, following MF negotiations with ministries. In the fall, estimates are made of all expenditure items to be presented to Parliament, *i.e.* both the ones covered by the Budget Bill and the ones brought forward in amendments to the Budget Bill. In the Budget Bill, the financial effects of these amendments are thus included. The reason for amendments is to draw attention to the matter, usually a major change in sectoral policy.

The outcome of the process is the Budget Bill containing the economic policy and budget statement, a survey of the national economy, the suggested appropriations and appendices prepared by the ministries concerning the appropriations, which is presented to Parliament in early January. As noted above, for some expenditure items no estimates are given in the Budget Bill, the fiscal proposals being presented in separate supplementary bills in February and March. Decisions are taken by Parliament on general policy guidelines in the area and on each vote.

Late in April, the Government presents a revised Budget Bill, summing up the various bills presented after the Budget Bill and containing a revised economic policy and budget statement, a revised revenue estimate, a revision of the economic survey presented in the Budget Bill, the multi-year budget projections and the 3-year economic policy assessment.

D. EXPENDITURE REVIEW

Ministries in Sweden are very small. Agencies perform their executive tasks quite independently; all communication between agencies and government is public. Directives are given by the government as a whole, not by individual ministries.

Reviews take place under various arrangements and authorities. From time to time, government appoints committees of experts. In some cases, members of Parliament may participate, for example when thorough preparation of new or altered legislation is involved. Reports are commonly circulated for comments by interested parties (such as government agencies, local governments, universities, trade unions, employers' associations etc.), the process being open to the public, and used by the ministries in the development of policy changes and associated legislation. Since the mid-1980's there has been more use made of less formal working groups, and generally shorter time frames for reports, with the aim being to have the reports available for consideration as part of the budgetary decision-making process.

The National Audit Bureau (about 200 professional auditors/researchers) which is part of the government, performs effectiveness reviews in addition to compliance reviews. The auditors are organised both in units reflecting the ministry organisation and in specialist functions (charges and fees, procurement, electronic data processing). They are formally responsible to the Minister for Finance, although they operate independently.

Parliamentary Auditors consist of twelve members of Parliament, backed up by a secretariat of some 20 auditors, and concentrate on issues of relatively general relevance to parliamentary decisions.

Finally, the expert group for studies in Public Finance (ESO) was set up to submit information for decisions concerning budgetary policy and public economy. A specific task was to study questions concerning productivity and effectiveness in the public sector.

The results of all the above-mentioned reviews are published. This does not always occur in internal review procedures, set up by MF and/or spending agencies.

E. IMPLEMENTATION OF THE BUDGET

1. Major instruments of in-year control

Immediately after approval of the Budget by Parliament, the government issues directives to all departments and agencies about the implementation of the budget; that is, how they can spend their funds. Under certain conditions, government can withhold funds appropriated by Parliament. In certain cases, funds can be exceeded, *i.e.* higher pension expenditure due to faster price increases.

In general, the implementation stage of the budget does not receive very much attention in the Ministries and MF. It is closely followed by the National Audit Bureau through its auditing and bimonthly forecasts for the outcome of the current budget. Preparation of the budget and multi-annual planning of activities are thought to be superior in terms of setting priorities and effectively controlling government expenditure.

The most important financial task in the implementation stage is to protect the projected budget deficit against unforeseen changes. There is a kind of reserve (the so-called additional expenditure requirement) available which is however limited for use in meeting unanticipated labour market expenditure. The government has the capacity to go to the Parliament for supplementary budget bills if unforeseen requirements arise in any area.

Parliament is informed about in-year developments of the budget through bimonthly reports by the National Audit Bureau. Government presents a current year review to Parliament.

2. Managerial discretion

Appropriations may be of four different kinds:
- appropriations that cannot be exceeded nor carried forward. There are very few such appropriations covering about 1 per cent of total expenditure;
- appropriations that can be exceeded but not be carried forward (principally appropriations relating to entitlements); this is the largest category, covering about 85 per cent of total expenditure. They can be exceeded only if within the use decided by Parliament. Expenditure overruns that are allowed are those relating to demographic changes, and price and wage developments and are controlled by the auditors;
- appropriations that cannot be exceeded, but that can be carried forward (for example, regional policies, energy saving measures and investment funds);
- appropriations which can be carried forward to future years with no limit, and which can be exceeded by borrowing from the next year up to a limit of 5 per cent. These appropriations cover all running costs – that is salary and administrative costs, including capital.

Transfers between votes without Parliamentary approval is not allowed.

F. RECENT REFORMS

As part of a continuing strategy to improve public management, greater emphasis is being put on the setting of targets, clearly specifying the required results, and analysing and evaluating the results achieved. Recent changes have built on earlier reforms.

Block-budgeting at agency level was introduced in the late seventies, with the regulation that goes with it being progressively reduced, so that the flexibility given Agencies in the management of their resources is now total. Within the budget frame allocated to them, agencies now have almost absolute freedom in the deployment of their resources, including staff numbers, and, from 1 July 1992, all accommodation costs. From FY 1991/92 budgeting has been framed more or less formally into a three year review cycle, although appropriations are still approved annually, and agencies' resources are, as a general rule, more deeply scrutinised once every three years and less in the other two years. Agencies can make longer range plans, adaptations can be prepared more at decentralised level.

However, significant changes were announced with the Government's 1992 Budget Bill, which proposed more analysis and evaluation at the sectoral level, as part of a budget making process designed to focus on longer-term expenditure strategy. This will be done by the introduction of budget frames at the level of the Ministries. The government also introduced a possibility for "rolling" an agency within the three year review cycle system by permitting the guidelines for an agency to be extended for an additional year, but subject to deep scrutiny of activity after the fourth year. There is an option for using this "rolling" alternative for an additional two years, however in the sixth year there must be an evaluation of the results which the agency has produced. The process of delegating responsibilities to the agencies will continue, but more will be demanded in terms of agency accounting for their performance. Many changes are proposed, designed to improve resource management including the introduction of new methods for cash management by agencies, allowing them to earn interest on funds at their disposal, and the replacement of appropriations for administrative investments with borrowings from the National Debt Office. The monopoly over central government payments held by the Postal Giro system is to be revoked. Other changes proposed relate to the management of fee-financed activities, and principles governing leasing practices in the state sector.

G.   FURTHER INFORMATION

1.   Documents related to annual budget

The fiscal year runs from 1st July to 30th June.

1. Budget Bill (*Budget propositionen*), January containing:
   - economic policy and budget statement, survey of national economy;
   - list of appropriations;
   - appendices by ministries on appropriations.
2. Popular version of the Budget Bill (*Regeringens budgetforslag*), January, containing:
   - economic policy and budget statement;
   - short description of sector policies.
   English translation available ("Swedish Budget").
3. Revised Budget Bill (*Kompletteringsproposition Reviderad Finansplan*), end of April year, containing:
   - revised economic policy and budget statement;
   - revised survey of national economy;
   - three year economic policy assessments;
   - multi-year estimates.
   The revised economic policy and budget statement is published in English.
4. Annual directives to agencies on how to prepare budget requests (*Aarliga direktiv*).
5. National Audit Bureau's presentation of government finances (*Statens finanser*).

2.   Other documents

6. Budget regulation (1989: 400, changed 1991: 1 029).
7. Regulation and Management in the Central Government Administration and Financial Preconditions for Government Agencies. 1992 Ministry of Finance, Budget Department.

SWITZERLAND

**Any changes which have taken place in Switzerland
since September 1993 are not reflected in this chapter**

A. INSTITUTIONAL STRUCTURE OF BUDGETARY DECISION-MAKING

1. Political and organisational structure of government

The Swiss Confederation is a federal republic comprising three levels of government: the Confederation or central government, the 26 cantons and some 3 000 communes.

Each canton has its own constitution, parliament and government. The way administrative responsibilities are divided between the cantons and their communes differs appreciably from one canton to another. Each level of government is legally autonomous and in principle independent as to how it exercises its constitutional powers, particularly in the financial field. Because of their scale, and also because many communes are small and hence have limited financial resources, many communal tasks (water supplies, primary and secondary education, waste water purification, etc.) are carried out at regional level by groups of communes (districts).

The powers of the Confederation, and hence of the federal government, are laid down in the Federal Constitution. They are split between 7 departments (ministries) and a number of federal bodies. The 7 federal departments are headed by a federal councillor. A general secretariat co-ordinates the business of the department, which is subdivided into several directorates.

The Federal Council (*i.e.* federal government, hereinafter FC) is headed by the President of the Confederation who is a federal councillor, elected to this post by Parliament for one year on a rota basis. It is above all an honorary appointment, each federal councillor remaining answerable to Parliament for the business of his own department. He thus acts as a member of the collegiate body that is the FC. A Federal Chancellery provides the administrative staff of the FC.

Parliament consists of two chambers, the National Council and the Council of States, which have the same prerogatives. The National Council has 200 members who are elected directly, while the Council of States is composed of 46 members representing the Swiss cantons (2 for each canton, 1 for each "half-canton").

Members of Parliament are elected directly for four years. The members of the Federal Council are also elected for a four-year period by the two chambers combined (Federal Assembly). Since 1959, the federal councillors have been chosen, in predetermined proportions, from among the Members of Parliament of the four biggest political parties.

A striking feature of Switzerland's budgetary federalism is the fact that the population decides directly what taxes may be levied. At Confederation level, taxes and maximum rates of tax are written into the Federal Constitution, and any amendments to the Constitution have to be decided by referendum. Thus, a change in the rate of tax must be put to the popular vote and, for it to be adopted, has to approved by a majority of both the cantons and the people.

2. Main budgetary organs

The Federal Finance Department (FFD) manages the Confederation's finances. It is responsible for securing the revenue needed to finance the Confederation's manifold activities, and for taking due care of public funds. Reporting to the FC, it examines all projects with financial implications in order to determine whether they are consistent with sound economic policy and if their cost is acceptable. It is in this respect that the FFD has an important role in the so-called "joint report procedure", for it is called upon to express its opinion on other departments' projects. The Federal Finance Administration (FFA), which comes under the FFD, is the main Confederation body dealing with all matters relating to federal finances. Its main responsibilities include preparing the budget and multi-year financial planning. Every year it draws up the targets and directives – requiring FC approval – which determine the thrust of budgeting and financial planning. On the basis of these instructions, the departments and agencies (about one hundred) plan their spending in the context of the coming year's budget and the financial plan for the following three years.

3. Role of the Government (Federal Council)

The FC administers the Confederation's finances, submits the budget and keeps revenue and expenditure accounts. It is even specified in the Federal Constitution that it is the Confederation's duty to pursue a sound financial policy in keeping with the economic situation, *i.e.* to ensure the long-term equilibrium of revenue and expenditure and to take the economic situation into account when shaping financial policy. The FC submits the budget to the Federal Assembly for approval every year.

4. Role of Parliament

The Federal Assembly draws up the annual budget on the basis of a draft message submitted to it by the FC. The National Council and the Council of States discuss the budget proposal and the approval of the central government accounts. In practice, each of the two Councils entrusts this financial supervisory role to their respective finance committees, *i.e.* the Finance Committee of the National Council and the Finance Committee of the Council of States, each of which is appointed for the duration of the parliamentary term. The Finance Committees are responsible for the financial management of the Confederation in general and look after the long-term trend in federal finances. They discuss the budgets, requests for additional appropriations, appropriations carried forward and accounts of the Confederation. They report on such matters to the legislative Councils whose task it is, in the final analysis, to approve them or not. Where financial surveillance is concerned, the constitution and the law give the Federal Assembly more extensive powers than they do with regard to administrative surveillance in general. Since the Assembly is empowered to authorise or refuse financial resources, it follows that it is able to exercise a direct influence in all areas of government activity.

The Finance Delegation, which consists of three members delegated by the Finance Committees of both the National Council and the Council of States, keeps a close and permanent watch over every aspect of the Confederation's financial management. In particular, it is empowered to approve urgent disbursement and commitment appropriations.

B. THE SCOPE AND NATURE OF GOVERNMENT FINANCES

Table 1 shows how the finances of general government, its borrowing requirement, debt and level of overall taxation (which includes compulsory social security contributions) evolved between 1975 and 1989. It should be noted that compulsory social security is not included in the following figures relating to general government finances.

General government expenditure rose at an average annual rate of 5.3 per cent between 1975 and 1989. However, the expenditure/GDP ratio remained constant throughout the period, standing at 26.9 per cent in 1989. Overall, general government finances were in deficit between 1975 and 1985 and in surplus from 1986 to 1989. 1990 saw a turnaround, with the start of a renewed deficit phase which could last for several years and apply to all three levels of government. General government indebtedness and the income tax and social insurance contributions/GDP ratio were well below the OECD average.

The Confederation, cantons and communes contribute almost equally to the financing of general government consolidated expenditure. Each level of government meets the expenditure incurred through the exercise of its responsibilities by means of tax revenue and other sources of finance such as compulsory levies and transfers from other levels of government. Indirect taxation is, in principle, the responsibility of the Confederation, whereas income and wealth taxes are the province of the local authorities (cantons and communes). In fact, the Confederation also levies direct taxes (tax at source, direct federal tax), part of which goes back to the cantons. It should be said that the communes also account for certain cantonal tax revenues. A federal redistribution system exists, the object of which is to ensure that the cantons can meet their responsibilities without their inhabitants having to shoulder an intolerable tax burden. The first plank of this financial redistribution involves the cantons

Table 1. **Trend of general government finances, 1975-89**

	Consolidated expenditure of general government (Confederation, cantons and communes)		General government borrowing requirement FF million	General government indebtedness FF million	Ration of income tax and social insurance contributions to GDP % of GDP
	FF million	% of GDP			
1975	38 066	27.2	−2 269	59 254	29.6
1980	47 240	27.7	−776	72 607	30.8
1981	49 956	27.0	−396	73 667	30.6
1982	54 384	27.7	−1 442	76 010	31.0
1983	57 443	28.2	−1 906	78 027	31.6
1984	59 779	28.0	−655	81 644	32.3
1985	62 773	27.5	−293	83 821	32.0
1986	65 364	26.9	+2 669	83 916	32.5
1987	67 647	26.5	+2 105	83 908	32.0
1988	73 267	27.3	+1 621	83 296	32.6
1989	78 028	26.9	+454	83 163	31.8

Source: Finances publiques en Suisse (1989)/Administration fédérale des finances; Revenue Statistics of OECD Member countries/OECD (1991).

sharing in certain federal revenues on the basis of their financial resources, which are reviewed every two years. The second plank consists of the fact that federal subsidisation of local authorities' investment and current expenditure is graduated on the basis of these same financial means. There are internal systems of financial equalisation specific to each of the cantons, and it is these that ensure intercommunal redistribution.

Table 2. **General government expenditure in 1989, by activity**

Expenditure of the Confederation, cantons and communes by area of activity (ranked according to outlay)

		Confederation	Cantons	Communes	Total
			In per cent		
1.	Education and research	9.1	27.0	22.5	20.0
2.	Social insurance	21.0	12.3	10.9	15.4
3.	Health	0.2	17.2	15.0	12.3
4.	Communications and energy	16.5	11.6	8.8	11.4
5.	National defence	19.0	1.4	1.8	7.4
6.	General government	2.9	5.0	9.1	6.5
7.	Expenditure of the finance department	10.9	6.5	7.0	5.1
8.	Protection of the environment	0.7	1.9	10.0	4.1
9.	Agriculture and food	9.4	3.9	0.8	3.9
	Miscellaneous	10.3	13.2	14.1	13.9
Total		100.0	100.0	100.0	100.0
		Breakdown of areas of activity between the Confederation, cantons and communes			
1.	Education and research	16.0	50.4	33.6	100
2.	Social insurance	47.9	29.8	22.3	100
3.	Health	0.6	64.6	34.8	100
4.	Communications and energy	51.0	23.9	25.1	100
5.	National defence	91.0	3.7	5.3	100
6.	General government	15.8	36.2	48.0	100
7.	Expenditure of the finance department	75.4	1.8	22.8	100
8.	Protection of the environment	5.7	16.8	77.5	100
9.	Agriculture and food	84.1	14.3	1.6	100
	Miscellaneous	26.0	42.6	31.4	100
Total		35.1	35.2	29.7	100

Source: Finances publiques en Suisse (1989)/Administration fédérale des finances.

The majority of administrative tasks are carried out jointly by the three levels of government. The main responsibilities of the Confederation are defence, foreign affairs and social security. Also, the central government plays an important role in agriculture and transport at national level. The cantons have a big say in education policy and health, and also ensure the smooth functioning of the legal system. Cultural activities fall mainly to the communes, which also have authority regarding the protection of the environment and water and energy supplies. The police, land-use planning and welfare assistance are catered for by both the cantons and the communes.

Table 3. **General government expenditure and revenue, 1975 and 1989**

	1975		1989	
	FF million	% of total	FF million	% of total
Expenditure				
Employee compensation	12 083	31.7	27 314	35.0
Goods and services consumption	9 235	24.3	18 891	24.2
Investment	6 794	17.8	9 652	12.4
Transfers to third parties	7 526	19.8	14 233	18.2
Transfers to public enterprises and institutions	2 020	5.3	7 146	9.2
Loans and equity investment	408	1.1	792	1.0
Total	38 066	100.0	78 028	100.0
Revenue				
Taxation	28 370	79.3	60 287	76.8
Income and wealth taxes	20 637	57.7	43 929	56.0
Tax on consumption	7 733	21.6	16 358	20.8
Monopolies, duties and business licences	405	1.1	677	0.9
Incomes	1 929	5.4	3 944	5.0
Indemnities (taxes, current sales, repayments, etc.)	5 094	14.2	13 574	17.3
Total	35 798	100.0	78 482	100.0

Source: OECD.

The federal social security offices draw up their own budgets. Their expenditure is covered by employees' and employers' contributions, and also by transfers from the Confederation and the cantons. The conditions of entitlement and contribution rates are the subject of federal laws and edicts.

Some federal entities operate like independent enterprises, but their budgets and accounts have to be approved by the Federal Council and Parliament. This is a reference to the federal railways and to the federal post, telephone and telegraph services (PTT). The Confederation grants operating and investment subsidies to the federal railways. The PTT transfer to the federal budget part of any net profit they may make.

C. BUDGET FORMULATION STRATEGY AND PROCESS

1. Strategic aims and global norms

With continuing stability being the key feature of its financial policy, the Federal Council adheres in principle to the objective of a balanced budget and controlled growth of expenditure. The latter has to be based on the development potential of the Swiss economy, and must not therefore exceed forecast GDP growth. For these targets to be achieved, priorities have to be clearly defined and strict spending discipline is vital. Where financial planning for the 1991-95 term is concerned, for example, the different departments were asked to be drastic in their selection and scaling down of activities that are to be extended. Under the same heading, the FC has announced different growth rates for different groups of activities. The various departments and agencies are expected to abide by these rates of growth and limits on spending, and to look for ways of cutting back on present expenditure levels.

2. Technical aspects of multi-annual estimates

Where work on financial planning is concerned, a distinction has to be made between the preparation of the legislative authority's financial plan and its annual review during the parliamentary term. There is a close link, in terms of objectives and duration, between the financial plan of Parliament on the one hand, and the broad thrust of government policy and the planning of staff numbers on the other. The financial plan covers a three-year period and is discussed every year in conjunction with the preparation of the budget.

3. Calendar of main points of decision-making and activities

The fiscal year FY (t) is the same as the calendar year (year t).

Months before start of FY (t)	Main events and activities
(Year t − 1)	
January-February	The FC lays down the principles governing the preparation of the budget and sets the budgetary targets.
March-April	The budget is prepared at agency and department level. Budgetary requests may be submitted to the FFD up till mid-May.
May-June	Budgetary requests are discussed at government level (FFA with the agencies concerned).
Early July	The FC is informed of progress with the budget; it decides on the procedure to be followed and may, if necessary, revise its budgetary targets.
July	The FFD, together with the other departments, is asked to make such adjustments as are required in order to achieve the budgetary targets.
Mid-August	The FC approves the proposed changes and, if necessary, adjusts the economic parameters.
End-August/September	On the basis of decisions taken by the Federal Council, the FFD draws up a draft budget message.
Early October	The FC adopts the budget message and submits it to Parliament for approval.
October-November	The budget debate in Parliament begins at end-October with discussions in the National Council and the Council of States.
December	The budget is debated and adopted (Federal Decree) by the National Council and the Council of States in their December plenary session.
(Year t)	
1 January	Start of fiscal year (t).

4. The annual budget cycle

The preparation and drawing up of the budget comprises the following phases:

Budget directives and budgetary targets

The preparation of the budget starts in January and February with the formulation of directives concerning the substance. The situation is then analysed from the financial policy standpoint, and it is on the basis of this analysis that budgetary targets and policy with regard to spending are spelt out. The FC issues the budgetary directives. When reviewing the Confederation account for the previous fiscal year, the FC informs the finance committees of the National Council and Council of States of the budgetary targets it has set itself. It is in early March that the directives and appropriation requests are sent to the Confederation's various general government agencies.

Preparation of the budget and requests at departmental level

In March and April the agencies are called upon to assess the appropriations needed for the various expenditure items, keeping to the ceilings set in the directives, and to estimate probable receipts under the different revenue items. Properly substantiated budgetary requests must be addressed to the FFD before mid-May.

Agreeing on the budget figures

The budgetary requests submitted by the agencies systematically exceed the ceilings set by the FC. The initial discussions take place at administration level. Requests for appropriations and revenue estimates are almost all discussed with the agencies, as is the effect that any adjustments might have. At the same time, the general secretariats of the departments are asked to establish priorities and sometimes to have bigger reductions made.

The FC is informed of progress on the budget before the summer break. It decides what action should be taken and, if necessary, revises its targets on the basis of a fresh analysis of the situation. Together with the other departments, the FFD is instructed to make such spending cuts as are required for the budgetary targets to be achieved. There is however limited scope for cuts in the context of the budget preparation exercise. About 80 per cent of the Confederation's expenditure can hardly be reduced because of legal prescriptions or contractua commitments.

Reductions which have not been achieved at administrative level are submitted, in a second working paper, to the FC for decision. At the same time, the FFD is asked to prepare the budget message. The FC's draft budget is drawn up on the basis of these preliminary decisions, and also of any changes which may prove necessary in the light of analysis of the assumptions made concerning economic developments (price rises, trend of GDP).

Preparation and adoption of the budget message

In the space of barely a month (between end-August and end-September), the Federal Finance Department draws up, on the basis of the FC's decisions, a draft budget message which, alongside the quantified budget proper, contains a detailed commentary on the budget outturn and on the trend in expenditure and revenue. It is in early October that the FC adopts the budget message and therefore submits the draft budget to Parliament for its approval.

Parliamentary debate and vote on the budget

The budget debate in Parliament begins in late October with the discussions in the two finance committees, and ends during the December session with the budget being voted in the plenum (Federal Decree).

D. EXPENDITURE REVIEW

In handling the financial management of the Confederation, the Federal Assembly, the FC and the administration have to ensure that funds are used in an effective and sparing manner (Art. 3, sub-paragraph 1 of the Federal Act on the Confederation's Finances – hereinafter FCF). The FFD considers, from this angle in particular, all the budgetary requests submitted by the administrative units (Art. 17, sub-paragraph 1 of the Order on the Confederation's Finances – hereinafter OCF).

In addition to this permanent monitoring, the FFD looks from time to time at all the Confederation's own or transfer spending when corrective programmes are introduced. Under the Federal Act on financial support and allowances, which came into force on 1 April 1991, the FC has moreover to check periodically – every 6 years at least – that the financial support and allowances paid by the Confederation are being used economically and efficiently to achieve their purpose.

In order to help the administrative units in their management efforts and facilitate the FFD's task in monitoring expenditure, plans to introduce a system of "controlling" in the Federal administration are currently being prepared.

E. IMPLEMENTATION OF THE BUDGET

1. Major instruments of in-year control

When an administrative unit has a payment to make which exceeds the balance on the disbursement appropriations at its disposal, it has to request an additional appropriation. Under the normal procedure, the request is considered by the FFD, by the FC and then, if the latter decides to submit it to the Federal chambers, by the chambers' Finance Delegation and then lastly by the chambers themselves.

These different authorities consider the material and formal justification for the request. In particular, they will ask why they expenditure was not budgeted for in the first instance and why it is not possible to wait until the next budget.

Generally speaking, the Federal Finance Inspectorate, which is the Confederation's top financial surveillance body, keeps permanent track of every phase of the budget process, including the drawing up of the central government account.

While the disbursement appropriations do give the FC and Parliament some control over expenditure, in the sense that they can reduce or increase it, this authority is nevertheless very limited. Room for manoeuvre in preparing the budget is severely restricted in particular by legal obligations (automatic functioning, bridging of deficits, set federal contributions), commitments already entered into and long-term sectoral plans. In 1989, for example, 80 per cent of the Confederation's expenditure was mandatory in nature. This is why the Federal chambers authorise commitment appropriations when it is important to know of and verify ahead of time the impact of complex projects which commit the Confederation for more than one fiscal year.

In contrast with the appropriations in the financial budget, which authorises expenditures to be made during the fiscal year (disbursement appropriations), commitment appropriations make it possible to contract financial commitments to carry out certain projects, the said commitments being in respect of subsequent years and up to the agreed amount. Commitment appropriations provide a framework within which it is possible not only to forecast and analyse over the long term, but also to assess all the financial effects of projected acquisitions and large-scale, complex work programmes. Within the traditional budget system, they remedy the drawbacks of annual budgets for larger-than-usual programmes.

The expenditure ceilings are merely federal decrees establishing a multi-year appropriation for clearly defined, expanding expenditures or sectors for which grants and disbursements take place the same year. These are quite simply financing decisions in the form of a simple federal decree, and presuppose the existence of a legal basis. From the point of view of their financial impact, they represent a sort of multi-year budget. But unlike the budget, they do not imply an expenditure authorisation; rather, the necessary appropriations have to be included in the annual budget and submitted for approval by Parliament. The latter has, however, to regard the expenditure ceilings as an upper limit, so in this sense it sets itself certain obligations.

2. Managerial discretion

The first opportunity to modify a disbursement appropriation allocated through budgetary channels consists of not spending the whole amount.

Conversely, when expenditure cannot be avoided during the fiscal year and an administrative unit does not have an adequate annual budgetary appropriation, an additional appropriation has to be requested. This is therefore a disbursement appropriation authorised on top of the budget. The additional appropriation is made available by the Federal chambers as part of the first or second supplements to the budget (during the June and December sessions, respectively).

An appropriation overrun is a temporary additional appropriation granted by the FC following the adoption of the message on the second budgetary supplement. Lastly, appropriations may be carried forward and used to pursue certain activities or projects when the appropriation made available for this purpose the previous year has not been entirely used.

F.   RECENT REFORMS

More frequent use of expenditure ceilings, coupled with the aim of setting maximum growth rates by area of expenditure, will enable the FC to exercise greater control over public spending by making it essential to establish clear orders of priority. At the start of the procedure for preparing the 1992 budget, for example, the FC set acceptable growth rates for the main groups of expenditure. Spending on military hardware, the promotion of research and development assistance, in particular, is now capped.

As noted above (Section D), a "controlling" system should make for improved political and financial planning and management. "Controlling" is a work method which allows optimum management surveillance so that officials can intervene where and when necessary. It will be possible both to highlight the objectives and to establish the extent to which they have been achieved. Also, the ongoing, systematic processing of information implied by "controlling" will make it possible both to assess any data which look essential for management purposes, and constantly to adjust the resources available to the objectives sought.

Without these being institutional measures, it is important to draw attention to the increasing collaboration, and distribution of tasks, with the private sector (upkeep of military hardware, research or data processing contracts, etc.).

Lastly, a plan to make senior civil servants' performance appraisal reports more flexible is under considera-tion. The idea would be to make them subject to private law, which would allow them to be terminated more rapidly – in return for compensation payments.

TURKEY

**Any changes which may have taken place in Turkey
since October 1993 are not reflected in this chapter**

A. INSTITUTIONAL STRUCTURE OF BUDGETARY DECISION-MAKING

1. Political and organisational structure of government

Turkey is a unitary state. Executive power is entrusted to the President and the Council of Ministers under the supervision of Parliament. Administrative organisation consists of central government, local administrations (special provinces of city municipality and village) and the State Economic Enterprises (SEEs).

Central government is headed by the Prime Minister and organised mainly in 17 ministries, 14 ministries of state, a deputy prime ministry and several agencies. Ministers of State are ministers without portfolio, usually with special tasks assigned by the Prime Minister. All ministers are members of Cabinet and usually also of Parliament. In every province (76 in total) a governor represents and is appointed by Central Government.

The single chamber Parliament is composed of 450 deputies. Five parties are represented in Parliament, the last election was held in October 1991.

2. Main budgetary organs

The following agencies are involved in central budgeting: Ministry of Finance (MF), State Planning Organisation (SPO), Under-secretariat of Treasury and Foreign Trade. The latter two under-secretariats are attached to the Prime Ministry.

The Ministry of Finance has principal responsibility for the preparation of the budget. The Ministry also exercises considerable influence on the implementation of the budget. The Ministry is composed of the General Directorate of Budget and Fiscal Control, the General Directorate of Revenues, the General Directorate of Accounting, the Research-Planning and Co-ordination Board and a number of other general directorates and boards. The General Directorate of Budget and Fiscal Control of the Ministry administers the budget. It is involved in the preparation, implementation and reporting stages of budgeting.

The General Directorate of Budget and Fiscal Control consists of five departments. Functionally, it can be grouped into three main departments.

- The *Department of Budget Administration* is responsible for preparation of the budget, it puts together the budget document for presentation to the Parliament. The release allocation, apportionment and cancellation of appropriated funds are other responsibilities of the department.
- The *Department of Public Administration* in collaboration with the State Personnel Office which is attached to the Prime Ministry, is in charge of personnel administration.
- The *Department of Financial Control and Expenditure Regulations* initially intervenes at the commitment stage of expenditure involving contracts by giving its approval. It also verifies all investment expenditures. The investment expenditures which are subject to this approval are regulated by the annual budget law. Another sub-department of the department examines the draft laws, regulation or other legislation concerning expenditures before they are submitted to the Parliament.

In addition, in all spending ministries and agencies there are 86 budget directorates and 11 Heads of Finance (which consist of budget directorates and accounting offices) in certain agencies functioning as a representative division of the General Directorate of Budget and Fiscal Control. They are responsible for preparing and implementing budgets of concerned ministries and agencies. The total staff of General Directorate of Budget and Fiscal Control is about 260 in the central unit and a further 1 000 in the budget directorates in spending ministries and agencies.

The Revenue side of the budget, which is included in the budget bill by the General Directorate of Budget and Fiscal Control, is prepared by the General Directorate of Revenue. It also administers tax collection and tax legislation.

The General Directorate of Accounting prepares the Financial Accounts Bill and it compiles revenue and expenditure transactions and arranges the general accounts for the Treasury.

The Research, Planning and Co-ordination Board prepares the Annual Economic Report which is submitted to the Parliament together with the Budget Bill.

The Under-secretariat of the State Planning Organisation is the secretariat of the High Planning Council. SPO makes assessments on the natural, social, economic and other resources of the country, and assists the government in drawing up the economic and social policies and targets, both in the short and long term. It also prepares the investment budget on a project basis which then is included in the budget documents by the General Directorate of Budget and Fiscal Control.

The Under-Secretariat of Treasury and Foreign Trade establishes the policies related to the state's domestic and foreign loans, short and long term debt management and also cash management.

3. Role of Prime Minister and Cabinet

The members of the Cabinet (the Council of Ministers) are collectively responsible for the formulation and implementation of the Government's general policy, while each minister is responsible for the expenditure of his or her ministry. The Prime Minister, apart from her role as chairman of Cabinet, also chairs the High Planning Council. Among its other members are a number of ministers including the Minister of Finance and the Minister of State for the State Planning Office.

The High Planning Council plays an important role in planning and budgeting. It defines the economic and social targets of the Annual Programme, by which the Five Year Development Plan is implemented. It is also the principal forum for determination of budget ceilings within the framework of the annual programme.

There is also a Money and Credit Council. This is headed by the Deputy Prime Minister.

Cabinet decides the draft budget bill and submits it to Parliament in October, 75 days before the beginning of the new financial year.

4. Role of Parliament

The Budget Bill is first considered by the Plan and Budget Committee composed of 40 members of Parliament. The members of this Committee can propose any amendment they wish to the Budget Bill. The Committee has to adopt a revised Budget Bill within 55 days, which subsequently is considered by Parliament in plenary session. During these debates, members of Parliament cannot propose amendments that would increase expenditure or decrease revenues. Parliament debates the Budget Bill as amended by the Plan and Budget Committee; members of Parliament may express their opinions on the budgets of individual ministries and agencies during this general debate. The various budget headings, and proposals for amendments are then read out and put to the vote without separate debates.

Parliament, as well as the Plan and Budget Committee, can change the budget at programme level, the same level at which the final approval of Parliament takes place. There are about 300 programmes in the budget, which are categorised according to departmental areas.

If, exceptionally, the Budget bill is not passed before the start of the financial year, Parliament may pass a provisional Bill that authorises Government to spend up to a certain percentage of the amount appropriated by the budget of the previous year, until a new budget is passed by the Parliament. The Budget Act is the only law the President cannot refer to Parliament for further consideration.

The appropriations granted by Parliament cannot be exceeded without prior authorisation from Parliament. Draft supplementary appropriation bills, and other draft legislation proposing additional financial commitments in the current or following year, must indicate the level of financial resources involved.

B. THE SCOPE AND NATURE OF GOVERNMENT FINANCES

There are 33 agencies (17 of which are ministries) in the general budget, while the annexed budget includes 65 agencies (53 of which are universities). Each annexed budget agency has revenues of its own. Around 85 per cent of the gross expenditures of agencies in the annexed budget is financed from the general budget.

The general budget also includes transfers to State Economic Enterprises (SEEs). There are about one hundred SEEs. Some of them operate on a normal commercial basis, while others produce and market monopoly and basic commodities like postal services and railways. The transfers to these public enterprises have been significantly reduced in recent years.

There are 107 extra-budgetary funds of which 63 have been included in the consolidated budget in the fiscal year 1993.

Data related to general government, functional classification of consolidated government expenditures is given in Tables 1 and 2.

Table 1. Administrative and functional classification of expenditure, 1988-93

Billion TL

Services	1988	1989	1990	1991	1992	1993 [1] Estimates
General services	10 915	17 674	27 297	56 870	85 044	180 933
Defence	2 529	5 097	9 110	16 074	30 291	49 555
Justice-security	801	1 747	3 484	6 830	11 847	16 447
Agriculture-forestry-village	985	1 984	3 904	8 739	13 897	19 635
Mining	71	141	233	566	951	2 842
Water affairs	1 545	2 517	3 824	7 148	11 718	15 747
Highways	675	1 134	2 109	4 241	6 999	10 662
Public works	390	579	1 018	1 716	3 897	4 851
Education	2 650	6 020	12 843	22 873	44 255	72 369
Health	641	1 482	3 213	5 222	10 462	18 031
Social services	138	260	723	1 162	1 857	2 827
Culture-tourism	106	236	596	960	1 838	3 281
Total	21 446	38 871	68 354	132 401	223 056	397 180

1. Programme.
Source: Ministry of Finance; General Directorate of Budget and Fiscal Control.

Table 2. Functional classification of consolidated budget expenditure as a percentage of total, 1988-93

Services	1988	1989	1990	1991	1992	1993 [1] Estimates
General services	50.9	45.5	39.9	43.0	38.1	45.6
Defence	11.8	13.1	13.3	12.1	13.6	12.5
Justice-security	3.7	4.5	5.1	5.2	5.3	4.1
Agriculture-forestry-village	4.6	5.1	5.7	6.6	6.2	4.9
Mining	0.3	0.4	0.3	0.4	0.4	0.7
Water affairs	7.2	6.5	5.6	5.4	5.3	4.0
Highways	3.1	2.9	3.1	3.2	3.1	2.7
Public works	1.8	1.5	1.5	1.3	1.7	1.2
Education	12.4	15.5	18.8	17.3	19.8	18.2
Health	3.0	3.8	4.7	3.9	4.7	4.5
Social services	0.6	0.7	1.1	0.9	0.8	0.7
Culture and tourism	0.5	0.6	0.9	0.7	0.8	0.8
Total [2]	100.0	100.0	100.0	100.0	100.0	100.0

1. Programme.
2. In round figures.
Source: Ministry of Finance; General Directorate of Budget and Fiscal Control.

Local administration's expenditures amount to 10 per cent of public expenditures. Revenue of such administrations partly comes from local government real-estate tax, operational revenues and municipal fees. They are also financed by transfers of tax revenues from Central Government.

Social security programmes are implemented by off-budget agencies. There are several types of social pension funds organised on an occupational basis. Revenues and expenditures of these funds are not included in the consolidated budget. Contribution and benefit rates are set by legislation. Government contributes to the fund for public employees.

The following table indicates the performance of budgetary indicators.

Table 3. **Fiscal indicators**[3]

	1988	1989	1990	1991	1992[1]	1993[2]
Total public current expenditure (real growth rate %)	1.9	3.3	17.0	1.0	1.9	4.9
Total public capital expenditure (real growth rate %)	−13.7	−6.6	8.0	3.8	1.1	−1.2
Revenues (% GNP)	28.5	28.3	27.9	25.4	26.6	29.6
Public expenditure (% GNP)	34.7	35.4	38.4	39.9	39.2	38.6

1. Estimate.
2. Programme.
3. Including SEEs. Social Security Funds are treated in net basis.
Source: State Planning Organisation.

C. BUDGET FORMULATION STRATEGY AND PROCESS

1. Strategic aims and global norms

Budgeting takes place within the broad framework of the fixed term Five Year Plan. According to the Constitution, government has to submit a Five Year Plan to Parliament. The approved plan and annual programmes are binding on the public sector and indicative for the private sector. The current (sixth) plan covers the years 1990-94.

The Five Year Plan specifies targets for economic, social and cultural development. Targets for public sector aggregates include total public current and capital expenditure and total public revenues. The plan also specifies ratios of total public expenditure to the GNP for each year, and corresponding real growth percentages.

2. Calendar of main points of decision-making and activities

Months before start of FY (t)	Main events and activities
(Year t − 1)	
7 (June)	Prime Minister's Budget Message. Guide to the Budget, prepared and issued by MF.
6 (July)	Preparation of individual ministry budgets.
5 (August)	Negotiations between ministries, SPO, and MF.
4 (September)	Series of meetings held among the SPO, MF, the Undersecretariat of Treasury and Foreign Trade high rank officials, preparing decision-making for the High Planning Council.
4-3 (September-October)	High Planning Council meetings.
3 (October)	Submitting the Budget Bill, Annual Economic Report, and Budget Memorandum to Parliament. Annual Programme announced as a Cabinet Decree.
3-2 (October-November)	Debates on the Budget Bill in the Plan and Budget Committee of Parliament.
1 (December)	Debates in the plenary session; approval of the Budget Law; and the promulgation of the Budget Law by the President. SPO issues the annual investment projects list as an annex to the Annual Programme.
(Year t)	
0 (1st January)	Start of fiscal year (t).

3. The annual budget cycle

The annual budget cycle begins in June, six months before the start of the fiscal year, with a Budget Call issued by the Prime Minister. The statement offers a broad statement of principles for the forthcoming budget.

On the basis of technical instructions from the Ministry of Finance in June, spending Ministries and other agencies prepare detailed budget proposals for current expenditure. These are the subject of discussion and negotiation with the Ministry of Finance over the next two or three months, culminating in decisions by the High Planning Council and the Prime Minister.

In parallel, Ministries and other agencies prepare and submit investment project budgets for negotiation with the State Planning Organisation and resolution again at High Planning Council and Prime Minister's level as required.

The High Planning Council settles a top down framework for the finalisation of the draft budget in September. It decides economic and social targets, and specifies the ceilings of current, investment and transfer allocations for the agencies. Within this framework, the Ministry of Finance and the State Planning Office finalise the draft budget in negotiations with agencies.

The draft budget bill is presented to the legislature in October, at least 75 days before the start of the fiscal year.

The appropriations granted by Parliament cannot be exceeded without prior authorisation from Parliament.

Ministers are responsible for the efficient use of appropriated resources. But the Ministry of Finance bears a general responsibility due to the authorities and duties vested in it by the Budget Act and General Accounting Law.

The Minister of Finance can regulate spending throughout the fiscal year. Shortly after the approval of the budget by Parliament, the Ministry of Finance issues a circular to all agencies stating the main principles governing commitments of funds and the maximum percentage of appropriations to be released.

The principles and percentages of this apportionment of funds depend on general economic conditions, recent trends in expenditures and revenues and the need to spread current expenditures throughout the year.

Parliament is informed about the implementation of the budget once a year, through the enactment of the Accounts Bill.

D. EXPENDITURE REVIEW

All expenditures and revenues are reviewed by the Ministry of Finance as part of the budgetary process, and the State Planning Office reviews investment proposals.

The Cabinet issues a decree related to the Annual Programme called "Decree about the Implementation Co-ordination and Surveillance of the Annual Programme". The ministries and agencies prepare several reports relative to their functions according to the decree. The Investment Realisation Report and the Major Investment Report are prepared quarterly and submitted to the SPO reviewing.

E. IMPLEMENTATION OF THE BUDGET

1. Major instruments of in-year control

Ministry of Finance publishes and monitors in the "Public Accounts Bulletin". This Bulletin includes information about budget appropriations, budget expenditure and revenue assessments stated on a general, annexed and consolidated budget basis together with the balance sheet of the Treasury.

The Budget Act authorises Ministry of Finance to regulate spending throughout the fiscal year. After the approval of the Parliament MF issues a circular to all agencies stating the main principles of commitments and the maximum percentage of appropriations to be released within the first 6 months. The second is usually issued in late June. The principles and percentage of apportionment of funds depend on general economic conditions, recent trends in expenditures and revenues, the need to spread current expenditure throughout the year and the nature of activities concerned. In addition, there is a separate control on the rate of cash outlays.

The Ministry of Finance also exercises a commitment control in current and future years. The Budget Act specifies the limits of commitment.

If there is a need to achieve savings, the Prime Ministry may issue a general savings guideline. The annual Decree of the Implementation, Co-ordination and Surveillance of the Annual Programme comprises a procedure by which investment programmes can be revised, if necessary, appropriation can be reallocated and cut back accordingly.

The budget of the Ministry of Finance includes a few contingency funds, such as a Reserve Fund, an Investment Acceleration Fund and a Personnel Reserve Fund representing about 3 per cent of total appropriations in 1993. They are utilised as emergency reserves for current and capital expenditure respectively.

Parliament is informed about the implementation of the budget once a year through enactment of the Final Accounts Bill. Members of Parliament, however, can ask to be informed about the budget implementation at any moment.

2. Managerial discretion

Parliament appropriates funds at the programme level, therefore appropriations can be only transferred between programmes with the approval of Parliament. Transfers of appropriations between the items of the same programme are only done by the Ministry of Finance. Personnel appropriations can only be transferred to personnel items within the same and other programmes. Investment appropriation can only be transferred with the consent of the SPO and by the Ministry of Finance within the same programme. If they are not utilised, all appropriations lapse at the end of the fiscal year.

UNITED KINGDOM

Any changes which may have taken place in the United Kingdom since November 1993 are not reflected in this chapter

A. INSTITUTIONAL STRUCTURE OF BUDGETARY DECISION-MAKING

1. Political and organisational structure of government

The UK is a unitary state. The Government is headed by a Cabinet of around twenty members which is formed by the Prime Minister, who is the leader of the majority party in the House of Commons. Most members of the Cabinet are responsible for one or more government departments and are usually supported by one or more junior Ministers. The Permanent Secretary of each department, or administrative head, is a non-political appointment, as are civil servants in general. Departments provide some services themselves, but they are increasingly doing so through departmental agencies formed to undertake their executive functions (see Section F below). In other cases, departments influence the provision of services by bodies such as local authorities.

The Conservative Party has had an absolute majority in the House of Commons since 1979. Two other UK-wide parties are currently represented, along with several smaller parties. Members of Parliament are directly elected by single-member constituencies. General elections take place when the Prime Minister advises the Queen to dissolve Parliament, but must be held at least every five years.

Parliament has a second chamber, called the House of Lords. This consists of hereditary peers and life peers appointed by the Queen on the advice of the Prime Minister. The House is mainly a revising chamber though bills can be introduced in it. Bills passed by one House are considered by the other. But bills dealing only with taxation or expenditure become law within a month of being sent to the House of Lords, whether or not the House agrees to them. If no agreement is reached with the House of Commons on other bills, the power of the House of Lords is limited to imposing a delay of a year, except that a bill to lengthen the life of a Parliament requires the assent of both Houses.

Many of the responsibilities of central government which relate to Scotland, Wales and Northern Ireland fall to their respective Secretaries of State. These responsibilities include health and education.

2. Main budgetary organs

Within central government, the lead in budgetary matters rests with the Chancellor of the Exchequer. Under him, the Treasury is concerned with both the revenue and the expenditure side of the Budget and with the formulation of economic and fiscal policies. The Treasury is also responsible for the pay of the civil service, and shares in its management alongside the Office of Public Service and Science, which is part of the Cabinet Office. Apart from the Treasury, the other departments reporting to the Chancellor include Inland Revenue and Customs and Excise, which are responsible for direct and indirect taxes, respectively; the Department for National Savings, which administers a range of personal saving schemes which finance part of the public sector borrowing requirement; and the Central Statistical Office.

The Chief Secretary to the Treasury normally leads on behalf of the Chancellor on public expenditure matters so that the latter can concentrate on economic, monetary and tax policies. The Chief Secretary, who is a member of the Cabinet, is supported by officials organised under a Second Permanent Secretary in the public expenditure sector of the Treasury. This comprises a General Expenditure Policy Group with some 40 staff dealing with forward planning, in-year control and statistics, and a number of specific expenditure groups which deal with particular spending departments. In total, some 400 people within the Treasury (including specialists and clerical support) are concerned with the planning and control of public expenditure, including departmental running costs and promoting value for money in departmental spending programmes; in addition, some 200 people are concerned with financial management in departments, civil service pay and conditions of service and industrial relations.

3. Role of Government and Legislature

The Government formulates its spending plans in the way described in Section C below. In recent years it has announced its plans for the next three financial years in an Autumn Statement, usually in November. (The financial year in the UK runs from April to March.) The Treasury and Civil Service Committee of the House of Commons then reports to the House for a debate in which it is invited to take note of the plans. Traditionally, tax rates have been announced by the Chancellor of the Exchequer in a Budget Statement, usually in March. From 1993, however, the Government announces its spending plans for the next three years together with its tax plans for the coming year in a Budget Statement in late November.

Parliamentary control is brought to bear because only Parliament can grant money for departments to spend. But only the Government can propose new areas of expenditure. Parliament can propose reductions but the Government can be expected to use its majority to protect its own proposals. In practice debates on expenditure usually concern strategy and priorities. Most central government expenditure is approved by Parliament on the basis of detailed statements, known as Supply Estimates, of the estimated expenditure of departments for the year ahead. Some expenditure, for example entitlements under the National Insurance Fund, payments to the European Communities and interest on government debt, rests on standing authorities given by Parliament.

Main Estimates are presented in March each year for the year ahead. An individual Estimate (or "Vote") may specify that certain levels of receipts can be "appropriated in aid" to reduce the net provision required. An annual Appropriation Act lists the total amounts of each of the 160 or so Votes and their coverage in broad terms (called the "ambit" of the Vote). An Accounting Officer, usually a Permanent Secretary, is appointed for each Vote and is accountable to the Public Accounts Committee of the House of Commons. In order for public services to be financed from the start of a new financial year until the Appropriation Act is passed in July, Parliament approves spending through Votes on Account before the year begins. These are normally for 45 per cent of the amount voted for the corresponding services in the current year.

B. THE SCOPE AND NATURE OF GOVERNMENT FINANCES

An analysis of general government expenditure by function is shown in Table 1 below.

Table 1. **Functional classification of general government expenditure, 1992-93**

As a percentage of total general government expenditure on services [1]

Social Security	33
Health and personal social services	17
Education	13
Defence	10
Law, order and protective services	6
Transport	4
Trade, industry, energy and employment	3
Other	13
Total	100

1. Excludes those elements of general government expenditure, *e.g.* debt interest, which are not attributable to a particular function.
Source: Statistical Supplement to the 1992 Autumn Statement (Cm 2 219).

Retirement pensions, invalidity and sickness benefit, unemployment benefit and certain minor benefits are financed through the National Insurance Fund, a government fund financed by employers, employees and the self-employed. This accounts for about 55 per cent of all social security payments, the balance being funded through the Supply Estimates. Changes in rates of benefits and contributions are proposed to Parliament by the Government, normally at about the time as it announces its public expenditure plans. They are usually intended to produce little change in the accumulated balance of the National Insurance Fund, which is not permitted to borrow to finance its expenditure.

Government departments are required to report annually to Parliament on actual and contingent liabilities above £100 000 except those taken on in the normal course of business as recognised by Parliament. This applies to all liabilities which may fall as a direct or indirect charge on the Consolidated Fund, and extends to liabilities which departments might acquire in respect of bodies which they sponsor. Guarantees and indemnities which do not have statutory backing must normally, if the liability could exceed £100 000 be notified to Parliament fourteen days before they are given in order to allow objections to be made.

Local authorities are responsible for a wide range of functions: education in schools (although individual secondary schools have been allowed to opt out of local authority control since 1989); personal social services; housing; police and fire services and civil defence; local transport; local environmental services; and some museums and art galleries. Local authorities also act as the central government's agents in paying certain social security benefits and student grants. (This description applies to England, Scotland and Wales. The functions of local authorities in Northern Ireland are more limited.)

Current spending on local authorities' own services is financed partly by grant, partly by non-domestic rates (a tax on non-domestic properties, which is set by central government but with the proceeds distributed to local authorities) and partly by the council tax, which is payable by nearly all households. The amount which is due will depend on the value of a property and the number of adults living in it. Central government has the power to limit, or "cap", excessive spending, and hence the level at which the tax is set by individual local authorities.

Local authority capital spending is financed from four sources. Capital grants and credit approvals (permission to borrow for capital spending) are controlled by central government. In addition local authorities can draw on the same resources as are available for current spending, including the council tax. They can also spend a proportion of their receipts from the sale of council houses and other capital assets, though legislation provides that a specified proportion of these receipts has to be set aside for the repayment of debt.

Following the success of the Government's privatisation programme, the size of the nationalised industries sector has been much reduced. Staff numbers fell from 1.8 million in 1980 to 0.4 million in 1992. Nationalised industries remain significant in the energy, transport and postal sectors but the Government has announced plans to privatise British Coal, Parcelforce and London Buses and to enable the private sector to operate rail services. In addition, the Government is reviewing the future ownership and structure of Royal Mail Letters.

The Government sets strategic objectives for the industries, lays down a Required Rate of Return on new investment (currently 8 per cent in real terms) and sets other financial targets. In its annual Investment and Financing Review, the Government agrees the investment plans for each nationalised industry and determines its external financing requirement. An industry's external finance is the difference between its capital requirements and the resources it generates from its trading activities. It is met by government finance (grants, subsidies, loans and equity) and the industry's market and overseas borrowing. External finance of nationalised industries scores in the government's control total (see Section C1 below). In 1992-93, it was estimated to amount to some £3.5 billion.

External financing limits also apply to Government trading funds, which although being parts of departments (or departments in their own right) are controlled separately on the basis of their net financing requirements. They also apply to NHS Trusts.

The estimated costs of tax allowances and reliefs have in recent years been shown in a Statistical Supplement to the Autumn Statement, published in late January or early February, and in the Financial Statement and Budget Report, published at the time of the Budget. The timing of publications will alter with the change to a budget covering both tax and expenditure in November 1993 (see also Section G).

C. BUDGET FORMULATION STRATEGY AND PROCESS

1. Strategic aims and global norms

The Government's budgetary policy is set within the context of the Medium-Term Financial Strategy (MTFS) which, since 1980, has provided the framework for monetary and fiscal policy. It is published in the Financial Statement and Budget Report (FSBR) at the time of the annual Budget. The MTFS is updated each year, but the defeat of inflation on a lasting basis has remained the central objective. The Government believes that in order to achieve this objective monetary policy needs to be supported with a firm fiscal stance. Thus monetary policy is complemented by setting fiscal policy with the aim of balancing the budget over the medium term. Automatic cyclical variations in public sector borrowing and debt repayment are consistent with this medium term approach to fiscal policy.

The Budget provides the main opportunity for reviewing fiscal policy so as to ensure that it remains on track for meeting the objective of balancing the budget over the medium term. Each MTFS presents illustrative fiscal projections for another four or five years ahead. These projections cover the Public Sector Borrowing Requirement (PSBR) and its main revenue and expenditure components. The PSBR is the difference between public sector payments to and receipts from the private domestic sector and abroad, including net lending, net cash expenditure on company securities (including privatisation proceeds) and some minor financial transactions. The Government forecast a PSBR of £35 billion for 1992-93 and £50 billion in 1993-94 in the Financial Statement and Budget Report in March 1993. A large part of the present PSBR is attributable to the effects of the economic cycle; in particular, social security expenditure and corporation tax receipts both lag behind the output cycle. The Government's objective is to bring the PSBR back towards balance in the medium-term. The objective for public spending (measured by general government expenditure excluding privatisation proceeds) is that, over time, it should take a declining share of national income, while value for money is constantly improved.

In order to achieve the objective for general government expenditure, (GGE), a more explicitly top-down approach to public expenditure control was adopted in 1992. Under this system a new spending aggregate – the New Control Total (NCT) – has been introduced. This covers about 85 per cent of GGE. It excludes social security spending which is directly related to unemployment and also central government debt interest. Both are highly cyclical and, if included in the NCT, could have an undesirable destabilising effect on other programmes. The NCT includes an unallocated Reserve for contingencies. It does not take account of privatisation proceeds.

Growth in the control total will be constrained to a rate which ensures that GGE (excluding privatisation proceeds) grows more slowly than the economy as a whole over time. On present assumptions this means that the Government is aiming to ensure that real GGE growth over time is no higher than 2 per cent. In 1992 growth in the control total was restricted to give average real growth over the three Survey years of no more than 1.5 per cent. This ceiling takes into account the trend rate of growth of items which are outside the control total but which score in GGE. It will if necessary be reviewed in the future.

Published figures, including plans up to 1997-98, are shown in Table 2.

Table 2. **Fiscal indicators**

	General government expenditure (excluding privatisation proceeds)		New control total £ billion	Public sector borrowing requirement	
	£ billion	% of GDP		£ billion	% of GDP
1987-88	178.4	41.75	148.6	−3.4	−0.75
1988-89	186.8	39.25	156.1	−14.7	−3.0
1989-90	205.0	39.75	175.2	−7.9	−1.5
1990-91	222.6	40.25	192.2	−0.5	0
1991-92	244.1	42.0	211.4	13.8	2.4
1992-93	268.0	44.75	230.9	35.0	5.75
1993-94	285.8	45.5	243.8	50.0	8.0
1994-95	302.0	45.0	253.6	44.0	6.5
1995-96	315.0	44.0	263.3	39.0	5.5
1996-97	330.0	43.75	274.0	35.0	4.5
1997-98	343.0	43.75	284.0	30.0	3.75

Source: Statistical Supplement to the 1992 Autumn Statement, Cm 2 219, and Financial Statement and Budget Report, March 1993.

2. Technical aspects of multi-year estimates

The Government's forward expenditure plans are drawn up in the annual Public Expenditure Survey on a three-year rolling cycle. Figures for the control total and its main components in each of the three years are expressed in cash terms. The figures for year 1 are translated before the start of the year into detailed spending controls, including cash limits, many of which are linked to Votes (see Section A) and external financing limits for nationalised industries (see Section B). These administrative controls are described in more detail in Section E below. Figures for year 2 and 3 are subject to review in subsequent Surveys. However, under the medium-term, top-down approach the presumption is that the aggregate cash plans should remain unchanged, and all departments are expected wherever possible to live within the cash allocations previously agreed.

Since the move to cash control in the early 1980s, spending plans no longer automatically compensate for general inflation. However, they do take into account the impact of inflation on specific areas of spending which are directly linked to price movements, such as index-linked social security benefits. Similarly, the plans also take into account the effect of other economic assumptions such as unemployment on other areas of demand-led spending.

The unallocated Reserve is intended to cover unforeseen policy initiatives, revised estimates of demand-led programmes and other overruns on spending within the control total, where these cannot be absorbed by the spending department concerned. Access to the Reserve needs the approval of the Treasury and, like overruns in cyclical social security, may give rise to Supplementary Estimates (see Section E1 below). The plans for 1993-94 include a Reserve of £4 billion in a control total of £244 billion. The Reserve for years 2 and 3 is usually set at a higher level than for year 1 because of the increasing uncertainty over time, and rises to nearly 4 per cent of the control total in the third year of the latest plans.

3. Calendar of main points of decision-making and activities

Months before start of FY (t)	Main events and activities
(Year t − 1)	
12 (April)	Departments submit position reports.
10 (June)	Initial Cabinet discussions of public spending outlook. Confirmation of NCT ceiling.
9 (July)	EDX begins to meet to discuss allocation. Chief Secretary holds bilaterals with spending Ministers and makes recommendations to EDX.
7-5 (September/November)	EDX continues to meet and makes recommendations to Cabinet. Cabinet discusses allocation.
5 (November)	Cabinet agrees allocation. Chancellor announces new spending plans as part of unified Budget.
(Year t)	
3-2 (January-February)	Detailed scrutiny of Ministerial bids for voted expenditure in FY (t). Publication of departmental reports and statistical supplement to unified Budget.
1 (March)	Publication of Estimates.
0 April	Start of financial year (t).
+4 before end-July	Completion of legislative process on both taxation and spending.

4. The annual budget cycle

Now that the Government sets firm aggregate limits on public expenditure in terms of the New Control Total the nature of the annual Public Expenditure Survey has changed. In recent years the overall level of spending in the period ahead has tended to emerge from a series of compromises on individual departments' programmes reached bilaterally between the Chief Secretary to the Treasury and Ministers in the spending departments. Under the top-down approach adopted in 1992, spending for the years ahead is constrained in advance by the annual ceiling set for the control total. The purpose of the Survey, which reviews plans for the next two years and sets them for the new third year, is to review the allocation between programmes of resources within the agreed overall limit to public expenditure. This allows for a more collective approach to setting priorities.

In February the Treasury requests position reports from departments assessing priorities and pressure points. If departments seek to increase spending in particular areas they must indicate how they would adjust spending within existing programme totals. In the early spring Ministers collectively endorse guidance on the conduct of the coming Survey, including the timetable and information requirements. Baselines are established, and for the first two years are normally the figures in the published plans. The baseline for the third year is usually the second year plans rolled forward. This may or may not be increased by a specific factor.

215

In June the Cabinet meets to discuss the outlook of public spending and confirm the ceilings for the control total. A Cabinet Committee (EDX), chaired by the Chancellor of the Exchequer, begins a series of meetings in July to discuss the allocation between programmes of resources within the agreed overall limits in order to make recommendations to Cabinet. Its discussions are informed by recommendation from the Chief Secretary to the Treasury based on a round of bilateral meetings with spending Ministers in July. EDX also takes into account the views of spending Ministers before submitting its preferred distribution to Cabinet for its consideration. The Chancellor has in the past announced a spending plan agreed by Cabinet in his Autumn Statement. From 1993 his announcement will form part of the unified Budget Statement (see also Section A3 above). More detailed analyses will be published subsequently in a Statistical Supplement and in individual departmental reports.

More detailed control is exercised over spending in the year immediately ahead. For the purposes of obtaining Parliamentary approval, Estimates covering the greater part of the expenditure in the plans are presented to Parliament in March, following Treasury scrutiny, as described in the Section A3.

D. EXPENDITURE REVIEW

The Government's policy of controlling public expenditure involves both reducing the share of public spending in money GDP in the medium term (see Section C1) and ensuring that value for money is constantly improved. Departments undertake critical review and analysis of policies and administrative activities throughout government and carry out "efficiency scrutinies" of how specific tasks, usually of an executive character, are performed. All new policies are required to have a policy evaluation framework and policies recently implemented are carefully monitored. Recent policy changes reviewed in this way include education and employment measures. Separate policy reviews, such as the recent review of the Health Service, look at large areas where changes are required. This work is in addition to the routine scrutiny of departments performed by the Treasury as part of the Public Expenditure Survey.

The National Audit Office, which reports directly to Parliament, both audits Government accounts and conducts enquiries into the efficiency, economy and effectiveness with which departments have used their resources. The reports are considered at oral hearings of the Public Accounts Committee of the House of Commons.

The Audit Commission, which is appointed by the Secretary of State for the Environment, acting with the Secretaries of State for Wales and for Health, has an important role in promoting value for money in local government and the NHS. In addition to ensuring that local authority accounts are properly prepared, an auditor appointed by the Commission needs to be satisfied that each authority has made proper arrangements for securing economy, efficiency and effectiveness in the use of resources. There is an Accounts Commission with similar functions for local authorities in Scotland.

The efficiency of some nationalised industries and other public sector trading bodies may be scrutinised by the Monopolies and Mergers Commission.

E. IMPLEMENTATION OF THE BUDGET

1. Major instruments of in-year control

As described in Section C1, the control total is the chief means of delivering the Government's expenditure objectives, and includes an unallocated Reserve. The Treasury monitors spending against the control total, and likely calls on the Reserve, throughout the year. Wherever possible, departments are required to find offsets for additional expenditure. If it seems likely that expenditure which is demand-led in the short term will exceed the levels planned, the Treasury may be more restrictive about proposals for other, more discretionary, expenditure.

The Government imposes cash limits on some expenditure, including that covered by two-thirds of Votes (see Section A3). In the case of a Vote, a cash limit indicates the Government's intention not to ask Parliament for supplementary provision later in the year. Cash limits cover expenditure which can be managed by setting predetermined limits, including general grants to local authorities; they exclude demand-determined services where, once policy and rates of payment have been set, expenditure depends on such factors as a number of qualified recipients coming forward. Limits on current spending on administration ("running costs limits") are also imposed, either on a gross basis by summing the relevant elements in the department's Vote(s) or, in the case of some areas within departments, net, so as to allow gross spending to vary in line with receipts.

Supplementary Estimates are presented to Parliament by the Treasury, normally in June, November and February. They cover movements of provision between Votes as well as additional requirements. Each set of Supplementary Estimates shows the impact on the control total and the charge on the Reserve. The Government publishes forecasts of the outturn of the control total in the current year when it announces its annual expenditure plans in the Budget in November and in the subsequent statistical supplement.

The provisional outturn on Votes is published in a White Paper in July after the end of the financial year. The White Paper also includes information on running costs limits and non-voted cash limits. The Appropriation Accounts are later presented formally to Parliament by the Comptroller and Auditor General and show how money voted in Estimates has been spent, subhead by subhead (some two thousand items).

The Treasury has in principle to give authority for all expenditure by departments. But in practice it grants them delegated authorities which cover much of it. These authorities are set taking account of departments' financial and management systems, both generally and in relation to the particular type of expenditure in question. They will be accompanied by arrangements regarding the provision of information to the Treasury on expenditure which is undertaken under delegated authority.

The use of a form of cash limit on the external financing of nationalised industries, trading funds and NHS Trusts is explained in Section B above.

2. Managerial discretion

The economy, efficiency and effectiveness of an individual spending department is the responsibility of its Minister. Within each department, the Permanent Secretary, or administrative head, necessarily has to delegate day to day responsibility. How far this is done varies between departments but in every case a Principal Finance Officer at or above a specified grade is chosen by the Permanent Secretary to oversee the arrangements. The appointment of an individual Principal Finance Officer at or above a specified grade is subject to the approval of the Treasury and the Office of Public Service and Science.

During a year a department may transfer funds between the items of a Vote subject to approval by the Treasury. It cannot transfer unspent funds from one Vote to another: such transfers require Parliamentary approval. (The Treasury will not normally approve transfers which allow increases in running costs.) The Permanent Secretary, as Accounting Officer, may be questioned by the relevant Parliamentary Committee on a department's spending.

Appropriations for current expenditure must be spent in the year in which they are voted, but under end-year flexibility schemes entitlements for carry-over from the preceding year are announced each July. These may amount to up to 5 per cent of capital provision and 0.5 per cent of running costs provision, respectively. Where appropriate, Parliament is asked to approve additional provision in the following year in respect of end-year flexibility entitlements.

F. RECENT REFORMS

The Treasury shares responsibility for the central management of the Civil Service with the Office of Public Service and Science (OPSS), which is part of the Cabinet Office. OPSS has a key role in improving the efficiency and effectiveness of public services, primarily through the creation of Next Steps Executive Agencies, following up the White Paper on the Citizen's Charter and taking forward market-testing within Government, as described below.

The main developments in public sector management in the last decade or so have been:

- the introduction of departmental manpower targets (1980), subsequently replaced by running costs limits (1986);
- the Financial Management Initiative (1982) which was concerned with the development of top management (corporate) planning procedures and systems for delegated budgeting; the latter was subsequently taken forward through the Multi-Departmental Review of Budgeting (1986);
- the Government Purchasing Initiative (1984);
- the Next Steps Initiative (1988);
- the Citizen's Charter (1991);
- ''Competing for Quality'' (1991);
- changes in the use of privately raised finance (1992).

1. Manpower targets; running cost ceilings

The overall target of reducing the number of civil servants from over 730 000 in 1979 to 630 000 was surpassed by the mid-1980s. Running cost limits were then introduced in order to continue the downward pressure on the size of the civil service while giving departments discretion in allocating administrative resources more efficiently as between manpower and other resources. The civil service now numbers around 560 000.

2. The Financial Management Initiative (FMI); the Multi-Departmental Review of Budgeting (MDR)

The FMI stressed the need for managers to have clear objectives and the means to measure output and performance; to be responsible for achieving value for money; and to have the necessary information and training. Building on the FMI, the MDR principles of budgeting focused inter alia on the need for management to set and review budgets which include measures and indicators which facilitate regular evaluation of achievements against objectives.

Departments have made good progress in carrying into effect the FMI and MDR. Work is continuing on developing and refining output and performance measures, and on improving the planning and monitoring systems of individual departments. Indicators and targets for departments and executive units increasingly cover an appropriate mix of economy and efficiency (including unit costs of output and improved purchasing), quality of service, and effectiveness.

Individual departments are seeking to move to more strategic and unified planning and monitoring systems, designed a) to improve the alignment of their aims and activities; b) to help them achieve the same rigour in pursuing value for money in spending on programmes as on administration; c) to reflect the more strategic role of the centre of departments vis-à-vis their Next Steps Agencies (see below); and d) to prepare for greater prospective flexibilities as the Treasury itself seeks to move to a more strategic role vis-à-vis departments.

One important flexibility was announced in 1991: henceforward, departments, including their Next Steps Agencies (see below), can gain greater responsibility for pay bargaining and greater scope for matching reward more closely to performance. From April 1994 Agencies employing 2 000 or more staff will assume responsibility for their own pay bargaining. Many agencies are planning their own pay and grading systems.

3. The government purchasing initiative

The recommendations of a 1984 efficiency review of Government purchasing subsequently became the framework for the Government Purchasing Initiative (GPI) which aims to develop professionalism in all aspects of Government procurement. The recommendation for a central focus for purchasing and supply resulted in the creation of the Central Unit on Purchasing (CUP) in 1986. Since then the role of the Unit has been expanded to include advice on the management of construction projects. The unit, which is now known as the Central Unit on Procurement, is located in HM Treasury.

The CUP's role is to:

- progress the GPI by advising departments on how to improve value for money, through the adoption of best practice, in all aspects of procurement and the management of construction projects;
- work with departments to develop professionalism in purchasing and create infrastructures to support departmental purchasing activities; for example, coherent organisation structures with identified responsibilities, adequate training programmes for developing staff and integrated purchasing information systems;
- monitor departments' progress in implementing the GPI; and
- report annually on departmental achievements to the Prime Minister.

The Unit does not have a central buying role or executive purchasing functions.

In 1991-92, on a reported purchasing spend of some £3.3 billion, value-for-money savings totalled some £176 million (5.4 per cent).

4. The Next Steps Initiative

Next Steps takes further the principles of the FMI and MDR, in particular through the enlargement of managerial discretion within a strategic framework of performance and accountability. The initiative involves the devolution, to the greatest extent practicable, of the executive functions of departments to Agencies within those departments.

Each Agency has a Chief Executive who is appointed by the departmental Minister and directly and personally responsible to that Minister for the performance of the Agency. The Minister, with advice from the permanent head of the department or one of his senior colleagues, sets a framework of resources, flexibilities and performance targets. As an Agency develops a favourable track record it can win progressively greater flexibilities.

The Minister remains accountable to Parliament for the conduct of the Agency. To underpin this accountability, the Chief Executive is appointed as Accounting Officer for the Agency, and as such is accountable to the Public Accounts Committee of the House of Commons. Agencies are required to publish full commercial-style accounts, audited by the Comptroller and Auditor General, together with an annual report.

By early April 1993, 89 Agencies had been launched and 60 per cent of the Civil Service, or some 350 000 people, were working on Next Steps lines. The aim is to complete the coverage as far as practicable by mid-1995.

5. The Citizen's Charter

In 1991 the Government published a White Paper on the Citizen's Charter, a set of initiatives "to make public services answer better to the wishes of their users and to raise their quality overall". The Charter is being supplemented by more detailed charters for individual services, and entails legislation in certain areas. The Citizen's Charter Unit, which is part of the Office of Public Service and Science, is responsible for co-ordinating follow-up to the White Paper.

The themes of the Citizen's Charter are:

- improving the quality of public services;
- choice wherever possible between competing providers;
- published standards of service and redress where these are not met; and
- value for money within a tax bill the nation can afford.

Measures already announced include guaranteed maximum waiting times for certain National Health Service treatments; the publication of league tables for schools results; new British Rail standards of service and compensation arrangements; and bringing the powers of utility regulators over standards of service up to the level of the strongest.

The Citizen's Charter notes the Government's intention to remove the monopoly of British Rail and to secure better services to customers by enabling the private sector to operate rail services, and also to reduce the monopoly of the Post Office in certain respects.

6. Competition in service delivery: market testing

The White Paper "Competing for Quality" of November 1991 set out objectives for greater competition in the provision of central government, National Health and local government services. One important tool in achieving those objectives is market testing.

This involves the precise specification of suitable activities before bids for supplying them are invited. In some cases there may be a strategic or practical decision not to have an internal bid. The successful bid is chosen on the basis of best value for money.

The November 1992 White Paper, "Citizen's Charter First Report: 1992" set market testing targets for each department to the end of September 1993. Those market testing targets covered activities valued at £1.5 billion. Future targets will be set building on experience. The areas to be market tested comprise a wide range of activities, from traditional support services such as catering and cleaning to areas closer to the core of government such as economic model building and the survey and certification of ships. To help encourage the expansion of market testing, departments and agencies can apply any resulting savings to other areas of programme spending.

The responsibility for driving forward the "Competing for Quality" initiative, including market-testing within Government, lies with the Efficiency Unit. This is also part of the Office of Public Service and Science. The Unit, which is guided by the Prime Minister's Adviser on Efficiency, has an established role in working with government departments to secure improvements in value for money. It has been best known for its scrutiny programme, which has produced savings of more than £1 billion since 1979.

7. Use of private finance

In the 1992 Autumn Statement the Government announced changes in the use of privately raised finance to enable the public and private sectors to work together more effectively, particularly on infrastructure projects. The Government intends to allow projects to proceed where the private sector takes responsibility and can recoup its costs by charges on the final user, without comparing them with publicly financed alternatives, as hitherto. The Government intends also actively to encourage joint ventures by making contributions in respect of benefits which the market cannot capture. The private sector will need to accept risk in such joint ventures, and will have a controlling interest in them. The Chancellor of the Exchequer announced in the Budget in March 1993 that the Government intended that the Channel Tunnel Rail Link should proceed as a joint venture and that Crossrail (a new rail link across London from east to west) would be reviewed with the aim of involving the private sector to the greatest possible extent.

G. FURTHER INFORMATION

1. Documents related to annual budget

The financial year runs from 1 April (year t) until 31 March (year t + 1).

The pattern of documents in recent years has been as follows:

1. *The Financial Statement and Budget Report* summarises economic background to the Budget,* describes the medium-term financial strategy, summarises the tax proposals and provides an economic forecast, with detailed projections for the public finances for the coming year, together with illustrative projections for inflation, money GDP, government revenues, expenditure, borrowing and monetary policy for a further three (occasionally four) years ahead; Budget day, year (t).
2. *The Autumn Statement* has (concluding with the document published in November 1992) given the outcome of the Public Expenditure Survey and presented new economic forecasts for a year ahead, including an updated estimate of the PSBR for the current year; November, year (t − 1).
3. *The Statistical Supplement to the Autumn Statement* has contained more detailed information on the governments expenditure plans for the next three years, with comprehensive descriptions of statistical and other conventions and definitions used in the Survey; early year (t).
4. *Departmental Reports* contain details of individual departments' spending plans and provide information on their objectives and performance; early year (t).
5. *The Supply Estimates,* which are summarised in the "Summary and Guide"; mid-March, year (t).

The list above relates to the position up to the March Budget in 1993. With the change to a Budget covering both tax and expenditure in November 1993 there will be some changes. Final decisions have yet to be taken, but the Government expects to publish a substantive document on Budget day on the lines of the current Financial Statement and Budget Report. This should cover much the same ground as the present document and the Autumn Statement, after eliminating overlaps. The earlier Budget may mean that some of the analysis currently published in the Financial Statement and Budget Report will have to held over to a supplement on the lines of the existing Statistical Supplement to the Autumn Statement, or more provisional figures substituted.

NOTE

The above publications, apart from departmental reports, are prepared by the Treasury. All are available from HMSO Publications Centre, PO Box 276, London SW8 5DT.

2. Other documents

6. *The Financing and Accountability of Next Steps Agencies* (White Paper Cm 914, December 1989): contents include the use of trading funds to finance certain activities.
7. *The Citizen's Charter* (White Paper Cm 1599, July 1991); a set of initiatives intended to make public services answer better to the wishes of their users and to raise their quality overall.

---

* The Budget (with capital B) currently refers to the Government's proposals for taxation. From November 1993 the Government will present its tax and spending proposals in a single Budget together.

8. *Competing for Quality* (White Paper Cm 1730, November 1991); describes steps to facilitate private sector participation in providing services to central government, local authorities and the National Health Service.

9. *The Next Steps Agencies Review 1992* (White Paper Cm 1760, November 1991); provides information on individual Agencies and Executive Units that are working on Next Steps lines.

10. *Budgetary Reform* (White Paper Cm 1867, March 1992); explains the intention to present the Government's tax and spending proposals to Parliament at the same time, beginning in November 1993.

11. *The Citizen's Charter First Report: 1992* (White Paper Cm 2101, November 1992); outlines the progress against the commitments set out in the Citizen's Charter White Paper and maps out future developments. All the above are available from HMSO (address as above).

UNITED STATES

**Any changes which may have taken place in the United States
since October 1993 are not reflected in this chapter**

A. INSTITUTIONAL STRUCTURE OF BUDGETARY DECISION-MAKING

1. Political and organisational structure of government

The United States of America is a federal republic consisting of 50 States. States have their own constitutions and within each State there are at least two additional levels of local government, generally designated as counties and cities, towns or villages. The relationships between different levels of government are complex and varied (see Section B for more information).

The Federal Government is composed of three branches: the legislative branch, the executive branch, and the judicial branch. Budgetary decision-making is shared primarily by the legislative and executive branches. The general structure of these two branches relative to budget formulation and execution is as follows.

The legislative branch includes the Congress, a number of committees made up of members of Congress and some legislative branch agencies such as the General Accounting Office (GAO) and the Congressional Budget Office (CBO). The Congress consists of two houses: the Senate and the House of Representatives. The major differences between the two are the number of members and the term of office. The Senate is composed of 100 members, two from each State, who are elected to serve for a term of six years. Direct Senate elections take place every two years, for one-third of all Senators. The House of Representatives comprises 435 members elected by the people for two-year terms, all terms running for the same period. Elections are held in November of even numbered years.

There are 22 standing congressional committees in the House of Representatives and 16 standing committees in the Senate. Among these, there are two Appropriations and two Budget Committees, one in each house.

The General Accounting Office provides an independent audit of Government agencies. The GAO is headed by the Comptroller General of the United States and is appointed by the President with the advice and consent of the Senate for a term of 15 years.

The Congressional Budget Office was established in 1974. The head of CBO, the Director, is appointed by the Speaker of the House of Representatives and the President pro tempore of the Senate. The term of office of the Director expires every four years, on 3 January.

The executive branch is headed by the President. The President is elected by the people for a four-year term. Presidential elections are held every four years and were last held in November of 1992.

The President's Cabinet is composed of the heads of the 14 executive departments. In addition, the President may accord Cabinet rank on other executive branch officials. Under this administration, the following officials have been accorded Cabinet rank: Director of the Office of Management and Budget (OMB) and the US Trade Representative. The Vice President also participates in Cabinet meetings, and from time to time, other individuals are invited to participate.

In addition to the Cabinet agencies, there are six large agencies and over 70 small agencies, boards, and temporary commissions.

Depending on one's definition of "executive", the estimated number of "executives" with political appointments varies, but it probably approximates 2 000 – of whom all are appointed by the president or by his appointees.

2. Main budgetary organs

Within the executive branch of the central government, the primary responsibility for budget formulation rests with the Office of Management and Budget (OMB). Primary responsibility for tax policy and tax estimates rests with the Secretary of the Treasury. Generally speaking, fiscal policy and economic forecasts are developed jointly by the Council of Economic Advisers (CEA), the Treasury, and OMB. The CEA is a three-member council appointed by the President to advise him on economic policy. The Council and its staff is part of the Executive Office of the President, as is OMB.

OMB's staff of approximately 600 is headed by a Director and two Deputy Directors who are appointed by the President, with the advice and consent of the Senate. One of the Deputy Directors focuses primarily on budget issues while the other focuses primarily on management issues. OMB is clustered into a set of budget divisions and a set of management divisions along with administrative and support staff.

The budget staff co-ordinates and reviews government programmes; prepares the budget; supervises spending authorised by Congress; prepares fiscal, economic and financial analyses and forecasts; and participates in developing budget, tax, credit, and fiscal policies. The staff is divided into programme resources, veterans, and labour; natural resources, energy and science; and economics and government. Each group is headed by an Associate Director who is a political appointee. Each group contains budget and special studies divisions that are headed by Deputy Associate Directors who are career employees. The budget divisions review the requests for funds from the various departments and agencies. The special studies divisions conduct in-depth studies of selected programmes to provide a better basis for making funding and policy decisions.

A unit that is headed by the Assistant Director for Budget compiles the work of the various budget divisions and undertakes analyses of the budget as a whole. This unit consists of two divisions: the Budget Analysis and Systems Division, which contains the Budget Analysis Branch and the Budget Systems Branch; and the Budget Review and Concepts Division, which contains the Budget Review Branch and the Budget Concepts Branch. Each division is headed by a Deputy Assistant Director who is a career employee.

The management staff is responsible for procurement, regulatory, and management matters. This staff seeks the most effective and efficient functioning of the Executive Branch. It is subdivided into a General Management Division and a Financial Management Division and each is headed by an Assistant Director.

The Office of Information and Regulatory Affairs was set up in 1981 to monitor and streamline Federal demands on the private sector. Its Administrator heads a staff involved in regulatory relief, paperwork reduction, statistical policy activities, and the sharing and distribution of information.

The Office of Federal Procurement Policy was established by statute in 1974 within OMB. It is charged with the development and monitoring of government-wide procurement and acquisition policies.

The Congress is heavily involved in the process of budget preparation; its main budgetary organs are dealt with in Section A4 below.

3. Role of President

The President makes the final decisions on an annual budget that is transmitted to Congress. The budget is transmitted early in each calendar year, eight to nine months before the next fiscal year begins on 1 October.

The process of formulating the budget begins not later than the spring of each year, at least nine months before the budget is transmitted and at least 18 months before the fiscal year begins.

During the formulation of the budget, there is a continual exchange of information, proposals, evaluations, and policy decisions among the President, the OMB, other units in the Executive Office of the President, and the various executive branch agencies. Decisions concerning the upcoming budget are influenced by the results of previously enacted budgets, reactions to the last proposed budget, and projections of the economic outlook that are prepared jointly by the Council of Economic Advisers, OMB, and the Department of the Treasury. For fiscal years 1991 through 1995, certain categories of spending and the maximum deficit amount are constrained by law. The President's budget proposals must be consistent with these constraints, which are discussed further under "Budget Formulation Strategy and Process".

4. Role of Legislature

The role of the US Congress in formulating the budget is more active and often more independent than the legislature's role in most other OECD countries. Congress considers the President's budget proposals and approves, modifies, or disapproves them. It can change funding levels, eliminate programmes, or add programmes not requested by the President. It can add or eliminate taxes and other sources of receipts, or make other changes that affect the amount of receipts collected.

Congress does not enact a budget as such. Instead, the budget is enacted in the form of several different types of legislation. Congressional procedures usually include an authorisation process, a separate annual appropriation process, and a concurrent budget resolution process.

In the authorisation process, organic legislation and appropriation authorisation legislation are considered and reported by the committees with legislative jurisdiction over the particular subject matter, usually referred to as substantive committees, and are considered by both Houses of Congress. Substantive legislation can create agencies, establish programmes, grant authority to perform functions, establish eligibility requirements, authorise the appropriation of funds to carry out the organic legislation and, in some cases, place limits on the amount that can be appropriated. With exceptions, substantive legislation does not provide any authority to spend money, although in the exceptional cases the amounts are large.

Most programmes are authorised indefinitely or for a specified number of years. In other cases, the substantive committees have required annual authorising legislation in an attempt to exercise control over programmes. Currently, most nuclear energy, space exploration, defence, foreign affairs, and some construction programmes require annual authorising legislation.

An appropriation is a law that permits Federal agencies to incur obligations and to spend funds for specified purposes. An appropriation act typically follows an enactment of substantive legislation. However, in some instances, funds can be made available through substantive legislation only.

In the appropriations process, Congress does not vote on the level of outlays directly, but rather on budget authority or other authority to incur obligations that will result in immediate or future outlays.

For many Federal programmes, budget authority becomes available each year only as voted by Congress in appropriations acts. Currently, most discretionary programmes (including the general operating costs of most agencies) receive annual appropriations.

However, in other cases Congress has voted permanent budget authority, under which funds become available annually without further congressional action. Most trust fund appropriations are permanent, such as the Social Security and health care trust funds; as are a number of Federal fund appropriations, such as the appropriation to pay interest on the public debt. In recent years, more budget authority has become available under permanent appropriations than through current actions by Congress. In turn, the outlays from permanent appropriations, together with the outlays from obligations incurred in prior years, comprise the majority of the outlay total for any year. Therefore, most outlays in any year are not controlled through appropriations actions for that year.

Congressional action on the budget is guided by the annual adoption of a concurrent resolution on the budget. Under this process, which was established by the Congressional Budget Act of 1974, Congress considers budget totals before completing action on individual appropriations and receipts measures. The Act requires each standing committee of Congress to report on budget estimates to the House and Senate Budget Committees within six weeks after the President's budget is transmitted. The budget resolution, which is scheduled to be adopted by 15 April, sets targets for total receipts and for budget authority and outlays, in total and by functional category. Like the President's budget, the budget resolution is subject to spending limitations imposed in law for 1991 through 1995.

Budget resolutions are not laws and, therefore, do not require the President's approval. However, there is consultation between the congressional leadership and the Administration, because legislation developed to meet congressional budget targets must be sent to the President for his approval. For some budgets prior to 1991, the President and the joint leadership of Congress formally agreed on the framework of a deficit reduction plan. These agreements, known as Bipartisan Budget Agreements, were reflected in the budget legislation passed for those years. A similar agreement process led to the enactment of the Budget Enforcement Act of 1990, which is designed to constrain spending for fiscal years 1991 through 1995.

Congressional consideration of requests for appropriations and changes in revenue laws normally occurs first in the House of Representatives. The US Constitution requires that revenue measures pass through the House of Representatives before being sent to the Senate. By precedent, appropriation bills also originate in the House and pass through all House review stages before being sent to the Senate. However, occasionally the Senate originates appropriations bills before the House has initiated or completed action.

The 13 House Appropriation Subcommittees study the requests for appropriations, examine in detail each agency's performance, and make spending-level recommendations to the House Appropriations Committee. The House Ways and Means Committee reviews proposed revenue measures. Each Committee then recommends the actions to be taken by the House of Representatives. After passage of the budget resolution, a point of order can be raised to block consideration of bills that would cause a committee's targets, as set by the resolution, to be breached.

When the appropriations and tax bills are approved by the House, they are forwarded to the Senate, where a similar review is conducted by the 13 Senate Appropriation Subcommittees and the Senate Finance Committee. In a case of disagreement between the two Houses of Congress, a conference committee (consisting of members of both bodies) meets to resolve the differences. The report of the conference committee is returned to both Houses for approval. When the measure is agreed to, first in the House and then in the Senate, it is ready to be transmitted to the President as an enrolled bill, for his approval or veto.

When action on appropriations is not completed by the beginning of the fiscal year, Congress enacts a joint continuing resolution to provide authority to continue financing operations up to a specified date or until their regular appropriations are enacted. Continuing resolutions must be presented to the President for approval or veto.

In each of the last several years, Congress has enacted omnibus budget reconciliation acts, which combine many amendments to authorising legislation that affect outlays and receipts. For example, the acts may change benefit formulas or eligibility requirements, the spending for which is often not controlled through appropriation acts.

B. THE SCOPE AND NATURE OF GOVERNMENT FINANCES

Compared to other OECD countries, general government expenditure has increased only marginally. General government net borrowing, however, shows a relatively large increase, mainly due to central government's budget deficit.

The relationships between the central government and State and local governments are complex and varied. For some of the largest categories of expenditure, such as social insurance and defence, the Federal Government makes payments directly to the public. However, in many instances, States and localities act as the agent of the Federal Government or share responsibilities, including costs. For example, States build and maintain highways, many of which are partly or largely financed by the central Government. Social service programmes, such as medical care for the poor and assistance to low-income families, are generally administered by the States and localities, which share a substantial portion of the costs.

The national Constitution guarantees autonomy to State governments and their local governmental subdivisions, though in practice a substantial admixture occurs. Each State has its own constitution, and its own Governor, legislature, judiciary, and civil service. Local governments are subsidiaries of State governments. States have the power to tax and borrow subject to State constitutions and laws, and local taxes and borrowing are locally determined but subject to State restrictions. States rely heavily on sales, income, and dedicated (especially motor vehicle) taxes; localities depend primarily on property taxes and user charges. The Federal Government provides grants, loans and tax subsidies to State and local Governments to aid them in providing government services. States and localities are responsible for their own debt.

Approximately 47 per cent of all federal outlays are for income transfers ("payments for individuals") in cash or in kind. These include medical care, food assistance, and housing assistance, as well as direct cash benefits. Most needs-tested benefits are administered by States and financed by grants from the National Government and by the States, or States and localities. In such cases, national law determines the general nature of the programme and conditions for eligibility, with States setting up additional conditions and sometimes paying benefits entirely from their own funds for people ineligible for Federal assistance. Less than 20 per cent of total payments for individuals is disbursed on the basis of a "needs" test; the remainder of these benefits are paid to eligible recipients – mainly elderly, sick, or unemployed – without regard to income.

Most of the non-needs-tested programmes are financed largely by earmarked social insurance taxes. Eligibility is mainly determined by age (for retirement), disability, or employment status; years of coverage and levels of payroll contributions usually are built into the formulas to determine benefit levels.

The Federal budget is composed of two major fund groups: Federal funds and trust funds. Starting with the 1969 budget, the latter were included within the "unified budget", but their separate identity has been maintained. Trust funds are generally financed by earmarked compulsory collections. The bulk of trust fund activities involve social insurance funds, but they also include dedicated highway and airport and airway taxes and the spending financed from those taxes.

The structure of Federal expenditures by function is shown below.

Table 1. **Federal government outlays by function (1990) including off-budget funds**

As percentage of total

National defence	23.9
International affairs	1.1
General science, space, and technology	1.2
Energy	0.2
Natural resources and environment	1.4
Agriculture	1.0
Commerce and housing credit	5.4
Transportation	2.4
Community and regional development	0.7
Education, training, employment, and social services	3.1
Health	4.6
Medicare	7.8
Income security	11.8
Social security	19.9
Veterans benefits and services	2.3
Administration of justice	0.8
General government	0.9
Net interest	14.7
Undistributed offsetting receipts	−2.9
Total	100.0

Source: *Mid-Session Review of the Budget*, 15 July 1991 (see Section G).

Legislation enacted in 1985 removed two major social insurance trust funds (the old-age and survivors and the disability insurance funds) from the budget. The other off-budget Federal entity is the Postal Service Fund which was removed from the budget by the Omnibus Budget Reconciliation Act of 1989. These off-budget funds are excluded from the maximum deficit amounts discussed in Section C below. However, the administrative expenses for social security are included in calculating the deficit. Also, the budget documents continue to focus on total receipts and outlays including these funds.

C. BUDGET FORMULATION STRATEGY AND PROCESS

1. Strategic aims and global norms

Limits on expenditures, receipts, and the deficit are established in law for fiscal years 1991 through 1995, as are procedures for enforcing the limits throughout the budget formulation process each year. These limits and procedures are determined by the Balanced Budget and Emergency Deficit Control Act of 1985 (commonly known as the Gramm-Rudman-Hollings Act), which was extended and amended extensively by the Budget Enforcement Act of 1990. The latter also affected the President's budget and the congressional budget process.

The law divides spending into two types: "discretionary appropriations" and "direct spending". These definitions are designed to distinguish spending that is generally controlled through annual appropriations acts from that which is generally provided in other, more permanent laws (most entitlement and other so-called mandatory spending). The law specifies processes, called "sequesters", for reducing spending. Different seques-ter procedures are prescribed for reducing the excess spending resulting from discretionary appropriations and for eliminating increases in the deficit resulting from legislation affecting direct spending or receipts. A third type of sequester applies to all types of spending if, after application of the discretionary and direct spending procedures, the deficit exceeds specified maximum deficit amounts. This third type can be applied beginning in FY 1994. However, the President, at his discretion, may decide to adjust the maximum deficit amount for economic and technical factors and thus avoid this third type of sequester. A substantial portion of spending (most notably the social insurance trust fund) is exempt from such sequesters.

The sequester process for discretionary appropriations and direct spending are designed to apply uniform reductions to the same kind of spending that caused the sequester. Discretionary appropriations are subdivided into three categories for 1991 through 1993. These are defence, international, and domestic. Spending limits for budget authority and outlays are specified for each category for each of those years. For 1994 and 1995, the limits apply to the total discretionary spending. From adjournment of a session of Congress through the following 30 June of a fiscal year, discretionary sequesters for the fiscal year take place whenever an appropriation bill causes the limit in a category to be breached. Under a sequester, spending for most non-exempt programmes in the category is reduced by a uniform percentage. Special rules apply in reducing some programmes and some programmes are exempt from sequester by law. Between 30 June and the end of a fiscal year, for practical reasons, the sequester is accomplished by reducing the limit for the category for the next fiscal year.

Sequesters of direct spending, called "pay-as-you-go" sequesters, occur following the end of a session of Congress (usually in the Fall of each year) if there is estimated to be a net increase in the deficit caused by laws enacted that affect direct spending and receipts. Under a pay-as-you-go sequester, spending for most non-exempt programmes in the category is reduced by a uniform percentage. Special rules apply in reducing some programmes and some programmes are exempt from sequester by law.

A deficit sequester occurs if it is calculated that estimated spending in all categories and estimated receipts will result in a deficit that exceeds the maximum deficit amount for the year by more than the allowed margin ($15 billion in 1994 and 1995). Under a deficit sequester, half of any excess must be taken from defence programmes and half from non-exempt non-defence programmes. Spending for most programmes is reduced by a uniform percentage that is calculated (separately for defence and non-defence programmes) to eliminate the increase in the deficit. Special rules apply in reducing some programmes, and some programmes are exempt from sequester.

The law provides that the estimates and calculations that determine whether there is to be a sequester are to be made by the OMB and reported to the President and Congress. The Congressional Budget Office is required to make the same estimates and calculations, and the Director of OMB is required to explain any differences between the OMB estimates and the estimates prepared by CBO. The estimates and calculation by OMB are the basis for sequester orders issued by the President. The President's orders may not change any of the particulars in the OMB report. The General Accounting Office is required to prepare compliance reports.

The Federal deficit is defined to cover the Federal Government's deficit, including the off-budget funds described in Section B above, although the funds are excluded from the maximum deficit amounts. Another common way of setting budget deficit targets is as percentages of gross national product (GNP). The Federal deficit in dollars and as percentages of GNP is shown below.

Table 2. **Federal deficits, 1985-94**

	1985	1986	1987	1988	1989	1990	1991	1992	1993	1994
In billions of dollars	212.3	221.2	149.8	155.2	152.5	221.4	269.5	290.4	254.7	203.4
As a per cent of GDP	5.4	5.2	3.4	3.2	2.9	4.0	4.8	4.9	4.0	3.1

Source: Historical Tables, Budget of the United States Government, Fiscal year 1995; Mid-session Review of 1995 Budget; and the Monthly Treasury Statement of Receipts and Outlays of the United States Government, 30 September 1994.

2. Calendar of main points of decision-making and activities

Months before start of FY (t)	Main events and activities
(Year t – 2)	
18 (April)	OMB issues planning guidance to the agencies for FY (t) to FY (t + 4).
14-16 (summer)	OMB and agencies discuss budget issues and options in preparation for FY (t) budget review and decision-making.
13-10 (September to December)	Executive Branch develops the President's Budget.
8 (not later than the 1st Monday in February)	Transmittal of President's Budget to Congress.
8 (15th February)	CBO submits report to Budget Committees.
8-7 (within 6 weeks of transmittal)	Each Committee reports its views and budget estimates to the House and Senate Budget Committees.
6 (1st April)	Senate Budget Committee reports concurrent resolution on the budget.
6 (15th April)	Congress completes action on concurrent budget resolution.
5 (15th May)	Annual appropriations bills may be considered in the House in the absence of a concurrent resolution.
4 (10th June)	House Appropriations Committee reports last annual appropriations bill.
4 (15th June)	Congress completes action on reconciliation legislation.
3 (15th July)	Transmittal of Mid-Session Review, dating the budget estimates.
(Year t)	
0 (1st Oct)	Start of fiscal year (t).

D. EXPENDITURE REVIEW

Policy analysis occurs at all levels within the executive branch. Operating agencies continually evaluate the effectiveness and efficiency of existing programmes. This analysis is an integral part of the agency budget justification that is submitted to OMB. In addition, OMB budget examiners conduct independent analyses that form the basis of their recommendations to the Budget Director and other policy-level officials. Efforts have been made to assure that programmes with basic similarities are treated equitably. An example is across-the-board policies regarding cost-of-living adjustments. In addition to policy analysis, management practices have received increased emphasis in the budget process during recent years. Specific management issues are discussed between OMB and major agencies, and the resulting decisions incorporated into the President's budget.

E. IMPLEMENTATION OF THE BUDGET

Once approved, the President's budget, as modified by the Congress, becomes the basis for the financial plan for the operations of each agency during the fiscal year. Under the law, most budget authority and other budgetary resources in each account are made available to the agencies of the executive branch through an apportionment system. The Director of OMB apportions (distributes) appropriations and other budgetary resources to each agency by time periods or by activities, to ensure the effective use of available resources and to minimise the need for additional appropriations.

In the apportionment process, OMB may establish reserves under certain circumstances to provide for contingencies, to effect savings made possible by changes in requirements or greater efficiency of operations, or otherwise withhold authority to obligate funds.

The Impoundment Control Act of 1974 further defines the process under which OMB may use the apportionment process. The act provides that the executive branch, in regulating the rate of spending, must report to the Congress any deferral of budget authority; that is, any effort through administrative action to postpone spending which has been authorised by law. OMB can also propose rescission (*i.e.* cancelling) of previously enacted budget authority, before it would otherwise lapse.

Once funds are apportioned by OMB, the responsibility for further control rests with the receiving agency. Each agency is required to maintain a system of internal controls, which assures that the funds are used properly, not only in terms of avoiding outright fraud, but in terms of meeting legislative intent, which is often non-binding.

Detailed reports on the use of funds are prepared monthly by the agencies for the Department of the Treasury and the Office of Management and Budget. The reports to OMB are called budget execution reports. The reports are by account, and are usually on a monthly basis. A copy of the report covering the last month in a quarter is sent to the House Appropriations Committee. The Treasury has central responsibility for revenue collection and disbursement and publishes monthly and yearly reports on the financial condition of the Federal Government.

Despite the apportionment process, changes in laws, economic conditions, or other factors may indicate the need for additional appropriations during the year. In such cases, supplemental budget requests may be sent to the Congress.

A comprehensive report on changes to the current budget is required each 15 July. It includes changes due to economic conditions, technical factors, new Presidential proposals, and legislation passed by the Congress and signed by the President.

F.   RECENT REFORMS

1.   Performance measurement

The most significant reform that is currently in progress is to introduce more performance measurement into decisionmaking and the budget process, as required by the Government Performance and Results Act.

As a first step, the Act requires that at least ten Federal agencies launch three year pilot projects, beginning in FY 1994, to develop measure of progress. They then must produce annual reports showing how they are doing on those measures.

At the beginning of fiscal year 1998, all Federal programmes must develop 5 year strategic plans – linked to measurable outcomes. By 1999, every agency will be crafting detailed agency performance plans, and integrating these plans into their operations and budgeting procedures.

2.   The National Performance Review (NPR)

In September 1993, the Vice President's National Performance Review issued a report recommending a number of changes in the way government operates to the President. The recommendations covered changes to crosscutting activities such as procurement, personnel policy, regulations, and the budget process, as well as specific changes affecting government agencies.

The recommendations affecting the budget process include:
- development of an Executive budget resolution;
- instituting biennial budgets and appropriations;
- minimising budget restrictions through allotments and apportionments;
- the substitution of operating cost budgets for controls on employment;
- minimising congressional restrictions on line items, earmarks and FTE floors; and
- allowing agencies to roll over 50 per cent of what they do not spend on internal operations during a fiscal year.

These budget process reforms, as well as other NPR recommendations, are presently being pursued, but have not yet been completed. Thus it is premature to report on the shape they will ultimately take.

G. FURTHER INFORMATION

1. *The Budget of the United States Government,* including the Budget Message of the President, January, year (t − 1).
2. *Economic Report of the President,* annual report on short-term and medium-term economic forecast and economic policy published by the Council Economic Advisors, January, year (t − 1).
3. *OMB Circular No. A-11,* annual instructions to agencies on preparing their budget submissions, June/July, year (t − 1).
4. *The Annual Report of the United States Government* for the fiscal year ended 30 September, issued by the Treasury in November/December, year (t + 1).
5. *OMB Circular No. A-34,* permanent instructions to agencies on control of funds.
6. *Mid-Session Review of the Budget,* July, year (t − 1).

MAIN SALES OUTLETS OF OECD PUBLICATIONS
PRINCIPAUX POINTS DE VENTE DES PUBLICATIONS DE L'OCDE

ARGENTINA – ARGENTINE
Carlos Hirsch S.R.L.
Galería Güemes, Florida 165, 4° Piso
1333 Buenos Aires   Tel. (1) 331.1787 y 331.2391
Telefax: (1) 331.1787

AUSTRALIA – AUSTRALIE
D.A. Information Services
648 Whitehorse Road, P.O.B 163
Mitcham, Victoria 3132   Tel. (03) 873.4411
Telefax: (03) 873.5679

AUSTRIA – AUTRICHE
Gerold & Co.
Graben 31
Wien I   Tel. (0222) 533.50.14
Telefax: (0222) 512.47.31.29

BELGIUM – BELGIQUE
Jean De Lannoy
Avenue du Roi 202
B-1060 Bruxelles   Tel. (02) 538.51.69/538.08.41
Telefax: (02) 538.08.41

CANADA
Renouf Publishing Company Ltd.
1294 Algoma Road
Ottawa, ON K1B 3W8   Tel. (613) 741.4333
Telefax: (613) 741.5439
Stores:
61 Sparks Street
Ottawa, ON K1P 5R1   Tel. (613) 238.8985
211 Yonge Street
Toronto, ON M5B 1M4   Tel. (416) 363.3171
Telefax: (416)363.59.63
Les Éditions La Liberté Inc.
3020 Chemin Sainte-Foy
Sainte-Foy, PQ G1X 3V6   Tel. (418) 658.3763
Telefax: (418) 658.3763
Federal Publications Inc.
165 University Avenue, Suite 701
Toronto, ON M5H 3B8   Tel. (416) 860.1611
Telefax: (416) 860.1608
Les Publications Fédérales
1185 Université
Montréal, QC H3B 3A7   Tel. (514) 954.1633
Telefax: (514) 954.1635

CHINA – CHINE
China National Publications Import
Export Corporation (CNPIEC)
16 Gongti E. Road, Chaoyang District
P.O. Box 88 or 50
Beijing 100704 PR   Tel. (01) 506.6688
Telefax: (01) 506.3101

CHINESE TAIPEI – TAIPEI CHINOIS
Good Faith Worldwide Int'l. Co. Ltd.
9th Floor, No. 118, Sec. 2
Chung Hsiao E. Road
Taipei   Tel. (02) 391.7396/391.7397
Telefax: (02) 394.9176

CZECH REPUBLIC – RÉPUBLIQUE TCHÈQUE
Artia Pegas Press Ltd.
Narodni Trida 25
POB 825
111 21 Praha 1   Tel. 26.65.68
Telefax: 26.20.81

DENMARK – DANEMARK
Munksgaard Book and Subscription Service
35, Nørre Søgade, P.O. Box 2148
DK-1016 København K   Tel. (33) 12.85.70
Telefax: (33) 12.93.87

EGYPT – ÉGYPTE
Middle East Observer
41 Sherif Street
Cairo   Tel. 392.6919
Telefax: 360-6804

FINLAND – FINLANDE
Akateeminen Kirjakauppa
Keskuskatu 1, P.O. Box 128
00100 Helsinki
Subscription Services/Agence d'abonnements :
P.O. Box 23
00371 Helsinki   Tel. (358 0) 12141
Telefax: (358 0) 121.4450

FRANCE
OECD/OCDE
Mail Orders/Commandes par correspondance:
2, rue André-Pascal
75775 Paris Cedex 16   Tel. (33-1) 45.24.82.00
Telefax: (33-1) 49.10.42.76
Telex: 640048 OCDE
Orders via Minitel, France only/
Commandes par Minitel, France exclusivement :
36 15 OCDE
OECD Bookshop/Librairie de l'OCDE :
33, rue Octave-Feuillet
75016 Paris   Tel. (33-1) 45.24.81.81
(33-1) 45.24.81.67
Documentation Française
29, quai Voltaire
75007 Paris   Tel. 40.15.70.00
Gibert Jeune (Droit-Économie)
6, place Saint-Michel
75006 Paris   Tel. 43.25.91.19
Librairie du Commerce International
10, avenue d'Iéna
75016 Paris   Tel. 40.73.34.60
Librairie Dunod
Université Paris-Dauphine
Place du Maréchal de Lattre de Tassigny
75016 Paris   Tel. (1) 44.05.40.13
Librairie Lavoisier
11, rue Lavoisier
75008 Paris   Tel. 42.65.39.95
Librairie L.G.D.J. - Montchrestien
20, rue Soufflot
75005 Paris   Tel. 46.33.89.85
Librairie des Sciences Politiques
30, rue Saint-Guillaume
75007 Paris   Tel. 45.48.36.02
P.U.F.
49, boulevard Saint-Michel
75005 Paris   Tel. 43.25.83.40
Librairie de l'Université
12a, rue Nazareth
13100 Aix-en-Provence   Tel. (16) 42.26.18.08
Documentation Française
165, rue Garibaldi
69003 Lyon   Tel. (16) 78.63.32.23
Librairie Decitre
29, place Bellecour
69002 Lyon   Tel. (16) 72.40.54.54
Librairie Sauramps
Le Triangle
34967 Montpellier Cedex 2   Tel. (16) 67.58.85.15
Tekefax: (16) 67.58.27.36

GERMANY – ALLEMAGNE
OECD Publications and Information Centre
August-Bebel-Allee 6
D-53175 Bonn   Tel. (0228) 959.120
Telefax: (0228) 959.12.17

GREECE – GRÈCE
Librairie Kauffmann
Mavrokordatou 9
106 78 Athens   Tel. (01) 32.55.321
Telefax: (01) 32.30.320

HONG-KONG
Swindon Book Co. Ltd.
Astoria Bldg. 3F
34 Ashley Road, Tsimshatsui
Kowloon, Hong Kong   Tel. 2376.2062
Telefax: 2376.0685

HUNGARY – HONGRIE
Euro Info Service
Margitsziget, Európa Ház
1138 Budapest   Tel. (1) 111.62.16
Telefax: (1) 111.60.61

ICELAND – ISLANDE
Mál Mog Menning
Laugavegi 18, Pósthólf 392
121 Reykjavik   Tel. (1) 552.4240
Telefax: (1) 562.3523

INDIA – INDE
Oxford Book and Stationery Co.
Scindia House
New Delhi 110001   Tel. (11) 331.5896/5308
Telefax: (11) 332.5993
17 Park Street
Calcutta 700016   Tel. 240832

INDONESIA – INDONÉSIE
Pdii-Lipi
P.O. Box 4298
Jakarta 12042   Tel. (21) 573.34.67
Telefax: (21) 573.34.67

IRELAND – IRLANDE
Government Supplies Agency
Publications Section
4/5 Harcourt Road
Dublin 2   Tel. 661.31.11
Telefax: 475.27.60

ISRAEL
Praedicta
5 Shatner Street
P.O. Box 34030
Jerusalem 91430   Tel. (2) 52.84.90/1/2
Telefax: (2) 52.84.93
R.O.Y. International
P.O. Box 13056
Tel Aviv 61130   Tel. (3) 49.61.08
Telefax: (3) 544.60.39
Palestinian Authority/Middle East:
INDEX Information Services
P.O.B. 19502
Jerusalem   Tel. (2) 27.12.19
Telefax: (2) 27.16.34

ITALY – ITALIE
Libreria Commissionaria Sansoni
Via Duca di Calabria 1/1
50125 Firenze   Tel. (055) 64.54.15
Telefax: (055) 64.12.57
Via Bartolini 29
20155 Milano   Tel. (02) 36.50.83
Editrice e Libreria Herder
Piazza Montecitorio 120
00186 Roma   Tel. 679.46.28
Telefax: 678.47.51
Libreria Hoepli
Via Hoepli 5
20121 Milano   Tel. (02) 86.54.46
Telefax: (02) 805.28.86
Libreria Scientifica
Dott. Lucio de Biasio 'Aeiou'
Via Coronelli, 6
20146 Milano   Tel. (02) 48.95.45.52
Telefax: (02) 48.95.45.48

JAPAN – JAPON
OECD Publications and Information Centre
Landic Akasaka Building
2-3-4 Akasaka, Minato-ku
Tokyo 107   Tel. (81.3) 3586.2016
Telefax: (81.3) 3584.7929

KOREA – CORÉE
Kyobo Book Centre Co. Ltd.
P.O. Box 1658, Kwang Hwa Moon
Seoul   Tel. 730.78.91
Telefax: 735.00.30

MALAYSIA – MALAISIE
University of Malaya Bookshop
University of Malaya
P.O. Box 1127, Jalan Pantai Baru
59700 Kuala Lumpur
Malaysia   Tel. 756.5000/756.5425
                            Telefax: 756.3246

MEXICO – MEXIQUE
Revistas y Periodicos Internacionales S.A. de C.V.
Florencia 57 - 1004
Mexico, D.F. 06600   Tel. 207.81.00
                            Telefax: 208.39.79

NETHERLANDS – PAYS-BAS
SDU Uitgeverij Plantijnstraat
Externe Fondsen
Postbus 20014
2500 EA's-Gravenhage   Tel. (070) 37.89.880
Voor bestellingen: Telefax: (070) 34.75.778

**NEW ZEALAND
NOUVELLE-ZÉLANDE**
Legislation Services
P.O. Box 12418
Thorndon, Wellington   Tel. (04) 496.5652
                            Telefax: (04) 496.5698

NORWAY – NORVÈGE
Narvesen Info Center – NIC
Bertrand Narvesens vei 2
P.O. Box 6125 Etterstad
0602 Oslo 6   Tel. (022) 57.33.00
                            Telefax: (022) 68.19.01

PAKISTAN
Mirza Book Agency
65 Shahrah Quaid-E-Azam
Lahore 54000   Tel. (42) 353.601
                            Telefax: (42) 231.730

PHILIPPINE – PHILIPPINES
International Book Center
5th Floor, Filipinas Life Bldg.
Ayala Avenue
Metro Manila   Tel. 81.96.76
                            Telex 23312 RHP PH

PORTUGAL
Livraria Portugal
Rua do Carmo 70-74
Apart. 2681
1200 Lisboa   Tel. (01) 347.49.82/5
                            Telefax: (01) 347.02.64

SINGAPORE – SINGAPOUR
Gower Asia Pacific Pte Ltd.
Golden Wheel Building
41, Kallang Pudding Road, No. 04-03
Singapore 1334   Tel. 741.5166
                            Telefax: 742.9356

SPAIN – ESPAGNE
Mundi-Prensa Libros S.A.
Castelló 37, Apartado 1223
Madrid 28001   Tel. (91) 431.33.99
                            Telefax: (91) 575.39.98

Libreria Internacional AEDOS
Consejo de Ciento 391
08009 – Barcelona   Tel. (93) 488.30.09
                            Telefax: (93) 487.76.59

Llibreria de la Generalitat
Palau Moja
Rambla dels Estudis, 118
08002 – Barcelona
            (Subscripcions) Tel. (93) 318.80.12
            (Publicacions) Tel. (93) 302.67.23
                            Telefax: (93) 412.18.54

SRI LANKA
Centre for Policy Research
c/o Colombo Agencies Ltd.
No. 300-304, Galle Road
Colombo 3   Tel. (1) 574240, 573551-2
                            Telefax: (1) 575394, 510711

SWEDEN – SUÈDE
Fritzes Customer Service
S–106 47 Stockholm   Tel. (08) 690.90.90
                            Telefax: (08) 20.50.21

Subscription Agency/Agence d'abonnements :
Wennergren-Williams Info AB
P.O. Box 1305
171 25 Solna   Tel. (08) 705.97.50
                            Telefax: (08) 27.00.71

SWITZERLAND – SUISSE
Maditec S.A. (Books and Periodicals - Livres
et périodiques)
Chemin des Palettes 4
Case postale 266
1020 Renens VD 1   Tel. (021) 635.08.65
                            Telefax: (021) 635.07.80

Librairie Payot S.A.
4, place Pépinet
CP 3212
1002 Lausanne   Tel. (021) 341.33.47
                            Telefax: (021) 341.33.45

Librairie Unilivres
6, rue de Candolle
1205 Genève   Tel. (022) 320.26.23
                            Telefax: (022) 329.73.18

Subscription Agency/Agence d'abonnements :
Dynapresse Marketing S.A.
38 avenue Vibert
1227 Carouge   Tel. (022) 308.07.89
                            Telefax: (022) 308.07.99

See also – Voir aussi :
OECD Publications and Information Centre
August-Bebel-Allee 6
D-53175 Bonn (Germany)   Tel. (0228) 959.120
                            Telefax: (0228) 959.12.17

THAILAND – THAÏLANDE
Suksit Siam Co. Ltd.
113, 115 Fuang Nakhon Rd.
Opp. Wat Rajbopith
Bangkok 10200   Tel. (662) 225.9531/2
                            Telefax: (662) 222.5188

TURKEY – TURQUIE
Kültür Yayinlari Is-Türk Ltd. Sti.
Atatürk Bulvari No. 191/Kat 13
Kavaklidere/Ankara   Tel. 428.11.40 Ext. 2458
Dolmabahce Cad. No. 29
Besiktas/Istanbul   Tel. 260.71.88
                            Telex: 43482B

UNITED KINGDOM – ROYAUME-UNI
HMSO
Gen. enquiries   Tel. (071) 873 0011
Postal orders only:
P.O. Box 276, London SW8 5DT
Personal Callers HMSO Bookshop
49 High Holborn, London WC1V 6HB
                            Telefax: (071) 873 8200
Branches at: Belfast, Birmingham, Bristol,
Edinburgh, Manchester

UNITED STATES – ÉTATS-UNIS
OECD Publications and Information Center
2001 L Street N.W., Suite 650
Washington, D.C. 20036-4910 Tel. (202) 785.6323
                            Telefax: (202) 785.0350

VENEZUELA
Libreria del Este
Avda F. Miranda 52, Aptdo. 60337
Edificio Galipán
Caracas 106   Tel. 951.1705/951.2307/951.1297
                            Telegram: Libreste Caracas

Subscription to OECD periodicals may also be
placed through main subscription agencies.

Les abonnements aux publications périodiques de
l'OCDE peuvent être souscrits auprès des
principales agences d'abonnement.

Orders and inquiries from countries where Distribu-
tors have not yet been appointed should be sent to
OECD Publications Service, 2 rue André-Pascal,
75775 Paris Cedex 16, France.

Les commandes provenant de pays où l'OCDE n'a
pas encore désigné de distributeur peuvent être
adressées à : OCDE, Service des Publications
2, rue André-Pascal, 75775 Paris Cedex 16, France

5-1995

QMW LIBRARY
(MILE END)

WITHDRAWN
FROM STOCK
QMUL LIBRARY

OECD PUBLICATIONS, 2 rue André-Pascal, 75775 PARIS CEDEX 16
PRINTED IN FRANCE
(42 95 01 1) ISBN 92-64-14476-5 - No. 47949 1995

WITHDRAWN
FROM STOCK
QMUL LIBRARY